SEVENTY - FIFTH ANNIVERSARY 1943

A Family of Thirty Million

A Family of Thirty Million

The Story of the
Metropolitan Life Insurance Company

by

LOUIS I. DUBLIN, PH. D.
Third Vice-President and Statistician

METROPOLITAN LIFE INSURANCE COMPANY

NEW YORK

1943

A Family
of Thirty
Million

Dedicated to

FREDERICK H. ECKER
Chairman of the Board

and

LEROY A. LINCOLN
President

WHOSE WISDOM AND ADMINISTRATIVE GENIUS
HAVE SERVED TO PROMOTE THE SECURITY
AND GENERAL WELFARE OF THE MILLIONS
OF METROPOLITAN POLICYHOLDERS IN THE
UNITED STATES AND CANADA

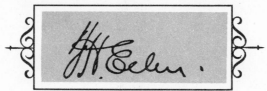

Chairman of the Board

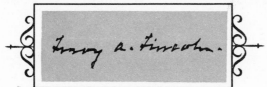

President

TABLE OF CONTENTS

TABLE OF CONTENTS—*Continued*

Part IV

Part V

LIST OF ILLUSTRATIONS

PREFACE

THIS VOLUME has been prepared in celebration of the 75th anniversary of the Metropolitan Life Insurance Company. It is fitting that this milestone in the life of a business institution which has become so widely known on this Continent, be marked by a record of events and accomplishments over the years. The country was already at war when the preparation of this history began. At such a time, one's thoughts turn naturally to a sober appraisal of the institution and of its relation to the way of life which we are fighting to maintain. It was in this spirit that the author approached his task. He was particularly fortunate in the abundant sources of information at his disposal. It was an even happier circumstance that he could also turn to a few men who not only remembered the early days, but who knew the founders of the Company and had worked beside them. Indeed, these veterans helped to lay new foundations and played a major role in the growth of the organization.

This history of the Company does not pretend to be complete. It would be impossible, in a single volume, to cover adequately the varied phases of so far-reaching a business. The author has, therefore, limited himself to a consideration of the principal characters and events in the story. He has tried to bring into focus those thoughts and policies which, over the years, have made the Metropolitan the leader that it is today. The significance of this history would have been lost without some reference to the background against which these events took place. The author has, therefore, sketched in roughly the economic and social development of the United States and Canada, and of the institution of Life Insurance which has contributed so richly to national progress.

This history has been written by one who has spent virtually his whole working life in the organization, and who is bound by many warm ties to his colleagues. Nevertheless, he has tried to be objective and to write an authentic story. He has made no attempt to gloss over the difficulties or the many problems that inevitably beset an organization over a period of 75 years. If at times the picture presented here appears too bright, it is not because it has been painted in glowing colors, but because the record of the Metropolitan is one of the most extraordinary in American business history. Its everyday operations have become an important element in the national economy, and through these activities, as well as through the extensive social services it has created and stimu-lated, the Company's influence has extended to homes and people in every part of the two neighboring countries. The author hopes that the reader will find this volume to be a truly human story, one that is peculiarly American, reflecting the national genius for enterprise, technical skill, and good business administration. Perhaps the volume will also serve to give the general public a clear conception of the theory and practice of modern Life Insurance.

At this time in our history, when the desire for security is greater than ever before, it is hoped that this volume will reflect what the American people have done through Life insurance to provide financial protection for themselves. They have achieved this security to a greater degree than any other people, achieved it voluntarily, and through institutions of their own making. This is in the American tradition. They have not depended upon Government subsidy, but have themselves taken the initiative. Americans apparently prefer this method, which takes into account individual needs and relies on the sense of obligation of the head of the family to look after his own.

To be sure, this effort has not reached perfection. But the record is one of constant improvement. Today fully one half the people of the United States and Canada depend in large measure upon the institution of Life Insurance for their program of family security. Nor is there any suggestion that the saturation point for the private companies has been reached. There are still many uninsured or inadequately insured individuals in the country who are the policyholders of the future.

The author desires to make acknowledgment of his indebtedness to his many colleagues, without whose help this volume could not have been written. So many have participated in the effort that it is impossible to name them all. Indeed, the chief task of the author has been to marshall the material supplied to him and to bring it into a uniform scheme. Especially helpful have been the Actuary of the Company, Horace R. Bassford; Second Vice-Presidents Samuel Milligan and Francis M. Smith; and Dr. William A. Berridge, the Economist—who were responsible for much of the original material. Associate Actuary James R. Herman undertook the checking of every item in the book. The author's sincere thanks are due to Vice-President Charles G. Taylor, Jr., who read the entire text and made many valuable suggestions. He is particularly indebted to his associates, Jacob Baar and Herbert H. Marks, who collaborated with him throughout the course of the work. With the help of these and many others, this has been a pleasant and stimulating undertaking.

Louis I. Dublin

February 1943.

A Family of Thirty Million

Part I

CHAPTER 1

Seventy-five Years of
Life Insurance

OR centuries men have seen in America the promise of a
better life for themselves and for their families. To them
this country has offered a share in its abundance, the
possibility of individual economic freedom, security in old age.
The essential dignity and worth of human beings is the
heritage of our people, and this ideal has colored all the efforts
of the men who have built the Nation. Our country has
grown and prospered because, from the very beginning, its
people learned to join together to plan for their future security
and have pooled their individual efforts to realize a better way
of life. These are the practices of democracy. They are also
the principles which guide Life insurance in helping to provide
and to safeguard these American values.

Although the need to protect the family against insecurity
is universal, it is in our country that Life insurance has enjoyed
its fullest and most vigorous growth. It has reached all classes
of people and has become organically part and parcel of our
economic life. At the present time about 70,000,000 Americans and Canadians own about 150,000,000 Life insurance
policies in legal reserve Life insurance companies, amounting
to the stupendous total of $140,000,000,000. Nowhere else
in the world has the average family achieved a comparable
degree of financial protection. Americans and Canadians
constitute about 7 percent of the world's population, yet
possess about 75 percent of the world's Life insurance. The
average amount of Life insurance in force in the United

3

States is nearly $1,000 per capita. Canada ranks second in this regard with nearly $700 per capita. Other leading countries fall far short of our accomplishments in this field; a wide gap separates us even from Britain, where the Life insurance business had its beginnings and where it has been developed continuously and skillfully over the centuries. The Americans and Canadians have selected this medium to exercise their native thrift and to provide by voluntary effort for the financial protection and security of their loved ones.

As a financial institution directly shared by more than half our people, Life insurance naturally plays an important role in the business life of the Nation. Of the 10 corporations in the United States which lead in assets, four are Life insurance companies. Each year all the Life insurance companies of the United States and Canada, in fulfillment of their contract obligations, are putting back into the hands of the American people about $3,000,000,000. During the decade 1931-1940, years dominated by the depression, the Life insurance companies paid to policyholders or their beneficiaries the vast sum of more than $28,000,000,000—funds which helped to save many a family from the relief rolls and many a business from bankruptcy. They have also provided comfortable incomes for many families. Today, these companies have assets of more than $37,000,000,000, a sum three times that of all assets of savings banks. This reservoir of money, invested in Government obligations, in prime securities of industry, in public utilities, and in bonds and mortgages secured by real estate, has given momentum to Life insurance and has served as a stabilizing force to our entire economic structure. The Life insurance business directly provides livelihood for about 300,000 people; indirectly, through its extensive investment operations, it gives work to millions more. By collecting and distributing these large sums along constructive channels, it acts as a catalyzer, stimulating economic activity on an impressive scale. In short, by the very nature of its business, Life insurance touches and benefits the day-to-day life of our citizens as do few other institutions.

4

The Metropolitan Life Insurance Company provides a good illustration of how the institution has developed and how it operates on this continent. Here is an organization which, within the lifetime of one man (happily still active as Chairman of its Board of Directors), has had its christening, its definition of policy and program, and its extraordinary growth. This year, on its 75th anniversary, it is not only the leader in its field but also the largest financial corporation in the world. It has kept pace with the development of our country, with its increase in population, with the growth of its cities, and with gains in national wealth and income. It is a thoroughly American institution; and its 75 years of development have paralleled the evolution of our national economic and democratic life. The Company has constantly sought to improve its procedures and its product. It has worked for lower costs, within the limits of sound insurance practice. It has afforded opportunity for advancement to thousands in its employ. It has been an aggressive and insti-gating force for social and medical progress. In short, it typifies the success of the enterprise system in protecting the security of the American and Canadian people.

The story of the founding and the history of this public service institution is largely the story of Life insurance in the two countries. Because its 75 years of growth have meant the unfolding of a better way of life for millions of working people and their families, it is a story worth telling. It is a record of forceful personalities, of dramatic changes, of social progress. It is a long story, rich in detail and economic significance. But behind this record, a living organization functions. Many readers, including the millions of policyholders who have a vital stake in the Metropolitan, would like to know a little of their Company's history. And so for them, this introduc-tory chapter will serve as a summary of the history of the Company and a glimpse into the essentials of what Life insurance is and does.

*   *   *   *

James R. Doug

President, 1868–1871

The Metropolitan Life Insurance Company received its Charter and began business on March 24, 1868, as one of eight such companies organized in that year in New York State. Its offices consisted of two small rooms on the second floor of the building at 243 Broadway, New York City—a small rear room for the President, Dr. James R. Dow, and a front room for the employees. The entire space was about 900 square feet, not much larger than a good-sized room. But in less than two years the little Company outgrew its first quarters and moved to 319 Broadway. From the very beginning the Metropolitan made a favorable impression on the insurance world and on officialdom, as is evidenced by the contemporary comments in the insurance press. Thus, in *The Spectator* of November 1872, appears the following: "With a complete and skillful official staff—one in every way qualified to maintain the enthusiasm of its field force and to guide its general interests with marked ability—we are justified in emphasizing the impression all along felt and expressed, that the Company's future is a bright one, and that it is making a record characterized by all the elements of stability and prosperity." *The Insurance Times* of the same date stated: "The Company is becoming daily a greater favorite with the American people, and is destined soon to overtake our largest companies in prosperity, magnitude, and wealth." How soon this prophecy became a reality astonished the entire insurance world.

By 1876, when the property at the corner of Park Place and Church Street was purchased for new and enlarged headquarters, the Company was a going concern. It already showed assets of more than $2,000,000, and it had more than $24,000,000 of insurance on the books.

When the Staff proudly took possession of their new quarters in 1876, they supposed that they were settling into a permanent home. How modest were these pioneers! Little did they dream that only 17 years later, at the end of their first quarter century of operation, they would be conducting a Company acknowledged as one of the leaders in the Life insurance field. It had expanded its quarters by that time into

Chapter 49.

AN ACT to amend the charter of the National Travelers' Insurance Company, and also to amend an act entitled "An act to authorize the National Travelers' Insurance Company to effect insurance upon the lives of individuals," passed April ninth, eighteen hundred and sixty-seven.

PASSED March 24, 1868.

The People of the State of New York, represented in Senate and Assembly, do enact as follows:

SECTION 1. The charter of the National Travelers' Insurance Company, and an act entitled "An act to authorize the National Travelers' Insurance Company to effect insurance upon the lives of individuals," passed April ninth, eighteen hundred and sixty-seven, are hereby amended so as to read as follows:

§ 2. The name of the said National Travelers' Insurance Company, from and after the passage of this act, shall be the "Metropolitan Life Insurance Company," and the same is continued and declared to be a corporation by that name. Its principal office shall be located in the city of New York.

§ 3. The business of the company shall be to make insurance upon the lives of individuals, and every insurance appertaining thereto or connected therewith, and to grant, purchase or dispose of annuities, as set forth in the first department of the first section of the act passed June twenty-fourth, eighteen hundred and fifty-three, by the legislature of the State of New York, entitled "An act to provide for the incorporation of life and health insurance companies, and in relation to the agencies of such companies," and this company shall possess and enjoy all the powers, privileges and franchises granted to, and shall be subject to all the regulations, restrictions and obligations imposed upon incorporations organized and existing under the said act of June twenty-fourth, eighteen hundred and fifty-three, and the amendments thereto.

§ 4. The capital of the said company shall be two hundred thousand dollars, and the capital stock shall be divided into four thousand shares of fifty dollars each, which shall be personal property, transferable only on the books of the company in conformity with the by-laws of said company.

§ 5. The corporate powers of the company shall be vested in and exercised by a board of directors and by such officers and agents as the board may appoint and empower.

§ 6. The board of directors shall consist of not less than thirteen, nor more than twenty-five persons, a majority of whom shall be citizens of the State of New York, and at least two-thirds of whom shall each own and hold in his own right at least ten shares of the capital stock of the company; and the remaining third may be holders of life or endowment policies, each paying a premium to the company of at least one hundred dollars per annum, or shall be entitled to an annuity of at least one hundred dollars per annum from the company.

§ 7. Seven directors shall constitute a quorum for the transaction of business, but a less number may meet and adjourn from time to time until a quorum is present.

§ 8. The board of directors shall have power to make and prescribe such by-laws, rules and regulations for the conduct of its affairs, not inconsistent with law or this charter, as may be deemed expedient.

§ 9. The board of directors shall also have all other powers usually vested in boards of directors of life insurance or annuity companies, not inconsistent with the constitution or laws of this state, or with this charter, and may at any time accept and exercise any or all additional powers and privileges which may be conferred by law upon this or in general upon life insurance or annuity companies.

§ 10. The following named persons, having been duly elected, shall constitute the first board of directors under this charter, to wit: James R. Dow, George C. Collins, H. A. Jones, S. M. Beard, John Caswell, Joseph F. Knapp, Watson Sandford, J. C. Dimmick, its magnificent new building at 1 Madison Avenue, an address which was soon to become known the world over. The business had then increased to 3,000,000 policies in force, insuring a total amount of $353,000,000, with assets well in excess of $19,000,000. This was an outstanding accomplishment within the short space of 25 years.

From this point onward, the development of the Metropolitan went on apace. Growth has been almost continuous, despite the seven major economic depressions experienced during the history of the Company. The Company seems to have contained within itself a perpetual source of new energy. When it passed its 50th anniversary in 1918, the Metropolitan was the leader among Life insurance companies both here and abroad, with 20,000,000 policies, for a total amount of $4,500,000,000, and with assets of more than $750,000,000—truly large figures for those days. At the present time, on its 75th anniversary, the number of its Life insurance policies (including Group certificates) approximates 43,000,000, representing insurance in force to the amount of $27,000,000,000 and assets of $6,000,000,000 guaranteeing the fulfillment of these contracts. The small business which began with six people in two rooms 75 years ago, is today an organization of close to 50,000 employees and Agents, who serve 30,000,000 men, women and children in every corner of this country and Canada.

What secret accounts for this unprecedented growth? Certainly the Metropolitan was not born with a silver spoon in its mouth. On the contrary, the early years of the Company were not without struggle and anxiety. The Metropolitan survived mainly because of the courage and resourcefulness of its early Officers—Joseph F. Knapp, President, and his associate John R. Hegeman. They had to meet the competition of larger and longer established companies, who could afford to pay their agents higher commissions. The cost of securing new business was also relatively greater for a new company. More than once Mr. Knapp had to step in and advance his own capital to tide over a temporary financial strain.

Yet despite the difficulties of these early days, they revealed a field later to have permanent significance for the Company. This came through an opportunity to underwrite the insurance for all members of the Hildise Bund, an organization of German-American wage-earners. Not only did this bring the new Company immediate business; more important, it gave the impetus for an entirely new approach to insurance sales— the Industrial field. The ease and success of underwriting their insurance proved that sales among wage-earners could be developed profitably. A little more than a decade after its founding, the young Company was already moving forward, well in its stride. It had taken the first steps toward its particular field of operations—the insurance of wage-earners and their families.

Here was unexplored territory, virtually untouched in America. (The Prudential Friendly Society had only a few years earlier, in 1875, introduced the Industrial business into New Jersey.) Millions of people of low or moderate income in need of Life insurance were not being served by the existing companies. In England, a number of companies had shown that Life insurance could be written for relatively small amounts, provided the weekly premiums were collected by agents in the homes. This mode of payment fitted into the scheme of weekly wages and the budget of working-class families. Moreover, all members of the household, the women and children as well as the head of the family, were eligible.

The first Industrial policy in the Metropolitan was issued on November 17, 1879. During the first full year more than 200,000 such policies were written, and the Company immediately took the leadership in this new field. Once the business "clicked," the Officers and the Agents of the Company became imbued with the tremendous possibilities of growth and usefulness inherent in their business. The spread of Industrial insurance became a gospel to them, and they operated with the zeal of missionaries. Branch offices were set up quickly in all the large cities of the country and Canada, and the business spread like a prairie fire. Without question, the introduction of Industrial insurance was the first and most important factor in the success of the Company.

The second factor lay in the intelligent and forceful management which it has enjoyed from the very beginning. After the death in 1871 of its first President, Dr. James R. Dow, who had served less than three years, five outstanding personalities in turn have dominated the Company's history. Joseph F. Knapp, one of the incorporators of the new Company, and a leading Director and Chairman of its Finance Committee from the beginning, became President in 1871. Mr. Knapp continued to mold the Company during its first two decades, ably seconded by his Vice-President, John R. Hegeman. This gracious personality worked side by side with his colleague, matured in power with the Company, and achieved the Presidency on Mr. Knapp's death in 1891. Mr. Hegeman continued as President until 1919, brilliantly assisted by Haley Fiske, who had come in as his associate in the management of the Company in 1891. Mr. Fiske's administration achieved a high-water mark, not only in the life of the Metropolitan but in the history of insurance in general. He continued in office until his death in 1929, and was succeeded by Frederick H. Ecker. It is of special interest that Mr. Ecker, who came into the Company as a boy of 16 in 1883, has been to the present day associated with the organization. He has seen virtually every step in its progress and has participated in the shaping of its policy over many years. In 1936, Mr. Ecker became Chairman of the Board of Directors, and Leroy A. Lincoln, who as Vice-President had assumed more and more the duties of Executive Officer, became the sixth President. A rare good fortune has determined the high character of the leadership of the Metropolitan from the beginning. Successful administration has been passed on from one able leader to the next, each schooled in the tradition and experience of his predecessors. This has given the Company a singleness of purpose and continuity of policy.

In the succeeding chapters of this history, we shall give in detail the significant items in each of the administrations.

319 Broadway
1869–1876

Early Home Office Buildings

243 Broadway
1868–1869

In this introduction we propose only to give a birdseye view of this extraordinary development and of the forces which have influenced it.

The first of these administrations, covering the years 1868 to 1891, was the period of the organization of the Company and the subsequent development of Industrial business. The second, that of Mr. Hegeman and Mr. Fiske, from 1891 to 1919, was characterized by the opening up of other fields of operation. When their administration began, the Metro-politan was almost altogether an Industrial company. It was the ambition of Mr. Fiske to create a strong Ordinary Depart-ment under adequate leadership, and vigorously to develop this branch of the business. It was characteristic of the man that he should hit upon the sound principle that the Agent, who carried the message of Industrial insurance each week into the homes of policyholders, should at the same time be the purveyor of Ordinary insurance. He recognized that Industrial insurance was not only a direct service to the wage-earning population; that it was in the nature of the case an extraordinary educator in the general insurance principle. Those who carried small policies and who grew up with them learned to appreciate the value of Life insurance and to want more of it. As these people increased their earnings and bettered their position economically, they became eligible for Ordinary insurance—that is, for insurance in larger amounts paid for quarterly, semiannually, or annually.

The wisdom of Mr. Fiske's beliefs was confirmed within a short time. The Ordinary Department, revived in 1892 and carried forward by an army of 5,000 Field-Men, was crowned with success soon after its beginning. Ordinary insurance could be written at lower cost than Industrial. It obviously cost considerably less to transact business in larger amounts and to have premiums forwarded by the insured directly to the Company, than to have Agents make weekly collections. Furthermore, it was found that those qualified for Ordinary insurance experienced a lower mortality than Industrial policy-holders, because they were a more strictly selected group and lived and worked under better-than-average conditions. Large numbers of working men were ready to take advantage of this new opportunity.

In the very first year the Company's Agents wrote more than $2,000,000 of Ordinary business, the next year over $6,000,000, in 1894 more than $14,000,000. The amounts continued to spiral upward in unprecedented figures. Few *new* companies could launch a fresh branch of the business with such spectacular success; but an established company with an adequate Home Office, an efficient organization, and a large clientele to draw upon could begin a new large-scale operation like this and succeed. And the Metropolitan did. In the course of the next 10 years what was equivalent to a sizable Ordinary company was established. At the end of 1902 there were on the books 278,360 Ordinary policies for more than $237,000,000. Only two decades thereafter, despite its late beginning, the Company arrived at the premier position in the Ordinary Life insurance field. Thus was launched the second major division of the Company.

The varied clientele which the Agents served brought into sharp focus the need for developing various forms of insurance on the Ordinary plan, adapted to persons who, because of occupational hazards or economic level, could not qualify for Standard insurance. Thus, in 1896, the Company began to issue Intermediate insurance—that is, policies on the Ordinary plan in units of $500. This type of policy was especially designed for workers who could not afford regular Ordinary insurance in amounts of $1,000 or more, but who were in a position to pay premiums on a quarterly or less frequent basis. Shortly thereafter the Company made available Special Class policies covering those in hazardous occupations or with certain physical impairments. A large business developed in this way, covering millions of lives and serving a sector of our people hitherto without such protection.

Another step in the long series to bring Life insurance coverage to salaried employees and wage-earners was the organization of the Group Division in 1917. Under this form, first inaugurated in America by the Equitable Life in 1911, a blanket policy is issued to the employer covering his employees, without medical examination, and at low cost. Group insurance contracts have had a phenomenal development since their introduction to American industry; and at present they provide, in addition to Life insurance, Annuities, Sickness and Accident insurance, Accidental Death and Dismemberment benefits, Hospital Expense insurance, and Surgical Operation insurance. Millions of workers, many of whom had had no insurance protection, welcomed this new medium. Group insurance has been an important instrument in promoting a spirit of cooperation and mutual good will between employers and employees, and has furthered their joint effort to better the conditions of the workers. Inasmuch as Group insurance operates in the wage-earning group, the domain which the Metropolitan has served over the years, it is not surprising that the Company has been particularly successful in this field. At the present time the Metropolitan has about 2,500,000 Group Life certificate holders insured for more than $5,000,000,000. It also has large amounts of other forms of Group insurance in force.

These developments, important as they are from the insurance standpoint, reflect the Company's leadership. The Chief Executives have been not only able men of affairs; they have also been men of broad vision and social sympathies—self-made men who had risen from the ranks and understood the problems of working people. It is obvious that these men were enterprising. But that their enterprises took the direction they did is proof of the essentially democratic character of the Metropolitan, which has always devoted the bulk of its efforts to wage-earning groups. The leaders wished so to conduct the business as to give it new values and to broaden the narrow financial relationship which had characterized earlier insurance. Contracts were liberalized throughout the entire history of the organization. Agents were taught to look upon their policyholders as their employers, as people to be served conscientiously.

15

The very intimacy of the relationship between Agents and policyholders has presented a variety of opportunities for useful service. Even in the early days the Agents carried valuable health literature to the homes of policyholders. Services of this type multiplied and reached their culmination in 1909 with the organization of the Welfare Division, a separate office working primarily in the field of health educa-tion and disease prevention. The launching of this broad social program, mainly through the decision of Mr. Fiske, was a landmark in the history of Industrial insurance in America.

We shall see later in greater detail how useful this venture has been. Here it is sufficient to point out that under the guiding genius of Lee K. Frankel, and with the wholehearted support of the Officers and the Field Staff of the Company, an instrument was created which has proved valuable to Industrial policyholders and to the business itself. The nursing of sick policyholders at the expense of the Company was especially welcomed. Contracts were made with local visiting nurse associations in various parts of the country. Where no local visiting nurse associations existed, the Com-pany assisted in the organization of new groups or employed its own Nursing Staffs if necessary. The Metropolitan insisted on high standards of nursing care, on good record keeping, and on businesslike administration of these welfare agencies; and this has had its salutary effect in shaping the character of the resulting services. Public health nursing is one of the real contributions of America to public health work; and much of this development can be traced to the partnership of the associations with the Metropolitan Life Insurance Company. During the period since its inception, the Nursing Service of the Company has made more than 90,000,000 visits to policyholders. Side by side, and supple-menting the Nursing Service, has been the creation and dissemination of a veritable library of health and safety in-formation. Pamphlets covering every phase of disease and accident prevention have been prepared so attractively and so authoritatively that they have served as models in form and content. This literature has been carried over the years into millions of homes by Nurses and Agents. Educators, public health officials, physicians, social workers, and laymen alike have acclaimed its value in spreading health knowledge among the general population. The huge figure of more than 1,200,000,000 pamphlets distributed to date, reflects the character of this contribution over the years.

It is no wonder that such services, plus many others, should affect favorably the life and health of the insured. Almost from the very beginning the mortality of Industrial policyholders reflected the effectiveness of the welfare campaign. Death rates began to retreat more rapidly for these insured than for the rest of the population. Today the mortality figures for Industrial policyholders are about half what they were at the inception of the effort. Among children the saving in mortality has been about 75 percent. The average child born today may expect to live 16 years longer than the one born a generation ago. These dramatic figures and the human values behind them have attracted world-wide attention. They have given tremendous stimulation to official and voluntary health activities on behalf of the entire Nation. This welfare service has more than paid for itself in deaths postponed, in many homes made happier, and in the ever increasing social point of view which has motivated the Agent.

The culminating achievement of the Hegeman-Fiske administration was the completion of the mutualization of the Company in 1915. In the beginning the Company was organized as a stock venture, as a business conducted for profit. That was in line with the spirit of the times, which encouraged the investment of capital for business expansion. Yet no one could have foreseen the extraordinary success of the organization, its rapid growth in number of policyholders and in assets, and the consequent influence of its position. It was exceedingly fortunate that the Charter of the Company limited the dividends of stockholders to 7 percent on their investment. Although the business ran into billions of dollars, piling up sizable reserves and surpluses, the stockholders were prohibited by charter from ever receiving more than $140,000 a year on the $2,000,000 of stock. Yet the danger was ever present that, in some future administration, efforts might be made to obtain control of the Company through purchase of a majority stock interest. There might thus result a directorate and management which would not so zealously protect the interests of policyholders. The administration realized this danger keenly; and Mr. Ecker, who then was Treasurer, was given the opportunity to carry on the mutualization negotiations with the stockholders. A word must be said for the generous and broad-minded attitude of Joseph P. Knapp, son of the former President, and one of the most active of the Board of Directors. His readiness to turn in his large stock holdings at the modest figure of $300 per share made a solution favorable to the policyholders quickly possible. Through payment of only $6,000,000, the Company once and for all removed any obstacle which stood in the way of complete ownership and control by its policyholders.

Such a fundamental transfer had been the hope of the administration for a long time; and in completing these delicate negotiations, the farseeing judgment of the management was demonstrated. From then on no individual could control the Company against the best interests of the policyholders who composed it. The Officers and the Staff were their employees not only in form but in substance; and thus was achieved the underlying democratic principle inherent in mutual Life insurance.

Mr. Fiske died in 1929, and was succeeded in the Presidency by Frederick H. Ecker, who, since 1883, had been in turn Office Boy, Clerk, Manager of the Bond Department, Comptroller, Treasurer, a member of the Board of Directors, and Vice-President. For 20 years he had shared with Mr. Fiske the responsibilities of administration. As the investment officer of the Company, he had guided the finances of the organization along constructive lines, assuring stability and sound business methods in the control of the Company's assets. He had achieved a notable position not only in the insurance world but in that of finance. He had become expert in the diverse problems of urban real estate, and especially its complexities in New York City. His advice was widely sought by leading railroads, and he was particularly constructive in reorganizing those in financial difficulties. In all these transactions he had safeguarded the interests of the Company.

Soon after Mr. Ecker took the helm, Leroy A. Lincoln, at the age of 49, was made Vice-President. He had come into the Company in 1918, and in little more than a decade had demonstrated his capacity to handle a variety of complicated administrative problems. He had a broad and intimate knowledge of the entire insurance business, having previously served as Counsel to the New York State Insurance Department. He brought to his duties not only a keen analytical mind but also a warm sympathy for the men in the Field, and especial enthusiasm for the social service program of the organization. When, in March 1936, Mr. Ecker became Chairman of the Board of Directors, Mr. Lincoln succeeded to the Presidency, continuing the policies of his predecessor in office.

Frederick H. Ecker became President of the Company at a period which then looked to many like a "Golden Era." All business was at a high peak, and the Metropolitan shared in the general prosperity. Toward the close of this period many people seriously believed that a new order of living had arrived in America and that prosperity was to go on forever. One measure of this buoyant state was the rise in prices of common stocks, particularly those dealt in on Exchanges. Under such promising conditions, it is not surprising that common stocks were seriously urged as suitable "investments" even for Life insurance companies; and one or two companies not subject to the restrictions of the New York Law purchased sizable blocks of well-selected common stocks for their portfolios. It was at this juncture, in September 1929, that President Ecker, in an address before the National Association of Life Underwriters at Washington, analyzed the proposal that Life insurance funds be put into common stocks, and took a firm position against such "investments" by the Life insurance companies. There were some who challenged his position; but not long after Mr. Ecker's address had been published and put into circulation there came, in October 1929, the first of the Stock Exchange crashes. His judgment as to the dangers of common stock investments for Life insurance companies was vindicated almost overnight.

The full import of this disaster was little understood at the moment. It was not for weeks and months that the country came to understand that its entire economy had suffered a shock which could not be overcome for years. As the first overturns in the Stock Exchange deepened into a well-defined national depression, the Life insurance companies shared the difficulties of the times with other financial institutions. Large numbers of people lost their savings on the Exchanges. Many banks closed their doors, foreclosures increased rapidly, and employment began to drop sharply. As a consequence, many people borrowed on their policies or surrendered their Life insurance to obtain the cash which they could find through no other source. This situation was further complicated by moratoria on policy loans and surrenders enforced in a majority of the States—limitations which were not sought by the Metropolitan. The Company continued to make all payments where no restrictions existed, and met every obligation as soon as the curbs were lifted. During the decade from 1930 to 1939 the Metropolitan paid out well in excess of $5,000,000,000 to policyholders or their beneficiaries. These payments saved from the ignominy of public relief many thousands of individuals who had set up their own protective plans through insurance during more prosperous years. Contemporary with the efforts of the Federal Government to afford relief to the destitute members of the population, they certainly lightened the public burden.

Still other difficulties of a financial character arose. The marked depreciation of urban real estate, farm lands, and bond values called for the rearrangement of the investment portfolio. President Ecker, with his long and varied experience in this field, addressed himself to the solution of this problem, made

20

particularly difficult by the continued decline in opportunities for the profitable investment of insurance funds. Money was accumulating in the treasury because it was almost impossible to find proper investment channels. Under these conditions and with a consciousness of civic responsibility, Mr. Ecker turned his attention to the field of moderate rental housing. At the age of 70 he launched a building program unprecedented in social character and magnitude, to provide homes for persons of medium income in New York City. He located a large tract in The Bronx, guided the planning of adequate buildings and services, and saw step by step the fulfillment of his hopes in the completion of a model community, Parkchester. Today 36,000 people live there, a splendid contribution to the moderate-priced housing program of the city and the Nation. Similar housing developments have been undertaken under Mr. Ecker's direction both in San Francisco and Los Angeles, and more recently in Alexandria, Va., near the city of Washington. Such building programs, without precedent in the United States for a private company, are recognized by national and private agencies as an important contribution to the housing problem in the period of war emergency. At the same time, they serve as an excellent investment field for the Company.

During the period of financial depression there were criticisms of every business; and the business of Life insurance in general and the Metropolitan specifically were not exempt. Notwithstanding the splendid record of the major companies, various movements for investigating the Life insurance business were initiated in Washington.

In 1938 the Congress of the United States responded to a message from President Roosevelt and included among the subjects to be investigated by the Temporary National Economic Committee certain investment phases of the business of Life insurance. The investigation was assigned to the newly created Securities and Exchange Commission. Those responsible for gathering evidence to submit to the T.N.E.C. lost no opportunity to seek out material for criticism in the

21

business and directed much of their attention to the Metropolitan. The Company took a firm stand in behalf of its policyholders and presented voluminous documentary evidence to show that it had conducted its many activities in the public interest, and that its size had not involved any abuse of economic power—that its position as investor of trustee funds as prescribed by Statute precluded such power. Nor had its size interfered with its effectiveness as a social organization. In fact, the Company had increased in initiative and in service as it had grown.

After the conclusion of the hearings, the comment of the Chairman of the T.N.E.C. was that the Life insurance business "has come through with flying colors." The failure of the effort to find serious fault with the administration of Life insurance in general is best evidenced by the character of the recommendations which were made by the Temporary National Economic Committee. These, for the most part, had to do with a number of suggestions as to modifications in the practice of State supervision. The impression made on the public by these hearings is to be measured by the fact that, during their progress and after their close, the amount of new insurance written by the companies and the lapse rate were exceedingly satisfactory. This was particularly marked in the case of the Metropolitan, which in 1941 reached the total of more than $25,000,000,000 of insurance in force, issued more business in both the Ordinary and Industrial Departments than in several years past, and achieved in both Departments the lowest lapse rates on record.

But if the insurance companies came through this Federal and other investigations unscathed, it must not be supposed that this business has been without its trials and tribulations. No human institution has ever sprung into perfection, like Athena from the head of Zeus; and the Life insurance business has had its growing pains. Three quarters of a century ago the Life insurance companies, including the Metropolitan, were launched as purely competitive business ventures with the profit motive well in the foreground, entirely in keeping

22

CHART I

Life Insurance in Force—All Departments
Metropolitan Life Insurance Company, 1868–1942

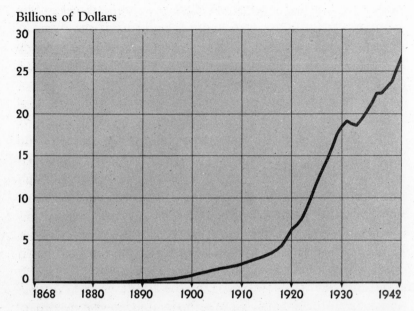

Billions of Dollars

with the aggressive, individualistic spirit of the times. Naturally, contracts at the beginning were not as liberal as they are today. Agents frequently were poorly trained and did not fully measure up to the responsibility of their calling. As a result, insurance was sometimes written in amounts disproportionate to the family income, haphazardly distributed, causing high lapse rates and excessive expense and loss.

As in every new and successful undertaking, practices developed which were subject from time to time to criticism both from within and without the insurance business. Some of these criticisms perhaps were unfounded; but others served a useful purpose by calling attention to the need for constructive changes. The history of Life insurance shows constant self-examination and improvement of practice. Throughout the years, certainly the Metropolitan has always been eager to try new fields and to better its service. The Company has lived through critical periods and has profited from them.

Beginning inauspiciously, in the course of the years it has continuously modified its point of view and its methods to adapt itself to the changing needs of its clientele. It has never ceased to raise the level of its Agency Force—to make them more expert insurance men, more thoughtful of the interests of their clients, more socially responsive. A business which began primarily as a profit-making venture has been converted, step by step, into one from which, ever since 1915, every vestige of profit has been eliminated. Early in the history of the Company was coined the happy slogan "A business above reproach." It is to the everlasting credit of the pioneers and their successors that they made this slogan a practical reality.

And yet in telling this 75-year story, we must not forget that the history of many other Life insurance companies has run a parallel course during these momentous years. The growth of The Prudential Insurance Company of America, another pioneer in Industrial insurance, parallels that of the Metropolitan. Throughout the years, the purely Ordinary companies like the New York Life, the Equitable, the Mutual, and many others have likewise maintained a fine record of integrity and public service. Together, the experience of these organizations illustrates a condition of life in America even more significant than the growth of the insurance business. We are concerned here with a development which is synchronous with the extraordinary industrialization of America and with the marked rise in the standard of living of huge numbers of people. No other business is more expressive of our fundamental democratic union, of our American ideals, energy, and resourcefulness. The changes we have described would have been impossible in any other country.

The story we are telling is, therefore, essentially the role which Life insurance has played in creating an American way of life. It reflects conditions which have made the working people of the country anxious and able to provide protection for their families. They have made the Metropolitan possible. The story behind the growth of the Company and of American Life insurance is essentially the story of America itself.

CHAPTER 2

The Cornerstones Are Laid:
1868-1891

THE WORLD of 1868, when the Metropolitan was born, was very different from the world we know today. There were no telephones in those days and no electric lights. The country had not yet been spanned by a trans-continental railroad. Records were kept in handwritten ledgers, and business letters were penned in longhand. The entire population of the United States was only about 37,000,000, as compared with 134,000,000 at present. The flag then carried 37 stars. Canada at that time contained only 3,500,000 people, as compared with more than 11,000,000 at present. She had only one year earlier (1867) achieved Dominion status in the British Empire. The two countries, although their frontiers were expanding, were still largely rural. At the census of 1870, the American population living on farms and in country villages numbered about 30,000,000. Persons engaged in agriculture, forestry, and animal husbandry constituted half the total working population.

The War of the States, to be sure, was over, but the struggle had left in its wake a variety of national problems— not only political but also economic and social. The Nation was still feeling most of these with full force. For instance, greenbacks were still in circulation, and specie payment was not to be resumed until 11 years later. With the emancipation of the slaves, the labor problem reached a new phase. The Government of a now united Nation was anxious to offer its citizens fields for expansion, and through the Homestead Acts and subsequent land grants made thousands of farm acres available to pioneers. To others more enterprising, new territories offered opportunity to exploit the resources of great plains and mountains. The primary need of the country was adequate transportation facilities, which were considered a key to further economic progress. However, all signs pointed to a great expansion ahead. The actual issues of the war itself had, for the most part, been settled. The country could now go forward to the fruitful destiny which its rich natural resources and its vigorous people promised.

Industry, commerce, and finance felt the new stimulus to surge forward. The business depression which immediately followed the close of the war proved short and was succeeded by a distinct upturn. By 1868 there was in progress a business revival which was to last five years. The Metropolitan was thus launched on a rising economic tide. Immigrants in large numbers were encouraged to come to add the work of their hands to the building of the country. They made up a new working population, which took root, for the most part, in the cities. Crossroads were becoming towns almost over-night. Towns were swiftly growing into cities. A deeper sense of permanence colored the thoughts of the American people, who began to think in terms of a future, a home, family security. The United States was rapidly coming of age.

The class of wage-earners was growing rapidly, a circum-stance which, as we shall see, proved to be a determining factor in the development of the Metropolitan. As inventions multiplied and factories grew, women and children were employed in greater numbers. The acceleration of industry and of urban life accentuated the economic insecurity which many felt in their new environment. City dwellers became conscious of the hazards of long working days, child labor, and industrial accidents. Mines and railroads and machines were being developed with consequent risk to human life. Health conditions in our cities were far from good. To provide a measure of security for this increasing urban population, Life insurance companies came into being.

The war decade of the 1860's gave opportunity for the great expansion of the Life insurance business. As a result, more than 100 companies were functioning by 1868. The New England Mutual and The Mutual Life Insurance Company of New York had already been in operation for 25 years. In fact, when the Metropolitan appeared on the scene, there were already in existence organizations with such familiar names as the New York Life, the Equitable Life of New York, the Mutual Benefit of New Jersey, the John Hancock, the Aetna, and the Connecticut Mutual. By present standards none of these companies was large, yet in their day they were important economic enterprises. At the end of 1868 the largest of these, The Mutual Life of New York, had gross assets of more than $30,000,000 and insurance in force amounting to nearly $200,000,000.

Thus, when the Metropolitan was founded, the Life insurance business had already achieved a fair degree of stability. The agency system, a typical American contribution, had been extensively developed in the previous 25 years. The agent had become a very influential element in the business. General agents were appointed to cover specific cities or, in the case of more sparsely populated areas, to represent a company in an entire State. These men personally contributed to the extraordinary growth of Life insurance in the United States, and much competition arose among the companies for good producers and reliable men. The principal policy plans used today were already developed. The straight Life policy was the most popular form of coverage, although the Endowment also had a measure of popularity. Term insurance constituted only a small part of the companies' business, while Annuity sales were negligible.

As was characteristic of all business ventures at that time, selling practices in Life insurance were much below present standards. It was a period of transition and growing pains. The increase in the number of companies had been too rapid. Many of these mushroom companies were offering extravagant commissions to their agents, and were so lax in the selection of risks and ignorant of methods of premium and reserve calculations that they were not able to meet their obligations. Doubtful assets had been permitted to appear in their balance sheets. Dividends were sometimes paid which had not been earned. As a result of such ignorance and maladministration, the great majority of Life insurance companies which were organized in the East from 1860 to 1869 passed out of existence before 1880. Those which remained in business, however, were, in the main, sound in their marketing practices and well managed.

That the institution of Life Insurance in America survived through aggressive, profit-seeking competition is due largely to the ability and integrity of many of its early leaders. There were men of stature and vision in the American insurance field—such men as Elizur Wright, the first Insurance Commissioner of Massachusetts, sometimes known as "the father of Life insurance in America"; William Barnes, the first Superintendent of the Insurance Department of New York State; Sheppard Homans, a pioneer in American actuarial science; and David Parks Fackler, who, in various actuarial capacities, served to keep many of the young companies on the right track. Among executive officers and directors of the companies were such vigorous personalities as Henry B. Hyde, of the Equitable; John F. Dryden, of The Prudential; Morris Franklin, of the New York Life; H. B. Claflin, Chauncey M. Depew, Cyrus W. Field, George F. Baker, and Leland Stanford.

It was in this bustling atmosphere of postwar activity that the Metropolitan Life Insurance Company had its beginnings. The roots of the Company, in fact, lead back directly to Civil War days when the National Union Life and Limb Insurance Company was launched in 1863 "for the purpose of making insurance upon the lives and limbs and health of the soldiers, sailors, and marines in the Army and Navy of the United States." This company, like so many others organized for wartime activity, had to be completely reorganized in the next few years. In 1866 it was divided into the National

Life Insurance Company and the National Travelers Insurance Company. The latter organization had planned to write Accident insurance, but in the words of its Secretary, it soon found this business "troublesome, so much in detail, and so beset with fraudulent claims that we concluded some time since to abandon it."

Accordingly, by an act of the Legislature of April 9, 1867, this Company changed its Charter to permit it to write Life insurance. Less than one year later it again changed its name and Charter, this time to become the Metropolitan Life Insurance Company. According to its first President, Dr. James R. Dow, it seemed advisable "to discontinue the Accident Department and pursue the Life insurance business exclusively, under a new and distinctive name, as the old name was not deemed appropriate to a purely Life insurance company." When the Metropolitan came into corporate being on March 24, 1868, it took over the small Home Office and Field organization of the National Travelers Insurance Company. The President and the Board of Directors continued their respective duties in the newly created Metropolitan and at the same location, 243 Broadway, New York City.

It is interesting to note that this Company, like its predecessor, was essentially a Brooklyn organization. The President, Dr. Dow, a retired physician of considerable means, was a highly respected citizen of Brooklyn. The majority of the stockholders and Directors were his close associates, not only in the business but in the religious and social circles of that city. Among these, Joseph F. Knapp was a leader. He had already made his mark in a lithographing business known as Major and Knapp Engraving, Manufacturing, and Lithographing Co. He owned 100 shares in the new organization, and was Chairman of its Finance Committee. Elias Jones was Vice-President; D. P. Fackler, Consulting Actuary; and Dr. James A. White, Medical Examiner. Similarly, H. A. Jones, S. M. Beard, Samuel W. Truslow, Watson Sandford, Howell Smith, all men of standing in Brooklyn affairs, saw in the organization of this Life insurance company an opportunity

President, 1871–1891

to invest their capital profitably and, at the same time, to render a public service.

The Metropolitan was organized and long operated as a stock company, beginning with a capitalization of $200,000, divided into 4,000 shares of $50 each. Provision was made in the Charter for a reduction in capitalization to $100,000 when the gross assets of the Company would reach $500,000. Although the Company was launched as a profit-making enterprise, the Charter limited the amount paid to stockholders to 7 percent on the capital stock, plus one tenth of any surplus remaining after providing for the outstanding liabilities of the Company. (Incidentally, the one-tenth provision was never put into effect and was dropped from the Charter in 1874.) The remaining nine tenths of the surplus was to be placed to the credit of policyholders in proportion to the amount of their respective premiums. Stockholders had a vote for every share of the capital stock they owned. Policyholders likewise were entitled to a vote, provided they were insured for at least one year and paid an annual premium of not less than $100, or were entitled to an annuity of $100 or more. Thus, from its very beginning, the Company was what is known as a "mixed" or a semi-mutual organization—a fortunate circumstance, as we shall see, for its future security.

The new Company was launched with vigor. Although it had few Agents, the Metropolitan from the start got more new business than most of the larger and older companies already in the field. By the close of 1868 the Company had issued 1,447 policies for $4,340,000, an extremely creditable total in a year. A stroke of good fortune, in 1869, was the opportunity to underwrite the Life insurance of the Hildise Bund, a sizable society of German-speaking working people. The Bund collected premiums weekly from its members and then transmitted them to the Metropolitan quarterly. In this step we have a suggestive forerunner of the Company's later interest in the insurance of working people.

Its resourcefulness and energy made the infant organization a strong competitor for business. It was expanding so rapidly that in the next year it was obliged to move from 243 Broadway to larger quarters at 319 Broadway. By the end of 1870 the Company had on its books in excess of $13,000,000 of insurance, an increase of 93 percent over the previous year. During 1870 the premium income had increased to more than $400,000; the reserve fund on policies to about $680,000; dividends, cash surrender, and death claim payments during the year amounted to more than $100,000. The Field Force numbered about 80, some of them eminently qualified and successful Agents. In a current reference to the administration, the important insurance journal, *The Spectator*, commented: "The managers of the Company are thoughtful, wide-awake men; yet with all their enterprise and push, they have been guided with a conservatism and foresight which have never to our knowledge induced them to forego character of business for mere volume."

It is interesting, in looking over the Company's early canvassing literature, to find that it emphasized the non-forfeiture clause in policies, evidently a popular move in a period when insurance companies were none too financially secure. All its contracts, whether Life or Endowment, carried a paid-up feature, available after three years' premiums had been paid, equal at least to the amount of premiums paid to the Company. Policies were "whole world policies" which permitted the insured to travel anywhere without canceling his insurance rights, although there were certain restrictions in the case of residence in specified regions. This at the time was a liberal provision. Another special feature of the Company's early operation, designed to encourage public confidence, was an arrangement with the State Insurance Department to countersign and to register certain policies indicating that the policy was secured by pledge of securities with the Department. All policies were incontestable after five years. A 30-day grace period for the payment of premiums was also an unusual concession. These items, which today are taken for granted in Life insurance practice and most of which are now required by law, were at that time liberal advances and indicated a skillful and progressive program for developing the young Company in line with the public interest.

The point of view and attitude of the Company are best characterized in a statement published on January 1, 1871:

> Above any mere addition therefore to its membership; above the pride of Assets rolling among the millions; above the matter of Dividends, "Special Features," &c., the chief concern of the Metropolitan shall be the *ultimate protection of the assured*.
>
> In these days of fierce competition, we are apt to disregard the old landmarks in the wild anxiety for business, but the management of this Company are determined to be guided only by those sound and conservative principles which can be the only basis of a *permanent* success; among them is the necessity of more solicitude for the *character* of its business than for its mere *volume*.

The first administration of the Metropolitan was destined to be shortlived, for Dr. Dow died at the end of February 1871. The management of the Company passed to Joseph F. Knapp, a man of extraordinary business capacity. As a leading Director and as Chairman of the important Finance Committee of the Metropolitan, Mr. Knapp had shown himself particularly equipped to steer the new business. He had a genius for detail, and his thoroughgoing, meticulous method of work assured a smooth-running organization. His was a hard-hitting, tireless energy. He possessed as well the intuitive faculty of judging men and placing them in positions best suited to their particular skills. It had been on his advice that John R. Hegeman had been appointed by Dr. Dow as Secretary of the Company. It was he who, with characteristic foresight, just before his death two decades later, arranged for Haley Fiske to take the office of Vice-President when Mr. Hegeman succeeded to the Presidency in 1891. It was he who recognized the ability of Frederick H. Ecker early in his career and gave it direction and scope. Joseph F. Knapp's hand guided the destiny of the Metropolitan during these crucial, formative years. Through those whom he selected as administrators, his vigorous influence has operated even up to this 75th anniversary year of the Company's founding.

An effective teammate for Mr. Knapp was John R. Hegeman, who had been selected to fill the Secretaryship of the Company caused by the resignation of Elias A. Jones in 1870, and who became Vice-President in 1871. Mr. Hegeman had received his training in the insurance business at the Manhattan Life Insurance Company, and before that had worked with the Bank of the Republic. He joined the Company at the age of 26, and for half a century was to be a forceful figure in its epic development. His genial disposition and polished manner admirably complemented the brusque manner of Mr. Knapp. His tact, personal magnetism, and persuasive eloquence carried the Company over many a rough spot in its early history.

Under such leadership, the sturdy young Company was well managed. Special effort was made to keep expenses low, to win public confidence and approval, to strengthen the financial status of the Company, to curtail lapses, and energetically to seek new business. As soon as Mr. Knapp took office, he announced that all business of the Company would be conducted on a cash basis. Prior to that, in accordance with common practice, the Company had accepted promissory notes in part payment of premiums. This credit practice was continued for many years more in other companies, with disastrous results to some.

The Metropolitan Officers were particularly careful in the selection of their Agents, and inquired in detail as to their abilities, character, and previous experience. They knew how important it was to look into every application for insurance, and they urged their Agents to exercise extreme care in the selection of clients. In spite of the sharp struggle for business, the Company emphasized and maintained high standards of ethics. It cautioned Agents not to offer improper inducements or make unauthorized promises. It instructed them to stick to the printed text in representing the plans, features, and record of the Company. Agents overstepping the bounds were reprimanded or dismissed. The Officers condemned the common recourse of running rival companies down in the wild scramble for business. This malpractice, they realized, was injurious to the entire institution of Life Insurance. They were not building for the day; they were building for the future.

It is obvious that they were also keen businessmen, and knew that generous and fair treatment of policyholders would win public recognition. Claims were paid promptly. As previously stated, policies were "registered," i.e., counter-signed by the Insurance Department, indicating that a special fund was deposited by the Company and held by the State as security for the payment of policies when they became due. In order to gain official confirmation of its sound financial status, the Company requested an examination by the New York State Insurance Department. In 1871, after such an examination, the Superintendent of Insurance, George W. Miller, stated that the Company was managed with "integrity, energy, and ability," and concluded with the following words: "From the thorough personal examination made, I am satisfied that the condition of the Company is such as to entitle it to the confidence of the policyholders and the public." Similarly, *The Baltimore Underwriter*, in referring to the business of 1872, wrote: "In its issue of 8,642 policies last year, the steady augmenting of its receipts, the economy of expenditure, the character of its assets, its watchful management, its large membership, the rigid scrutiny of its risks, the public apprecia-tion of its distinctive plans of insurance, etc.—in all these, we say, is the assurance that whatever solid Life assurance contemplates the Metropolitan is abundantly able to supply."

Intelligent management and energetic prosecution of the business by the new administration bore results. By the end of 1871, after less than four years of existence, the Company had on its books more than 11,000 policies totaling almost $15,000,000 of Life insurance, a considerable sum for that time. Only two years later the figures increased to 18,600 policies in force, and to more than $26,300,000 of business.

35

The official returns for 1873 revealed that, in the number of policies written, the Company held third place among the 56 companies transacting business in New York State. By this time, the Company had already entered 17 States and the Dominion of Canada. Its business extended to all the States in the New England, the Middle Atlantic, the East North Central areas, as well as to Iowa and Missouri.

This sound growth is all the more remarkable in that it occurred during a period of economic and financial excesses. Speculation and "frenzied finance" were rampant. The post-Civil War demand for commodities was gradually letting up and prices declined as a result. Excessive railway building and the too rapid development of the trans-Mississippi West had brought about a glut of foodstuffs and thrown older areas out of cultivation. A sudden crisis developed which broke into the lavish prosperity of the country and was immediately felt by all insurance firms. Partly owing to deficiencies of management, accentuated by the general economic crisis, no less than 22 Life insurance companies in New York State had ceased business in the six years ending with 1873.

It must not be assumed, moreover, that the Metropolitan's early success was achieved without many difficulties or that it continued indefinitely. The task of building a functioning organization and a Field Force was an arduous and expensive one. Competent Agents were difficult to find. Many of the men engaged produced insufficient business, and a considerable number of the applications submitted were on questionable risks. In spite of every effort, the lapse rate was high, reflecting the adverse business conditions which were gripping the country. As the depression deepened, insurance company after insurance company went to the wall. Of the more than 15 Life insurance companies incorporated in the State of New York in the three-year period 1866 to 1868, the Metropolitan alone survived.

One obstacle which the Officers had to overcome was the fierce competition of the older companies in the field. These could afford to pay higher commissions because their greater assets and surplus gave them a more solid financial position. The Metropolitan was unable to compete in commissions with these better-established companies without seriously impairing its assets. This situation was accentuated by the growing depression throughout the country. As a result, the Company's business began to drop sharply in 1874, and continued downward for five years until 1879. In this short period, the number of policies issued annually declined from 8,280 to 510. The insurance in force decreased rapidly from $27,300,000 in 1874 to less than $12,000,000 in 1879. The Company, to any outsider, would have seemed to be on the way to dissolution.

But even in these darkest hours the Officers retained their vigor and faith. They were no mere summer soldiers. They had shown their confidence in the ultimate success of the organization by obtaining a leasehold and moving into the spacious building at Park Place and Church Street in 1876. They were confident that the Company would soon return to the highroad of success. It was the ever-resourceful Mr. Knapp who pointed the way. He proposed opening a new and immense field of operation—Life insurance for wage-earners and their families—where the Metropolitan would not be compelled to compete at a disadvantage with other companies. In 1879 the Company entered the field of Industrial insurance. Thus began the establishment of the close ties it has always maintained with the working people of this country, a relation which has determined the distinctive character of the organization and its services. By entering this vastly enlarged theater of operations, the Company was to influence the entire course of the business in this country. The year 1879 is indeed historic for American Life insurance.

The decision to write Industrial insurance was by no means a sudden inspiration, but a carefully planned move. Both Mr. Knapp and Mr. Hegeman were keen students of the business, and for a decade they had been following the discussions on the need for Industrial insurance in this country in *The Insurance Monitor*, the *Spectator*, and especially in *The Insurance Times* under the distinguished editorship of Stephen

37

Third Home Office: 32 Park Place
1876–1893

English. This branch had already achieved signal success in England, where the Prudential of London was carrying on a considerable Industrial business. Meanwhile American insurance officials had been warmly debating the pros and cons of Weekly Premium business. Such an outstanding personality as Elizur Wright agitated against it; on the other hand, Julius L. Clark, Insurance Commissioner of Massachusetts and a leading figure in the insurance world of that day, advocated it in his annual report for 1874.

The theme "insurance for the masses" runs like a hopeful thread through the Metropolitan's early correspondence. President Knapp discussed it often and at length with Vice-President Hegeman; he talked to the Agency Staff about it. Year after year the same note creeps into his letters. "I have not forgotten insurance for the masses," he wrote to one of the General Agents in 1872. "On the contrary, it is upper-most in my thoughts. I have several good thinkers at work who will no doubt soon produce something which will take." In fact, by 1879, the Company already had had a decade of experience with Life insurance on the lives of working people, sold on the basis of weekly premiums. It will be recalled that in 1869, almost before the ink on the new Charter was dry, the Metropolitan underwrote a type of insurance on working people who paid their premiums weekly, and found this business both feasible and profitable.

The most convincing argument for undertaking the new business was the success of the Prudential Assurance Com-pany of London in popularizing Industrial insurance among the wage-earners in the cities of England. Both Mr. Knapp and Mr. Hegeman had watched this organization with avid interest. In the Company's Archives there is still an old scrapbook, big as an unabridged dictionary, labeled "Pru-dential of London," which contains booklets, pamphlets, corre-spondence, annual statements, newspapers, magazine and insurance paper clippings about the English organization. It shows the evidence of painstaking study by these Metro-politan Officers. They commented on the various forms of policies. They studied the annual reports of the Prudential. On its quinquennial report for the period ending December 31, 1876, are notations in Mr. Hegeman's handwriting, comment-ing on the vastness of the Prudential's Industrial compared with its Ordinary business. The premium income from Industrial was 11 times that of Ordinary. He noted the size of the average weekly Industrial premium, about $3\frac{1}{2}$ cents. "Very heavy loading," is his cryptic note on the figures giving the expense of the business. He underscored the stipulation that the full benefit was not to be paid if death occurred during the first year of insurance. He studied carefully the ratio of expense to income. The Metropolitan Officers learned also that while the Prudential had achieved phenomenal prosperity, it had gone through difficult years before the initial surplus was built up.

Accordingly, those who knew Mr. Knapp were not surprised when, early in 1879, he packed his bags and sailed for London. He was not the kind of man to be content with armchair studies; characteristically, he headed right for the fountainhead of information on Industrial Life insurance, Henry Harben, of the Prudential. Mr. Knapp was given a cordial reception. His studies at firsthand confirmed his previous decision to enter the business. His next step, one without parallel in the annals of insurance history, was executed with typical boldness. He arranged with Brice Collard, a British insurance man, to become his local deputy and to send over a sizable number of Englishmen experienced in conducting Industrial insurance, to launch the Metropolitan's new effort in the United States. Between 1879 and 1884 Mr. Collard commuted back and forth from London to New York, bringing to our shores several hundred able men, together with their families. Once located in key centers, these men had a heroic task to accomplish—to hire and train local Agents in the new approach, and to organize and establish District Offices from the very ground up—all at top speed. They had to teach a technique of selling policies for small amounts, of receiving the premiums weekly in the homes of the insured, and of accounting for this multitude of transactions to the Home Office.

Many circumstances conspired to make formidable the building of an Industrial insurance business in this country. The depression of 1873 and its aftermath of liquidations and bankruptcies had seriously disturbed the economic life of the Nation. This was the most disastrous period in American insurance history. Policyholders lost many millions of dollars in company failures, and public faith in the institution of Life Insurance dropped to a low point. Moreover, the American people had little or no knowledge of the advantages of Industrial insurance—the large majority had never even heard of it. Only The Prudential Insurance Company of America and the John Hancock Mutual Life Insurance Company were already in the field, and their operations were very restricted.

There had been few fraternal organizations such as the English Friendly Societies to popularize among working people the practice of saving funds for the expenses of death.

Despite these difficulties, the Company flourished from the very beginning, probably because of the experienced technique of the English Agents. The first Industrial policy was issued on November 17, 1879, and before another year had passed more than 200,000 such policies were issued. The insurance in force multiplied by leaps and bounds. At the end of 1880, in a little over a year, the Company had on its books more than $9,000,000 of Industrial insurance. This figure was virtually doubled during the next year. At the close of 1882 the Industrial business in force exceeded $34,500,000. The Company passed the $100,000,000 mark early in 1886, a little more than six years from the inception of the business. As the volume of business increased, so did the Field Force. A few weeks after Industrial insurance was launched the Company had three District Offices, with 130 Field-Men. The following year the strength of the Field Force increased to 750. By 1883 more than 1,600 men were operating from nearly 50 District Offices; and the expansion of business and personnel continued apace. The insurance world viewed this development with amazement. The Company's success had proved the enormous popular demand for this type of protection, previously almost altogether ignored.

Paradoxically, the very success of the Company brought with it serious financial difficulties. The establishment of many new District Offices, the forging of a Home Office organization, the setting up of reserve funds, and the payment of commissions to Agents, all entailed an outlay of considerable money. The situation in 1883 reached a point where in its high flush of prosperity the Company was probably insolvent; certainly the capital stock was impaired. Faced with this situation, Mr. Knapp set about to increase the Company's capital. He solicited his friends; he even mortgaged his own home. In these ways he brought in $400,000 in new money, increasing the Company's capitalization to

$500,000. The Company was still expanding so rapidly that even this additional cash did not immediately put it upon a sound basis. Notwithstanding the fact that $400,000 had been added during the year, at the end of 1883 the surplus was slightly more than $300,000—an increase of less than $33,000 over the previous year. With the passing of another year, the surplus was further reduced, due partly to the expenses occasioned by the substantial increase in new business, and by the end of 1885 it had dropped to just under $140,000. The Company had a bookkeeping loss of $560,000 in three years. In effect, all the new capital was wiped out. Then the tide turned. In 1886 the surplus increased to $258,000 and grew rapidly thereafter. Never since has there been any question as to the financial stability of the Company.

When Mr. Knapp was seeking new funds in 1883, the Company's precarious financial condition obliged him to offer the prospect of a good-sized profit to the investors. This was especially true since the Charter limited annual dividends to 7 percent of the capital stock. His inducement was a provision that if the business succeeded, the capital stock could be increased to a maximum of $2,000,000, yielding four shares for each one purchased. Mr. Knapp himself contributed so large a portion of the added funds that he came to control a majority of the stock—51 percent, to be exact. It is important to note that despite these generous terms to the investors, the dividends were limited to $140,000 a year at a maximum. Actually, even after the Company had grown to giant proportions, never a penny more than $140,000 a year could be paid to stockholders. The full significance of this provision will be apparent when we discuss the mutualization of the Company in the following chapter.

Through these ups and downs, Mr. Knapp was steadfast in his belief in the ultimate success of the venture. His efforts for business went on vigorously even during the period of critical financial difficulty. During 1883, for example, the Industrial business on the books increased by almost $22,000,000. With an average amount of each policy only a little

42

more than $100, one can realize what a prodigious achievement this was. Once the financial stability of the Company was assured, the business grew at an even more rapid pace. In 1886 the Industrial in force increased by more than $28,000,000, and by 1890 the annual growth mounted to $30,000,000. In the short period between 1883 and 1891 the amount of Industrial insurance in force, despite a high lapse rate, increased from $56,500,000 to more than $250,000,000; the number of policies jumped correspondingly from 526,000 to more than 2,200,000. Nothing like this had ever before happened in the field of Life insurance.

The warm and spontaneous response of the people to Industrial insurance clearly demonstrated the widespread need for this new form of protection. Wage-earners and their families were quick to realize that this type of insurance was suited to their pattern of life. These people could not afford to buy Ordinary policies, but they were glad to purchase insurance in small amounts and to pay premiums weekly to an Agent who called at the home. Moreover, all members of the family, including the husband, wife, and children, were eligible. Insurance officials were equally quick to recognize the value of Industrial insurance. As early as 1881 the Superintendent of Insurance of New York State wrote in his annual report: "This class of insurance is somewhat new and is yet an experiment in this country, but thus far it seems to meet with success which promises well for its future growth and prosperity." And four years later, the Hon. Ephraim Williams, the Insurance Commissioner of Connecticut, actually recommended Industrial Life policies as an antidote to poverty. He said: "If people so circumstanced would generally avail themselves of its benefits, the tendency would be to diminish the population of poorhouses and decrease the public burden in this respect."

Such public approval helped to throw open even more doors to Life insurance companies offering this type of family protection. The contemporaries of the Metropolitan—The Prudential Insurance Company of America, which had begun operations as an Industrial company in 1875, and the John Hancock Mutual Life Insurance Company, which started in August 1879—were also forging ahead. As the Industrial business prospered, several other companies entered the field. It was indeed fortunate that the bulk of Industrial insurance was conducted by companies which were managed with high integrity and skill.

Sowing the seeds of Industrial insurance over a rapidly widening area required an unprecedented expansion of the Company's Field Force. When the Industrial business was launched late in 1879, the Company had only one branch office in New York City and two in Brooklyn. During 1880 no less than 23 offices were opened in such widely separated cities as Providence; Baltimore; Boston; Pittsburgh; Philadelphia; Rochester, N. Y.; Portland, Maine; and Washington, D. C. Each year saw the cultivation of new areas. Offices were opened in Chicago and in Newark during 1881, and by 1883 the Company had pushed as far west as Milwaukee, Wis., and as far south as Richmond, Va. The business was pursued most energetically where the need for Industrial insurance was most urgent—in industrial cities with large concentrations of wage-earners. In the five-year period between 1886 and 1891, the number of District Offices grew from 65 to almost 100; the Field Force increased from nearly 2,700 to almost 5,000 men.

True pioneers those who managed these early offices! Their names are still mentioned with reverence when the Veterans get together to reminisce about "the good old days." There was William G. Staniland, one of the first over from England. He was assigned to the Pittsburgh District, and became the first Metropolitan Superintendent to go west of the Allegheny Mountains. There was W. G. Roberts, of Philadelphia, an older brother of James S. Roberts, who later became Secretary of the Company; James W. Walker, who did spade work in the early Industrial business; Allen Lee Bassett, who had been President of The Prudential of Newark, and who for years managed the Metropolitan's Newark District;

JAMES M. CRAIG

GEORGE H. GASTON

JAMES S. ROBERTS

John H. Crankshaw, who played an important part in training the Field Force. Especially effective was Joseph Grosner, who, as Agent, then as Superintendent, and later as Chief Supervisor at the Home Office, played a vital role in inspiring the Field-Men to an understanding of the service they could render. All these men not only did yeoman service in opening territory for Industrial insurance, but also trained literally hundreds of new men to take over leadership as Superintendents in the ever-expanding operations of the Company.

Meanwhile the growth of the Industrial business brought equally knotty problems of control to be solved in the Home Office. It is to the credit of the first Officers and their associates that at the inception of the business they evolved a system of record keeping and management so efficient that it has been carried over, with few changes, to present-day use. A trio of brilliant and effective men were responsible for this solid working foundation—James M. Craig, James S. Roberts, and George H. Gaston. Mr. Craig, who came into the Company in 1872, had much to do with the efficient setting up of the card records and the bookkeeping system, and later with the calculation of premium rates in Industrial insurance. He took on ever-increasing responsibilities as the Actuary and devoted a half century to the service of the Company, until his death in 1922. James S. Roberts, one of the English group, came over in 1880 with his father and two brothers, all of whom were employed by the Metropolitan. He too helped develop the record system, specializing in auditing the accounts of Agents, and left his mark by the invention of many short cuts and devices by which the cost of the work was materially reduced. Mr. Roberts had, when he retired in 1928, served the Company 48 years, and continued occasional visits there until he died in 1939 at the ripe old age of 80. The third of the group, George H. Gaston, joined the organization as a Clerk in 1879, having been previously employed in a similar capacity in The Prudential of Newark. He grew up with the young Company, and worked particularly with the early organization of men in the Industrial

Field Force. Great was the jubilation in his office when the Weekly Industrial balance sheet showed a profit for the first time. He was appointed Secretary in 1891, and soon there after was made Vice-President in charge of the Agency Division. Forty-three out of his 64 years were spent with the Company, until the moment of his death in 1922. The lives of these three men spanned the critical years of the Company's development of the Industrial business. They laid its founda-tions in terms of efficient techniques and a productive and loyal Agency Force.

As the volume of business multiplied and premiums flowed into the Company in an ever-widening stream, the assets rose rapidly. Whereas, prior to 1885, these were never much over $2,000,000, by 1887 they had increased to about $5,000,000, and in the next five years reached the impressive total of over $16,500,000. This rising tide of money created the problem of finding safe and profitable investments. In the decade of the 1880's a substantial part of the investment portfolio of the Life insurance companies was devoted to loans on and ownership of real estate. Loans on real estate secured by mortgage and properties owned amounted to about one half

Fred Ecker at the age of 16

47

of the invested assets of the Metropolitan throughout the '80's, and rose to three quarters of the Company's investments by 1891. In the early years of the decade the cities made large bond issues to finance internal improvements. These city bonds and United States Government securities accounted for a little more than a quarter of the investment portfolio, but they soon diminished in importance. The widespread repudiation by municipalities of their debts resulted in the virtual elimination of these securities from the Company's portfolio in the next few years. With this change came a rapid rise in the purchase of railroad securities. These entered the investment picture for the first time in 1882, and then only for a small amount. Two years later, however, following the enormous railroad expansion to meet increasing population, this type of security accounted for more than 10 percent of the Company's invested funds, and shortly thereafter it jumped to almost 30 percent. By 1886 the Company was holding the bonds of more than 20 railroads operating in various parts of the country. These securities were purchased under the general guidance of Vermilyea & Co., one of the larger investment houses of the period. Shortly thereafter, Mr. Ecker, although still a very young man, began to take an increasing part in the Company's investment activities. He was thus initiated into the intricacies of railroad investment, a field in which he was later to become one of the country's outstanding figures.

No wonder that the Company, growing like a young titan, toward the end of the 1880's began to feel cramped in its quarters at Park Place and Church Street. A new Home Office was definitely needed to house the vastly increasing Staff and to give the public some idea of the rising importance of the Company as an insurance institution. With the enterprise and vision that had always characterized him, Mr. Knapp went ahead and purchased a sizable plot on the corner of Madison Avenue and 23d Street facing Madison Square Park, in what was then one of the more fashionable uptown residential areas of the city. The move was an adventure, for at the time there was not an office building north of 14th Street. The noted architects, the Messrs. Le Brun, who had reconstructed the building at Park Place in 1876, were commissioned to draw plans for a new building. In 1890 was laid the cornerstone on which was to rise, within three years, a magnificent structure, the building at 1 Madison Avenue. It has remained, with progressive additions, the Home Office to this day—a symbol of the dignity and size of the organization, a beautiful landmark known throughout the world.

In the midst of this happy planning, a tragic note was sounded. Early in 1891 Mr. Knapp's health failed, and he went to Europe to recuperate. On the way back to New York on the steamer *La Champaigne*, he died on September 14th of that year at the age of 59. Through his successful management of the Company he had so ardently believed in and to which he had devoted his energy and judgment, Joseph F. Knapp had become one of America's rich men; but he was never to see the culmination of his labors.

President, 1891–1919

CHAPTER 3

A Social Institution Emerges:
1891-1919

AT THE NEXT MEETING of the Board of Directors, on October 7, 1891, John R. Hegeman, the affable and capable colleague of Mr. Knapp, was elected to the Presidency of the Company. Haley Fiske, who was to carry the chief burdens of administration for nearly 40 years, was made Vice-President. For a decade prior to 1891 he had handled the legal affairs of the Metropolitan in the office of the Company's counsel, Arnoux, Ritch, and Woodford, and in that capacity had worked closely with the Officers and had acquired a thorough knowledge of the insurance business. Mr. Knapp, two years before, had urged young Mr. Fiske to join the ranks of the Company. This was not feasible at the time, but Mr. Knapp did arrange that on his death Mr. Fiske was to take on the administrative responsibilities of the organization. Mr. Hegeman, as President, was to attend to financial problems, and to be the spokesman for the Company in its relations with the public. In this regard, his picturesque and gracious personality was a distinct asset. It was agreed to let the task of management fall on the shoulders of the younger, harder-hitting man. From 1891 to 1929 Mr. Fiske, first as Vice-President and later as President, was the dominant force in the Metropolitan. The president of a fellow company termed him "the Jupiter of Life Insurance Heavens." His forcefulness was akin to thunderbolts. To him as much as to any single man, the Metropolitan owes its eminence in the insurance world. Nor was his influence limited to his own Company.

His vigorous personality and his constructive intelligence left their indelible mark upon the whole institution of Life Insurance in America.

Haley Fiske was born in New Brunswick, N. J., on March 18, 1852. His father was a blacksmith and, later, a foundryman; his mother, a keen-witted woman known for her fine spiritual qualities. She inspired reverence in her son and evidently played a large part in giving direction to his life. Young Fiske attended Rutgers College, and although he made no particular mark as a student his fine personality stood out; his carriage and courteous bearing brought him the sobriquet Sir Haley. In a real sense, he was Sir Haley for the rest of his life to all who knew him. His first job was as a local newspaperman, but at the same time he studied law with Judge Woodbridge Strong. Early in May of 1873 he entered the New York office of Arnoux, Ritch, and Woodford as a clerk. He advanced rapidly and soon became an outstanding figure in the firm. Young Fiske, it was noted, possessed an amazing astuteness and sound judgment. The firm made him its trial lawyer, and his eloquence was such that even the famous Colonel Bob Ingersoll met defeat at his hands. Vigorous and incisive, he put his teeth into everything he did. He was assigned by his firm to handle the increasingly important affairs of the Metropolitan, and thus made himself expert in Life insurance problems and, more particularly, in those pertaining to the Industrial business.

Mr. Fiske became Vice-President of the Metropolitan before his 40th birthday, and soon became the dominating personality in the management of virtually all Departments. He was unmistakably Boss. He looked into every detail of office management. He required frequent and detailed reports from his heads of Departments; claims were reported to him daily. Under his militant direction the rapidly growing Home Office was galvanized into an even more efficient organization. He inaugurated the "Triennial Conventions," where he personally reported on the Company to the Field Force in every State in the Union and in every Province in Canada in which it did business. He gathered together the District Superintendents and Agents for personal instruction. A naturally gifted speaker, he acquired, with the years, an extraordinary eloquence which he used in moving descriptions of the program of the Company and its increasing contributions to the public welfare. He was at once administrator, chief salesman, and ambassador of good will.

Almost as soon as he took office, Mr. Fiske addressed himself to widening the field of the Company's operations with a reorganization of the practically defunct Ordinary Department. The little Ordinary business which had been on the books prior to the opening of the Industrial Department had shrunk to even less by 1891. The Metropolitan had become virtually an Industrial company. The Agents were concentrating on the writing of the Weekly Premium business. However, Mr. Fiske, with a farsighted view of the general improvement in standards of living, was convinced that the more than 4,000 Agents in the Field, coming into frequent contact with hundreds of thousands of families, had a rich opportunity to serve many of these people more effectively. Large numbers of policyholders, schooled from childhood in the value of Life insurance through their Industrial policies, would also be in the market for larger policies on the Ordinary plan. To such persons, the lower cost of the latter type of insurance would make available a larger amount of family protection.

To launch this venture was a stupendous undertaking. The Agents then were, for the most part, a poorly trained and shifting group. Could they be trusted to carry the message of Ordinary business convincingly to a more exacting public? Many had their doubts. But Mr. Fiske made a decision from which he never deviated: that every Agent of the Company must henceforth be of such high caliber that he could also conduct the Ordinary business successfully. He laid out permanent plans for instructing the Agents regarding every phase of the new business, including the types of policies and plans available in competitive organizations as well as in the Metropolitan. Most Agents welcomed this enlarged opportunity to increase their usefulness and to write the new line of business. As the earnings of the men increased, and the scope of their work widened, the job of Agent attracted men of higher and higher caliber.

Yet it was no easy matter in the early 1890's to branch out into the field of Ordinary insurance. Many of the evils which had driven the Metropolitan out of that field more than a decade before were still rampant. There was this difference, however: the Company had now been built up to the point where it was financially stable enough to make a forceful bid for business in the face of the competition of tontine and semi-tontine insurance. These speculative policies promised to those policyholders who continued their insurance for a specified period, the surpluses accumulated by the dividends and paid-up values forfeited by those who dropped out of the group in the interim. This type of insurance, which paid large commissions to agents and promised large future dividends to the insured, was still in the full tide of popularity. Mr. Fiske knew that this was a dangerous practice, and he would have none of it. In this, he anticipated by 15 years the exposures of the Armstrong Investigating Committee. The new Ordinary policies of the Company were to be without such speculative frills—written at the lowest possible cost, preferably in limited amounts, on better circumstanced wage-earners and salaried workers.

The keynote of the new Department was sounded in the first manual issued to the Agents: "The Metropolitan believes the time has come when the plain, common-sense men who make up the bulk of Life insurance policyholders are looking for a plain business contract. By plain business contracts we mean those that tell their story upon their face; which leave nothing to the imagination; borrow nothing from hope; require definite conditions and make definite promises in dollars and cents." The Company would have no part in the current extravagances of the business. This early doctrine has been called the "Creed" of the Company, and it has been

54

the platform to which the Company has steadfastly adhered. As we shall see later, it enabled the Metropolitan to stand out as a veritable fortress for the proper conduct of Ordinary insurance.

The Ordinary business prospered anew soon after 1892. This new lease on life was due not only to the low cost of the contracts, but also, in large measure, to the wide variety of plans available and to the many liberal features Mr. Fiske had incorporated in the policies. During 1892, 1,704 Ordinary policies were written for approximately $2,000,000, as compared with 178 policies for less than $200,000 the year before. The Ordinary insurance on the books jumped rapidly from approximately $5,300,000 in 1892, to almost 10 times that sum only five years later. Before the turn of the century more than $110,000,000 of such business was in force, representing close to 125,000 policies. Whereas in 1891 the Metropolitan was at the bottom of the list of Ordinary companies operating in New York, it had reached fourth place as regards business written in this Department by 1900. After the Armstrong investigation the Company forged ahead at an even more rapid pace, narrowing the margin between itself and the older, larger companies. Between 1906 and 1913 the Ordinary business in force gained $609,905,310. In the same period the New York Life gained $243,493,494; The Mutual $81,208,898; the Equitable $94,417,206. The Metropolitan thus gained nearly 50 percent more than all these three combined. Only a decade later, in 1923, the Metropolitan had become the largest Ordinary insurance company in the world as well as the largest in total insurance in force. This standing, moreover, had been achieved without general agents or salespeople other than the men who represented the Company on the so-called Industrial "debits," that is, the territory which each Agent serves.

Shortly after the Ordinary business was reestablished and the Company's Agents began to canvass for this type of insurance, they found that a considerable number of working people were able to pay premiums quarterly, but could not afford to buy insurance in sums as large as $1,000, the minimum amount for Ordinary. To provide this group with protection, the Company in July 1896 began to issue Intermediate insurance, i.e., policies for $500, with premiums payable annually, semiannually, or quarterly. It is not surprising that the Metropolitan should have pioneered in this field, since it has always blazed trails in bringing insurance protection to the lower-income groups. This new form of insurance likewise found a ready market. After the first six months 5,110 Intermediate policies were on the books for $2,555,000. At the end of 1901, only 5½ years after this department was launched, there were nearly 110,000 Intermediate policies in force for an amount close to $55,000,000. Within the next three years these figures more than doubled, and continued to increase rapidly. The use of Intermediate insurance has been subsequently extended to include persons in somewhat hazardous occupations and for those with physical impairments which make them ineligible for standard Ordinary policies. To widen even further the circle of protection, the Metropolitan in 1899 inaugurated Special Class policies for those who, because of occupation or physical impairments, could not meet the standards of Ordinary or Intermediate insurance.

An even more formidable task than building the Ordinary Department confronted Mr. Fiske when he joined the Metropolitan. Industrial insurance was under severe attack. Even before the Hegeman-Fiske administration came into office, the storm clouds had begun to gather. Late in the 1880's a number of attacks were directed against Industrial insurance. Incredible, but nevertheless true, was the fact that some worthy citizens of the day actually charged that Life insurance on children endangered their lives because a number of parents would let their children die of neglect, or murder them for the insurance proceeds. This was an era of muckraking, and the sensational attack on Big Business, Life insurance companies included, found a sympathetic response among certain legislators, newspapermen, and others who took up the cry.

The attack on child insurance, if not adequately answered, threatened the very life of Industrial insurance. Weekly Premium business was for the family; and unless the young-sters who formed so large a part of the family were included, the basic principle of this type of coverage was defeated. This result was abundantly evident from the experience of the Prudential of London, the expansion of which had been radically hindered by a temporary ban on child insurance. In 1889 the Pennsylvania Legislature introduced a bill to pro-hibit insurance on children. The idea spread to New York, Ohio, Massachusetts, Connecticut, and to Canada. For six long years legislative inquiries into Industrial insurance con-tinued their challenge. The most serious of these attacks was that of the Massachusetts Legislature of 1895. Charles Coolidge Read was spokesman for the Massachusetts Society for the Prevention of Cruelty to Children and other organiza-tions supporting the bill for the abolition of insurance on children. Sensational newspaper headlines inflamed public sentiment with stories of starvation, extreme poverty, and suffering alleged to result from Industrial insurance. When Mr. Fiske offered to answer the accusations through the columns of the newspapers, they refused to accept his state-ments except as paid advertisements. To put the facts before the public, his statement was printed at regular advertising rates. Next Mr. Fiske spoke in the chambers of many State Legislatures. With the tact and eloquence which had charac-terized him as a trial lawyer, he called attention to the flimsi-ness of the accusations, showed that even their few isolated cases when investigated had proved to be false. He success-fully challenged his opponents to present one authenticated instance of the terrible effects they charged. His simple weapon was fact. He knew that ignorance and prejudice would be thrust aside by the power of truth. And it was.

In connection with the hearings, Mr. Fiske outlined the accomplishments and the benefits of Industrial insurance and discussed the misconceptions that had grown up around it. He emphasized that a business which had been established for 40 years in England and which in two decades in the United States had resulted in the writing of nearly 7,000,000 policies by the three leading companies must certainly meet a fundamental need. He proved that Industrial Life insurance was a real necessity to wage-earners.

His review of the situation brought about a change in public sentiment. He cited previous investigations of Industrial insurance here and abroad. Pennsylvania had had a legislative inquiry in 1889, and after hearings were held, threw out the bill attacking Industrial insurance. The movement in Ohio brought the same result. New York State had conducted an investigation in 1890, and the Legislative Committee's hearings convinced the man who introduced the bill that he had made a mistake, and the Committee then killed it. Mr. Fiske quoted the action of the Province of Ontario, Canada, in which the bill to prohibit infantile insurance was not enacted into law. Connecticut, Illinois, and Tennessee all had had the same experience. After weeks of the sharpest interrogation, the Massachusetts committee shelved the bill. Everywhere the inquiries that threatened Industrial insurance came to an end. At these hearings Mr. Dryden, of the Prudential, and Mr. Rhodes, of the John Hancock, gave valuable testimony, but it was Mr. Fiske who carried the main burden for the defense, and the signal victory was his.

Although the absurd charges that Industrial insurance led to crime and poverty were definitely and finally answered, there remained the hard core of truth in certain serious defects in the conduct of this type of insurance. It was true that the lapse rate was high and that the provisions of the policy were far from liberal. Mr. Fiske saw these as well as any of its sharpest critics, but he was also convinced of the essential good which Industrial insurance was doing. He firmly believed that the weak spots in the Industrial business could, with time, be removed.

Apparently a stirring religious experience of self-searching was also at work within the man himself. It was about this time that he became an ardent and devout churchman. If

1 Madison Avenue
First Unit—1893

this were the biography of the man as it is of the Company, we would take more time to probe into the character which was being reforged during these critical years. Those who knew him during his tempestuous career as a successful trial lawyer could hardly recognize the new personality of the insurance executive. He was just as militant as before, but that militancy was now directed essentially toward making himself a useful instrument for the public good. He felt deeply the social responsibility which his power as head of a great Life insurance company serving men and women gave him. Henceforward it became his consuming desire to improve the life and health of the American people. He worked unceasingly, as one with a holy mission. Those who knew him during the last 20 years of his life recognized a man poured in heroic mold, dedicated to the task of making the world a better place in which to live and grateful for the Metropolitan as the instrument through which he might work.

His sense of social responsibility was translated into practice through increasing activities which broadened the scope of Industrial insurance and reduced its cost. Life insurance as a business was crossing the threshold into Life insurance as a social institution. An impressive step in this direction was taken in 1893. A major depression was fastening itself upon the country. Railroad building had been accompanied by inordinate speculation. Credit was generally inflated and many banking institutions failed. With their failure, some important railroad systems and the coal and iron industries were involved in the general distress. As unemployment increased, many people were unable to pay their premiums and were losing their protection when they needed it most. In September of that year the Company startled its Field Force with the following announcement: "Meanwhile we say to Superintendents, that if there should come under your notice the case of the death of any policyholder who kept his policy in force for a considerable length of time, and then was forced to let it go solely by being thrown out of work during the recent panic, we invite you to call our attention to the case with the special facts and circumstances concerning the deceased and his family that have come to your knowledge, so that we may consider what, if anything, we can do in the way of receiving a claim."

Without publicity, Agents investigated deaths on their debits, and many claims were paid on policies that had lapsed during the hard times. According to a strictly legal point of view, the Company was under no obligation to pay these claims; but a new spirit of service was abroad. It was felt again when toward the end of 1893, with better times in sight, the Company made sweeping concessions to policyholders in order to restore their insurance protection. Under these concessions, where a policy had lapsed during the business depression with premiums paid for certain minimum periods, the policyholder was given the option of receiving a new policy on a more favorable basis than either a reinstatement of his old policy or an independent application for new insurance. Hundreds of thousands who had been forced to forfeit their policies through hardships renewed their insurance without any loan or lien against it. These concessions, first adopted in November 1893 after five months of depression, were discontinued in July 1894, since the occasion for them had passed in view of the general improvement in national conditions.

In January 1892, when the paid-up privilege was first included in new policies, it was extended to all existing policies provided they remained in force five years from January 1, 1892. In 1894 the paid-up privilege was made a feature of all Industrial policies which had then been in force five years. Thus this privilege was granted three years before it should have been put into effect had the promise made in 1892 been strictly followed.

The Company continued its efforts toward the progressive liberalization of the Industrial policy. Year after year additional concessions were made to policyholders, and many of the increased benefits were made retroactive. Thus, in 1909, since mortality and expenses were reduced, the Company was able to increase its benefits on the average about 10 percent and to make the increase retroactive to policies issued from the first of January 1907. On death claims which had been paid in the intervening years on a number of policies, it sent checks for the amount of increased benefit. Restrictions as to cause of death (including suicide), occupation, and military service, were discontinued. Policies were made incontestable after two years. Revival of lapsed policies was facilitated. Paid-up and cash surrender privileges were provided where premiums were discontinued after certain minimum periods. A refund of 10 percent of the premiums was established for policyholders who paid premiums personally at a Company Office. The entire trend was toward larger benefits at lower cost, so that the disparity between Ordinary and Industrial insurance was constantly reduced. Many of these provisions were made voluntarily by the Metropolitan, and then were considered so valuable that they were incorporated into statutory requirements.

The announcement in 1896 of a plan to pay a cash bonus was the most sweeping concession which had ever been made to policyholders by any Industrial insurance company. The Metropolitan, as a stock Company, had issued nonparticipating insurance and hence was under no obligation to share its profits or savings with the policyholders. Nevertheless, the Company paid back to the insured $600,000 for the year 1897 alone. Actually, the law did not permit dividends on non-participating policies, but Mr. Fiske noted that it said nothing about profit-sharing bonuses. He thus avoided conflict with the law to make this huge gift to the Company's policyholders, recognizing them as participants in a cooperative venture. "Bonuses" continued to be paid until the mutualization of the Company in 1915, after which regular annual dividends were declared. Voluntary payments to Industrial policyholders over and above any contractual and implied obligations amounted to $49,000,000 during this premutualization period.

An outstanding step in the effort to increase the benefits to Industrial policyholders was the inauguration of the Company's welfare program in 1909. In January came the announcement: "Insurance, not merely as a business proposition, but as a social program, will be the future policy of the Company." The Welfare Division was organized under the direction of Dr. Lee K. Frankel, a man of broad social service experience who had just completed his studies of various forms of workingmen's insurance here and abroad, especially in Germany, where the movement had made great progress. The first meeting of Mr. Fiske and Dr. Frankel was a momentous occasion. Mr. Fiske had gone to the Charities Building in New York City to answer an attack on Industrial insurance.

As he came out, he was introduced to Dr. Frankel who had been one of the speakers. In the course of the conversation, Mr. Fiske learned that Dr. Frankel was contemplating the organization of a social insurance bureau for the Russell Sage Foundation. His ideas so impressed the Metropolitan Executive that shortly after Mr. Fiske proposed that he work out a welfare program for the Company. He accepted, recognizing that here he had favorable soil and a ready-made organization for setting his plans into rapid and effective operation. Dr. Frankel saw in the large Agency Staff an organized group of willing and useful co-workers, who in their close weekly contacts with the policyholders could carry vital health information into millions of American homes. He realized that both the Company and its policyholders would profit by preventing disease and extending the length of life. A decrease in mortality would lower the cost of insurance. All social workers knew that large numbers of wage-earners and their families were dying prematurely because of their ignorance of simple laws of healthful living. Here was a mechanism at hand with which to attack a waste of human life.

The story of the welfare activities, thus inaugurated, is so important in the history of the Company that we have assigned an entire chapter of this volume for its fuller treatment. At this point, it is necessary only to say that it was launched with eager enthusiasm by the personnel of the Company, both at the Home Office and in the Field. Almost overnight a campaign of education began which, in its broad scope and intensity, was unique in public health history. The Company's first step was the distribution into millions of homes of a series of pamphlets written in popular style on various preventable diseases. Within a few months the Company organized a visiting service of graduate public health nurses, which was made available to Industrial policyholders without charge. A variety of activities followed apace —publications on general care of the health and on accident prevention; campaigns and demonstrations for the reduction of the more important preventable diseases, including tuberculosis, diphtheria, and pneumonia. All have been successful far beyond the not inconsiderable bounds of the Metropolitan clientele; indeed, they have contributed to the health and welfare of the entire populations of the United States and Canada.

*   *   *   *

But now the scene shifts. We must retrace our steps a bit and go back to 1905—a year of great import in American Life insurance history. For some time it had been clear to leaders of public opinion that all was not well with the practice of Life insurance as it had been conducted by some of the larger companies. In that year the New York Legislature appointed a joint committee, with Senator William W. Armstrong as Chairman, to make a sweeping inquiry into every phase of the industry. The inquiry concentrated upon the alleged mismanagement of the companies, their vast accumulations of wealth, their treatment of policyholders, their cost of operation and administration, the methods and character of their investments, their legislative activities, and practice of contributions to political parties. The investigation was conducted by distinguished counsel headed by Charles Evans Hughes, later Governor of the State of New York and Chief Justice of the United States Supreme Court. Much that was unsavory was disclosed in the activities of some, though not all, of the larger companies. The report of the investigation was followed by drastic legislation which cleansed the business of questionable practices which had sprung up during the years. Two decades later the business had earned from Mr. Hughes, in an address before the Association of Life Insurance Presidents, the commendation: "I believe that there is no safer or better-managed business in our country than yours."

In so far as the Metropolitan itself was concerned, the Armstrong investigation and the legislation which ensued were, with exceptions mentioned below, a happy vindication of the practices which the Company had previously estab-

64

lished. Tontine, or deferred dividend insurance, which Mr. Fiske had proscribed when the Ordinary Department was reestablished in 1892, was outlawed. Expenses in the acquisition of new business were definitely limited. When other companies argued that the restriction of expenses imposed a hardship upon them, the Legislative Committee cited the Metropolitan as an example that business could be done within the proposed limits. As regards Industrial Life insurance, the Committee referred to what were called "serious evils which have been disclosed by this inquiry," but stated that it was not prepared to make recommendations with reference to that business. This was regarded by Mr. Fiske as a personal triumph. He had impressed the Committee with his views as to the importance of Industrial Life insurance as an institution and with the value of the service which it rendered, and he had urged that the companies be permitted to seek remedies of the features criticized, without legislative interference. The only applicable changes in the law were to put the reserve liabilities on the basis of Metropolitan Industrial mortality, and to provide paid-up values to lapsed policies after three instead of after five years. The result of the investigation as a whole was to add to the prestige of the Company, a fact evidenced by the sharp increase in its business in the years that followed.

Nevertheless, the Armstrong investigation was not without unpleasant effect upon the head of Metropolitan's official family. Sharp criticism had been directed against some of the Company's practices and, more particularly, against some of the acts of its President, Mr. Hegeman. It was disclosed on examination that it had been the custom of the Company to sell its collateral loans at the close of each year and to repurchase them at the beginning of the following year, and thus to give the impression in the Annual Statement that no such loans were outstanding. It was also pointed out that Mr. Hegeman had deposed in the Annual Statement that a certain account in the Hamilton Trust Company was an interest-bearing account but had omitted to report that on a part of the balance no interest was credited. For this he was charged with third degree forgery and perjury.

In the perspective of years it is only fair to say that the action of the District Attorney of New York County in bringing indictments against Mr. Hegeman was officious and probably trumped up, playing into the political scheme prevalent at that time of "getting the big fellows." How flimsy the charges were is clear from the decision handed down by Justice Dowling of the Supreme Court of New York in dismissing the forgery indictments against Mr. Hegeman. "I have read carefully every line of testimony submitted to the grand jury and there is nowhere a suggestion of criminal intent in anything that was done. There is no proof that the loans were not amply secured by collateral; nor that the interest was not sufficient; nor that in any way the transaction was unlawful. The loans, as a matter of fact, have been shown by the testimony to have all been paid in full, nor is there any claim that the syndicate participations were unlawful, productive of loss, or even suspicious." Thus the charges of forgery were dismissed at the end of 1907, but the trial on the perjury indictments dragged on for several more years, finally to be dismissed in June 1910. This was Mr. Hegeman's official vindication; but in spite of his great native strength, being a sensitive and honorable man he never quite recovered from what he considered the undeserved disgrace which had come to him.

The legislation following the Armstrong investigation also included restrictions on the amount of new Ordinary business which Life insurance companies were permitted to write in any one year. This restrictive legislation was by degrees much modified in later years. But in the light of subsequent developments, it now seems strange that when, in 1906, the largest New York company had a little more than $2,000,000,000 of Ordinary business in force, the second in size a little more than $1,500,000,000, and the third somewhat in excess of $1,000,000,000, the Legislative Investigating Committee should include in its report a statement that no useful purpose would be served by these companies becoming larger. Since that time similar strictures on the score of size have occasionally been made as the companies grew, demonstrating how relative a concept is "size." Today, all the leading companies are many times as large as they were then, and operate at much lower expense and more beneficially. Growth has given them increased usefulness and stability.

But as these companies grew and as they extended their protection over an increasing part of the population, many became conscious of an added obligation to the policyholders. The conception that Life insurance was not only a commercial enterprise but also a public trust, found effective expression in the mutualization of the Company in January 1915. It is true that the Company had been guided by the spirit of mutuality for many years. Its original Charter made provision for the limited participation of the policyholders in the election of Directors; dividends to stockholders had been limited to 7 percent of the capital stock; and it had been an established practice that surplus be returned in the form of "bonuses" to policyholders. Moreover, a large majority of the stock was in the hands of Mr. Knapp's heirs and of President Hegeman, who could be counted on to maintain the traditional protective relationship between policyholders and Company. There existed, however, the potential danger that through the death of these stockholders or through other means, control of the Company might fall into the hands of those who would use it to further their own interests. Haley Fiske, ever a trail blazer, as far back as 1902 was instrumental in amending the Company's Charter to give all policyholders— Industrial and Ordinary—the privilege of voting for members of the Board of Directors. This move was intended to serve as a barrier to future attempts to control the stock. For who would be so foolish as to think, even though he controlled all the stock—80,000 votes—he could outvote 10,000,000 policyholders?

Nevertheless, the situation was a potentially dangerous one. A surplus of many million dollars under stock control was a great temptation; and there was no certainty that at some time in the future legal artifices would not be used by a group of ruthless manipulators to exploit this huge fund, which was increasing rapidly. It was clear that mutualization was in order.

The major credit for carrying through the conversion of the Metropolitan from a stock to a purely mutual company belongs to Frederick H. Ecker, then Treasurer and later Mr. Fiske's successor in the Presidency. It was he who persuaded Joseph P. Knapp to sell his stock to the Company. The purchase was wholeheartedly supported by Mr. Fiske and by John G. Milburn, the Company's counsel. With the majority of the stockholders consenting, it was a foregone conclusion that the Company would acquire the rest of the shares. The purchase price was determined by a fair and judicious formula—the stockholders were to receive an amount which, safely invested, would bring the same interest return as the Metropolitan stock had yielded. It was agreed that the Company would pay them three times the par value per share, although much higher offers had been made by outside investors. Accordingly, for a payment of $6,000,000, the Metropolitan Life Insurance Company was turned over completely to its policyholders.

This action, completed at the end of 1914, electrified the insurance world. The policyholders, the press, and insurance officials, all acclaimed a generous act which made the Metropolitan truly a Company of the people.

The Superintendent of Insurance of New York, Mr. Hasbrouck, hailed the mutualization as the most noteworthy event of the insurance year. Regarding the ownership of the surplus, which was the essential issue in the transaction, he wrote as follows: "The situation was not without its disquieting features, although at no time was the issue of ownership, or right to a distribution, raised. The point is here alluded to for the purpose of emphasizing the significance of what took place. Without compulsion, and even without public agitation, but because it was recognized by the stock-

68

Public Interest in Mutualization of the Company

holders and the management of the Company that, as years went on and the assets of the Company increased still more, the very existence of the question, together with the dangers of a shifting stock control, might create a situation where the usefulness of the Company would be seriously impaired, it was decided to determine the ownership of the surplus in favor of the policyholders. Hence, section ninety-five of the Insurance Law was invoked to mutualize the Company and settle the question."

With this step, all the doubts and uncertainties involved in the old setup were removed at one stroke. The Company and all its assets once and forever belonged solely to the policy-holders. There was no need hereafter for "bonus" techni-calities, for all divisible surplus would go back to policyholders. A clause providing for a distribution of surplus was added to all new policies. But what was more important was that participation in dividends was extended to the *existing* policies issued previously on the nonparticipating plan. Altogether, in the years preceding mutualization, the Metropolitan re-turned in cash or premium credits close to $49,000,000—and since mutualization about $350,000,000 more—to policyhold-ers whose contracts as written entitled them to not one penny of such refunds.

The most pressing decision as a consequence of mutualiza-tion was the Company's program in its Ordinary Department. Heretofore, like other stock companies, it had issued policies at nonparticipating premium rates which were much lower than those offered by the mutual companies. The question arose as to what the Company would do now that it was mutualized, a matter of no small importance to competing organizations. The Company went right ahead and made the unexpected and unprecedented announcement that here-after it would issue participating policies at the old non-participating premium rates. Thus, it would now sell low-premium insurance and pay dividends too. This step nat-urally raised a welter of opposition from other companies who feared such competition. The Insurance Department, however, recognized the justice of the Metropolitan's position and suggested appropriate changes in the insurance law. In 1916 an amendment was passed by the Legislature which made possible the continuance of the old rates for Ordinary policies (except for the $5,000 Whole Life and a few other policies on which a moderate increase was made). The Company thus substantially won its point and has continued to operate on the basis of providing insurance at the lowest possible cost to the policyholder. The steady adherence to this principle made it possible by 1923 for the Ordinary Department, although a latecomer in the field, to outdistance all other Ordinary companies. Today it has nearly $14,000,-000,000 of such insurance in force.

So far in the story of this administration, we have made little reference to the personalities who shared with Mr. Hegeman and Mr. Fiske in the management of the Company. Major achievements, after all, reflect the efforts of an able organization. It was possibly Mr. Fiske's most important single contribution as an administrator that he knew how to pick leaders and to place them effectively in the many-sided Company structure. Even if he reserved for himself the last word in all important decisions, he gave his lieutenants ample opportunity for the expression of their talents. We have already seen how wisely he acted in his choice of Dr. Frankel to carry the new Welfare Division. He had previously shown the same judgment in picking Frank O. Ayres as the executive to develop the Ordinary Department of the Company, and George B. Woodward to supervise the endless detail of the Industrial Department and Home Office operations. Mr. Woodward was the author of the low-cost $5,000 Whole Life policy which created a sensation when it was introduced in 1909, and which has ever since enjoyed a huge sale. When the time came for the launching of the Group Division in 1917, Mr. Fiske picked from among the Superintendents of Agencies James E. Kavanagh, a man who was ably equipped through sympathies and past contacts to bring to the attention of American industry this new method of protection for

GEORGE B. WOODWARD

working people. Some years earlier, a chance meeting with
Dr. Augustus S. Knight in Boston, during the exciting days
of the Massachusetts legislation, resulted in an invitation for
him to join the Company as Medical Director. These were
exceedingly able men, each in his own sphere; and if the
Company grew rapidly and its operations ran smoothly, it
was because the Chief Executive had pondered the qualities
required to operate the varied departments and had found
them in these men.

During this administration and the next, the Metropolitan
made a contribution to the stability of the Life insurance
business through its action in taking over a number of companies which were in financial distress. It thereby increased
in great measure the soundness of the institution as a whole
and protected the insurance of hundreds of thousands of
families. In some instances, this reinsurance was done at the
request of public officials and insurance departments; in other
cases, certain small companies, which were in difficulty or

anticipated difficulty, sought the assistance of the Metropolitan to relieve them of pending embarrassment. Because
of the size of the Company, its national character, and its
position in the insurance world, it has been in an exceptional
position to render this service to such policyholders.

From 1893 through 1929 the Metropolitan took over all
or part of the business of 34 Life insurance companies, affecting
852,632 Life insurance policies, more than 90 percent of which
were Industrial. The bulk of these assumptions were made
during the Hegeman-Fiske administration. The Sun Life
Insurance Company of Lexington, Ky., taken over in 1902,
and involving 170,858 Industrial policies, was the largest of
these. Although the aggregate number of policies assumed
at various times was never large as compared with the policies
in force in the Company, the number of individuals concerned
made up a considerable group who would undoubtedly have
suffered loss had not the Metropolitan been willing to lend
a hand.

The reinsurance of the Pittsburgh Life and Trust Company in 1917, involving 50,477 Ordinary insurance policies,
and more than $91,000,000 of insurance, was important both
because of the size of the company and because the plan under
which this business was assumed was unique in the history
of Life insurance. When the Metropolitan took over this
company, at the urgent invitation of the New York and
Pennsylvania Insurance Departments, the assets of the Pittsburgh Life were so badly impaired that it was found necessary
to place a lien on all policies fixed at 33⅓ percent of the
reserve. Provision was made, however, that all death claims
during the succeeding five years would be paid without deduction of the principal of the lien. So successfully was this
assumed business administered that the liens were cut in half in
1922 and entirely removed in January 1925. Thus, in less than
eight years after the transfer of the business, all the policies
were restored to full benefit. In addition, Endowments which
had matured up to that time were reimbursed for liens previously deducted. In 1926 the Metropolitan went one step

73

further and placed all the business on a participating basis. Through this demonstration, the Metropolitan furnished a new pattern for dealing with companies whose reserves had been found to be impaired, a pattern which has virtually become the standard practice.

Toward the end of the Hegeman-Fiske administration two events occurred, the impact of which was sharply felt in the Life insurance business. First came the active participation of the United States in the World War, from April 1917 to November 1918, followed by the devastating world-wide epidemic of influenza which swept the country in 1918–1919. These occurrences brought into sharp focus the value of Life insurance, and at the same time demonstrated beyond doubt the basic soundness of the American Life insurance structure, which met the crisis unflinchingly. About 25,500 Metropolitan policies became death claims as a result of the first World War. Eighteen thousand of these were on lives of men in the service of the United States, and 7,500 on lives in the Canadian forces. The first American soldier to be killed after this country entered the war, Corporal James R. Gresham, was a Metropolitan Industrial policyholder. He was killed on November 3, 1917, "somewhere in France," and the claim was paid to his mother living in Evansville, Ind., on November 15th. In the time of America's participation the Company, following very liberal practices, paid more than $8,250,000 in war claims.

The ravages of the influenza epidemic, superimposed on the war catastrophe, took a far larger toll of life than the war itself. Between October 1, 1918, and June 30, 1919, the disease carried off more than 83,000 Metropolitan policyholders; the claims on these lives amounted to $27,600,000, or $24,000,000 in excess of those to be expected under normal conditions. The Company's Claim Division was taxed far beyond its capacity, and those of the Staff who themselves were not stricken toiled long beyond regular hours to pay the claims as soon as possible. Further to expedite payments, the Company allowed Superintendents of Districts to honor claims up to $300. After the epidemic the Company organized an Influenza-Pneumonia Commission, composed of specialists in the field, to study the causes and ways of combatting these diseases. The results of their labors are described in Chapter 20.

President John Rogers Hegeman, after many years of illness, died on April 6, 1919. He would have reached the age of 75 on the 18th of the month, and in June would have passed 49 years as an Officer of the Company. He had seen and participated in the entire development of the Metropolitan from its meager and most unpromising beginnings. The Company to which he had given himself had overcome every obstacle until, at the time of his death, it was unquestionably in the premier position in the business. Even during his own Presidency of less than 28 years, he had seen the Company's assets multiply 55 times, its business in force and its income 17 times. The Life insurance outstanding at the time of his death was $4,500,000,000, and of this amount more than $2,000,000,000 was in the Ordinary Department. A source of keen satisfaction to him was the culmination of the building program of the Company: the impressive Home Office on Madison Square. The completion of the Tower which was his conception, in 1909, gave him especial joy. In his address dedicating the Tower with its "Light That Never Fails" he said: "Tonight we give it dedication; and here and now, in holier words than mine, we dedicate it, and the great building of which it is the fitting climax, to 'whatsoever things are honest; whatsoever things are just; whatsoever things are pure; whatsoever things are of good report,' in the grand business for which it was conceived, designed, and completed."

But as vital as these evidences of material growth, was the new spirit which was permeating the entire organization in the later years of Mr. Hegeman's life. A new social philosophy was evidently at work in the insurance field. During his administration the Welfare program was fully established and warmly accepted for its humanitarian value, especially among the Industrial population. In the Ordinary Department as well, innovations were conceived to make that business more useful and attractive. Through the development of its Group Department the Company pioneered in bringing the benefits of Life insurance to American industry. On all fronts the Metropolitan, guided by Mr. Hegeman and Mr. Fiske, had become a great public service institution, and a constructive influence on the life and health of the country.

CHAPTER 4

An Era of Expanding Public Service:

1919-1929

THE ELECTION of Haley Fiske to the Presidency on April 22, 1919, involved no major changes either in the character of the administration or in the general policy of the Company. As Vice-President, Mr. Fiske had been clothed with full executive authority, and for 28 years had vigorously directed the destinies of the organization. Nor did any new personalities enter the picture in 1919, although the year before had seen the appointment as General Attorney of Leroy A. Lincoln—a man who in the course of the next decade was to make his mark in the Company's administrative history. It was inevitable that Frederick H. Ecker should succeed to the Vice-Presidency. He had been for many years the executive Officer in charge of investments, and had achieved a commanding position in the world of finance. He had developed, moreover, an increasing interest in general Company management. He had literally grown up with the business; his ability and judgment reflected 36 years of valuable service. Mr. Fiske was in his 67th year when he took office, and Mr. Ecker in the prime of life at 52.

This administration, which continued for a decade until the death of Mr. Fiske in 1929, was cast in what many have called the "Golden Era" of American business. It was a period of rapid growth, during which the commercial life of

77

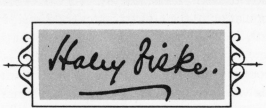

President, 1919–1929

the Nation, including the Life insurance business, reached unprecedented heights. For the Metropolitan it was a decade of great expansion. When the Fiske-Ecker administration began, the total amount of Life insurance in force in the Company was about $5,000,000,000; only one decade later this figure had more than trebled, the business on the books having reached the sum of $17,000,000,000. There had been an average increase in force of about $1,200,000,000 each year. It was not until 1902, a third of a century after the founding of the Company, that the insurance in force had reached the total which in the decade 1919–1929 was actually being added each year. During these 10 years the business of the Company grew four times as rapidly as in the decade immediately preceding. Although the number of Life insurance companies operating in the United States increased appreciably in the postwar years, the Metropolitan continued to get a very substantial proportion of the total business issued. By 1928, the last full year that Mr. Fiske was President, the Company wrote 10 percent of the Ordinary business in this country, more than 30 percent of the Industrial, and 33 percent of the Group. During the decade the Company's assets increased by $2,000,000,000, reaching the $3,000,000,000 mark before the end of 1929. Three years before, the Metropolitan had already achieved the leading position among the financial corporations of the world. At the close of 1926 the assets of the Company totaled $2,108,004,385.

The population of the United States and Canada increased by one sixth in the postwar decade. Metropolitan policy-holders grew at a much more rapid rate, namely, 82 percent. In 1919 about one in every eight persons in the United States and Canada was insured in the Company; 10 years later the ratio was one in five. In some areas, in the late 1920's, Metropolitan policyholders comprised an even larger proportion of the population. In New York City, Montreal, Memphis, and a number of other cities the Company had insured every third person; in some cities, like Syracuse, every other man, woman, and child was a member of the Metropolitan. In other cities, such as Troy and Cohoes, N. Y., the number of Metropolitan policies in force actually exceeded the total population, since some farsighted citizens owned several policies of different types.

Nothing gave Mr. Fiske and his associates greater satisfaction than to see the benefits of Life insurance brought to an ever-increasing number of families. Year in and year out the President urged the Managers and Agents to reach to the entire population, and to utilize their opportunities for the betterment of human conditions. His statement at the Company's Annual Convention in 1927 is typical of the viewpoint which permeated the organization during his administration:

"The desire that we have for the future is not aggrandizement. We are distributing all the money we have. It is not power, except to be used as men with power should use it. No, it is for the bettering of human conditions; it is for a reaching out of a heart as big as Mother Metropolitan to better the condition of working men, to lengthen their lives, to improve their domestic relations, to bring up children better, to educate them, to make them live longer lives, to make happiness." To those who heard this speech, it was a stirring call to action.

Mr. Fiske's desire to spread Life insurance to every nook and corner of the United States and Canada found fertile soil in the general economic prosperity. Money flowed freely in the decade prior to 1929, more freely than wisely. People in moderate circumstances bought all the commodities within their means and frequently beyond their means, optimistically depending upon continued and even greater prosperity. Instalment buying reached unprecedented sums, constituting a heavy mortgage on future earnings. In his Convention address of 1926 Mr. Fiske had already called attention to this development and expressed fears of impending disaster. Even more reprehensible was the rampant speculation. Men and women in all walks of life gambled their income and savings on the stock market. The virus of speculation had got into the blood of the American people, and toward the end of the decade the disease reached epidemic proportions.

The curve of stock market prices became the fever chart of the Nation. But it is to the great credit of the American people that while they were speculating freely, they were also making provision for their future security through the purchase of Life insurance. Total Life insurance in force in all American companies increased from $36,000,000,000 in 1919 to more than $100,000,000,000 in 1929. The number of policyholders rose to 67,000,000 persons at the end of the decade. When the tide began to turn, this huge volume of protection helped serve as an anchor to stabilize the entire economy.

The working people of the country shared liberally in the prosperity of the postwar decade. Increased earnings afforded wage-earners and their families an opportunity to provide themselves with Life insurance, Industrial for the most part, although more and more of them now purchased protection on the Ordinary basis. During the 10-year period, the amount of Industrial business on the Company's books increased by about $4,000,000,000, coming close to $6,500,-000,000 at the close of the administration. In other words the figure in 1929 was more than $2\frac{1}{2}$ times that of a decade before. And the growth in Ordinary was even larger!

The developments of this decade provided an eloquent answer to the arguments against child insurance propounded just before the turn of the century. What a vindication for Mr. Fiske and his colleagues, who had defended the business against heavy odds! It was not until 1921 that the controversy was finally settled. Colorado was the only State where the insurance of children under 15 years of age had been prohibited by law. Acting in accordance with public sentiment, the Colorado Legislature in April 1921 amended the law so as to permit parents to insure children over 1 year of age, with limitations on amounts similar to those provided by New York State. Of even greater significance was the law enacted in New York State in March 1923, permitting the insurance of children under 1 year. Soon thereafter Life insurance began to be issued on the lives of infants in virtually all areas of the United States and Canada. The business at once proved to be exceedingly popular. Industrial insurance at last embraced the entire family.

While the Industrial business was expanding, the contract continued to be liberalized; costs declined as the benefits to policyholders increased. The number of additional concessions granted are too numerous to give in detail, but a few examples will serve. Near the end of 1921 all Industrial policies issued on adults were put in full immediate benefit from the date of issue. For a number of years before this, many policies had been in only half benefit during the first six months. The significance of this action is clear from the fact that in 1922, the year immediately following this revision, more than $1,150,000 were paid in death claims on Industrial policies in force less than six months. Benefits for loss of eyesight or limbs were also liberalized in 1921. Heretofore, upon proof of such loss, one half the face value of the policy was paid in cash, and a fully paid-up policy was issued for the balance. However, in November 1921, it was decided to continue the cash payment as before, and to issue a paid-up policy for the full amount of the original insurance. At the end of 1928 a Double Indemnity clause was added to Industrial policies without any additional premium, the provision being made retroactive. This clause provided for double the amount of insurance to be paid in case of death by accidental means. As a result of this concession the Company paid to beneficiaries some $2,800,000 in the year 1941 alone.

The necessity of bringing down the cost of Industrial insurance was always uppermost in Mr. Fiske's mind, and his administration was eminently successful in doing so. A number of favorable factors were at work to help bring this about. With the new health program the mortality among Industrial policyholders was declining appreciably, with resulting savings in the amount of claim payments. Another important factor in the cost of insurance is the interest rate. During this period earnings on investments increased, and were well in excess of the earnings assumed in the premium

82

calculations. Still another item was the more rapid increase in business than in personnel, so that the expense ratio dropped. Such is the economy of large-scale operation. Finally, better management contributed to the reduction of administrative costs. The increasing practice of issuing Industrial insurance without medical examination resulted in considerable savings. The practice of increasing the size of the Agent's debit, or the number of families and individuals he was to serve, was another factor in reducing the expense ratio in the Industrial Department.

These savings were at once reflected in larger dividends. In 1918, the last full year of the Hegeman administration, Industrial policyholders received dividends amounting to about $6,250,000. In a banner year of dividend revision— 1929—the Company's announcement read: "The total amount of dividends declared will be about $37,000,000, which makes dividends and bonuses paid or credited to Industrial policies $230,000,000 in 33 years." Although the total dividends paid naturally increased from year to year during the decade due to the growth of the business, the dividends themselves were substantially increased. It is interesting to observe how effective the dividend policy of the Company was in reducing the cost of Industrial insurance, especially on older policies. Thus, in accordance with the program announced for the year 1929, for example, a dividend credit equal to one half the total annual premium was returned to policyholders whose insur- ance had been issued in 1894 or earlier. Policies issued in 1900 were given a dividend credit equal to 20 weeks' premiums; Industrial policies in force only 10 years were given a dividend equal to 10 weeks, or a return of about 20 percent of their annual premiums. Even policies only five years old were credited with a dividend equal to seven weeks' premiums—no small item in lowering the cost of insurance to workingmen's families.

Other features of the dividend programs of this period are worthy of mention. At the end of 1927 it was announced that all policies issued in the years before 1907 on the Whole

Life or $500 Endowment at Age 80 plans would be made paid up in full after premiums had been paid to the anniversary of the policy preceding the attainment of age 75 by the insured, even though the policies as written had called for the payment of premiums throughout life or until age 80 respectively. Moreover, there was inaugurated at the beginning of 1928 a program of equalizing, by various forms of dividends, the amounts of insurance in policies issued under the Company's older tables of rates with the larger benefits provided by the later tables. At the end of 1927, for instance, equalization dividends were declared on premium-paying and fully paid-up policies becoming due in 1928 (as death claims or loss of eye-sight or limbs claims or matured endowments), in an amount sufficient to "equalize" the claim payment with the amount that would be provided under the Company's then current tables of rates. At the end of 1928 dividends were declared in an amount sufficient to provide for a permanent increase in the amount of insurance under such policies, thereby guar-anteeing for the lifetime of the policies a part of the difference in benefit covered by the equalization dividends. Similar permanent increases were declared from time to time in the years following. Mortuary and maturity dividends, which had been an integral feature of the program of Industrial bonuses and dividends since 1906, were continued at high levels throughout this period. Such dividends are payable upon termination of the policy by the death of the insured or at maturity of an Endowment policy, and represent the pay-ment of part of the surplus funds maintained for all policies which is no longer needed when a policy ceases to be in force.

During this period a simple and effective procedure was developed under which the Agency Force could credit Indus-trial dividends directly on the Premium Receipt Books of the insured—no small matter in the management of 22,000 Agents and many millions of Industrial policies. Many difficulties of an administrative character had to be ironed out, but the result was to establish a routine method of making dividend pay-ments and of proper crediting with the least amount of bookkeeping and expense. The Company has always been among the first to take advantage of the invention of new labor-saving and time-saving devices. A receipted bill for $125 paid for its first typewriter in 1878 is still preserved in its archives, significant of its early willingness to try out new inventions. In fact, long before the general public was even aware of the telephone, the typewriter, or the adding machine, they were already in active use at the Metropolitan. During the Fiske administration and thereafter the Company's eagerness to adopt technological improvements, including many intricate business machines, in its vast task of record-keeping, has resulted in far greater efficiency and consequent lowering of expense.

Side by side with the liberal dividend provisions was another concession which materially reduced the cost of Weekly Premium Industrial insurance. This was an arrangement whereby Metropolitan policyholders could pay their premiums directly at District Offices or at the Home Office of the Company. By thus saving the cost of collection by the Agent the Company allowed a reduction of 10 percent on their premiums. Introduced in 1911, the practice became extremely popular during the following decade. In the year 1928 alone such savings in premiums amounted to well over $3,000,000, and over the decade from 1919 to 1928 policy-holders who took the time and trouble to pay their premiums directly saved more than $14,000,000. At the present time close to one third of all Industrial Weekly premiums are paid in this way.

Another constructive step in Mr. Fiske's effort to lower the cost of insurance for working people was the introduction in 1927 of Monthly Premium Industrial policies. Obviously, the collection of premiums monthly instead of weekly reduced the cost of transacting the business, with the result that premiums on Monthly policies were about 15 percent lower than on corresponding Weekly policies. Such an appreciable cut in the cost of Industrial insurance would have been thought visionary a decade before. The step made it possible for

85

families on the same insurance budget to buy a greater amount of protection. Monthly Premium business prospered at once. In three years — that is, by the end of 1929 — there were in force on this plan well over 600,000 policies for nearly $340,000,000. By the end of 1942 the policies totaled almost 3,000,000 and the amount of insurance more than $1,350,-000,000. With such large volume of Monthly Premium Industrial business, the saving to policyholders has run into many million dollars.

These significant developments in the Industrial Department during the decade of the Fiske-Ecker administration served to lessen the differences in cost between Industrial and Ordinary insurance. Larger dividends, continued concessions and liberalizations, and lower expenses were all effective answers to the criticism of high cost which had always been directed at Industrial insurance. Today the chief difference between the two types reflects only the higher mortality prevailing among Industrial policyholders, the smaller size of Industrial policies, and the additional service which they receive to keep their policies in force.

Under the stimulation of boom conditions in the decade of the 1920's, it was natural that Ordinary insurance should also spurt forward and reach new high levels. In fact, the Company's Ordinary Department expanded at an even more rapid rate than the Industrial, for the business of the former more than trebled during the decade. In the course of 1919, when the Fiske-Ecker administration began, the Ordinary business had just caught up with the Industrial, and there were about $2,500,000,000 in force in each Department. Before the end of 1919 the Ordinary Department definitely took the lead, and in the early part of 1929, when this administration closed, its business totaled close to $8,000,000,000, exceeding the amount of Industrial by $1,500,000,000. About one fifth of this Ordinary insurance was on the very low-cost $5,000 Whole Life Plan. During the 10-year period the net cost of Ordinary protection was substantially reduced as dividends continued to increase. In 1918 Ordinary policy-

86

holders received $4,000,000 in dividends; in 1928 the total came to $32,000,000. For the decade as a whole no less than $140,000,000 were returned in dividends to Ordinary Department policyholders.

During the decade, new contracts were introduced to meet a variety of human needs. Monthly Premium Ordinary insurance with premiums collected at the homes was introduced in 1926 and proved to be very popular. At the same time insurance on women was extended and liberalized. An added service to the Company's Ordinary policyholders was the organization, in 1920, of a unit later named the Insurance Advisory Bureau. Without any charge, this Bureau gives policyholders expert advice on such insurance matters as appropriate changes in plans or options to meet changed conditions; designations of beneficiaries; insurance for trust funds; settlement options; provision for college education through Life insurance; monthly income to continue a salary or part of it; annuities to provide security for old age; and budget systems for providing premiums. Policyholders, through their Agents, have availed themselves of this valuable service.

But the most spectacular increase in business during this administration came in the field of Group insurance. Actively entering this field in 1917, the Company had nearly $60,000,000 of Group Life in force by the beginning of 1919. Only one decade later well in excess of 35 times that amount was on the books—a total of about $2,250,000,000, covering some 1,300,000 lives in more than 3,000 organizations. At the end of 1919 the Metropolitan ranked as a poor fourth in Group insurance among the leading companies. By the beginning of 1929 its Group business stood well above that of any other company.

This amazing development under the supervision of Vice-President Kavanagh reflected in large part the accelerated tempo of industry and commerce in the postwar decade. But it meant more than that. It meant unusual advantages in service and materially lower costs for Metropolitan Group policy-

JAMES E. KAVANAGH

holders, especially through the contributory system of sharing premium payments. Three gigantic Group contracts were signed during this 10-year period—General Electric insured its employees in 1920 for $46,000,000, the Southern Pacific Railroad for $117,000,000 in 1923, and General Motors for $130,000,000 in 1926, which amount was increased to $400,-000,000 two years later. It was a dramatic moment indeed when news of the signing of this largest Group policy in insurance history was telephoned across the ocean to Haley Fiske, who was on a visit at the time to the Company's British Head Office in London. Mr. Fiske followed the expansion of the Group business with eager expectancy. He envisioned Group insurance as an instrument for improving the security of working people and for promoting more harmonious relations between capital and labor. Through the cooperation of employer and employee, workers could be provided not only with Life insurance at low cost, but also with protection against accidents and sickness, and with pensions at retirement. The Metropolitan issued its first Group Health contract in 1914 and its first Group Annuities contract in 1921.

The Company's free Nursing Service and other welfare activities were also extended to employees insured under Group policies. Furthermore, in 1919, the Policyholders Service Bureau was organized to study a wide range of problems arising in industry and to give advice to Group policyholders on such matters as industrial hygiene, accident prevention, personnel management, production engineering, and general business management. Both employers and employees have made frequent use of the research information issued by the Service Bureau.

The Metropolitan not only expanded its business in each of its functioning Departments, but also rounded out the "circle of protection" by adding a new type of coverage. At the end of 1921 the Company organized its Personal Accident and Health Division under the supervision of Stewart M. LaMont, widely experienced in this type of business. The individual contracts issued in this Department were unique in many respects. They were the first policies of their kind to be issued on a participating basis. A grace period of 31 days; scientific graduation, according to age, of premium rates for health policies; and reduced commissions to Agents after the first policy year were all departures from current practices. The low cost and attractive provisions of these policies resulted in a gratifying public response. By 1942 the Company had in force Personal Accident and Health policies calling for payment of well in excess of $5,000,000 in weekly benefits in case of sickness and accident, and principal sum benefits of more than $1,000,000,000 in the event of accidental death or dismemberment.

At the same time, the Company's Welfare program under Dr. Lee K. Frankel was growing in size and influence. By 1929 the Metropolitan Nurses were making 4,800,000 visits a year to the homes of policyholders in some 4,500 cities and towns. There was an ever-increasing demand for Company literature on health and safety, and by the end of the

LEE K. FRANKEL

decade about 50,000,000 pamphlets a year were being distributed. In addition to expanding its existing activities, the Company during this period initiated a whole series of new welfare projects. In 1919 a Commission was organized to study the control of influenza and pneumonia. This Commission in the subsequent years made many valuable contributions in the field of pneumonia control. The Company also conducted practical demonstrations on a wide scale, showing in Framingham, Mass., how tuberculosis could be reduced drastically, and in Thetford Mines, Quebec, how the lives of many infants could be saved by proper care. These demonstrations have had widespread effect in stimulating similar health activities in other communities throughout the United States and Canada. In order to reach the widest audience, the Company has pioneered in carrying on its health campaign through advertising in national magazines of large circulation, through motion pictures, and through radio broadcasts. This work has reflected favorably on the health of the American people, and on the Company's policyholders in particular. Between 1911, when the Company first began to keep detailed records of mortality, and 1929, the death rate among Metropolitan Industrial policyholders decreased by one third. In this period the average length of life among these insured increased about nine years, whereas in the general population of the United States the increase was only slightly more than five years.

These expanded services to policyholders, as well as the Company's vastly increased business, called for a larger staff both in the Field and at the Home Office. In the short span of the 1919–1929 decade the Company's branch offices expanded in number from 557 to 830. The number of Agents grew at an even more rapid rate, totaling more than 22,500 in 1929, or more than 75 percent in excess of the 1919 figure. Moreover, with larger gains in business Agents' earnings increased from an average of about $37 a week to $56 a week. This naturally made possible the securing of men who would make Life insurance salesmanship a life career. To raise the work of the Agent to a professional status, the Company began to give the Field Force more and more concentrated training. Only a beginning was made in this direction, however, during the Fiske-Ecker administration; the most effective work in this field was accomplished later, as we shall see, under the aegis of Mr. Ecker and Mr. Lincoln.

The feverish activity of the decade also had its repercussions at the Home Office, where the number of employees in the 10-year period increased from less than 6,500 to well over 11,000. The volume of work at the Home Office had increased so rapidly that there arose the problem of sufficient work space. To give Canadian policyholders better service and to help relieve the congestion in the Home Office, the Company decided to establish a Head Office for the Canadian business in Ottawa. Under the executive direction of Mr. A. F. C. Fiske, the Canadian Head Office was established in April 1924. Thus the far-flung business of the Company was directed not only from the Home Office in New York, but also from Head Offices in San Francisco, in Ottawa, and in London, where the Group insurance business issued by the Company on workers in Great Britain and on the Continent was handled.

At the same time that the Company moved along with the turbulent era, restraining forces within the organization made themselves felt to an increasing degree. Toward the end of the decade selling practices were beginning to change fairly rapidly. Less emphasis was being put on quantity of business sold and more on fitting the insurance program to the needs of the average family. Detailed studies were made on average groups of policyholders, on the amount and distribution of insurance in their families. The Field Force was urged to emphasize Life insurance on the head of the family, even if this meant less insurance on the other members. Above all, there was to be no overloading of Industrial insurance. Increasing consideration was given to the amount of the total premium in relation to the family income. Agents were, of course, encouraged to obtain new business by contacting the still large number of uninsured. Yet, when Monthly Premium Industrial insurance was introduced in 1927, Agents were permitted to write only a limited amount of Weekly Industrial business on any one person during a year, thus encouraging the writing of lower-cost insurance on the Ordinary or on the Monthly Premium plans. All these measures were directed toward writing insurance which would persist because it was properly adapted to the family needs and budget. When the financial crisis came after 1929, these measures undoubtedly were instrumental in keeping the lapse rate much lower than it would otherwise have been.

In fact, over the years the Metropolitan had placed great emphasis on the prevention of lapses. The Company was sensitive to the criticism of the high lapse rates which had been leveled against the business in general, although the criticism was for the most part exaggerated. Methods of compensating the Field Force had been so fixed as to reward them for persistent business. The first step in reducing the expense of putting policies on the books and soon thereafter taking them off is to see that Agents do not write such business. Much depends upon the attitude and the ability of the Agent to serve his families intelligently. Although the matter of lapses was one of the principal topics of President Fiske's addresses to the Field Force, the most effective work in this field was accomplished, as we shall see later, in the administrations of Mr. Ecker and Mr. Lincoln.

During the era of industrial prosperity Mr. Fiske, in his eagerness to cover the entire field of providing security for wage-earners, considered even the possibility of writing unemployment insurance. It was the one major hazard in the economic life of working people against which they were still unprotected. Authority to write this new type of business required an amendment to the insurance law, and this the Company did not obtain. Moreover, there were within the organization specialists on the subject whose studies convinced them that unemployment insurance was not an insurable risk within the framework of sound actuarial practice. As a consequence, in spite of Mr. Fiske's solicitude for men and women threatened with this hazard, the Company did not underwrite unemployment insurance, and thus it saved itself an unhappy experience in the depression which was to develop only a few years later.

One of the notable achievements of the Company, as well as of the institution of Life Insurance during the decade, was the continued adherence to sound investment principles. In a period of seeming affluence the officers of the large majority of insurance companies rejected the blandishments of high returns held out by investments in stocks, and thus made their organizations immune to the speculative fever which was raging among people throughout the country. It was this careful policy which contributed so largely to the ability of the Metropolitan and of other companies to weather the economic crisis. Mr. Ecker's sound investment program, which he lost no opportunity to expound and to popularize during the boom years, will remain one of the proudest pages

93

in the Company's history. He stood firm as the movement gained momentum to amend the laws to permit Life insurance companies to make common-stock investments. In commenting on this trend in an address before the National Association of Life Underwriters on September 26, 1929, he said: "Speaking for myself, and with the background of an active contact with Life insurance investments of over 40 years, I am not prepared to advocate any substantial change in the limitations which now prevail in the laws of some of our principal States. ". . . Life insurance investments are held to insure faithful performance of the Life insurance contracts. So far as possible the element of chance should be eliminated, and the funds should not be subject to the hazard of speculation."

Mr. Ecker's insight into the situation at that time was prophetic. At the Company's Annual Convention early in February 1929 he made the following observation: "In the present-day movement, stocks are enjoying public favor. Investments in equities are regarded as leading to more profit than the interest paid on obligations or bonds which have heretofore been preferred for their greater security. Preference is now to be partners or stockholders in an enterprise at less interest returns than to be bondholders. The shares of the best-rated institutions are selling on a 2- or 3-percent basis in the expectation of richer future returns through the capitalizing of earnings in the business, and, to be sure, the experience of the last few years entirely justifies this position. It is characteristic of the American people, however, to do nothing by halves, but to go to extremes, and it may be that the pendulum swing in this cycle is reaching the end of its travel in that direction." The accuracy of his prediction was evident to everyone before the year was over.

While during the decade the Metropolitan continued its traditional program of sound investment, it was, as always, responsive to the contemporary economic and social needs of the country. An analysis of the Company's investment portfolio shows how this attitude was translated into practice. A shortage of housing facilities at the end of the first World

94

Children's group at the Astoria Apartments

War led to a great expansion in building during the postwar decade. The Company financed the construction of residential and business buildings on a large scale, with the result that mortgage loans increased from slightly less than 35 percent of its total assets in 1919 to 45 percent in 1929. In addition, under a special enactment of the Legislature, the Company invested $7,000,000 in the construction of model housing accommodations for 2,125 families in Long Island City and Astoria, N. Y. This was a successful pioneer effort to provide low-cost housing for families of modest income. The Company's funds also aided the development of cities and the wider use of public utilities. In the latter field the Company's investments increased from almost nothing in 1919 to about 9 percent of its assets a decade later. During the first World War the Metropolitan aided the Governments of the United States and Canada through purchase of their bonds, and by the end of 1919 these securities formed 16 percent of the Company's investments. In the course of the postwar decade these bonds were gradually paid off, and comprised only a little more than 2.5 percent of the portfolio in 1929. Railroad

95

securities during the decade remained fairly constant and accounted for one fifth of the invested funds. The Metropolitan also contributed to the economic welfare of our agricultural population through its farm loans. The Company entered this field in 1917, and by 1929 these funds amounted to nearly $197,000,000, or 6.5 percent of the total assets.

The country was at the height of its feverish activity when Haley Fiske died suddenly on March 3, 1929. In 15 days he would have reached his 77th birthday. His lifetime had spanned an era of economic expansion without parallel in all human history. The modest organization he had joined in 1891 had become by a wide margin the world's largest financial corporation. Yet Mr. Fiske prided himself not so much on the material expansion of the Company as on the development of its social services. He saw in the growth of insurance protection a practical means for improving the living standards of working people. The passing of Haley Fiske symbolized also the end of an era. The solid accomplishments of that period will remain a valuable contribution to our way of life; but here, as in all times of rapid growth, there were excesses and dislocations. It became the task of the administration which followed to retain the accomplishments and to correct the errors.

CHAPTER 5

Life Insurance Weathers the Depression:

1929-1943

FREDERICK H. ECKER became President of the Metropolitan on March 26, 1929, and associated with him as Vice-Presidents were Robert L. Cox and Leroy A. Lincoln. Mr. Cox died in January of the following year, and Mr. Lincoln immediately assumed the position of second in command. He succeeded to the Presidency in March 1936, when Mr. Ecker became Chairman of the Board. When the new administration took office in 1929, the country was enjoying what appeared to be great prosperity. Many men in business and in public life believed that we had attained a depression-less economy. Corporate earnings were at a high level. There was frenzied activity in the stock market and in the flotation of new securities. Prices of common stocks reached dizzy peaks. Credit was easy to obtain. The growth of the Metropolitan and of other Life insurance companies reflected the optimistic spirit of the times. All prospered as a result of the great business activity and the high rate of employment at good wages then prevalent throughout the country. The first hundred billion dollars of Life insurance in force had been attained; predictions were being confidently made that within another 10 years the second hundred billion would be added.

But in October 1929 came the first manifestation of a series of cataclysms which shook the country and the world. The first stock market crash came almost out of a clear sky. The full significance of this indication of economic distress was little understood at the time. Many people suffered immediate losses. Many held on to their securities while prices were dropping sharply, only to sell them at even lower figures at a later date, or to be closed out for lack of margin. Nevertheless, there were many in high places who refused to believe that this was more than a temporary financial setback. Although the national income fell in 1930 and 1931, it was still at a fairly high level. Because of the low prices to which common stocks had fallen, various recommendations were made in the late autumn of 1929 urging the Life insurance companies to make such purchases in anticipation of rapid economic recovery. The State laws governing Life insurance investments specifically forbade such venturing. Undoubtedly great havoc would have been wrought in the financial structures of many companies and great losses suffered by policyholders if such advice could have been taken. The market quotations as they dropped from month to month thoroughly confirmed the prophetic warnings of Mr. Ecker, and justified his insistence that the law limiting the character of the investment portfolio of Life insurance companies should remain essentially unchanged.

The Life insurance companies stood firm. Because of the character of their portfolios, they were not seriously affected by the declining values. In some respects, the very nature of the upset at the close of 1929 reacted favorably upon the companies. Many individuals who had lost heavily in the stock market felt called upon to increase their Life insurance in order to make good the losses to the estates which they had hoped to build up for their families. Thus, in the years immediately following the first stock market crash, Ordinary insurance made unparalleled gains. In 1930 the Metropolitan issued, exclusive of business revived or increased, close to $1,400,000,000 of Ordinary insurance, the highest annual figure in the history of this Department up to that time. But even this figure was exceeded by a considerable margin the following year, when a total of more than $1,460,000,000 was achieved.

In fact, 1931 has remained the banner year for the writing of Ordinary insurance in the Metropolitan. Even in the Industrial Department there was an issue of $1,110,000,000 in 1930, only 8 percent less than in its peak year of 1929. In 1931 the Industrial insurance issued still exceeded $1,000,000,000. In both the Ordinary and the Industrial Departments, the total insurance in force continued to increase without interruption through the year 1931. Apparently, the economic situation up to that time had not yet seriously affected the ability of the American people to purchase or maintain Life insurance.

However, as the months passed, the seriousness of the financial situation became more acute and more widely felt. As commodity prices continued to drop, industrial plants reduced operations or shut down altogether. Employment fell to unprecedented low levels, and by the fall of 1932 it was estimated that more than 12,000,000 were out of work. With the further toppling of security values, many financial institutions were compelled to close their doors. The distress which reached millions of families increasingly affected the operations of Life insurance. It was now clear that this depression was the most severe, as it later proved to be the longest, in the history of the United States and Canada. New writings declined and lapses increased perceptibly. Many of the insured who had equities in their policies naturally turned to their companies for loans and cash surrender values. In none of the previous depressions had there been such a volume of demand on Life insurance companies, because the provisions for releasing such funds had not been so liberal in the earlier policies. Now the situation was quite different. Here was a security which did not fluctuate with the market, assured by a type of institution which was under no selling pressure and could meet all normal liabilities.

Loans in the Ordinary Department of the Company reached new levels toward the end of 1931, and for the year as a whole totaled almost $130,000,000, or 25 percent above the figure for the year before. In 1932 the figures reached the highest point on record, and in June of that year the monthly loans came to almost $16,000,000. During this year, about $167,000,000 was loaned to Ordinary policyholders—more than double the amount recorded in 1929. In the Industrial Department, the surrender of policies for cash showed an even greater increase. While in 1929 Industrial cash surrenders amounted to but $33,700,000, in 1932 the figure rose to $145,200,000, or more than four times as much.

Following the declaration of bank moratoria in a number of States, the Executive Committee of the National Convention of Insurance Commissioners called a meeting in Chicago in the spring of 1933 to consider the effect of a possible general extension of these bank moratoria upon the cash situation of Life insurance companies. At that time it was recommended that the various State authorities who might be contemplating the extension of bank moratoria be reminded of the fact that, as a matter of fairness, there were financial institutions other than the banks, particularly Life insurance companies, having like obligations to the public. It was also urged that these companies be given the same consideration as would be given to the banks, in any legislation that might be adopted. The Executive Committee, however, was unable to agree unanimously upon the recommendations and consequently no action was taken.

The situation under consideration by the Executive Committee reached a climax when, almost immediately after the inauguration of President Roosevelt on March 4, 1933, a proclamation was issued, effective March sixth, closing the banks and stock exchanges throughout the country. The immediate effect of this action was at once to increase the demand for loan and cash values on Life insurance policies. The Metropolitan and other companies had met the needs of policyholders, and it was the consensus of opinion that the companies could continue to meet all the demands that were being made upon them. Nationwide closing of the banks, however, presented a new situation. There was a general realization that the problem was country-wide, and that there were companies which might be embarrassed if enormous demands for cash payments continued. The Superintendent of Insurance of New York called a meeting of Life insurance company presidents to consider the matter. Viewing the institution of Life Insurance as a whole, it was felt that steps should be taken to assure the ability of companies to meet all payments in full. Discussion of the general situation by the Superintendent of Insurance with the Governor and with the leaders of the Legislature resulted in the passage of emergency laws, under which restrictive regulations on loans were issued. Similar laws or regulations were eventually in force in 29 States.

The companies operating in New York State were forbidden to make any policy loans or to pay any cash surrender values in the State, unless these sums were used for payment of premiums. Only on the proof of extreme need could the companies make a loan or cash surrender payment, and then the amount was limited to $100 in the aggregate on Ordinary policies. No such limitation, however, was placed on Industrial insurance. Although at that time cash surrender values were not contractually available on Industrial policies until premiums had been paid for 10 years, the Company for some years past had purchased these policies, in cases of extreme need, at the full cash value of the paid-up insurance, after they had been in force for only three years. This privilege was continued and in this way many million dollars were paid out by the Company as concessions on policies having no contractual cash value at the time. It should be pointed out also that the restrictions by Superintendents of Insurance were never sought nor required by the Metropolitan, which stood ready and able at all times to meet any demands, and which did continue to meet such demands in the States where permitted. Furthermore, in every State, even in those which enacted emergency regulations, death claims, disability benefits, matured endowments, and annuities continued to be payable and were promptly paid.

It was not long before these restrictions were removed in many of the States, and the companies, including the Metropolitan, continued to serve their policyholders as sources of ready funds. During the 10-year period from 1930 to 1939, payments to policyholders or beneficiaries by the Metropolitan alone amounted to more than $5,000,000,000; and for all American companies, the amount was more than $26,000,-000,000. These payments, made during the time when the Federal Government, as well as State and local governments, had to make large outlays for relief, served to maintain the morale and independence of many families and to lighten the public burden. No one can exaggerate the constructive part that Life insurance companies played in these depression years. The voluntary security which millions of families had created during the period of business prosperity was now a bulwark of protection in time of great need.

Immediate financial problems more serious than any which had confronted the business in its entire history now had to be faced. No individual company, no matter how careful its management, could avoid the effects of an economic revolution which had engulfed not only the United States but the entire world. The rental value of real estate dropped, consequently undermining the position of mortgagors. Precipitate declines in commodity prices affected the ability of farmers to meet their payments of interest and principal. Land values dropped with a thud, and subordinate liens added to the perplexities with a consequent increase of defaults on farm mortgages. Shrinkage of business and subsequently of freight tonnage affected the earnings of railroads, bringing about sharp declines in the value of their securities. This situation, arising out of the collapse of business, demanded immediate attention. Fortunately, President Ecker had had a long and varied experience in the investment side of the business, including the panic years of 1893 and 1907; and he addressed himself to the solution of the problem.

His was essentially the task of adjusting the Company's portfolio in the light of prevailing conditions. Here Mr. Ecker's extensive knowledge of securities, and his quickness and accuracy of decision, stood the Company in good stead.

Because of the uncertain position of real estate, city mortgage lending was rapidly reduced. Farm lending, too, was temporarily curtailed. In many instances it became necessary for the Company in the interest of policyholders to foreclose mortgage loans. But in each instance this final step was taken only after the borrower had been given every opportunity to retain his property. The Metropolitan did not forget its social obligations merely because hard times had arrived. The proportion of railroad securities in the portfolio dropped appreciably. On the other hand, as we have already pointed out, loans to policyholders increased. Bonds of public utilities and particularly the Company's investment in Government securities grew in relative importance. With the constantly growing difficulty of finding desirable securities for investment, the amount of cash in the Company's hands rose materially. This likewise assured the ability to meet any demands for cash payments. Reserves for losses were increased, and writedowns in value were taken where needed. In this way, advantageous and well-timed adjustments in investments were made. Values ultimately proved to be well conserved. When the tide turned and the economic upswing began in 1934, the Company was in a sound financial position. It should prove interesting to future students of finance to look into the careful changes made during this period, which made possible the stability of the Company in the face of financial cataclysms. A similarly heartening story could be written for the Life insurance business as a whole. The maximum potential losses through failure have already been reduced to less than $\frac{1}{2}$ of 1 percent of the reserves. The industry has weathered the storm.

But as the clouds cleared, it was realized that an old era had closed. The soundness of the Metropolitan's investment practices during these years had been practically demonstrated. Yet values, not only of securities but of ideas current in business, had been challenged and severely deflated. Hereafter, those in authority in business and in government had infinitely more responsibility thrust upon them. No longer could one move complacently with the tide. A new epoch had set in, and fortunately the men at the helm in the Company had demonstrated their capacity to meet it.

Nor did the multiplicity of financial problems limit Mr. Ecker and his associates in their efforts to improve other phases of the business, particularly that of Life insurance distribution. In Home Office and Field meetings the President placed renewed emphasis upon quality rather than on volume of business. The keynote of the first Convention of the Managers and Field-Men over which he presided was described as "Conservation — Conservation of Business and of Men." Stress was laid upon the vigilance that should be exercised to preserve the business in force and to sell business which would persist and meet the insurance requirements of the heads of families. In a Circular Letter to the Field, Mr. Ecker at this time wrote: "I want you to feel the responsibility for protecting the families on your debits by covering the breadwinner with sufficient Life insurance. Again I urge you to make a special effort to meet the fathers of your families, to learn how much insurance they carry, and not to be content until they have been insured for a sufficient amount, having in mind the income and the number and circumstances of the dependents. In my judgment, such an amount should be what will tide the family over for at least two or three years in the event of the death of the breadwinner."

In following this program, rules of practice have been developed to guide Agents to place insurance more judiciously —in the amounts and in the form best suited to the economic capacity of each family. Those in better circumstances are to be provided with Monthly Industrial or Ordinary policies. The writing of Weekly Premium insurance on children is limited to a total premium of 25 cents a week in all companies; for adults not more than $500 of Weekly Premium insurance is issued by the Company within six months. Special attention is given to applications for the larger amounts of Industrial insurance to determine whether these people would not be better served by Ordinary insurance. Further restrictions are now placed on the writing of insurance on housewives and other dependents, in relation to the amount in force on the head of the family. Moreover, the Industrial application form has been changed to require information regarding existing policies in the family and family earnings, from which data the Home Office is in a better position to judge whether the total premium payable by the family would be in due proportion to its income. The effect of these rules and of other instructions to Agents has been to eliminate, at the source, unsuitable insurance that would presumably not stay on the books. Industrial applications submitted by Agents in good faith are rejected where the insurance appears to be unsuitable as a result of these considerations. This has been an important factor in the continuous decline in the lapse rate of Industrial policies, now at the lowest point in the Company's history. The plans of the Company for better selection and training of Agents have resulted in greater stability in the Agency organization and a marked reduction in the Agency turnover. The percentage of "controllable terminations" was reduced from 33 percent in 1930 to less than 7 percent in 1940. Little by little and step by step, Industrial insurance has been made over. Criticisms have been met, and today it stands out as a form of Life insurance carefully planned to meet the needs of working people and to give them the utmost in service and in financial return.

Yet, as is usual in times of depression, there was criticism of business generally; and the business of Life insurance came in for its share of investigation and study. Industrial insurance was the object of particular criticism in a number of States. In 1937 a new Life insurance code became effective in the State of Illinois, containing for the first time a section requiring standard provisions to be included in Industrial policies. Similarly, in 1938, the Legislature of New York made a thorough study of the Insurance Code with a view toward its revision. In this connection it undertook, through an extensive questionnaire, an investigation of all companies transacting Industrial business in this State. The recommendations for revision of the code were made with great understanding of the problems involved and, with few exceptions, were sound and workable. It is significant that Metropolitan forms and practices were adopted in many cases.

Although the practices of the Metropolitan in the conduct of the Industrial Life insurance business had been constantly liberalized and improved, some of the liberalizations in practice had not been incorporated in the policy form. Under the guidance of Mr. Lincoln, a general revision of the provisions and guarantees of Industrial policies was inaugurated in 1937, adding some new features as well as bringing the printed policy forms into conformity with the already existing practices of the Company. The most important change was a provision for automatic non-forfeiture value in the form of Term insurance after premiums had been paid for as short a period as six months. Beginning in 1935, new policies had provided cash values after premiums had been paid for five years, and this provision was continued in the 1937 policy editions, but later the period was reduced to only three years. It is noteworthy that the legislation in Illinois and the subsequent legislation in New York required no substantial change in the revised form of Metropolitan Industrial policies. The changes put into effect brought the Industrial contract as nearly as possible into conformity with the provisions of the Ordinary policy; and what is equally important, the Company, as far as and as soon as it was practicable, granted to the holders of policies previously issued the privileges currently provided by the new policies.

Of national significance was the investigation of the institution of Life Insurance begun in 1938 by the Temporary National Economic Committee authorized by Congress. The administration in Washington had launched a program of increased control of economic affairs, which included greater jurisdiction over large-scale business. The move involving insurance companies was made in response to a recommendation from President Roosevelt, which suggested for investigation certain investment phases of the business. More particularly, it called for inquiry into the possible concentration of economic power in the large assets of the insurance companies.

The Securities and Exchange Commission was assigned to study this problem. The counsel and special staff set to work to investigate not only insurance investments, but also practically every feature of the general management of the companies. It was obvious to those who followed the course of the investigation that some of the participants were not without prejudice. The entire inquiry was colored by the assumption that there was fundamental mismanagement in the Life insurance industry. Great emphasis was placed on the tremendous size of the companies, and testimony was sought to show that this might interfere with the effective operation of the business. Criticism was leveled at the cost of Industrial insurance and on the manner of its distribution. An attempt was made to show that State supervision was inadequate, with implications of the advantages of Federal supervision. Not only was no opportunity lost to seek out matters for criticism, but much of this was assiduously "played out" to the press prior to the presentation of testimony before the Commission.

Encouraged by public support and conscious of the soundness of their industry and its management, the executives of the insurance companies organized under the chairmanship of President Lincoln of the Metropolitan and jointly presented their side of the case. It was pointed out that the institution of Life Insurance had presented a remarkable record of stability in the years during which the economic foundations of the country had been shaken. During the decade 1929 to 1938 the insurance companies of 30 of the 45 States (three States have no local companies) had a perfect record of solvency. Not a single company in these 30 States had suspended operations; and this group accounted for over 85 percent of the total assets of all legal reserve companies in the whole country. The assets of companies which did suspend operations during the decade amounted to only 2 percent of the Life insurance assets in the United States, and the potential loss to policyholders was less than 1 percent of the policy reserves. Even this small proportion of impaired reserves was then being rebuilt through assumption by other companies, and has been reduced to less than ½ of 1 percent.

Another proof of the strength of the Life insurance industry was the extremely small amount of emergency borrowing it required from the Reconstruction Finance Corporation. The amount of loans to all Life insurance companies was less than $45,000,000. This was less than 2 percent of the Corporation's lending during the depression to all types of business combined, and was only ⅕ of 1 percent of all Life insurance assets. Moreover, these loans were largely repaid during the next few years. The Metropolitan, however, was never obliged to borrow a single cent from that or any other source during the depression. It was proved that as the result of the strong financial position of the companies, the American people might look as confidently to their Life insurance organizations during disastrous and critical years as they could during more favorable times.

If, as the T.N.E.C. inquiry stated, the companies were large, their size only reflected the confidence and respect which the American people had for their Life insurance institutions. Their size had not stood in their way; in fact, it added to their resourcefulness, to their initiative, and to their ability to serve their clientele well. Their very size, indeed, had enabled them to undertake tremendous welfare activities which smaller companies could not have afforded. It was furthermore pointed out that the current trend was not toward, but away from, the concentration of Life insurance assets. Smaller companies, little heard of at the beginning of the 20th century, had been able to rise to a position of prominence, and the leaders of yesterday were not necessarily the leaders of tomorrow. The companies, because the overwhelming share of their investments carried no voting rights, could in no way exert influence over the Nation's business. Only a modest fraction of the outstanding bonds and mortgages of the country and an insignificant fraction of the stocks were held by the Life insurance companies. They did not and could not control the economic life of the country.

In general, it was evident that some of the investigators were thoroughly disappointed with the lack of evidence of anything but a healthy condition in the Life insurance business. The Chairman of the Congressional Committee, after the conclusion of the hearings, commented: "The business has come through with flying colors." The investigation as a whole unquestionably left the public with a sense of assurance that the business was being conducted soundly and conscientiously, in the interest of policyholders. This was fully demonstrated the year immediately following, the most satisfactory in American Life insurance history. Confidence was especially marked in the case of the Metropolitan, which in 1941 reached the total of more than $25,000,000,000 of insurance in force, issued more business than in several preceding years, and achieved the lowest lapse rates on record in both its Ordinary and Industrial Departments.

Despite the bias which was displayed during parts of the hearings, the results proved to be a source of satisfaction to the institution of Life Insurance as a whole and to the Metropolitan in particular. From the point of view of public relations, the outcome was gratifying. The good will and respect of the public is a vital thing for the industry. The T.N.E.C. inquiry in 1939 proved an opportunity to confirm in the public mind the soundness and integrity of the industry in which it put its trust.

Another fact—and an important one—in the Company's relations to the public was the makeup of its Agency Force. From the beginning the Ecker-Lincoln administration had placed a new emphasis on the selection of the Field workers. Managers were urged to exercise more and more care in the choice of Company representatives; and in September 1931 the announcement was made of the establishment at the Home Office of a separate and well-staffed Division exclusively devoted to Field training and sales promotion. Every new Agent was expected to be thoroughly familiar with the plans and programs of the Company. Managers, even those with long service, were brought to New York for "refresher" courses. Field representatives were encouraged to take instruction leading to the Chartered Life Underwriter (C.L.U.) designation and to take insurance courses at colleges and commercial schools. Life insurance salesmanship in the Metropolitan has thus become increasingly a professional career attracting men of higher qualifications. At the same time the public has been informed, through a long series of advertisements in magazines of nationwide circulation, of the functions of the Agent, and how these representatives can render service in working out the most desirable form of insurance for each individual. Better-trained Agents, with their clients' welfare increasingly in mind, have been an effective means of providing better service to policyholders and greater economy of operation.

In March 1936 the Board of Directors established the office of Chairman of the Board, and Mr. Ecker was advanced from the Presidency to fill this position. Mr. Lincoln, who had been Vice-President and General Counsel, was elected to succeed him in the Presidency. This change was made in response to Mr. Ecker's desire to share with his colleague more of the exacting burdens of administration, particularly those pertaining to the work in the Field. For Mr. Lincoln the previous 18 years of service in the Company were an invaluable preparation for the administrative responsibility of his new office. At the same meeting of the Board a group of younger Executives were advanced to ranking positions in the Company. These men were all products of the Metropolitan's training program; they knew their way about and added new vitality to the several Departments to which they were appointed. The complexion of the official family was thus given additional youth and vigor, guaranteeing a long period of continuous and productive management. At the close of 1937 the Board of Directors, in anticipation of Mr. Ecker's retirement (under the Company's Insurance and Retirement Program) after nearly 55 years of service, took cognizance of his experience and extraordinary ability, of his gratifying vigor of mind and body, and insisted on his continuing in office. Their announcement read: "Mr. Ecker has yielded to the insistence of the Board, but upon the express condition, imposed by him, that his continuance in office shall be without salary." Throughout the Company and throughout the insurance world, this happy rounding out of a career which had influenced every phase of its development was received with satisfaction. No one in the history of the Life insurance business has ever won for himself a larger measure of esteem and respect.

Mr. Ecker as President had continued and had extended the Fiske tradition of meeting with the entire Field Force in their respective home areas. But he emphasized and humanized this personal relationship with the Agency Staff, developing his own technique of leadership. He encouraged free discussion with the Managers, for improving supervision and directing their many Field activities. He brought Home Office Executives into closer touch with Field problems and thus promoted a better understanding between the two. For the first time in the history of the Company he sat down with the men and listened to their problems. They liked him, his lack of pretense, his simple friendliness. He saw every Field-Man during the first three years of his Presidency. These closer Field contacts resulted in a consideration of joint problems and a pooling of ideas. Through such man-to-man talks, certain changes in the Agency contract were made which, with later revisions, have had a fundamental influence on the recent course of the business.

Mr. Lincoln, likewise, set for himself a program in the Field and spent a large part of his first years as President traveling from city to city, getting to know the Managers and Agents. Their welfare became one of the President's absorbing interests. Mr. Lincoln, keenly aware of the vital position of the Agents in the business, soon inaugurated the practice of conferring with them in small groups, encouraging the full and free discussion of their problems. The obvious

Mr. Lincoln meets the Agents

sincerity, friendliness, and directness of the President wiped out any possible constraint which might have existed previously between Agents and the management. By the establishment of such contacts, the President himself obtained a clearer insight into Field work and was enabled to bring about further improvements in Agency contracts.

At the same time, forces of dissidence were at work. The intensive drive for unionization in almost every field of activity which followed the enactment of the National Labor Relations Act and the several State Labor Relations Acts, encouraged outside groups to attempt the unionization of the Agents of the Company, particularly throughout the East. On representation of a group of Agents who had joined such a union, an election was ordered by the New York State Labor Relations Board among the Agents of Metropolitan Territory in New York. The Company believed that its Agents were not within the scope of the New York Act and that the occupation of a Life insurance Agent was not a proper field for unionization, and sought to have the New York Supreme Court set aside the order of the Labor Board directing the Company to bargain with the union. The case was eventually taken to the Court of Appeals of New York State. The

Company's contentions were not fully upheld; but the Labor Board's order was sustained by only one judicial vote, with five against the Company's position and four for it. The period for which the union was certified as the bargaining agent expired before the conclusion of bargaining and was not renewed. The controversy with the union was settled out of court. The impetus for unionization was essentially from without; and in this regard it is significant that the majority of the Company's Agents in Metropolitan Territory subsequently submitted to the New York Labor Relations Board a statement that they did not desire union representation. In June 1942 another election was ordered by the New York State Labor Relations Board, and the union was recertified as the collective bargaining representative for Agents in Metropolitan Territory. At this writing the Company is engaged in bargaining with the representatives of the union.

So far as the Company as a whole is concerned, there never was a friendlier and more understanding relation between the management and the whole Field Force than now exists. This is all the more gratifying when one considers another contemporary development, the venture in business of self-styled "Life insurance counsellors" or "insurance advisors." These are usually ex-Agents who, for their own profit, strive by radio, direct representation, or other means of solicitation to dissatisfy Life insurance policyholders with their existing programs, and to undermine confidence in the integrity and services of Agents. The so-called "counsellors" attempt to sell "specialized advice" which usually leads either to the cash surrender of existing insurance or to its change to some form calling for a lower premium. By bringing about some cash payment or some reduction in the premium as a result of a change to policies with reduced benefits, the "counsellor" attempts to justify his fee. Unfortunately, the policyholder is frequently unaware of the injurious effect of the changes suggested. Many policyholders are clearly imposed upon by misrepresentations of skill and of objectivity which the "counsellors" do not possess. Moreover, they do not render any service which the Company is not ready to perform with greater perspective and without charge to the policyholder. It is a matter of satisfaction to record that the devious operations of one "counsellor" came finally before the courts, through a libel action brought by him against the Metropolitan and one of its Managers. The character of his operations was exposed, and after a verdict in favor of the Company and the Manager, the minutes of the trial were ordered referred by the Presiding Justice to the District Attorney of the county for action. This, it is hoped, will lead to the termination of an utterly destructive and spurious development in recent Life insurance history.

A major problem confronting the Metropolitan, as well as other Life insurance companies and investors generally, has been the continued decline in the interest rate on investments. The downward movement began even before the inception of the 1929 economic crisis and has continued virtually un-abated. Many causes, such as agricultural overproduction, world-wide deflation, and the loss of foreign markets, have operated to bring this about; and the effect on Life insurance is significant. Inasmuch as the operations of a Life insurance company are based on assumed interest earnings necessary to fulfill its obligations to policyholders, the decreased yield has presented a serious problem. Interest earnings have, in fact, dropped to the lowest point in the history of the business. Thus, the net investment income of all American Life com-panies was almost $2,500,000,000 less during the 10-year period from 1931 to 1940 than it would have been had the 1930 interest level continued. In recent years the net returns on Metropolitan investments have been approximately $3\frac{1}{2}$ percent; and on new funds the earnings have averaged only about $2\frac{1}{2}$ percent. The inevitable consequence of this situ-ation has been to increase the cost of insurance. Here was a situation completely beyond the control of the Officers but one which, nevertheless, called for both knowledge and wis-dom in handling. The problem was met first by a downward revision in the dividend scale and, later, by an increase in premium rates on policies issued after January 1, 1942. These inevitable steps are being followed by other Life insurance companies and have been accepted by the body of policy-holders as eminently justified.

As the opportunities for profitable investment became fewer, Mr. Ecker turned his attention toward the field of large-scale housing into which, it will be recalled, the Company had made an initial successful venture in the early 1920's. In such a course he saw the double advantage of a fair interest return to the Company and, in view of the lack of moderate-cost housing, a needed service to the community. In 1938 the Chairman announced plans for the construction of a huge new housing project to be owned and operated by the Company. A desirable property in the Borough of The Bronx in New York City, consisting of 129 acres, was bought. In this location an attractive and complete community providing housing for more than 12,000 families has been created under the guidance of a Board of Design consisting of leaders in the fields of architecture, engineering, and city planning.

Parkchester has been cited by housing experts and by all interested in public welfare as an important civic contribution. It is the largest housing project ever undertaken either by private or public agencies in the United States. Parkchester has demonstrated that convenient location, attractive surroundings, and comfortable living can be provided at moderate rentals and can still net a reasonable return on capital. It has proved the feasibility of providing such housing without Government subvention of any sort. Since the completion of Parkchester the Company has launched three other sizable housing developments, one in San Francisco, another in Los Angeles, and a third in Alexandria, Va.

At the same time the new Home Office building program of the Company has continued. By 1941 all but the last quadrant of the building between 24th and 25th Streets on Madison Square had been erected. A large and imposing office structure has taken shape across the way from the

FREDERIC W. ECKER
Resigned in January 1942 to serve as Special Assistant to the
Lend-Lease Administrator.

Tower, a fine addition to the skyline of New York. Under two roofs more than 15,000 employees of the Company care for the ever-increasing volume of its business. It is a source of gratification to the Executives that even during the period of disturbed economic conditions, the Company has continued to grow and has continuously found it necessary to increase the Staff at the Home Office. On the other hand, because Agents have been taught how to make more effective use of their time and energies, because Ordinary insurance constitutes a larger proportion of the business as a whole, because Monthly Premium insurance has grown and a larger percentage of Industrial weekly premiums are paid directly, the Company has found it possible to handle the growing volume of business with a smaller Field Force. This adjustment has been made without dispensing with the services of any man properly performing his duties. It has been so conceived as not to

CHARLES G. TAYLOR, JR.
Vice-President

impose any hardship upon faithful representatives of the Company, and has been effected only as retirements, deaths, and resignations have occurred. At no time has it been necessary for the Company to let anyone go for the want of useful employment in the Home Office or Head Offices or in the Field.

As it has been aware of peacetime responsibilities, the Company has dedicated itself with even greater resolution to its wartime obligations. It has contributed to the financial resources of the two countries it serves through the purchase of large blocks of Federal and Dominion securities. In the year after Pearl Harbor, the Company increased its holdings of United States Governments by more than $550,000,000, bringing the total to nearly $1,700,000,000. Also during the past year it increased its holdings of Dominion Government securities to a total of about $130,000,000. It has also encouraged the purchase of War Bonds and Stamps by policyholders through the efforts of the Field Force and by its own employees.

The Company has made available to the Government a number of its experts, who have given valuable advice and technical assistance in various fields. In addition, Frederic W. Ecker resigned his positions as Vice-President and member of the Board in January 1942 to give his full time to the Lend-Lease Administration as Special Assistant to Mr. E. R. Stettinius, Jr. Both these important positions were filled by the promotion of Charles G. Taylor, Jr., formerly Second Vice-President. A total of over 3,000 members of the Home Office and Field Staffs have joined the armed forces. The entire organization, and the institution of Life Insurance as a whole, has been geared to the fullest effort in support of the Government at war.

A Family
of Thirty
Million

CHAPTER 6

Industrial Insurance

From the preceding pages it is clear that Life insurance service to the wage-earners of the United States and Canada has been the central theme of Metropolitan history. It has determined the character of the Company's development as has no other single factor, and its imprint is clearly marked upon the pattern of the Metropolitan's activities. It explains the development of the Industrial Department, which continues to be a very effective medium for meeting the insurance needs of this group. The Metropolitan was not the first company in this country to write Industrial insurance. The honor rightly belongs to the Prudential Insurance Company of America whose operations as the Prudential Friendly Society antedated those of the Metropolitan by four years. It is true, however, that the Metropolitan began to serve the wage-earners of this country a full decade before the launching of its Industrial business in 1879. Within the first years of its founding, the Company underwrote the Life insurance of a workingmen's organization which received premiums weekly from its members and transmitted them quarterly to the Company. Thus the Metropolitan from its inception devoted special attention to working people, and has retained this as a primary and absorbing interest throughout the years.

Industrial Life insurance has been variously defined. It is essentially Life insurance for the great majority of people who make up the industrial or wage-earning population. It took form and direction as our mighty cities grew and as more and more people became wage-earners. They had probably more need for Life insurance than the better-circumstanced groups, but they could buy it only in small amounts and could pay for it only out of wages usually received weekly. Experience has indicated that the families for whom Industrial insurance has been designed, generally did not find it convenient to remit the small premiums directly to the Company, or found the cost of that method out of all proportion. It was essential that someone receive the premiums each week at their homes. Here, then, is the essence of Weekly Premium Industrial Life insurance: insurance in relatively small amounts on the lives of working men and their families, paid for out of wages, to Agents who personally receive the premiums weekly. Such insurance has the same objectives as Ordinary insurance, but in more modest degree; and both forms are based on the same scientific principles of level premium and reserve.

In view of the pressing need of Life insurance by working people, it is surprising that this branch of the business developed so late in our insurance history. It was inaugurated in America, as we have pointed out, in 1875, by the Prudential of Newark. Workingmen, not sought by the insurance companies, at first attempted to meet their needs through cooperative assessment societies. Unfortunately, these societies suffered from the defects inherent in the assessment plan of operation, and they failed, as the assessment plan has generally failed, both in England and in America. Following the Civil War, feeble attempts were made by one company or another to furnish insurance to wage-earners, but they did not succeed, either because of the unsoundness of their plans or because they did not recognize the necessity of receiving the premiums at the homes of the insured. The fact is that Industrial insurance did not take hold in America until the Prudential, the John Hancock, and the Metropolitan launched it, following the essentials of procedure—actuarial, managerial, and administrative—which the Prudential of London had worked out during more than 20 years of operation.

It is a matter of record that both President Dryden of the Prudential and President Knapp of the Metropolitan were close students of the Prudential of London. Both went to

London and witnessed the functioning of the business at first hand. In fact, Mr. Knapp and the Metropolitan's Attorney, Stewart L. Woodford, and an expert they took with them, were shown every courtesy. They brought back with them a clear conception of the details of management, and implemented this with a complete file of the forms essential to a business as intricate as Industrial insurance. The records of the Company show that the procedures and the forms of the Prudential of London were followed to a large degree, and these undoubtedly contributed to the immediate success of the venture. Of course, important adjustments to American conditions had to be made. There was a fundamental difference, for instance, in the basis on which the reserve liability was computed. To be permitted to transact business in the United States, a company was required to maintain reserves computed on the net premium basis, which made it necessary for American companies to maintain larger reserves than those on similar business in England. The computation of premiums in the earlier days, before the mortality experience on this class of risks or the expense rate of conducting such business was known, was not easy. It was due to the good sense and skill of James M. Craig, Actuary of the Company, that the business was launched properly and safely.

The Metropolitan's Industrial business was begun with the issuance, on November 17, 1879, of 34 Industrial policies for weekly premiums totaling $3.95. Before the end of that year a total of 5,143 policies for $516,618 face amount were on the books, and those at the helm knew that their new venture was meeting a real need. By the end of 1880 the Industrial business of the Metropolitan had already outstripped that of the two other companies then operating. There was no sign of uncertainty as the new enterprise expanded in many directions. The greatest advantage which the Metropolitan enjoyed arose from the decision to bring from England a large number of men already well trained in the business, a decision of historic interest, as the most direct transfer of old-world marketing methods in the history of

D/122

New York
Jany. 23rd/80

William Inman Esq.
Liverpool

Dear Sir:

I enclose copy of a letter from Mr. Knapp president of the Metropolitan Life Ins. Company, and also of a letter of introduction I have given to their Mr. B. Collard, which explains itself.

Please furnish Mr. Collard passage for as many Cabin or Steerage passengers as he may require, advising me by same Steamer of the number shipped and we shall collect the passage money here, crediting same to the ship at our p.p. rate of $28. per adult for Steerage, + $55. for Cabin. Children 1 to 12 years half price. Do. under 1 year $3. steerage, and free in Cabin. Very respectfully yours

Signed: John L. Dale

Arranging for passage of English Agents

the industry. The first contingent of 21 men appears to have arrived early in the year 1880. All the men were experienced, most of them having previously been with the Prudential of London. Among these were the vigorous old-timers Goldthorpe, Higginbotham, Booth, Selkirk, Shackleton, Roberts, Staniland—men who made Metropolitan history in the early days. Most of them were placed as Superintendents or Assistant Superintendents of District Offices in the larger cities of the country, and set to work at once to build up a solid Field organization. The importations from abroad rapidly increased in number. Brice Collard literally commuted between New York and London, signing up more than 800 likely Field-Men in the old country. Altogether, including their families, it is estimated that some 2,000 persons came over in this directed migration. As Mr. Craig said in his Company history of 1897: "To these, in addition to its own Home force, was assigned the task of laying the foundation; of educating a body of efficient co-workers; training them to the best methods of house-to-house canvassing and collecting; perfecting them in the intricate matters of bookkeeping, accounts, and the numerous forms inherent to a business of so much detail."

The young Company moved with vigor. Not a local or a sectional, but a national service was envisioned. At the close of 1879 the Company had 124 Agents in its service. By the end of the next year the number had increased to 637. At the close of 1884 there were 1,566 Agents operating in 56 different key centers. The vast tenancy of busy cities of the United States and Canada had been opened to Industrial insurance. Many of the pioneer Superintendents who served this new territory were to become leading figures in the Company, not only as great producers but as trainers of men. Over the years, some had the satisfaction of "graduating" a great many trained Superintendents.

The speed with which the business grew reflected the real need of the people for this type of insurance. The existing old-line organizations had afforded them neither the insurance nor the service that they required. Yet the need for protection was urgent, and the Company was obviously able to meet it. In no other way can we explain the fact that a business with limited resources, which had barely survived the panic difficulties of the 1870's, could in a decade have attained major size. The firmest kind of a foundation had been laid. When the Company moved from its Home Office in Park Place to the new quarters on Madison Square in 1893, there were in operation 146 District Offices with nearly 8,000 Superintendents, Assistants, and Agents serving a clientele whose Industrial insurance in force included nearly 3,000,000 policies for close to $350,000,000.

It was not that the Metropolitan alone enjoyed such extraordinary expansion. The Prudential, operating from Newark, soon got into vigorous stride, as did the John Hancock. An increasing number of companies subsequently began to cultivate the field, because of the insistent demand of wage-earners everywhere for insurance they could afford and on a weekly basis. Its availability in small units—a policy could be bought for a minimum weekly premium of 5 cents or less—and its method of servicing made it unique and desirable. Throughout the years this form of insurance continued to spread, reaching all parts of the Nation. Today in the United States and Canada there are about 90,000,000 Industrial policies in force in more than 100 companies, for a total of $22,000,000,000. About 50,000,000 people are insured. This is more than twice the number owning Ordinary insurance. A large proportion of the country's total Industrial clientele, more than 22,000,000, are insured in the Metropolitan.

It must not be supposed that this has been an adventure without its trials and difficulties. Many companies failed in their effort to write Industrial insurance. Furthermore, there is little doubt that in the case of some other companies the insurance would have been lost to thousands of policyholders had not the Metropolitan come to their rescue by assuming the business. But, as shown in earlier chapters, the Company survived its own difficulties and continued to grow, so that by the end of 1909 it had more aggregate insurance (Ordinary and Industrial) in force than any other Company, a position which it has held ever since.

In tracing the major developments in the Industrial business during the course of the 60-odd years since its inception, one sees that the change in the policy itself has been primary. The contracts of today, with their wide range of privileges and benefits to the policyholder, are related in name only to the policies first issued. Step by step the Industrial contract has been liberalized, resulting in a revolutionary change in this branch of the business. The lack of experience in this country made the inauguration of Industrial insurance a venture into the more or less unknown, so that it was natural that the early policies should be hedged about with restrictive clauses. For any misstatement in the application, the early insurance could be voided by the Company at any time during the life of the insured. A policy once lapsed for nonpayment of premiums carried no provision for reinstatement and no cash or paid-up values. However, as experience was gained, such restrictive clauses were eliminated or liberalized, and policy provisions and practices were adopted which provided more and more benefits and a wider range of services to the insured. It is gratifying to note that this development has taken place not alone in the Metropolitan but in the business as a whole.

The first major step in liberalizing the Company's Industrial policy came in 1892 with the introduction of nonforfeiture paid-up values. These applied in the event of a lapse after premiums had been paid for five years, provided the insured had reached the age of 18. Strange as it may seem to us today, this was a far-reaching step at the time. Subsequently the nonforfeiture feature has been greatly liberalized. In policies currently being issued, Paid-up Term insurance for the full amount of the policy is provided automatically after premiums have been paid only half a year, with the option of cash values or a reduced amount of Paid-up Life or Endowment insurance after only three years. Loss to the insured when a policy lapses is thus largely eliminated.

Not only have other rights and privileges been added to new contracts, but time and again the Company has generously added benefits and valuable concessions to policies already in existence which had not the slightest legal claim to such benefits. The contractual amounts on such policies have been voluntarily increased by millions of dollars. In the days before the Company was mutualized, contracts were nonparticipating —that is, the Industrial policyholder had no contractual right to share in the divisible surplus. As early as 1896, however, the Company took the unprecedented step of declaring bonuses

127

on Industrial policies which up to 1915 totaled about $49,000,000. After mutualization the right to receive dividends annually was written into the policy, and this right was extended to policies already in force. Since 1916 the Company has continued to pay dividends to Industrial policyholders each year without interruption. More than $800,000,000 has been paid in dividends to such policyholders from 1916 through 1942.

From time to time the Company has granted additional benefits. For example, in March 1916 a special benefit in case of loss of eyesight or of limbs and, in December 1928, an additional benefit in case of death by accidental means was added to the Industrial policies in force, as well as to those to be issued thereafter. No increase was made in the premium rates in either case because of the addition of these benefits. Other liberalizations have been made in both these provisions since their adoption. Payments to Industrial policyholders under these benefits since they were inaugurated total more than $56,000,000. It is significant that where safety permitted all the concessions to policyholders have been made retroactive on existing policies.

The entire trend has been for the provisions of the Industrial policies more and more to approximate those of Ordinary policies. At present the provisions in both are quite similar, except for the absence of optional modes of settlement, choice of the form in which the dividend is received, restrictions as to assignments, and the privilege of receiving policy loans (features which would add substantially to the cost on smaller amounts of insurance without commensurate advantage). In fact, in some respects the Industrial provisions are more liberal.

There has likewise been a fundamental change in the character of the Agency Force. As we have already pointed out, the Agent is the keyman in the business. He is responsible in large degree for the quality of the service given and likewise reflects the Company's attitude to policyholders. When Industrial insurance was introduced the Company was particularly concerned with an aggressive policy of production so as to extend its benefits to as many people as possible. This required rapid expansion of the Field Force. Scientific methods of selecting Field-Men and comprehensive training programs were yet a thing of the future. Hence the turnover of men in the Field was very high. At present the situation is different. Over the years a program of selection and training of Field personnel has been developed; careful judgment is exercised in the choice of men, with emphasis on character, previous background, and experience. Only those who may be expected to find in their employment a life career are accepted by the Company. Agents' schools, which give a thorough course in insurance principles and practices and the plans and policies available, have been established. Greatly increased earnings have attracted men of higher qualifications and greater devotion to their work. At the turn of the century the average income of the Metropolitan Agent was about $10 a week; in 1942 the weekly average was more than $60. The controllable turnover has been reduced to about 9 percent in 1942. Few business organizations can show as excellent a record for sales personnel. Better trained, more intelligent, and more experienced men give better service to policyholders, write the proper kind of business, and keep in mind their obligation to arrange a suitable distribution of policies and premiums consistent with a family's income and needs.

Nor has the policyholder himself remained unchanged over the years. He is a party to the contract, and the character of the business reflects him as it does the Agent and the Company. The Industrial family today is very different from that of 60 years ago, when our cities were crowded with poor immigrants who eked out an existence on the barest margin. The standard of living has risen enormously in the intervening decades. National wealth and personal income have increased so appreciably that working men and women have been able to use a larger proportion of their earnings for insurance and savings. At the same time the need for protection has been so widely impressed on the land that individuals have learned to plan more intelligently for their future security. The

marked decrease in the size of the average family, moreover, allows for better care and provision for each of the
members. The pressure on the worker's family income is,
therefore, less today per unit than formerly. There is more
money available for insurance and greater ability to continue
it. The American people today accept Life insurance as one
of the basic necessities; and, in meeting that need, the Agent
has served to an increasing degree as an advisor and counselor
rather than as a "go-getting" salesman.

In an earlier chapter we have called attention to the attack
on the business in the critical days in the early 1890's, when
Industrial insurance fought for its very life. The sensational
charges against child insurance were fully disproved, and the
Industrial business was recognized as socially useful. It
experienced another period of attack during the depression
that started in 1930. While this economic upset affected all
lines of business and all parts of the population, the widespread
unemployment had its severest effect on the wage-earners and
their families. Their reduced incomes resulted in widespread
cash surrender and lapse of Industrial policies. The critics
seized upon this unfortunate situation to launch an attack on
the companies. Their principal grievance was the high lapse
rate. This obviously was due primarily to unemployment and
curtailed incomes, matters over which the companies had no
control. Moreover, the insurance companies relished a large
lapse rate as little as did their critics. Inasmuch as most policies
which lapsed had been in force for only a short time, the
claim of financial loss to policyholders was much exaggerated.
Entirely overlooked by most critics was the payment of more
than $2,500,000,000 (more than $1,000,000,000 by the Metropolitan alone) as cash surrender values under Industrial policies
during the years 1930–1939, and the momentous aid that this
amount of money gave to the wage-earners—money which
would not have been available had it not been for the wide
distribution of Industrial policies among working people. Including all settlements made under Industrial policies, the
Metropolitan paid nearly $2,400,000,000 to policyholders

or their beneficiaries under their Industrial insurance during that decade. Had this money not been available to them, the public relief load would have been greatly increased.

Nevertheless, the high lapse rate was a serious problem and the leaders, both in the Metropolitan and in the other large companies, exerted continuous effort to improve this unfortunate feature of the business. Certainly the record of the Metropolitan is one of persistent effort toward reduction of lapses, and despite the widespread unemployment of the past decade, its measures have met with gratifying success.

Several factors have contributed to this achievement. First and foremost has been the development of basic underwriting rules through which the Company has avoided lapses by avoiding business which experience has shown would be of doubtful persistency. Agents are instructed to place insurance first where it is most needed—namely, on the breadwinner— and to apportion it on dependents with due regard to the family's ability to maintain the premiums. The amount of Industrial insurance on women and children has been defi-nitely limited. The Home Office Underwriters review all applications to detect the possibility that the premium may be beyond the means of the family. Finally, emphasis has been placed on the writing of Monthly Premium Industrial insurance or of Ordinary insurance wherever the family's situation would warrant it. A Weekly Premium policy will in no event be issued on an adult for more than $500, thus encouraging the applicant to purchase lower-cost forms of insurance if he is in a position to do so.

Not only has the Company in recent years sharply revised its underwriting practices, but it has likewise completely changed the basis of compensating its Agency Force. One purpose of these revisions was to encourage the writing of lasting business and the conservation of old business. For many years prior to the depression, the compensation for Agents in the Metropolitan, as well as in other Industrial companies, depended in large part upon the "increase" made on their debits—that is, the excess of premiums for policies newly issued over premiums on policies lapsed. With the large surrender of insurance during the depression the lapses exceeded the issues, and many Agents had "decreases" rather than "increases." This situation was unsatisfactory to the Agents because it removed in large degree their financial incentive to write or conserve business. As early as 1931, experimentation was started with a new form of Agency agreement, and two years later Mr. Ecker announced an improved method of compensation that eliminated the factor of "increase." This agreement was further revised in 1938. Under the current agreement the Agent's compensation for writing Industrial business has been brought more into line with that for corresponding Ordinary business; furthermore, he receives a conservation commission determined by the relative persistency of his business. Mr. Lincoln, who was responsible for this revision, in which he was ably assisted by Second Vice-President Francis M. Smith (in charge of the Industrial Department), takes great pride in the current agreement. This encourages the writing of sound business and the maintenance of existing insurance, and does not place undue emphasis upon new production. Thus, in addition to the rules which guide the Agent to the right kind of programing for his clients, there is additional incentive to write business which will persist.

These measures have had excellent results. While it was to be expected that the lapse rate of Industrial insurance would decrease as business conditions improved, the actual improvement has been beyond the fondest expectations. In 1942 it was the lowest in the history of the Company, not only on new business but also for the aggregate. The persistency of the Metropolitan Industrial insurance is now about the same as the combined experience of purely Ordinary companies. It is a matter of interest, in studying the lapse rates according to the duration of the insurance, to find that the greatest improvement has occurred at the early durations. In connection with the two most recent triennial examinations of the Metropolitan by the New York State Insurance Department,

FRANCIS M. SMITH
Second Vice-President

detailed studies were made of the policies lapsed in the years
1935 and 1939. It was found that in this four-year period
Weekly Premium lapse rates during the first three years of
policy duration decreased by 37 percent, but during the
first four weeks of insurance the decrease was 60 percent.
Similarly, Monthly Premium Industrial lapse rates during the
first three years of policy duration decreased by 27 percent.
Although formerly the early lapse rate of Weekly Premium
business was considerably less favorable than that on Monthly
Industrial insurance, in recent years the two have drawn
closer together. Since 1939 further substantial reductions in
the lapse rate have been achieved, especially at the early
durations. In view of the fact that the heaviest lapse has
always been in the first few weeks of insurance, these sizable
improvements indicate a real accomplishment; and there will
be no letup in efforts for further improvement.

However, it must be realized that while lapses are being
reduced to a minimum, they can never be wholly eliminated.

The most important factors causing the termination of insurance are unfavorable economic conditions, which are equally beyond the control of the insurance company and of the individual. During financial crises and widespread unemployment, the lapse rate and cash surrenders always increase. To meet some of the problems arising from this situation, the Metropolitan, in cooperation with the Prudential and the John Hancock, established in 1931 what is known as the Life Insurance Adjustment Bureau. This office, managed by an experienced social worker and an adequate staff, advises social agencies regarding the best adjustment of insurance programs for families whose circumstances have changed to the point where they are no longer self-supporting. During the decade in which this Bureau has been in operation a total of more than $29,000,000 has been returned to policyholders through various adjustments; and what is equally important, much insurance on breadwinners and other members of the family has been conserved. The Metropolitan has made liberal concessions beyond contractual obligations to policyholders in need.

Still another factor in the lapse rate beyond the control of the companies is the fact that Life insurance is subject to the same vacillations of human nature as characterize other types of financial commitment. After all, only a small fraction of those who originally subscribe to building and loan associations continue to pay on their shares to maturity. Instalment payments on automobiles are defaulted in many cases. Christmas Club accounts in savings banks show a heavy lapse tendency. Whether lapsing is due to the inability of the insured to continue payments on his policy through unfortunate financial circumstances, or whether it results from the fact that the insured has changed his mind, the factors are beyond the control of the Company. It is important to note, however, that throughout its history the Metropolitan has repeatedly taken steps to facilitate the revival of policies lapsed. At present, Agents in most instances are authorized to reinstate lapsed Industrial insurance without medical examination; and where the situation warrants, the premium arrears may be carried as a lien on the policies. Thus, many families that discontinue premium payments during periods of temporary financial difficulties are able to reinstate their insurance when their finances improve.

Another point of attack during the depression decade concerned the writing of Weekly Premium Industrial Endowment policies. In the early days Industrial insurance was written only on the Whole Life plan but, as an added service to policyholders, Limited-Payment Life and Endowment forms were later developed. Both these types proved very popular. The wage-earning families particularly favored Endowment insurance for their children, since it provided both protection and some measure of saving. It is true, of course, that Endowment policies call for a higher premium per unit of insurance than Life policies. This was the basis of the attacks which alleged that an unduly large proportion of Industrial insurance was written on Endowment forms. Agents were charged with exerting pressure toward this end, influenced by the commission motive rather than the interest of policyholders. These allegations were disproved by a Field investigation made by Examiners of the New York Insurance Department in 1938, which showed that it was the conscious choice of its purchasers. This report, however, was submitted after the New York Legislature had in that year passed a law prohibiting the writing of any form of Industrial Endowment insurance by any company doing business in the State. For such companies the prohibition, in effect, extended to all States in which they did business. While the Superintendent of Insurance favored the continuance of the new law temporarily as an experiment, he had some doubts as to the desirability of the prohibition, and in 1938 stated the objections to such legislation as follows:

> . . . to entirely prohibit it seems somewhat arbitrary and paternalistic. Those who buy ordinary insurance are permitted to exercise their discretion and choose the kind of insurance they want. There seems to be no sufficient reason for telling the poor man that he can only choose certain types irrespective of his own desires.

In 1939 the New York Law was amended, and opened to all, except residents of New York State, the purchase of Industrial Endowment insurance. The Company, glad of the opportunity to meet the need for Endowment insurance of wage-earners once more, announced several new forms of such policies. These were issued outside of New York State at the beginning of 1940, when the modification of the prohibition became effective. They comprised Weekly Premium forms of Endowment policies of comparatively long term, and Monthly Premium Industrial 20-Year Endowment policies for amounts of $250, as well as for amounts that could be purchased by monthly premiums of $1 and $2. The Company did not return to writing Weekly Premium Endowment policies for as short a term as 20 years, because the decline in its interest earnings would have resulted in a marked decrease in benefits on such policies. They could, however, be sold at attractive rates on a Monthly Premium basis because of lower servicing costs.

In 1940, 1941, and 1942 the New York Legislature passed, by an almost unanimous vote, an amendment which would have permitted the writing of Monthly Premium Industrial Endowment policies in the State on substantially the same basis as that outside. While each of these amendments was vetoed by the Governor, the situation has since been ameliorated. A law passed in May 1942 permitted the writing in New York State of small Ordinary Endowment policies without loan values and without options as to the method of dividend payment—provisions which are unduly costly in small policies. Such insurance, written in the Intermediate branch, is now offered in New York State. Thus, people are afforded the same service in this State as elsewhere.

Over the decades, well-meaning but often misinformed persons have decried what they have called "the high cost of Weekly Premium Industrial insurance." Any off-hand comparison with the cost of Ordinary insurance would be, of course, to the disadvantage of Industrial. There can be no escape from higher costs in view of the nature of the business.

Three factors determine the cost of Life insurance, whether it be Ordinary or Industrial—mortality, operating expense, and the interest earned on the invested funds of the Company. Of these, the first two operate to make Industrial insurance cost more than Ordinary. Because it is sold chiefly to the families of working men, Industrial insurance must provide for the higher mortality prevailing among this group. Despite marked improvement in recent years, the death rate of Industrial policyholders still shows an excess of about 20 percent as compared with the holders of Standard Ordinary policies. The second item, operating expense, is higher in the case of Industrial insurance, not only because of the small units in which these policies are issued but also because it must cover the cost of the additional services which Industrial policyholders receive. The premiums are received in the homes weekly, and the Agent must often call more than once to find the policyholder at home and in funds. His time is at the disposal of the people on his debit, and the policyholder is saved the trouble and expense of having to pay at the office of the Company. The services of the Agent must be paid for, and they are well worth what they cost. No wonder that the operating cost of Weekly Premium insurance is higher than that of Ordinary.

Nevertheless, progress has been made consistently to reduce the difference between the cost of Industrial and Ordinary insurance, and this reduction has been in large measure the result of definite planning and conscious effort. As we shall show more fully in the chapter on mortality, death rates of policyholders have declined throughout almost the entire span of life. At the younger ages they are now only about one fifth of the former levels. The Company's broad program of welfare activities, including its extensive Nursing Service, has undoubtedly reflected favorably on the longevity of the Industrial policyholders. More and more their life expectation has come into line with that of the population as a whole. There is still a sizable difference, however, in favor of the Ordinary policyholders.

Better management has also reduced the expense ratio of the business. The employment of better-qualified Agents, their greater stability, the improved persistency of policies, the better control of details of the business, the new devices of record-keeping, the extension of insurance without medical examination—all have helped to bring the expense ratio down, although the services given have been greatly extended. In fact, the proportion of the Industrial premium devoted to expenses today is only about one half what it was about 50 years ago, and is smaller than that required by the majority of purely Ordinary companies for conducting their business.

Two further developments have reduced the cost of Industrial insurance. As early as 1911 the Company inaugurated a plan whereby Industrial policyholders willing to pay weekly premiums directly and continuously to the Home Office or to a District Office would receive a refund of 10 percent of the premiums. The following year this provision was included in the policy and became a contractual right of the insured. The Metropolitan was the first company to grant this allowance. Large numbers of policyholders have taken advantage of this provision; in fact, more than 30 percent of the weekly premiums in force are now paid directly to the Company, without collection commissions to Agents; and the amount returned to policyholders in 1942 for such direct payment was about $7,700,000. It is interesting to note that almost 30 years after this practice was adopted by the Metropolitan, it became a statutory requirement for companies in New York State, illustrating once again how the Company's voluntary provisions for the benefit of policyholders have later become part of the insurance law.

The second development was the introduction in 1927 of Industrial insurance on the Monthly Premium plan. This form of insurance was designed primarily to meet the requirements of men and women who could afford to buy policies for between $500 and $800 and to pay their premiums monthly. In the main, the Monthly Premium Industrial policy was intended for better circumstanced wage-earning families. In

138

recent years this type of insurance has also been made available in smaller amounts and on the lives of children. The Monthly Premium policies are similar in their provisions to the Weekly contracts. From its very inception this insurance has been participating and has had the benefit of the Company's Nursing Service. Yet current rates for Monthly Premium insurance are 12 percent lower than on corresponding rates for Weekly Premium policies. In fact, Metropolitan Monthly Premium Industrial insurance compares very favorably in cost with Ordinary insurance in many other companies. It is not surprising, therefore, that its growth has been phenomenal. At the end of 1942 there were nearly 3,000,000 Monthly Industrial policies on the books for a total amount of insurance of nearly $1,400,000,000. In recent years an increasing proportion of the Company's Industrial business has been on the Monthly plan. Notwithstanding its relatively recent development, it represents, at present, about 17 percent of the Company's Industrial insurance.

We may conclude this section on cost by referring to a report made in 1938 by the Insurance Department of the State of New York, after an intensive study made of Metropolitan Industrial insurance. The State Examiners concluded that the net cost of Weekly Premium Industrial insurance exceeds the cost of comparable substandard Ordinary insurance, on the average, by only approximately 15 percent of the Industrial gross premium. The report pointed out that this figure may be further reduced to about 5 percent if premiums are paid to a District Office under the privilege of the 10-percent refund. The Examiners of the State Insurance Department, after 18 months of study, reached the conclusion that "these costs are not excessive in view of the service rendered." Their conclusions were reaffirmed as the result of a later examination.

Equally important in providing Life insurance to working people at low cost has been the increasing trend to write Ordinary instead of Industrial insurance on their lives. An important step in this direction was taken by the Company in 1925 when it began to issue Monthly Premium Ordinary insurance at practically the same rates as for its corresponding quarterly premium policies. The holders of these Monthly Ordinary policies receive the same broad Agency service that is rendered the Weekly Industrial policyholders. Thus, Ordinary insurance especially adapted to their circumstances was placed within the reach of many wage-earners. Moreover, Industrial policyholders have a privilege of converting their insurance into Ordinary when circumstances warrant the conversion.

As a result of the revisions in underwriting practices and the emphasis on lower-cost forms of insurance, the composition of the Company's business has undergone a marked change in recent years. At the end of 1930 there was $6,400,000,000 of Weekly Premium business in force in the Metropolitan. By the end of 1942 this total had increased only slightly to $6,500,000,000. At the same time the Monthly Industrial business much more than tripled, increasing from $396,000,000 to nearly $1,400,000,000. Similarly, in that time Monthly Ordinary insurance rose from $986,000,000 to $3,250,000,000. Group insurance increased from $2,703,000,000 to $5,350,-000,000. Thus, of the insurance particularly designed for wage-earners and their families, 61 percent was on the Weekly Premium plan at the end of 1930, as compared with less than 40 percent at the end of 1941.

In addition to the insurance companies, other socially minded organizations have endeavored to furnish lower-cost Life insurance. But Weekly Premium and Monthly Premium Industrial insurance continue to be the types that best meet the circumstances of large numbers of wage-earners. Perhaps the best-known of these outside efforts is the plan of Savings Bank Life insurance in operation in three States. This insurance is on sale in a number of banks at the request of qualified purchasers. However, the total amount of such insurance is extremely small in comparison with the Industrial insurance issued by the Life insurance companies. It is, moreover, doubtful that a large proportion of the insurance issued by the banks is on the lives of persons for whom Industrial

CHART II

Industrial Life Insurance in Force*
Metropolitan Life Insurance Company, 1879-1942

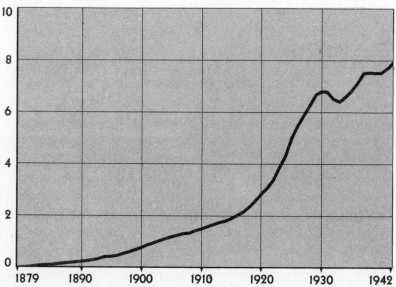

Billions of Dollars

*Includes Weekly and Monthly Premium Industrial business.

insurance is designed. These efforts have not resulted in the supplanting of Industrial insurance, because cheaper insurance can only be furnished by eliminating the broad services of the Agent—services which experience has indicated are necessary for the majority of workingmen's families.

One of the valuable services rendered by the Agent is to revise the family insurance program as circumstances require. Families frequently begin their program with Industrial, and as their economic conditions change they are able to purchase Ordinary insurance. Sometimes it is to their interest to convert the Industrial to Ordinary insurance; but if the Industrial insurance has been outstanding for a number of years it is often desirable to retain this form because of advantages accruing through the age of the policies. Thus, as time goes on, many families own both types of policies. Industrial insurance is the educator, which gives their children, as they grow up, a sense of insurance values. This development of the family program and the graduation of individuals from one type of insurance to another, is reflected in the fact that almost one fourth of Metropolitan Ordinary policyholders also carry Metropolitan Industrial insurance, and about one in every five of Group policyholders also owns Metropolitan Ordinary or Industrial policies. In many families the bread-winner owns Ordinary or Group insurance, while smaller amounts of Industrial insurance are maintained on the dependent members.

It is, therefore, less and less true that only the lower-income groups are Industrial policyholders. Industrial insurance, far from providing only burial funds, is now generally part of a larger family program. Today, for example, a white male Industrial policyholder who dies in his late 30's, leaves his family on the average close to $615 from his Industrial insurance alone. Moreover, the average payment rises to about $1,000 when the benefits payable from other Metropolitan insurance are included. While the average amounts paid on the lives of white women are less—and properly so—the benefits are considerable, reaching a total of $585 for all Metropolitan policies when death occurs between the ages of 35 to 39. In addition to the funds that are provided in case of death, Industrial insurance provides valuable benefits to living policyholders through Endowments and through the availability of cash surrender values.

Today, after some 60 years of development, Industrial insurance is deeply rooted as an American institution. It has lived and grown because it has served the needs of our people, and it has served them well. There is no doubt that, in the beginning, Industrial insurance was a crude instrument; but as time went on it was forged and refined in the crucible of experience. The New York Insurance Department recently stated in referring to Industrial: "Certain it is that at no other time in its history has the business been on a sounder or more equitable basis." It has now become an essential means by which the majority of the American people protect their families. During the pioneer days much of the ground was uncharted and the founders of the business had to proceed cautiously, lest some false move bring the entire enterprise to economic disaster. But as experience accumulated and the business developed, more and more substantial benefits have accrued to policyholders. Industrial insurance has become an important financial mechanism which has helped to stabilize the finances of wage-earner's families during critical periods.

And it is an institution which will continue to serve the American people. In years to come it will continue to be the form of Life insurance for people who can pay only weekly or monthly premiums, who can afford to pay only small amounts, and who need an Agent to service their insurance. Industrial insurance, as so many of our other established institutions, has not always been beyond criticism; but in its effort to serve our people it has gone through many changes which have resulted in improvement of its service. From an enterprise originally operated for profit it has become very largely a mutual institution conducted for the benefit of the policyholders. In the Metropolitan this development has gone even further. There, the concept of Life insurance as an instrument for social good has been expanded to include extensive activities in the fields of welfare and public health. Symbolic and expressive of this attitude has been the Company's extensive welfare program, the largest ever launched by a private agency, developed primarily for Industrial policyholders. The viewpoint of social responsibility has permeated the entire organization.

CHAPTER 7

Ordinary Insurance

ORDINARY INSURANCE on sound actuarial principles became effectively available to the insuring public in this country a hundred years ago. The New England Mutual was chartered in 1835, and a few months before it began doing business, in 1843, the Mutual Life Insurance Company of New York opened its doors. These companies, and the many others that followed in their path, have built up the Life insurance business in the United States according to the level-premium plan first developed in Great Britain by the Equitable of London in 1762. Ordinary insurance was originally designed as a means of providing financial security for people of the middle and upper income groups, who could afford to buy insurance in fairly large amounts and who were in a position to leave substantial estates. In this respect it differed from Industrial insurance, which was developed later to care for workingmen's needs. Not only did Ordinary insurance serve a different sector of the population; its methods of operation likewise were quite distinct. Underwriting requirements for large policies were much more rigid in occupational and physical qualifications. Ordinary was meant primarily for the head of the family; Industrial was essentially family insurance, embracing within its scope women and young children as well as the breadwinner. Despite these differences, which lie chiefly in administrative details, Ordinary and Industrial insurance have common objectives.

In the history of the Metropolitan, especially, the distinction between these two branches of the business has been rather tenuous. While the two are distinct entities and have been conducted by separate Home Office Departments, Ordinary and Industrial insurance have gone hand in hand to serve, in large measure, the same insurable groups and have been conducted by the same Agency Force. Such development could only have occurred in a democratic country where there are no hard and fast class lines, and where, as a normal process, people are constantly progressing from the lower income to the higher-income groups. As our wealth and resources have been developed and as national income has multiplied over the years, the wage-earners themselves have developed an economic status which is equivalent to middle-class standards in other countries. The history of Ordinary insurance in the Metropolitan reflects the American way of life, and the development of security on a fairly substantial basis among large numbers of our wage-earning population.

When the Metropolitan began operations under its present name in 1868, it was solely an Ordinary company. We have already pointed out the vigorous efforts of President Knapp to catch the public eye through attractive forms of policies and effective sales campaigns. Here we need only recall that the provisions of the early policies were very liberal for that period. Premium rates were moderate; no restrictions were placed on travel; 30 days' grace was allowed for the payment of premiums; paid-up values were granted after two or three years; loans to pay premiums were available after three years.

These early policies were sound and attractive; but they were offered by a new Company that faced the severe competition of stronger and older rivals, who were selling deferred-dividend contracts on most liberal estimates as to future dividends. The Company's Ordinary policies had, therefore, only a small measure of success. In the competitive struggle of those early years the Metropolitan, with its slight resources and its limited Agency organization, could not have survived but for its fortunate association, almost from the beginning, with the Hildise Bund. The Company entered into an agreement to underwrite the Life insurance on the members of this society. This arrangement continued for about 10 years and, as we have seen, had a lasting influence upon the future of the business. It eliminated the expense of building up a large sales organization and secured a larger volume of insurance comparatively free from competition and at smaller expense than would have been otherwise possible.

From 1869 until the liquidation of the society in 1878, Life insurance on its members accounted for the greater portion of the Ordinary insurance written by the Metropolitan. The Company's business reached a peak in 1873 with an issue of 12,242 policies for $17,753,399. Thereafter, however, because of the serious economic depression then prevailing, new insurance declined rapidly, and later, ceased almost altogether. An effort was then made to continue writing business through a somewhat similar society, the Prudential League, but the plan did not succeed. Only 510 policies were issued in 1879, and at the close of the year the total Ordinary in force had declined to $11,150,349, from a peak of $27,385,145 only five years earlier. The Metropolitan was in a serious position; business continued to drop, and no Field organization of any vigor had been established.

To any other group of insurance men, this discouraging decline would, in all probability, have meant the early dissolution of the Company. Such had been, in fact, the fate of all the other companies founded about the same time. But to President Knapp and his colleague, John R. Hegeman, this experience brought home a very important lesson. The relationship of the Company to the society of working people already insured was convincing proof that Life insurance in America could be written in sizable amounts on the lives of wage-earners, if the convenience of the policyholder could be met in the payment of premiums. It was these considerations, without doubt, which influenced the Company in its decision to enter the Industrial field. However, with the problem of small policies and frequent premium payments, it was necessary to build as quickly as possible a staff of competent Industrial Agents.

We have seen in the preceding chapter how this decision was translated into an extraordinarily successful development.

From 1879 to 1891 all the energy and resourcefulness of the Company was directed into its Industrial business, and virtually no attention was paid to new Ordinary insurance. The in-force of this Department continued to decline, and by the end of 1891 was down to $3,767,882. But some important lessons with regard to the management of a Life insurance organization, and to the insurance needs of the mass of American people had been learned in this period. By the beginning of 1892 the success of the Industrial business was assured; the Company was on a sound financial basis; it had developed a Field Force of 5,000 men. Under Mr. Fiske's leadership it was then decided to revitalize the Ordinary business and to pursue it aggressively.

In many respects this was a heroic decision. The Agency Force, although large and extensive in its operations, was wholly untrained in the writing of Ordinary insurance. The men had, to be sure, been successful in the Industrial field, but it was a serious question whether they could learn the Ordinary business and whether they would even be willing to make the effort. Each Agent had an Industrial debit to service, and his duties left him little time or opportunity to contact Ordinary prospects. Would he be able, therefore, to find enough suitable prospects on his debit to justify the new effort? Would the class of Ordinary prospects secured by Industrial Agents measure up to the physical and occupational requirements? Could the Ordinary business be conducted at reasonable expense, and would it persist?

It was in the midst of such uncertainties that the Metropolitan launched its Ordinary business anew on March 1, 1892. Despite the difficulties resulting from the inexperience of its Agency force, the Officers had faith in the local Superintendents and in their own ability and judgment. Time has shown the wisdom of their decision. The country was ready for the idea; and the Company, once it began to write Ordinary insurance in earnest, soon outdistanced its rivals, reached an enormous public, and provided it with a measure of security without precedent in the history of Life insurance.

What was behind this extraordinary success? In the interplay of a number of fortunate factors, probably the most important was the wise decision of Mr. Fiske to concentrate on the insurance needs of people of moderate means through the issue of Ordinary policies on the nonparticipating plan. This was a complete departure from the prevailing practice of the leading mutual companies, which issued high-priced policies coupled with extravagant promises of huge dividends. The Metropolitan took a firm position against the issuance of tontine or semitontine policies—that is, policies under which the dividends were deferred for a period of years, usually 20, and in which claims paid within the period did not share in the surplus—both a temptation and a gamble. In announcing its return to Ordinary business, the Company formulated a principle which during the early years passed as its Creed: "The Metropolitan believes the time has come when the plain, common-sense men who make up the bulk of the Life insurance policyholders are looking for a plain business contract. By plain business contracts we mean those which tell their whole story upon their face; which leave nothing to the imagination; borrow nothing from hope; require definite conditions and make definite promises in dollars and cents."

This decision was particularly opportune because of the character of the group among whom the Agency Force was operating. The Metropolitan organization then consisted of more than 4,000 Agents working under the direction of nearly 700 Superintendents and Assistant Superintendents in the leading population centers of the United States and Canada. Through Industrial insurance they had already established close and cordial contacts with millions of people—working folk and small businessmen who had been almost entirely neglected by the leading Life insurance companies. As the country prospered and working conditions improved, more and more of these people were ripe for Ordinary insurance, if it could be had at low cost; and obviously they would be interested in sound protection rather than in speculative "tontine" promises.

Furthermore, the very character of the Company's sales organization made the decision all the more practicable. The Metropolitan Agent was constantly in the Field reaching large numbers of people in all walks of life, rather than canvassing a small group of well-to-do businessmen, as did the usual Ordinary Agent. Perhaps more important was the fact that he was working full time for the Company and already receiving an income from his Industrial business. Moreover, the Metropolitan Agent, in constant contact with his prospects and policyholders, could service the insurance better than the Ordinary Agent and help keep it in force. The Company was careful to provide in its Agency contract that commissions would be paid only to the men who either wrote or serviced the business. If a man left the employ of the Company, all renewal commissions ceased. Under prevailing arrangements with general agents as practiced by purely Ordinary companies, the man who wrote the policy received renewal commissions as long as the business was in force, even though he was not in a position to service it. In the Metropolitan, on the other hand, the Company retained the same degree of control over its Ordinary as over Industrial insurance, and the plan of compensation recognized not only the writing Agent but also any other who might subsequently be entrusted with the care of the business on the debit. The result was to produce a close and mutually useful relation between the Agent and his policyholders, which helped to keep the insurance in good standing and subject to continuous review as to adequacy.

When the Field Force, early in 1892, began to write Ordinary insurance, it offered a variety of attractive contracts, in amounts of $1,000 or more, designed to meet a range of needs and situations. All these contracts were not only low in cost but they were also, for that period, liberal in their provisions. Paid-up values were provided after premiums had been paid for only three years, and there were no restrictions regarding travel or residence. Within the next few years the policy contracts were revised, giving the insured additional advantages. Restrictions as to Army and Navy service and as to change in occupation were removed; incontestability was provided after two years; loan and cash surrender values were made available after premiums had been paid for three years; the suicide clause was reduced to two years; and a grace period of 30 days in the payment of premiums was allowed. Moreover, women, previously excluded, were given the opportunity of buying insurance, but at an extra premium for most plans. (The extra charge was later reduced and finally eliminated.) Many of these farsighted liberalizations later became standard provisions of Ordinary policies by the laws of New York and other States.

With the announcement of the reorganization of the Ordinary Department delayed until March, the accomplishments for the year 1892 were moderate. Yet the business written, amounting to 1,704 policies for $2,002,641, was sufficient to stop the downward trend of the business in force in the Ordinary Department. In 1893 the writings totaled more than $6,000,000. Only two years later, in 1895, almost three times that amount was produced, the total coming close to $18,-000,000. As the stream of applications continued to flow into the Home Office, the business in force naturally began to mount rapidly. The number of Ordinary policies on the books jumped from 3,153 in 1891 to 23,253 by the end of 1895; the amount of insurance in force increased correspondingly from less than $4,000,000 to more than $26,000,000. These were creditable figures for a new effort in the years before the turn of the century. In fact, the Ordinary Department was rapidly growing into a Life insurance company of good stature.

But as the Ordinary Department was moving forward with increasing momentum, a number of perplexing problems arose, having their origin in the character of the purchasers of the insurance and of the Agency Force. Embarking, as it did, on a pioneer venture in introducing Ordinary insurance to the industrial population, the Company had no assurance as to what its mortality experience would be. It did know that the environment in which these people lived and worked

ISAAC J. CAHEN

exposed them to a number of health hazards, and that these operated to shorten life. Because of the low premiums charged by the Company, the mortality had to compare with that experienced by strictly Ordinary companies. Thus, the problem of underwriting and the selection of risks was of paramount importance. It was not surprising that at first the mortality was fairly high; but as the Field-Men and the Home Office became better educated in sound underwriting, the mortality among Ordinary policyholders soon improved.

Credit for the early success of the Ordinary Department belongs to three men: James M. Craig, Actuary of the Company; George H. Gaston, Secretary and head of the Field Force; and Isaac J. Cahen, who headed the Ordinary Department at the Home Office. The Actuary's sound judgment was responsible for the conservative setting of the whole operation. Mr. Gaston's vigorous and enthusiastic leadership of the Agents led them to mastery in the new field. His confidence in their ability was contagious. Mr. Cahen was a man of extraordinary gifts, combining keen insurance judgment with administrative talent. By 1892 he was already a Veteran in the Company's service, his association with the organization antedating even Mr. Hegeman's. Since the earliest days and during the expansion of the Industrial Department from 1879 to 1892, he had been charged with responsibility for the Ordinary business of the Company. Under his guidance a competent Staff was assembled and trained, and a sound foundation was laid for the successful administration of the Department which functions with little change to this day.

Almost as soon as the Company launched its Ordinary business, the Agency Force, canvassing among the wage-earners, came in contact with many who were in a position to pay premiums at least quarterly, but who could not afford policies for $1,000 or more. In order to open the door of Ordinary insurance to this large group of the population, the Company in July 1896 began to issue Intermediate policies (a name derived from the fact that this type of insurance occupied a middle position between Industrial and the regular Ordinary). Not long after Intermediate insurance was inaugurated, its scope was widened to include applicants who did not measure up to the physical and occupational standards required for regular Ordinary insurance but who were good risks on a somewhat higher premium table. As the men in the Home Office under Mr. Cahen acquired greater underwriting skill, they saw in this type of insurance the means of providing for those not acceptable as "standard risks."

Intermediate policies were issued for $500 or multiples thereof, with premiums payable annually, semiannually, or quarterly. Knowing that practically all applicants for Intermediate policies would be the better-paid wage-earners, the Company correctly anticipated that their mortality would be lower than that for Industrial policyholders but higher than that for owners of Ordinary policies—just how much lower or how much higher, no one could tell with certainty. Since this was a pioneering venture, the Company determined to steer a safe course. Premiums were based on the Industrial mortality table, but with a loading for expenses similar to that used in the Ordinary Department. Realizing that Inter-mediate policyholders would be overcharged if, as anticipated, the mortality experienced was less than that called for by the Industrial table, the Company decided that Intermediate policyholders should have returned to them any savings from mortality or any other source. Intermediate policies, there-fore, were issued on a participating basis. The mortality among those insured proved to be very favorable, and payment of dividends on the Intermediate contracts was inaugurated in 1901. Within the next few years substantial amounts were returned to policyholders. As a result of legislation following the Armstrong investigation, the Company in 1907 found it necessary to issue Intermediate policies on a nonparticipating basis. However, by this time it had already had a decade of experience in this field and was, therefore, able safely to compute its new premium rates on the basis of its own mor-tality experience.

Intermediate insurance from the very beginning proved very popular. During the first six months alone, 5,110 policies were put on the books for an amount exceeding $2,500,000. At the end of 1897, the very next year, more than 20,000 policies were in force for $10,000,000. By the end of 1906, just over a decade after the inauguration of the business, more than $155,000,000 of Intermediate insurance was in force. These contracts had a special appeal to women, because they were not subject to an extra premium charge, as in regular Ordinary policies.

The Intermediate Branch of the Metropolitan business was also fortunate in its leadership. Soon after the Depart-ment was organized, it came under the guidance of Francis O. Ayres, who had been associated with Mr. Fiske in the law office, and who followed him to the Metropolitan in 1892. In due time Mr. Ayres became one of the great personalities of the Company. He gave impetus and direction to the development of the Intermediate business. In 1903 he was advanced to Fourth Vice-President in charge of the Ordinary

FRANCIS O. AYRES

Department, and for the next three decades spent a major part of his time in the Field, devoting an untiring vigor and constructive skill to building, first, the Intermediate Branch and later the entire Ordinary Department. Able, energetic, and democratic, his friendships were legion; no man more beloved than he ever represented the Company. It is difficult to appraise the extent to which he was responsible for the extraordinary development of the Ordinary Department until his retirement in 1932.

As the Ordinary business grew, it became apparent also that there was a considerable group of people who could not qualify for regular Ordinary or for Intermediate insurance because of their impaired physical condition, or because of their extra-hazardous occupation, but who, nevertheless, were insurable at higher premiums. In order to provide them with Life insurance protection the Metropolitan again pioneered, and in June 1899 inaugurated what was called the Special Class Branch. For the want of a reliable gauge of their

154

mortality, a conservative procedure was again evolved. At first the premium charged was the same as that for Standard insurance, but as an offset a lien was placed against the policy for an amount believed adequate to cover the extra risk. These policies were issued on the participating plan, and the dividends were applied to reduce the liens year by year. The Company's mortality experience with these risks also proved to be favorable. Liberal dividends were paid, and the liens were wiped out in periods varying from 10 to 20 years. The policies were then free of lien and entitled to future dividends and subject to the same premium rates as policies issued to individuals without impairment.

However, as had happened in the Intermediate Branch, the enactment of the Armstrong laws necessitated the dis-continuance of participating policies, and Special Class insur-ance was thereafter issued on the nonparticipating plan. Fortunately, by 1907 sufficient substandard experience had been developed by the Company to enable it to prepare new mortality tables and new premium rates and loan and sur-render values for both the Intermediate and Special Class Branches. The business has been continued on the revised basis since that year. In this way these two important new branches of the Metropolitan provided insurance to many substandard risks who had heretofore been beyond the pale of most Ordinary companies.

From substandard risks the Metropolitan next turned its attention toward the economically favored groups. Foremost among those guiding the Company in this new direction was George B. Woodward, an actuary by training, but by choice and position an all-around insurance executive of versatile experience. It was his belief that professional men and busi-ness executives physically above average and engaged in occupations of little or no hazard, who could purchase $5,000 or more of insurance and pay premiums annually, would con-stitute a group of very low mortality. Coupled with the saving in mortality, he pointed out, would be the reduced expense of doing business on policies of large average size.

The Company accepted Mr. Woodward's proposal, and in May 1909 presented to the public the so-called $5,000 Whole Life policy. This offered to "super-risk" applicants a policy for which the rate was not only lower than that charged for the usual Whole Life contract, but actually lower than was ever offered by any other Life insurance company. In addition, loan and surrender values, constituting the full reserve under the contract, were available after three years.

The policy created an immediate sensation in the insurance world. Its low premium cost and liberal values placed it in a class by itself. From May 1909 to the end of the year, $14,700,000 of this business was put on the books; within four years, more than $100,000,000 was in force. The figures continued to increase at a phenomenal rate. The billion-dollar mark was passed during 1926, and by the end of 1942 the American people had in force more than $2,250,000,000 of insurance under this advantageous policy. The original expectation of favorable mortality and low expense ratio for this picked group has been fully realized, and over the years the low net cost has won for this policy premier rank in the Life insurance world.

It is, therefore, not difficult to see why the Ordinary Department prospered. The Executives of the Company were resourceful, leaving no important group in the community out of the new plan of protection. If the large group of better-circumstanced working people constituted the principal source of business, ample provision was also made to include sub-standard risks, on the one hand, and business executives and professional people, on the other. For each of these groups there was an attractive program of insurance suited to their needs and to their buying power.

We have already considered the mutualization of the Company and its effect on the various operations. Here we need note only the repercussions on the Ordinary Department. They were immediate and rather difficult to handle, especially as they impinged on premium rates. The new legal status of the Company on January 6, 1915, made all policies partici-

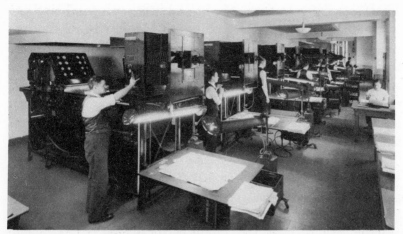
Photostating Ordinary Applications

pating. Despite this change, it was the natural desire of the Executives to retain the same low premiums which were in operation before mutualization. This could not be done under the New York Insurance Law as it was then written, because the low loading in the premium rates of the Metropolitan prevented the Company from doing business within the provisions of the New York law pertaining to mutual companies. New legislation to permit the continuance of the Metropolitan's low rates met with the determined opposition of other companies. Nevertheless, the 1915 Legislature of New York State passed a compromise bill affording temporary relief to the Company and gave an opportunity for further investigation of the subject. The Legislature in the following year finally passed an amendment that made possible the continuation of the old low rates except as to some few contracts, including the $5,000 Whole Life policy. On these policies, a moderate increase became necessary from July 1, 1916. On all others the premiums remained as they were before mutualization. A notable victory was thus won by the Company for the principle of low premiums in Ordinary insurance.

With mutualization, all existing policies, as well as those issued subsequently, became entitled to dividends. The continued reduction in cost of Ordinary insurance has been one of the striking features of the business, and has helped to account for the universal popularity of the Company among all classes of the population. When the Company was forced to raise premium rates in July 1919, following the World War and the influenza epidemic, again in January 1935 and once more in January 1942 because of the decline in interest rates, it endeavored in every instance to continue to provide Life insurance at the lowest cost commensurate with safety.

The Metropolitan has been keenly interested not only in writing, but also in maintaining, the Life insurance protection of the family. It has foreseen the contingency that, as the result of accident or disease, a policyholder may become totally and permanently disabled, with consequent loss of income. In such cases, economic necessity usually forces the lapsing of insurance at the time when it is most needed. To give policyholders an opportunity to cover these hazards, the Company in 1912 began the issuance of a Waiver of Premium benefit in the event of total and permanent disability. This took the form of a supplemental agreement which was attached to the policy, and called for the payment of a small extra premium. The purchase of this additional benefit was entirely optional with the insured; but because of its unquestioned value and low cost, the benefit proved very popular. Beginning with 1914, it was incorporated in virtually all Ordinary and Intermediate contracts without extra premium and, in addition, the benefit was made retroactive for all such policies then in force. This practice continued until the disability income benefit was introduced.

In 1918 the Metropolitan, following the lead of some other Ordinary companies, extended the Disability clause to include, in addition to waiver of premium, a cash annuity of $10 a month for each thousand dollars of insurance in cases of total and permanent disability. Although a substantial extra premium was charged for this coverage, it likewise proved an exceedingly popular feature. At the beginning the experience proved reasonably satisfactory, which created a feeling of false security regarding the adequacy of the rates. There were further extensions of the benefit, liberalizations which were to prove costly during the period of widespread economic depression, during which the rate of disability multiplied. During periods of financial crisis, when income is sharply curtailed or lost and savings are exhausted, claims for disability benefits increase. Ailments become seriously magnified, and many policyholders are tempted to seek compensation under their Disability clause. In addition there has been a decided tendency on the part of the courts to interpret "disability" far beyond the scope contemplated by the companies in fixing the premiums. It is not surprising, therefore, to find that as the depression progressed, the disability experience, not alone in the Metropolitan but in practically all companies, became more adverse. It should be pointed out, however, that serious as the losses were, policies with the Disability provision have not as a whole involved a deficit to the Company.

Looking back over the experience with the Disability Annuity clause, it now seems questionable whether it really belonged in a Life insurance policy or whether it should not have been restricted to the domain of Accident and Health insurance. Of all the Company's innovations throughout its history, the Disability clause remains the only really unsatisfactory venture. In 1931 the Metropolitan discontinued writing the Disability Annuity feature, and since that time has issued only the Waiver of Premium benefit. Life insurance as a whole has learned an important lesson from this experience —not to advance too quickly or too boldly into any line of business, the success of which may be jeopardized by unpredictable economic conditions.

The possibility of sudden death by accident is a source of serious concern to applicants for insurance. These fears are well founded, for accidents take a heavy toll throughout life and at ages 20 to 34, when family responsibilities rise to a peak, are the principal cause of death among men. To meet this contingency, the Company, in June 1919, introduced the Double Indemnity benefit, now known as the Accidental

159

Means death benefit. This provides, at a very small extra cost, an additional payment equal to the face amount of the policy in the event of death resulting solely from accidental means. At first, the Double Indemnity provision was not available to certain classes of policyholders, chiefly those in the Special Class and Intermediate Branches. A few years later, however, this feature was extended to those persons. The benefits paid under this Double Indemnity benefit since its inauguration have totaled $24,000,000.

The issuance in March 1923 of policies on a Monthly Premium plan proved another forward step by the Company to provide low-cost Ordinary insurance to people of modest income. This innovation has had far-reaching consequences. In the beginning the monthly premium was required to be at least $10, and collections were effected by the same premium receipt system as prevailed under other policies in the Ordinary Department, payable annually, semiannually, or quarterly. This experiment was continued for three years and proved so workable that the Company extended the facilities for writing Ordinary insurance on this basis. As a result of the experience gained, it was decided that for receiving monthly premiums of $10 or less the same method as that used in the Industrial Department—through the Agent directly at the homes of the insured—would be most feasible. The Metropolitan was thus the first company to launch Ordinary insurance on a Monthly Premium Debit plan. This put low-cost insurance within the reach of huge numbers of good risks, whose financial condition still did not give them the assurance of meeting larger premium payments at longer intervals.

The success of this plan was instantaneous, and by the beginning of 1942 there were on the Company's books Monthly Debit Ordinary policies amounting to $3,000,000,-000; this represented 23 percent of the entire insurance in force in the Ordinary Department. The popularity of monthly premium payments led the Company, in 1927, to issue Industrial policies on the same plan, with consequent savings to this large group of insured. It was not long before other companies followed the lead of the Metropolitan in this innovation.

The Company was thus in the enviable position where it could reach virtually every group of the insurable population. It wrote policies for small and large amounts; insured men and women, young and old; those in hazardous as well as in nonhazardous occupations; and provided premium-paying facilities to meet the convenience of all classes of policyholders. Only a few Life insurance companies had achieved a similar scope. It is not difficult to understand, then, that under this setup and with the type of leadership that Mr. Ayres and his associates could give, and with an Agency Force bound to the Company with ever-increasing ties of loyalty and devotion, the business should grow to enormous proportions. It is a matter of pride that throughout the recent depression the Company made a gain each year in the amount of Ordinary insurance in force. By 1923 it had already reached the first position in this field of American Life insurance, a position which it has held ever since.

It is obvious, then, that from the business standpoint the growth of the Ordinary Department has been an achievement far exceeding the fondest dreams of its founders. But has this development been as effective as it has been huge? Has the Company conscientiously met its extraordinary opportunity to serve its policyholders? These are pertinent questions. In the broadest sense, the efficiency of any Life insurance organization may be measured by the persistency of its business and by the cost of the protection. Let us see how these two criteria of effective operation shape up with reference to the Ordinary Department of the Metropolitan.

Many factors are responsible for the lapsing of Life insurance. Economic conditions, frequency of premium payments, and the quality of service all influence persistency. During periods of depression the wage-earning members of a community, who constitute the majority of Metropolitan policyholders, are the most seriously affected. This fact notwith-

CHART III

Ordinary Life Insurance in Force*
Metropolitan Life Insurance Company, 1868–1942

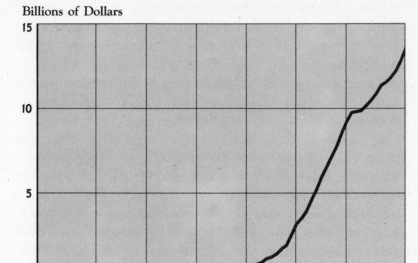

*Includes Standard, Intermediate, Special Class, and Monthly Premium Ordinary business.

standing, the Ordinary lapse rate of the Company has been remarkably low, comparing favorably with the best rates among the strictly Ordinary companies. In fact, in 1942 the amount of insurance voluntarily terminated by policyholders in the Ordinary Department declined to the extraordinarily low rate of about 2½ percent of the average amount of insurance in force during the year.

This excellent record of persistency reflects the fact that the insurance sold satisfies a real need; that it has been written on the proper plans and for suitable amounts. In other words, the business reflects the conscientious underwriting of a well-trained Field organization. In addition, there is the factor of service and the individual responsibility of the many thousands of Agents to furnish it. The Metropolitan was the pioneer in developing concentrated debits of regular Ordinary business. Under this system, each of the 800 Districts handles the Ordinary insurance of policyholders residing within its confines. In turn, the District is subdivided, and each Agent is required to service the Ordinary insurance within his debit. This concentration of business, carrying with it personal responsibility for service, is a Metropolitan product, although the method is now used by other companies writing both Ordinary and Industrial business.

In any mutual company the ultimate objective is to furnish policyholders with protection at the lowest cost commensurate with good service and safe and progressive management. The Ordinary Department yields to no company in this test of all-round efficiency. The subject of cost of Metropolitan insurance is more fully treated in Chapter 10. Here we need only note that the unprecedented low cost in this Department has been achieved despite serious handicaps. It must not be forgotten that the average Ordinary policy in the Metropolitan is considerably lower in amount than in purely Ordinary companies. This is a notable item. Few Metropolitan policyholders buy large amounts of insurance, and for this reason it is imperative that expenses per policy be reduced to a minimum. New methods have been devised to improve efficiency. Much effort has gone into building a skillful organization in the Home Office to overcome the handicap of small policies.

The mortality experience is also a major factor in determining net cost of insurance. Low mortality is, in fact, the major cushion or factor of safety in Company operations during the present period of low interest rates. Offhand, it might be assumed that Metropolitan mortality would be higher than that of strictly Ordinary companies, because its policyholder group is composed largely of wage-earners who suffer greater exposure to occupational hazards. Despite this factor the type of Metropolitan selection and underwriting of risks has produced a very favorable experience. Virtually all Metropolitan insurance is written by its full-time representatives, who have a natural interest in good service to their own Company. Furthermore, with policies of small average size, the element of selection against the Company and the adverse speculation so frequently associated with insurances for large amounts, so-called "jumbo" cases, are reduced. The net result has been an excellent Ordinary mortality experience.

Underwriting problems are, of course, complex for a Company like the Metropolitan, which has such a variety of insurance as the Whole Life policy, the standard policies, and the three substandard branches—Intermediate, Special Class, and Special Class B. When an application is received, it must be reviewed in the light of the information given as to the health, habits, occupation, and financial condition of the applicant, and appraised as to his comparative status in these respects. Insurance in the proper standard or substandard branch is issued on the basis of this appraisal. In the interest of complete justice to applicants, it is imperative that the Underwriters' judgment be based upon sound and up-to-date information on the factors influencing the level of mortality. For that purpose, the Metropolitan alone, or in association with other companies, regularly conducts investigations into the mortality of various classes of insured persons—especially on those in occupations presenting any type of hazard and those with various impairments or with adverse medical histories. The underwriting practices are modified from time to time as the result of such studies.

It is significant that the proportion of men and women eligible for standard insurance, both on occupational and medical grounds, has increased steadily over the years. Today, more than 90 percent of the applicants for insurance in the Ordinary Department are medically eligible for standard insurance, and all but 3½ percent are eligible for either standard or substandard policies. Many classes of workers, who in earlier days were ineligible for Ordinary insurance because of occupation, are now accepted as standard risks. It may be noted, too, that the Company keeps its methods of medical examination up to date, with the result that the medical selection of applicants is increasingly accurate and liberal. Those in charge of underwriting—the Medical Directors, the Actuaries, and the Application Approvers—have the responsibility of making sure that every applicant pays the premium for his protection which is commensurate with the degree of risk undertaken by the Company. The Underwriters in the Metropolitan have carried their responsibility toward the successful administration of the Ordinary Department with flying colors. This phase is presented in detail in Chapter 21.

The Field Force likewise deserves full credit for its part. It has constituted, over the years, a conscientious and skillful group of insurance men. The very nature of the Metropolitan's organization and the wide range of its activities are conducive to the development of rounded and competent insurance salesmen. The Metropolitan Agent, viewing the insurance needs of the family as a whole, no longer sells mere policy plans. He acts as insurance advisor and counsellor, helps the prospect to think through his family requirements in the light of the various contingencies of life, and to plan an insurance program consistent with the family income. He realizes that there is room for periodic revision of such programing as the requirements and capacities of the individual insured change. Fortunately, the close contact between the Agent and the families he serves on his debit makes such time-to-time adjustment feasible. To qualify the men for these important tasks, the Company conducts a comprehensive program of instruction and training for the entire Field Force—Managers, Assistant Managers, and Agents. We discuss this educational effort in Chapter 12, and here need only indicate that through this continuous training, the Field Force has developed a new approach to insurance salesmanship. That the method has proved effective is demonstrated by the extraordinary increases of insurance in force, even during depression years; by the low lapse rate, and by the good will which Metropolitan policyholders have toward the Company which serves as the instrument of their security.

During the momentous years of the past half century, the Ordinary Department has moved forward, embracing every new opportunity to serve the Life insurance needs of the

SAMUEL MILLIGAN
Second Vice-President

American people. Each new development was designed to help the policyholder to realize the main objective of his family protection and to increase the effectiveness of his Life insur-ance. Since 1927 the Department has been under the admin-istrative direction of Second Vice-President Samuel Milligan, who was promoted to that post after demonstrating his ability and judgment in the Company's Actuarial Division. During the decade and a half of his administration, Mr. Milligan has not only carried on the splendid tradition of his predecessors, but has also inaugurated numerous innovations which have kept the Metropolitan Ordinary Department in the forefront of the insurance world. The Company now counts in this Department nearly 7,000,000 policyholders insured for the huge sum of $13,500,000,000. This epic achievement reflects in large measure the broad vision and the competent direction which the Ordinary business of the Company has enjoyed throughout its history.

CHAPTER 8

Group Life Insurance

THE IDEA of Group protection may be traced to the sense of responsibility felt by employees and employers toward their fellow workers who fall prey to sickness, death, or other misfortune. At first this feeling of sympathy often took the form of "passing the hat." However, this practice, while commendable, was generally haphazard and inadequate, and smacked too much of charity to be satisfactory. Hence there developed various types of employee benefit plans designed to give a more definite measure of protection, in a manner which would retain the self-respect and dignity of the beneficiary. In some cases these plans were initiated and operated solely by employees, in others by the employer, and in still others jointly, with both parties sharing the cost. The first employee benefit plans were self-insured—that is, oper- ated by the individual groups. These, however, usually lacked actuarial guidance and a broad enough basis for safety, so that many of them turned out to be unsound and in due time ran into financial difficulties. The sponsors of these plans then turned increasingly to actuaries and to insurance com- panies for assistance. Group insurance was the logical and effective result.

The years have seen a marked expansion both in the scope of benefits and in the number of employees covered by Group insurance plans. Though only three decades old, Group Life insurance now covers 11,000,000 employees in more than 30,000 separate organizations in the United States and Canada, for a total of $20,000,000,000 of insurance. It comprises about one seventh of the total Life insurance now in force in old line companies in these two countries, and is not far below the total for Industrial insurance. Like Ordinary and Industrial insurance, it has become an integral part of our American way of life. Group Life insurance is designed to provide a basic minimum amount of protection during an employee's wage-earning years. It is intended to supplement and not to replace individual insurance. By providing a measure of security it has strengthened the self-reliance of the individual employee and his family.

Group insurance has likewise become an important aid in building a sound program of industrial relations. Many employers have come to appreciate more and more that joint friendly and cooperative projects not only promote the welfare of the employee but also tend to cut labor turnover and to increase the efficiency of operation. In a democracy like ours it is to be expected that systematic protection against adversity should have been developed primarily through voluntary individual enterprise. It is to the credit of American industry that it has done so much to make available to workers and their families protection against death, accident, sickness, and insecurity of old age.

In line with its tradition of pioneering, the Metropolitan was among the first to develop Group coverage. The experiment began in 1909, when the Company offered Life insurance benefits more liberal than those in its regular Industrial policies, to organizations—such as labor groups and fraternal societies—in which 100 or more members were insured and in which the premiums collected were turned over to the Company in one sum. It was expected that the increased liberality would be justified by savings in commissions, collection fees, etc. While a few policies were issued on this plan, the experience proved unsatisfactory, and nearly all the contracts subsequently lapsed. This and other trial efforts indicated that this type of Group Life insurance would not operate satisfactorily.

The first Group policy to attract widespread attention was that issued by the Equitable Life Assurance Society in 1912 on 3,000 employees of the Montgomery Ward Co. for more than $6,000,000 of insurance. In 1914 the Metropolitan issued a Group Life policy covering 4,500 of its own employees at the Home Office and another on 13,000 in the Field. A little more than two years later the Metropolitan extended its operations to cover commercial groups. This delay was due largely to the fact that Group insurance was included as Ordinary, and that the insurance legislation in New York State following the Armstrong investigation limited the amount of Ordinary insurance that a company was permitted to write in any one year. In 1916, however, the law was amended to exclude Group insurance from such limitations.

Premium rates and policies had been prepared on a number of different plans, of which the One-Year Renewable Term plan and the Endowment at Age 90 plan were the most prominent. As the yearly Renewable Term plan proved much the more practical and adaptable to actual operation in employee groups, the other plans fell into disuse. At first individual policies were issued at prevailing rates. Soon, however, the practice was adopted of issuing a master policy to the employer with a certificate to each insured employee, setting forth the principal provisions of the policy as they affected him and his beneficiary.

In January of 1917 the Company established its Group Insurance Division for the active development of the business. It was put under the direction of James E. Kavanagh, then Fourth Vice-President, who had already thoroughly demonstrated his ability as a creative insurance executive. By the end of 1917 the Metropolitan had some $21,000,000 of Group insurance in force, covering employees of 74 companies. The total in that year for all Life insurance companies in this country and Canada came to about $350,000,000.

Despite this substantial beginning, the business was still far from stabilized. There was little standardization, and many questions and problems arose. It was at this point that the National Convention of Insurance Commissioners appointed a committee of their members to draft a definition of Group Life insurance. The convention invited the cooperation of the Actuarial Society of America and asked it to select a committee to represent insurance companies; Mr. James D. Craig, then Assistant Actuary of the Metropolitan, was a member of this committee. The Convention at its December 1917 meeting adopted its committee's report recommending the following definition, which, in substance, has been subsequently enacted into the laws of most of the larger States:

> Group life insurance is that form of life insurance covering not fewer than fifty employees, with or without medical examination, written under a policy issued to the employer, the premium on which is to be paid by the employer or by the employer and employees jointly, and insuring only all of his employees, or all of any class or classes thereof determined by conditions pertaining to the employment, for amounts of insurance based upon some plan which will preclude individual selection, for the benefit of persons other than the employer; provided, however, that when the premium is to be paid by the employer and employee jointly and the benefits of the policy are offered to all eligible employees not less than seventy-five per centum of such employees may be so insured.

This soundly phrased definition has served until this day, with only a few minor modifications, as the basic code for underwriting this form of insurance. It brought into focus the main differences between Group Life and other branches of Life insurance, and helped to crystallize it as a distinct operation. Of primary importance was the fact that an employer-employee group of sizable magnitude, rather than the individual, was the unit of selection for coverage. This provision has made it reasonably certain that both average mortality and a substantial saving in expenses will be experienced because of wholesale underwriting and administration. In the absence of individual underwriting, and in order to preserve the essential simplicity of Group insurance, the amount issued to each employee is based on a uniform schedule, according to employee classes. In general, the most satisfactory plan has been found to be one based on earnings in rather broad income groupings, thus related to the employees' economic status and insurance needs. Then, too, the insurance may be, and usually is, issued without medical examination or any other form of individual investigation. Instead, the underwriting is determined by the size of the insured group (at least three fourths of those eligible, with a minimum of 50 lives), the findings of the inspection report on the group as a whole, and the statements of the writing agent and the employer. The only individual qualification usually required of the employee is that he be actively at work on the date his insurance becomes effective.

The usual Group Life policy affords an employee leaving the service of the employer an option to obtain, without medical examination, some permanent form of individual insurance of not more than the face amount of the certificate, upon payment of the premium applicable to his age and class of risk at that time. Most Group policies provide, moreover, that upon continued payment of the premium, employment may be deemed to continue indefinitely in the event of absence due to sickness or injury, and for a limited period during layoff or leave of absence.

While the boundaries of the Group insurance field were being surveyed and charted 25 years ago, the organization of the Group Division in the Metropolitan began to take more concrete form. Mr. Kavanagh and his associate, Mr. A. C. Campbell, both of whom had been called to Washington in the service of the Government during the first World War, returned to the Home Office and energetically set about building the new Division. Mr. J. M. Campbell returned from naval service and assumed responsibility for the development and operation of an efficient clerical and administrative Staff. The year 1919 marked the real beginning of a coordinated and well-considered effort, of which the organization of a specialized sales force was an essential feature.

The Group salesman was originally conceived as an instructor who would, in addition to personal sales work, teach the existing Field Force how to sell Group insurance. Accordingly, specially trained Group sales representatives were put in charge of some 25 large centers throughout the United

ALEXANDER C. CAMPBELL
Second Vice-President

States and Canada. In addition to selling Group insurance, these men directed classes for Metropolitan Managers and Assistant Managers in their respective areas. The Field Force of some 16,000 men, located in every strategic industrial center of the two countries, could make many contacts with employers, explore possibilities, and in other ways open opportunities for the concentrated follow-up canvass which the special representative of the Group Sales Division could make. While many Group cases have been written by members of the regular Metropolitan Field Force, the canvassing and selling of the larger Group contracts have been carried on largely by the men of the Group Sales Division, who are specialists in this form of underwriting and are well informed concerning employer-employee relationships.

The Group Division soon began to reap the harvest of its well-directed and aggressive efforts. During 1919 nearly five times as many Group Life policies were issued as in the previous year, the amount involved being $77,096,360. Policies were written on groups in factories, as well as in various business, financial, and publishing institutions.

The year 1920 was also one of notable achievement. It opened with the issue of a $46,000,000 policy on 42,000 employees of the General Electric Company. A few months later a policy was written on the employees of the Westinghouse Electric and Manufacturing Company. The year closed auspiciously with $125,450,000 of new Group Life insurance written, and the Metropolitan the leader in Group sales for that year. At the end of 1920 the Company had in force 1,179 policies for Group insurance covering almost 280,000 lives and amounting to $280,000,000 out of a total Group Life insurance in force in the United States and Canada of approximately $1,687,000,000.

Up to this point Group insurance had been sold to employers mainly as something to present to their employees as a gift. In the great majority of cases the employer paid the entire premium, and with a few exceptions only Group Life insurance was negotiated. This arrangement had some distinct shortcomings, and during the 1921 depression many employers found it burdensome to carry the cost. Toward the latter part of 1922 and during 1923 there was a sharp change in a new direction. Group programs were often broadened to cover Accident and Health policies, including Accidental Death and Dismemberment; and the enlarged plan, comprising all three of the coverages, was submitted to employees as a voluntary offer contingent on their paying a substantial share of the cost.

These "contributory" policies, as they were designated to distinguish them from those in which the employer paid the entire cost, called for a somewhat different form of contract from that previously in use. The employee had to make written application, at the same time designating a beneficiary and authorizing the employer to make weekly or monthly deductions from the pay roll. Application had to be made within 31 days after date of eligibility, failing which a medical examination was required. The contract stipulated that it would become effective only when at least 75 percent of the eligible employees applied for the insurance, and would remain in force only as long as that proportion continued to participate.

The contributory plan met with immediate and widespread approval. Employers, relieved of part of the financial burden, were now more readily interested in the benefits of Group insurance. At the same time, these benefits were made more attractive and inclusive. Employees, on their part, welcomed the new insurance program in which they enjoyed greater benefits with enhanced self-respect as a result of sharing in the cost.

The first large Metropolitan contributory policy, effective January 1, 1922, was on the employees of the Delaware and Hudson Company. It covered nearly 12,000 persons for Group Life insurance as well as Accidental Death and Dismemberment insurance and weekly Accident and Sickness benefits. This example was soon followed by a number of the Nation's outstanding business organizations, among them the International Paper Company, F. W. Woolworth Company, Armour & Company, and the Pressed Steel Car Company. Indeed, the roster of Metropolitan Group policyholders, even in that early period, covered a wide range of industries and business enterprises throughout the United States and Canada, including important banks and financial institutions, department stores, coal mines, meat packers, public utilities, and manufacturing companies. Nor did the Metropolitan confine its activities in the contributory Group field to large concerns only. By 1928 about 60 percent of its contracts were with firms of not more than 100 employees, and widely representative of American industry.

There can be little doubt that the introduction of the contributory plan was one of the touchstones of success in Group insurance. Of the Group Life insurance issued by the Metropolitan in 1922, 54 percent was on the contributory plan. The very next year the figure jumped to 87 percent, and a year later reached 90 percent. The business continued to grow rapidly as individual contracts were issued for unprecedented sums. Thus, in 1923, the Southern Pacific Railroad Company bought approximately $117,000,000 of Metropolitan Group Life insurance, covering 71,170 employees. In December 1926 more than 100,000 employees of the General Motors Corporation were insured under the largest Group Life insurance policy issued up to that time, the negotiations being conducted for the Company by Mr. A. C. Campbell. Within two years the benefits were made available to almost 200,000 General Motors employees, providing for the gigantic total of over $400,000,000 of Life insurance with Group Accident and Health benefits added. The contract has since been extended to include Hospital Expense and Surgical Operation benefits. Since its inception, the protection under the contract has kept pace with the growth of the corporation. This has consistently remained the largest Group Life insurance contract in force with any insurance company.

These are only two striking cases among many. Included among the some 3,300 Group Life insurance policies now in force in the Metropolitan are those on employees of Curtiss-Wright Corporation, Continental Baking Corporation, Eastman Kodak Company, Electric Bond & Share Company, Monsanto Chemical Company, R. H. Macy & Company, National Biscuit Company, Republic Steel Corporation, Sears Roebuck & Company, and the United States Steel Corporation. It is significant that these and many other important companies, as well as many hundreds of smaller ones have, through the friendly cooperation of their workers, taken an increasingly prominent role in promoting the security of the American family.

Prior to the inauguration of the contributory plan the Metropolitan Group business was developing at about the same rate as that of other leading companies. By 1924, however, it attained, and has since maintained, leadership in the field. At the half-year mark in 1942, out of about 130 Life companies in the Group field, the Metropolitan had one fourth of the total business and had insured about 2,500,000 lives for more than $5,000,000,000 of Group Life insurance.

First and foremost among the underlying reasons for this extraordinary record are, of course, the general considerations, already noted: that Group insurance offers a ready means of meeting safely and economically the great need of workers for protection against the primary hazards of life; and that it provides employers with a cornerstone for a structure of sound industrial relations. There are, however, a number of more specific reasons, in large measure peculiar to the Metropolitan. The Company for many years had already been the leading organization in the Life insurance field, and employers and workers alike knew it, and had confidence in its methods and proposals. In particular, it had long been closely associated with the industrial populations of the United States and Canada. By 1923 its clientele numbered 20,000,000 people, many of whom had been policyholders of the Company for years. The good will that had been built up was often reflected in the action of employers when deciding on the carrier of their Group insurance. Moreover, as already emphasized, the Company's large Agency Force, working in populated areas throughout the land, was in a strategic position to locate and develop Group prospects.

In the keen competition for the business, an important reason for choosing the Metropolitan lay in the special services the Company could bring to industry. From the very beginning, it was realized that if Group Life insurance was to be sold on an adequate and fitting scale, the Company's service should be broadly conceived and freely rendered. An obvious step was to extend to employees covered by Group policies the welfare services already available to the Company's Industrial policyholders, namely, nursing by trained graduate nurses, and participation in well-considered plans of health education. Over the years about 900,000 employees insured under Group policies have received the benefit of the Nursing Service for a total of approximately 2,300,000 visits; 86,000,000 pamphlets on health topics have been distributed, many of them at critical periods when needed to meet threatening situations either in the community or within the plant.

The Company, however, did not stop there. It created new organizations specifically to serve its Group policyholders. The Industrial Health and Hygiene Service, with a laboratory staffed by experts under Dr. A. J. Lanza, Assistant Medical Director, was set up to bring to industrial plants authoritative information on health supervision, to assist in stamping out the preventable causes of sickness among employees, and to correct existing hazards. Its studies and recommendations have covered such subjects as ventilation, lighting, sanitation, control of toxic dusts and gases in mines and factories, protective devices in hazardous processes, the role of physical examinations in industry, effect on workers of toxic substances, and the planning of industrial plant dispensaries. Services of this nature have played a constructive role in raising the level of industrial health in this country. Associated with them has been the Accident Prevention Service offered by the Metropolitan Safety Bureau in connection with accidents both on and off the job.

The Policyholders Service Bureau, organized in 1919, has directed its efforts toward assisting employers to achieve better relations with their employees. Many of the largest companies in the country have availed themselves of the broad services of this Bureau, which tries to anticipate the needs of business both in the preparation of reports and the collection of information valuable to executives. To this end it maintains for distribution an up-to-date list of 350 reports on a large variety of subjects, and issues an *Executives Service Bulletin* to 22,000 business managers. Since the second World War began, the Bureau, under the able management of Mr. W. J. Barrett, Assistant Secretary, has developed a timely and constructive program to assist industry in solving various important problems arising from the war effort.

The Metropolitan's success in the Group Field stems in large measure, too, from its efforts not only to sell insurance but to keep it satisfactorily in force. This has been especially important under the contributory system, where the contract persists only so long as a satisfactory participation is main-

Group Division Sales Managers' Conference
White Sulphur Springs, W. Va.

Back Row—A. C. Campbell, W. J. Barrett, N. R. Perry, H. P. Mills, E. A. Tomlinson, Fred Ulmer, E. C. McDonald, J. E. Kavanagh, F. R. Whelan, E. O. Dunlap, R. A. Hohaus, J. M. Campbell.

Front Row—G. F. Johnston, D. D. Power, Gerald Priestman, H. W. Frey, P. F. Bouquet, C. W. McGinnis, E. R. Seese, H. E. Clarke.

tained. In actual practice, the percentage of employees insured under most Group policies is very high. A special Staff has been established to service Group policies. Each policy is reviewed periodically in order to make sure that policyholders are receiving adequate attention and service, and to uncover any unsatisfactory features in the underwriting or experience. The review includes a check of employee participation, terms of the contract, and use of the various services, as well as the development of recommendations for increased coverage. A group of Field Service Supervisors periodically call on policy-holders for the same general purposes.

This periodic check-up of a Group policy serves to antici-pate and to correct difficulties that might arise, and to promote the cooperative understanding of all parties concerned. Convincing evidence of such mutual satisfaction is to be found in the extraordinarily low rate of master policy termination. Even during the depression years, both employers and employees saw fit to continue their Group insurance contracts. In the year 1941 the master Group Life policies terminated covered only $\frac{1}{4}$ of 1 percent of the total amount of insurance under all such policies, and a large part of even this small fraction resulted not from dissatisfaction with the contract, but from discontinuance of the business or reorganization of the employing company.

Further impressive evidence of the success of Group insurance lies in the character and amount of the benefits paid to those it is designed to protect. In 1941 a total of $120,000,000 of death benefits was paid by American companies to beneficiaries of Group certificate holders, and since the inception of this form of protection such payments have added up to over $1,300,000,000. In the Metropolitan alone the benefits paid under Group Life insurance in 1941 reached a total of some $32,000,000 on 14,500 lives, the average benefit being in excess of $2,000. Only 20 years earlier the average benefit was but little above $1,000. This has been an important contribution to the welfare of the working people of the United States and Canada.

Another factor in the extraordinary success of Group Life insurance, not only in the Metropolitan but also in other companies, has been the low cost of the benefits provided. It was fortunate that the actuaries discovered early that the yearly Renewable Term plan could be applied readily and safely to cover this type of Life insurance. Premiums under this plan are at a minimum, sufficient to cover the cost of current mortality and the small item of management expense. Moreover, the average premium based on the age distribution in a going concern generally does not change materially from year to year, because owing to normal turnover the average age of the group does not vary greatly over a period of time, the additions of new employees whose average age is generally younger being sufficient to balance the normal aging of the others. The employees' contributions in practically all cases are less than their premiums would be for individual Term insurance even at the youngest age in the group. This advantage minimizes the possibility that younger members of the group might withdraw and thus increase the average age and, consequently, the average premium rate of the group.

Minimum initial gross-premium rates for each age are promulgated by the Superintendent of Insurance of New York State, in accordance with a statute prescribing the American Men Ultimate Table of Mortality, with $3\frac{1}{2}$ percent interest as the basic net premium plus a loading to be computed by a formula approved by the Superintendent. At the end of each policy year the actual financial experience is reviewed for the individual Group policy and for the business as a whole, to determine whether the scale of premium rates by age should be continued for the ensuing policy year. In most cases no change is necessary.

The actual experience under the Company's Group Life One-Year Term insurance in non-hazardous industries has been extremely favorable. The mortality has been better than that expected on the basis of the American Men Ultimate Table, the ratio of actual to expected claims, during the last five years, varying from under 50 percent for ages under 30, to approximately 80 percent for ages 45 and over. The total mortality has averaged approximately 70 percent of the Table. Despite the fact that risks are accepted without medical examination, the death rate from tuberculosis among Group policyholders is about the same as for those insured in the Ordinary Department. Only the diseases of middle life and old age show higher rates. As might be expected, deaths from accidents are considerably higher than among Ordinary policyholders.

This favorable mortality has been coupled with very low management expense. Moreover, as the Group insurance business grew and methods of administration improved, operating expenses have been reduced. Thus, in 1941, the total expenses in the Group Life Division were only 7 percent of the premium income, the actual expenses for the respective groups varying, of course, by size and other factors. Savings have been effected in part by the increasing role which the office of the employer has played in the clerical administration of the insurance. In many respects the employers do for their workers the job that Branch Offices and Agents of the insurance company do for the individual policyholders. The employer contributes these clerical services without any compensation. In addition, thousands of important business executives, actuated by deep interest in the welfare of employees and their families, have given generously of their time in the development and improvement of Group insurance protection.

As usually arranged, the insured employee pays a fixed premium, generally not more than 60 cents per month, or $7.20 a year per $1,000 of insurance, irrespective of age. Anything required in addition to the payment made by the employees, falls on the employer.

Dividends are computed at the end of each policy year, taking into account the actual experience of the group and the mortality experience of the Group business as a whole. They are payable, when earned, to the employer, who uses them as a partial offset to his premium contribution; in other cases, he uses part or all of them for the benefit of the employees. Of course, if the aggregate dividends paid to an employer are in excess of his contribution, the extra amount must be returned to the insured employees in cash, or be used to waive their contributions for a certain number of months, or to help pay the cost of more insurance or of new forms of Group coverage.

The story of Metropolitan Group insurance would be incomplete without reference to the Company's experience with this branch of its business in foreign countries. During 1925 and 1926, important Group policyholders in the United States urged the Company to explore the possibility of arranging for the extension of Group insurance protection to the employees of their branches abroad. In the summer of 1927 Second Vice-President J. E. Kavanagh and Actuary J. D. Craig visited England to arrange for the establishment of a Branch Office in London, through which the Company could conduct Group insurance business. In November of that year Mr. Kavanagh sailed for England with a small staff of trained men, together with their immediate families, and organized working quarters in Bush House on the Strand. Through this London Office arrangements were made to extend Group insurance protection to the British employees of various American Group policyholders. Soon contracts were made available for purely British companies, and it was not long before the business was large enough to require a staff of approximately 70 employees.

In the winter of 1928–1929 Mr. L. A. Lincoln, then General Counsel, and Mr. A. C. Campbell, then Third Vice-President, explored the same problem in Chile, the Argentine, Uruguay, and Brazil. After extended investigation they reached the conclusion that it would be more advantageous and practical to have local insurance companies handle our Group insurance in those countries, through the medium of reinsurance contracts. The result was the development of a reinsurance program which still continues to operate successfully in Argentina and Brazil.

Profiting by this experience, the Company decided not to undertake the direct underwriting of Group insurance in Continental European countries. Accordingly, Mr. A. C. Campbell, and Mr. H. R. Bassford, then Assistant Actuary, went abroad to effect Group reinsurance programs in several European countries, on the basis adopted in South America. With the advent of the war some of these reinsurance arrangements have necessarily been discontinued.

After careful weighing of the relative merits of the Group reinsurance plan versus the direct operating procedure that had been adopted in England, the London Office was closed. The Company's American employees were brought back to New York at the end of five years of direct underwriting experience in Great Britain. Simultaneously, arrangements were made with the Legal & General Assurance Society, Ltd., to assume the Company's purely British business and to extend the reinsurance arrangement to the British branches of American Group policyholders. The consent of every interested policyholder to this revised procedure was secured in advance, and the program was approved in its entirety both by the British High Court and the Insurance Department of the State of New York. Thus ended the only direct Metropolitan operations ever attempted outside the American continent.

Reference should also be made to a feature known as the Permanent Protection Plan developed very recently in connection with Group insurance on the Renewable Term basis. The purpose of this plan is to meet the demand for low-cost Life insurance on a Group basis, and at the same time to provide older and more permanent employees with a specified amount of fully paid-up Life insurance upon retirement or termination of employment. The program is a combination of Term insurance purchased on a year-to-year basis and permanent insurance purchased each year in small units by single-premium payments.

Under a typical policy, the permanent insurance feature becomes automatically available when the employee has completed certain requirements, such as a specified period of continuous service and attainment of a specified age (normally 40 or 45). Prior to that age his entire Group insurance is on the usual Term basis. Beginning with the specified age, however, a fixed amount of permanent insurance is purchased each year for each employee in a given salary class, so that while his total amount of insurance remains constant, his permanent insurance increases and his Term insurance decreases correspondingly. The unit of permanent insurance to be purchased each year may, for example, be such that after 25 years a contributor (age 40 to age 65) would have accumulated approximately half the total Life insurance for his salary class. Apparently a worth-while development, this permanent protection feature is still in the experimental stage, and it is too early to forecast its probable results.

A discussion of Group Accident and Sickness insurance, Group Accidental Death and Dismemberment insurance,

Group Hospital Expense insurance, and Group Surgical Operation insurance appears in the chapter which follows. At this point consideration will be given to the Group Annuity coverage, inasmuch as it is in many ways closely related through its dependence on life contingencies to the main topic of the present chapter.

The Group Annuity is that type of coverage under which an employer makes provision for retirement incomes for his employees through an insurance contract. In most cases, the cost is borne on a cooperative basis by the employer and employees, although in some instances the employer pays the entire cost. Only during the last 20 years have many employers and employees developed a clear recognition that retirement plans involve costs of very substantial magnitude which should be met by funding during the active working years of the employees. Without such advance provision the out-of-pocket disbursements increase steadily over the years, until a point may be reached at which the payments become a burden and it may become necessary to discontinue or to greatly curtail the plan.

Characteristically, the Metropolitan was the pioneer in developing practical and sound methods by which a Life insurance company could underwrite employee retirement. This pioneer work, which started about 1921, required much experimentation, study, and consultation with employers, as well as constant close collaboration of the Group and Actuarial Divisions. As a result there emerged a basis of operation which has met the needs and desires of employers and employees and has become an accepted method of underwriting retirement plans on the Group principle.

Contributing to this result were James E. Kavanagh, head of the Group Division, and Ingalls Kimball, who in the fall of 1922 headed a new unit organized for the sole purpose of developing Group Annuity plans acceptable to industry. There were many technical and actuarial problems to be solved, and to this phase of the work Edwin C. McDonald, now Vice-President in Charge of the Canadian Head Office, the late James D. Craig, Actuary and Reinhard A. Hohaus, now Associate Actuary, devoted much of their time and talents.

Under the typical Group Annuity contract now offered by the Company, both employee and employer make contributions during the employee's active service. In most cases the annuity becomes payable at age 65, though arrangements may be made for postponing retirement until a later age, as well as for "optional" retirement at some earlier age, or for normal retirement ages other than 65 (such as 60 for women). At an employee's death the total amount he himself has contributed (with or without interest, depending on the terms of the plan) is paid to his beneficiary, less any retirement income already paid to him. On withdrawal the employee may receive his total contributions, or he may take a Paid-up Annuity based on these contributions. Most plans provide that if an employee who meets certain specified conditions, such as a minimum period of years as contributor, elects the paid-up option, the amount of the annuity will be based on the employer's contributions as well as his own.

Many organizations included under the old-age benefit provisions of the Social Security Act are using Group Annuity plans as a means of supplementing retirement incomes arising from the Act. Although these plans operate independently of the Act, they take its prospective benefits into account in their total income objective. Many of them aim to provide for the typical employee a total annual payment at retirement equal to from 40 percent to 60 percent of an employee's average salary. For organizations not subject to the old-age provisions of the Social Security Act, the annuity for the insured in most cases approximates 1½ percent to 2 percent of each year's salary over the working period.

Since 1927, when the experimental period ended, there has been a considerable expansion in the volume of Group Annuity business both in the Metropolitan and in the country as a whole. It is estimated that in 1933 some $40,000,000, and in 1941 some $200,000,000, was received by the companies

CHART IV

Group Life Insurance in Force
Metropolitan Life Insurance Company, 1917–1942

Billions of Dollars

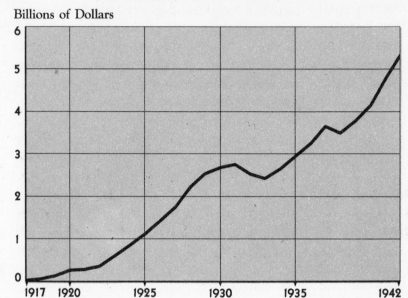

under Group Annuity contracts. At the close of 1941 the Metropolitan had in force 271 pension contracts covering 269,101 persons for $74,670,500 of annual retirement annuity.

The present volume of Group Annuities in force would undoubtedly have been very much greater if in recent years the Metropolitan and many other Life insurance companies had not materially reduced or suspended their activities in underwriting Group retirement plans. The reason for this action was the greatly increased difficulty of satisfactorily investing the substantial reserve funds which were rapidly being built up.

Group insurance is indeed an indispensable phase of a still broader movement involving two other essential components—individual insurance and social insurance. Together these three forms, conceived as complementary and not as competing activities, can provide a rounded and balanced structure capable of meeting the needs and desires of our people for protection against the major threats to life, health, or earning power. Like the three legs of a stool, each has an essential function to perform in providing the desired security. Social insurance aims to furnish the individual with a basic protection to keep him off the roll of public charges. Group insurance enables him, through cooperation with a farsighted employer, to amplify this basic modicum in a manner more in accordance with his normal standards of living. Individual insurance obtained on personal initiative permits him to round out his protection in line with his own individual needs, responsibilities, and capacity. This insurance trio constitutes in large measure America's answer to the problem of creating a socio-economic climate in which democratic freedom can achieve a truly healthy growth.

Group Life insurance and the affiliated benefits which have sprung from it during the past 25 years represent, in their entirety, a great humanitarian effort. They are an eloquent expression of the deepened social consciousness of American industrial management reflecting the good will of a large number of employers translated into an effective service for their employees. This is a distinctly American institution, in line with our best and most cherished tradition of free enterprise. It is altogether a voluntary and cooperative arrangement between management and labor. Employers, on their part, feel a sense of responsibility for their co-workers, and recognize that obsolescence of man power is a proper charge on industry. Workers, self-reliant and enjoying the American system of high wages, willingly contribute their share of the cost. In view of these facts, it is not surprising that once this system was put into working order it grew rapidly, and today it covers about 40 percent of all employees that are eligible for Group insurance under the definition prescribed by law. Altogether, Group insurance has advanced the security of American wage-earners, and has made significant contributions to our way of life.

An important factor in the extraordinary growth of Group insurance in the Metropolitan has been the deep and sus-

187

tained interest of three successive Presidents—Haley Fiske, Frederick H. Ecker, now Chairman of the Board, and Leroy A. Lincoln. Within the Group Division itself, former Vice-President James E. Kavanagh served with conspicuous success as directing head from its beginning until his retirement from active service at the end of 1941. Effective January 1, 1942, A. C. Campbell, Second Vice-President, who had been closely associated with him during this entire period, was placed in charge of the Group Division, his associate Executives being J. M. Campbell, Third Vice-President, in charge of Group administrative affairs in the Home Office and Field, and Gale F. Johnston, Third Vice-President, in charge of Group sales work both in the Field and Home Office.

CHAPTER 9

Accident and Health Insurance

ROM THE BEGINNING of the modern industrial era, loss of
family income and consequent distress has often resulted
not only from the death, but also from the serious sickness
or injury of the breadwinner. For this reason workers often
banded together for their mutual protection in friendly societies, lodges, and other organizations, and made provision for
disability benefits as well as for death benefits. It was natural
for men facing common hazards to be drawn together. Thus,
in many instances, mutual benefit associations of working
people were organized in one plant or in a number of plants
engaged in similar lines of business. When Group Life insurance became a common and approved way of handling the
risk of death, it was natural that the risk of injury or sickness
should be covered along much the same lines. The most rapid
development in Group Accident and Health insurance has
been in recent decades and in close association with the growth
of Group Life insurance.

The Metropolitan was among the pioneers in this country
in developing Accident and Health insurance on the Group
plan. At the time of the launching of the welfare program
in 1909, Vice-President Fiske announced the intention of
the Company to engage in the business of Health insurance.
His announcement dwelt upon the increasing role that the
Metropolitan was playing in the field of social service and
indicated that, if the demand were adequate, the Company
would be prepared to enter the field of insurance against
sickness, disability, and old age. This was a part of a broad
program which Mr. Fiske envisioned to make the Metropolitan a more effective instrument for the security of the

family, whose protection was increasingly engaging the attention of the American people. The plan was hailed as an important step forward in meeting the needs of working people, who up to that time had few of the protections which social insurance schemes had made available to the industrial population abroad. Mr. Fiske had great faith that an organization like the Metropolitan, with its high order of technical skill and extensive Field organization in contact with millions of people, could, on a voluntary basis, extend the necessary coverage rapidly and effectively.

The Charter under which the Metropolitan was then operating limited the Company's business to Life insurance and Annuities. Before the Company could enter the new field of Accident and Health insurance, it was necessary that the New York Insurance Law be amended to permit the required changes in the Company's Charter. These became effective in 1913, and permitted the writing of Accident and Health insurance. An additional change in the Charter was required when the Company was mutualized in 1915. These amendments enabled the Metropolitan to write, first, Group contracts providing benefits in the event of disablement from sickness or accident, or loss of life, limb, or sight by accidental means, and related coverages; and, second, individual Personal Accident and Health policies. We shall begin by discussing the Group coverage, leaving the subject of Personal Accident and Health to a later section of this chapter.

When the Company first explored the possibilities of writing Accident and Health insurance, it was confronted by the fact that the field had not been fully developed in this country, and that there was a scarcity of basic data. Accordingly, in 1912 the Company sent some of its Officers, including James D. Craig, then Assistant Actuary, to Europe to study the subject and to seek the advice especially of the leading British actuaries. The Friendly Societies and other organizations in England had by this time accumulated a large experience and had already established a groundwork for the business. A considerable amount of material was collected and brought back, but there was no way of knowing how closely the rates of sickness abroad would represent conditions prevailing in our country. Despite these difficulties, the Company decided to undertake the transaction of Accident and Health insurance on the Group plan, beginning on a limited and more or less experimental scale. Accordingly, in July 1914 the Disability Insurance Division of the Company was created, and put under the charge of Dr. Lee K. Frankel, then Sixth Vice-President, who was responsible for the Company's welfare activities. In 1921 this work was absorbed by the growing Group Division under the leadership and direction of Mr. J. E. Kavanagh, then Third Vice-President, and of Mr. A. C. Campbell, then Superintendent of the Group Division.

The Company's first Group Accident and Health policy was issued on its own Home Office employees on July 1, 1914, and two months later this protection was extended to the Field Force. The contract was issued on the contributory basis, the Company and the employees sharing about equally in the cost of the disability coverage. The disability insurance provided employees with a weekly income in the event of incapacity due to illness or nonoccupational accident. For the first 26 weeks of disability the benefits were, in general, two thirds of the average weekly salary; when disability continued beyond this period, benefits were provided until the age of 65 on a decreasing scale. This coverage was in force almost a year before the Company issued a similar policy to another employer.

In June 1919 the Company announced a new type of policy, which is of particular historical interest because it was issued to every eligible employer in the newly developed industrial center of Kingsport, Tenn. Every working man and woman so employed in that city was offered Group Life and Accident and Health insurance. This newer type of policy attained some popularity, and whereas only a few of these contracts were placed in 1919, there were more than 200 in force by the end of 1923. Most of these policies were written with the employer paying the entire cost. Considerable stimulus for the development of this new type of business came from the rapid growth of Group Life insurance on the contributory plan.

In 1924 a new era was inaugurated in Group Accident and Health insurance. In response to a growing demand for this type of coverage, especially from the railroads, the Metropolitan in November of that year prepared a simple, comprehensive, and flexible policy providing for contributions to the cost by the employees as well as by the employer. This form, in its essentials, has continued to serve to the present day. As in Group Life insurance, a blanket master policy is issued to the employer, and the employees receive individual certificates reciting the benefits payable to them. The policy is applicable either to all the employees or to all employees of a given class determined by conditions pertaining to the employment. An essential proviso is that at least 75 percent of those eligible must elect to be insured. This and other features preclude individual selection, either of the persons insured or the amount of insurance. There is no medical examination, but an employee must be actively at work in order that his insurance become effective. There is usually a "probationary period" for new employees, in many cases three months of active employment, before the insurance goes into effect.

Under the most popular plan, benefits begin on the eighth day of incapacity and continue for a maximum period of 13 weeks. Payments are usually a uniform weekly amount, which may vary according to salary or class of employment. To prevent overinsurance the benefits are limited to approximately two thirds of the employee's weekly earnings, and to a maximum of $40 a week. Occupational accidents and diseases covered under Workmen's Compensation laws, are not covered in most Metropolitan Group Accident and Health policies, inasmuch as all States other than Mississippi now have some form of such protection for workmen. However, in the case of workers not protected under such laws— for example, many railroad employees—the policy, with an extra premium, can be made to cover accidents arising out of employment.

Premium rates, with certain restrictions, are computed without taking into account the ages of those covered under the Group Accident and Health contract. This can be safely done because, within the variations in age distribution among employees of different companies, accident and sickness rates do not differ as widely as do mortality rates. Experience has shown that the rate of disability, unlike mortality, is considerably higher among women than among men, and the premium rate, therefore, increases with an increased proportion of women employees. The premium is also increased for certain industries or other special classes of risk where experience has indicated that, on account of special conditions, a higher disability rate is probable. The premium is paid directly to the Company by the employer on either a monthly, quarterly, semiannual, or annual basis. Either the employer or the employees may pay the entire premium, or it may be shared by both. Policies are participating.

Metropolitan Group Accident and Health contracts have become increasingly popular. By the end of 1941 the Company had in force insurance on 2,105 groups comprising 1,404,782 lives, providing a total weekly benefit of well in excess of $20,000,000. The Metropolitan, moreover, has always been well in the lead of other companies operating in the Group Accident and Health field. In fact the current yearly premium is almost double that of the company transacting the next largest volume of this type of business. The success of the Company has been stimulated in no small measure by the special services it offers—by its extensive welfare work, including the Visiting Nurse Service, and by the cooperation of the Policyholders Service Bureau. This has been accompanied by the progressive lowering of the premium rates for the coverage by virtue of improved claim experience and economies effected in administration. The minimum basic initial premium rate for the eighth day-thirteen weeks plan of benefit has decreased from 84 cents a month for a $10 weekly benefit in 1923, to 60 cents at the present time. Such reductions have been made not only for new groups, but have also been extended to many existing policies where the experience warranted. In addition, a total of $33,529,512 had been returned in dividends to the policy-holders by the end of 1941. In the years since the inception of this protection to the end of 1941 the Company paid to the insured employees in claims no less than $95,147,530. It is obvious that this form of insurance has served a basic need.

Side by side with the Group Accident and Health contract, the Company has also developed another form of Group Disability insurance. On May 15, 1919, Accidental Dismemberment insurance was introduced, and about three years later was expanded to include Accidental Death benefits as well. Group Accidental Death and Dismemberment insurance provides a lump-sum payment, but no weekly benefits. Subject to the provisions of the policy, the full amount of insurance is paid in case of death by accidental means, or in case of loss from accidental cause of both hands, both feet, of a hand and a foot, the sight of both eyes, or of either hand or foot in conjunction with the loss of the sight of an eye. One half the amount of the policy is paid in the event of accidental loss of one hand, one foot, or the sight of one eye. Benefits are usually paid for occupational as well as for nonoccupational accidents.

Accidental Death and Dismemberment coverage may be issued in combination with either Group Life or Group Accident and Health policies. When written in conjunction with Group Life, Accidental Death and Dismemberment insurance is usually issued for the same amount as the Life insurance, provided this does not exceed $5,000 on any employee. Premium rates vary for different industries, ranging from 10 cents to 35 cents monthly per $1,000 of principal sum for most industries, but may be higher in the relatively more hazardous enterprises. Paralleling the experience for Group Accident and Health insurance, the cost of Group Accidental Death and Dismemberment insurance has been progressively lowered.

The most recent of these reductions occurred in March 1941 and resulted in an actual decrease in the total premiums received by the Metropolitan in 1941 despite a substantial increase in the amount of insurance, as compared with the previous year.

Starting with a single group in 1919, this branch has expanded until, at the end of 1941, 387 organizations were covered by this type of protection in the Metropolitan, comprising 382,096 lives for a sum well in excess of $500,000,000.

The plans of disability insurance which we have just discussed had been designed primarily to compensate the insured or his family for loss of income resulting from sickness or accident. No special provision was made, however, for expenses incurred by cases requiring hospitalization or surgical care. For some years prior to 1929 a few fraternal societies and employee organizations provided coverage for such services, but it was not until recent years that group hospitalization plans began to flourish. In response to the rapidly increasing demand for this type of protection, the Metropolitan has developed both Group Hospital Expense and Group Surgical Operation insurance, both of which, offering essential services at very moderate cost, have attained widespread popularity. In both these recent developments, Third Vice-President Earl O. Dunlap, an actuary by training and experience, has played a major role, as he had earlier in the development of the other forms of Group insurance.

Group Hospital Expense insurance is issued to an employer, either in the form of a separate policy or as a supplementary agreement to a Group Life or Accident and Health policy. The contract provides, with certain limitations, for the payment of a daily benefit or reimbursement, such as $4 or $5 a day, for hospitalization up to a maximum of 31 or 70 days, according to the plan of benefit. The plan is distinctly flexible as to the amount of daily benefit to meet the variable cost of hospitalization in different localities and the kind of accommodation desired by the insured. The policy also covers charges for anesthesia, special laboratory service, use of oper-

195

ating room, and similar expenses—not including physician's fees—up to a total of five or ten times one day's benefit, depending upon the contract provisions.

Although the Metropolitan had included Group Hospital and Surgical Operation benefits in the Insurance and Retirement Program for its own Home and Head Office employees as early as January 1, 1928, the first Hospital insurance contract for the employees of another employer was issued in June 1935, covering almost 800 employees. Because adequate data were lacking at the beginning, the business at first was conducted on a closely controlled experimental basis. This naturally changed as experience developed, and policy provisions, underwriting requirements, and premium rates were revised, generally in the direction of lower premiums for equivalent benefits. Early in 1942 a new plan of benefit with more complete coverage was introduced, increasing the reimbursement for special services and reducing the minimum period of hospital confinement required in certain cases. The minimum initial premium for this improved and more liberal plan was set at 14 cents a month per dollar of daily benefit, a higher premium rate than for the old plan, which is still offered as an alternative.

Group Hospital Expense insurance has enjoyed a very rapid growth, particularly in the past five years. At the end of 1941 the Metropolitan Hospital Expense insurance covered 688 groups, comprising 526,459 lives, for daily benefits totaling $2,133,916.

The first Group Surgical Operation contract issued by the Metropolitan to an employer other than itself became effective on October 1, 1938, for a group of about 100 employees. The subsequent growth of this coverage has paralleled that of Hospital Expense insurance. It is generally issued only as a supplement to Group Hospital Expense or Group Accident and Health insurance, and the limitations in the policy and the underwriting requirements are essentially the same as for Group Hospital Expense insurance. The contract provides for reimbursement to the employee of the actual fees charged for designated operations, subject to specified limits. The maxima for different operations are set forth in a schedule included in the policy and are graded according to the type of operation, usually up to a maximum of $150. The original contracts carried limitations of benefits to one half the schedule reimbursement for operations performed while the employee was other than an in-patient in a hospital. On January 1, 1940, a new schedule was introduced removing this limitation. In addition the new contracts no longer excluded from coverage all employees age 70 or over. This more comprehensive form of coverage was accompanied by an increase in the basic scale of premium rates from 35 cents to 40 cents per month. Further modifications in the rates were made in 1941 and 1942, with the rates in some circumstances increased to 45 cents.

In 1939 Hospital Expense and Surgical Operation insurance were extended to protect the dependents of workers. On January 1st of that year, these two new forms of coverage were made effective for office employees and Field-Men of the Metropolitan. The Company's first contract of this type with other employers was made in June 1939 for Hospital Expense insurance, and in May 1940 for Surgical Operation insurance. Dependent Hospital Expense and Surgical Operation insurance are issued only as supplementary coverage for the worker himself. Provisions for the dependents are similar to those for the employees, except that the schedule of benefits selected is often lower.

A list of the companies that have enabled their employees to protect themselves through the medium of one or more of the Metropolitan Group Disability coverages reads like a Who's Who of American business. Among the larger ones are: General Motors Corporation, Republic Steel Corporation, Union Carbide and Carbon Corporation, Jones and Laughlin Steel Corporation, Caterpillar Tractor Company, Armour & Company, Continental Baking Corporation, International Paper Company, Standard Brands, Great Northern Railway Company, and American Can Company. The great success that has attended the development of the Group business in the Metropolitan and in the other companies would have been impossible but for the readiness with which many thousands of employers have contributed, not only consider-able sums of money but also a substantial amount of clerical and auditing work.

There could be no better evidence of the soundness of the Group programs outlined in this and in the preceding chapter, and of the confidence which employers and employees alike have reposed in them, than is provided by the extent to which they have permeated American industry and business. Today these programs stand at the peak in volume largely because of the support accorded them by both employers and employees. Group protection against death and disability has reached such huge proportions that current premiums for the country as a whole, made up of pay-roll deductions and employer contribu-tions, total $240,000,000 a year. Altogether, the development of Group insurance in its various branches has given immense benefit to thousands of working groups and has contributed materially to the security of the country.

The spread of Group insurance, moreover, hastened the day when Social Security came into being in America. Certain it is that the rapid extension of Group insurance and the experience gained in this field furnished most valuable aids in formulating and developing the Federal Security pro-gram. It will be recalled that several of the Metropolitan Officers were delegated by the Company to make a study of social insurance plans in Europe before legislative action was consummated by the Government. The first-hand knowledge gathered by Dr. Frankel, Mr. Craig, and Mr. Olzendam was of invaluable assistance in formulating the program of Social Security under Federal auspices. The Life insurance business, as a whole, has been sympathetic in forwarding the Social Security program. In point of fact, the leaders in the Group insurance business were in the forefront to guide and direct the new movement into practical and useful channels. It is altogether gratifying to note that two phases of protection for workingmen in our country, Group insurance on the one hand and social protection under Government agencies on the other, have at no time been in conflict. There has always been the closest cooperation, which has ensured the harmonious development of Social Security plans side by side with voluntary Group insurance as its partner and supplement, to the great benefit of both.

Personal Accident and Health Insurance

Valuable as Group insurance is as a means of protecting large numbers of individuals against the consequences of accidents and disease, there are many who, because they work in organizations not covered by Group insurance, or are self-employed, must provide for their own protection. A large and important branch of the insurance business has grown up to meet the needs of these people. Limited coverage for disability arising from sickness or accident had been available to individual policyholders, as supplementary to their Ordinary Life insurance contracts, since 1912. This consisted of a provision waiving all further premiums due on their Life policies during the continuance of total and permanent disability incurred prior to age 60. In 1918 the Company extended the benefits available under this supplementary contract, to provide for monthly income payments in addition to a waiver of premiums in event of total and permanent disability. Additional coverage against death by accidental means was also introduced in the form of double indemnity in 1919. But it was not until 1921 that disability protection on an individual policy contract could be obtained in the Metropolitan independently of a Life insurance policy.

On June 22, 1921, President Fiske sent a letter to the Managers of the Company announcing the intention to issue individual Accident and Health policies. A few months were spent in careful preparation, and on October 7, 1921, on the 30th anniversary of his election as Vice-President in 1891, President Fiske personally approved an application and secured delivery on that same day of Policy No. 1. The application, on file in the Company archives, was made on behalf of Mr. Frederick W. Chaney, and written by Agent B. H. Wade, of Danville, Va., District. These individual contracts were designated "Personal Accident and Health" policies, thus distinguishing them from the Group Accident and Health contracts. In providing, through the various forms, specific indemnities for the loss of life, limb, or sight by accidental means, and weekly benefits for disability resulting from accidental means or sickness, they served to broaden and round out the circle of individual insurance protection. This type of coverage became available to Canadians in the latter part of 1922, when an amendment to the Dominion Insurance Law permitted the issuance of such policies by a Life insurance company.

The organization and development of the Metropolitan's Personal Accident and Health business was placed in the hands of Mr. Stewart M. LaMont. When President Fiske was convinced that there was a broad opportunity for the Company to meet the accident and health hazards of individuals, he sought the best qualified man available to head the new Division, and his choice fell on Mr. LaMont, an outstanding figure in this field. Mr. LaMont, from the very beginning, had the advantage of the advice and assistance of Actuary James D. Craig and his associate, H. R. Bassford, who has subsequently become Actuary of the Company. The new Division began to function on a modest scale with a staff of eight people, among them Mr. L. K. Farrell, now Assistant Secretary, and Mr. T. F. Hickey, now Superintendent of Claims, both of whom had had experience in this field with other Accident and Health companies.

The Metropolitan introduced a number of innovations in Personal Accident and Health insurance. One important departure from the practice of other companies related to participation in divisible surplus. As the Company was already mutual when the Division was instituted, it was in a position to offer the first participating policies in this field. The records show that the initial dividend on these policies

STEWART M. LaMONT

was paid in 1924. According to present practice, dividends
on Standard Personal Accident and Health policies are paid
after they have been in force three years or more, and on
policies covering accident only, after four years. This participation continues to be a special Metropolitan feature. Another attractive feature is the grace period extending the time
for payment of premium 31 days beyond the due date. Other
companies following the lead of the Metropolitan have since
incorporated this privilege in their policies.

An important deviation from common practice was introduced by the Metropolitan in grading premium rates on all
forms of individual Health insurance policies according to the
age *at issue*, and charging a level premium from the time the
policy is issued until the limiting age is reached, just as is
done in Ordinary Life insurance. The limiting age for the
issuance of Health insurance is 55 years. This practice has
been carried on by a few other companies on noncancelable

policies only; but on the standard or One-Year Term type, the usual practice of Accident and Health companies has been to issue Health insurance at flat rates for all ages up to a fixed point, which in most cases is age 49, and then to provide for a substantial increase in rate at age 50 or 55, or both. The higher rates are charged when a policyholder attains these ages, regardless of the age at which the policy was issued or how long it has been in force.

A distinct departure was also made by the Metropolitan in the matter of Agents' commissions on Personal Accident and Health policies. The custom with other companies in this field has been to allow the same commission on renewals as on the first year's premium, and to continue these relatively large commissions throughout the life of the policy. The Metropolitan, on the other hand, applied to Accident and Health insurance the practice usually followed by Life companies, of paying a first-year and renewal commission. This saving naturally has inured to the benefit of the continuing policyholder through the operation of the participation feature of the contract.

When the Personal Accident and Health business was inaugurated in 1921, seven forms of policies were provided. Of these, two have stood the test of time, namely, the Standard Accident policy and the Standard Accident and Health policy. Four of these policies were of so-called "noncancelable" type, which meant that the Company did not retain the option, as under policies of the Standard type, to cancel or refuse to renew the policy at any time. While there was not a great demand for these policies, the experience was unfavorable and in November 1924 the issuance of these forms was discontinued. The seventh policy provided only indemnity for death or dismemberment by accidental means. This contract never had a great appeal and was discontinued in August 1939. The Standard Accident policy insures against injuries caused by accidental means, and provides specific lump-sum benefits for loss of life, limb, or sight, and weekly benefits for a specified maximum period for total or partial disability, with such indemnities doubled for injuries sustained while in or on any public passenger conveyance (except aerial), or in a passenger elevator or a burning building. Additional payments are provided, within specified limits, for the cost of medical treatment for nondisabling injuries. The Standard Accident and Health policy includes the provisions just enumerated, with the addition of weekly benefits for total disability and for partial disability following at least seven days of total disability, which results from sickness, and of a lump sum payable at the end of a year of total disability in the case of total and permanent disability resulting from blindness or paralysis due to sickness.

Originally, the Standard Personal Accident policy included a limited benefit for specified surgical operations for bodily injuries by accidental means, and the Standard Personal Accident and Health policies included limited alternative benefits for specified surgical operation or hospital expenses. In 1942 each of these policies was revised so as to offer the insured a choice of a policy with or without benefits of this nature, the premium rates differing accordingly. The noninclusive policies continued to be called "Standard" policies, while those including the new Hospital Expense and Surgical Operation Expense benefits were called "Comprehensive" policies.

The Simplex Personal Accident and Health policy, introduced in 1940, is designed to furnish only the primary form of protection—namely, against loss of income due to total disability from injury or sickness lasting more than one week. Its coverage is more limited than that of the Standard Accident and Health policy, and the premium considerably less. There seems to be a definite demand for this type of coverage which fills specific needs.

The Metropolitan has never followed the practice of some other companies which issue "special risk" or "limited" policies to cover only narrowly specified accident hazards or diseases. Neither has it adopted the common practice of reducing either the amount or duration of weekly indemnity if the insured is not confined to his home. On the other hand the Metropolitan limits the issue of Personal Accident and Health policies to persons in the less hazardous occupations. Acceptable occupations are divided into four classes, according to their respective hazard. The Company does not attempt to write Personal Accident and Health policies in the Industrial field, which is reached by Group insurance on a much more satisfactory basis.

Metropolitan Personal Accident and Health insurance, with its many innovations, liberal provisions, and low cost, has naturally attracted a large clientele. In two decades this Division has risen to a high position among the leaders in the field. By 1929 it had jumped to ninth place among the companies writing this type of business. Since then it has continued to advance in rank, and for the past few years has occupied sixth place. At the end of 1941 the Company had in force Personal Accident and Health insurance under which the annual premiums amounted to $6,799,556.

The Division at the Home Office, under the leadership of Mr. LaMont, grew from the original staff of eight to more than 200. In 1937 Third Vice-President A. W. Trethewey assumed direction of Accident and Health production, although Mr. LaMont retained supervision of the Accident and Health Division in the Home Office. When the latter retired in 1938, Second Vice-President Samuel Milligan took over the Home Office administration of the Division, which was directly supervised by Assistant Secretary Farrell.

That Personal Accident and Health insurance is performing a useful function is clear from an analysis of the extent and character of the illnesses and injuries for which claims have been paid in this Division. For example, in the five-year period 1934 to 1938, sicknesses occurred at the annual rate of close to 230 and accidents at the rate of about 120 per 1,000 policyholders covered for each type of risk. Of the sicknesses reported it is noteworthy that 56 percent, or considerably more than half, were due to respiratory diseases. The accident figures show how common are everyday injuries, even to the average man not engaged in a hazardous occupation. Of the

ARTHUR W. TRETHEWEY
Third Vice-President

injuries reported, some 27 percent occurred within the apparently safe confines of the office or shop and some 18 percent on home premises. Thus, close to half of the cases represent persons injured inside buildings or on private premises where they might feel reasonably secure from danger. Even recreation has its serious hazards. The record shows that over 13 percent of the aggregate injuries occurred while the men were bathing, bowling, riding horseback, playing baseball, tennis, golf, or other games. These figures bring into sharp focus the fact that danger lurks everywhere, and the vital need for protection against the financial loss that may result from injury by accidental means.

The Company takes particular interest in the growth of its Accident and Health business, because the establishment of this Division fulfilled a long-cherished ambition to offer its policyholders an all-inclusive service. The point has frequently been made that this form of protection is properly a part of the ideal family insurance program. For Accident and Health insurance is security at a small annual cost that can conveniently be budgeted, and directed against misfortune not adequately provided for under any other form of insurance. Designed as protection against loss of time and of earnings, and against unexpected expense suddenly incurred, it supplements the security afforded by Life insurance. Together, the various forms of Life and Accident and Health insurance enable the policyholder to obtain what has been termed "the Complete Circle of Protection."

CHAPTER 10

The Cost of Life Insurance

NEXT TO SAFETY, it is the cost of Life insurance which is of primary interest to the policyholder. He wants the insurance which is best suited to his needs and is low in cost, taking account of all the benefits and services rendered by the company. This phase of Metropolitan history has been particularly gratifying, for throughout the years the Company has made every effort to bring Life insurance to large numbers of people at the lowest cost consistent with safety. Herein lies one of the reasons for the Company's extraordinary success, be it in terms of Industrial, Ordinary, or Group Life insurance.

The question of cost seems never to have escaped the attention of the Executives. The reader will recall the limitations placed on dividends to stockholders when the business was launched in 1868. Later, as the Industrial Department grew, costs were materially reduced by increasing benefits and liberalizing policy provisions. When the Ordinary Department was reorganized in 1892, the appeal to the public was largely on the score of low-cost insurance. The introduction in 1909 of the $5,000 Whole Life contract was a landmark in this continuing program. The fight which the Company carried through and won for the maintenance of low premiums at the time of its mutualization was another important step in the same direction. Later the Metropolitan's favorable experience permitted a liberal dividend policy which, coupled with low initial premiums, won for the Company an unrivaled reputation on the score of costs. The introduction of Monthly Premium Ordinary and Industrial policies further reduced the cost of Life insurance to large numbers of wage-earners and their families. Truly, the many efforts to provide American and Canadian families with an increasing amount of insurance protection per premium dollar have been milestones in the Company's history.

Fundamental to a consideration of the cost of Life insurance protection as currently provided is an appreciation of the several factors which enter into it. The three important ones are: the mortality experienced, the rate of interest earned on funds accumulated for the benefit of policyholders, and the expense incurred in running the business. Of the three, mortality is the basic element. In earlier days attempts were made to provide limited amounts of Life insurance in which the mortality accounted for virtually the entire cost. These efforts were generally unsatisfactory and were a far cry from modern Life insurance, which provides level-premium protection to millions of insured persons for long periods of time and with a large variety of necessary services. The fact that the death rate, and hence mortality cost, increases with advancing age created the need to equalize premiums over the long-term contract, and as a result the level-premium plan was established. With it came the reserve accumulation for the benefit of the policyholder, and the profitable investment of these funds gave the opportunity for interest earnings to reduce the cost of insurance.

Life insurance is soundest when conducted as a business enterprise. As has been pointed out, various types of policies must be created to meet the specific needs of the insured. The policies must be sold and they must be serviced; hence the item of management expense. In actual practice the premium is fixed at a conservative amount not only to cover the cost of the insurance, taking account of the three factors referred to, but also to provide a reasonable margin of safety to meet unforeseen contingencies.

In a discussion of cost it is necessary, furthermore, to make a distinction between the two prevailing types of Life insurance companies. The mutual companies uniformly sell participating policies; the stock companies for the most part sell nonparticipating policies. In a mutual company such as the Metropolitan, the policyholder receives in the form of annual dividends such amounts as are found not to be needed to cover the current cost of insurance and to provide the necessary reserves. Under nonparticipating insurance the gross premium is generally fixed at a somewhat lower amount than under participating insurance. The additional safety margin needed is furnished by the capital contributed by the stockholders. No dividends are paid to policyholders, and the stockholders may receive dividends on their stock if earned. The cost of insurance to a person holding a non-participating policy is, therefore, the annual premium he pays. The cost of insurance to a person holding a participating policy is the premium he pays less the dividends he receives. This distinction is all the more necessary in following the history of cost in the Metropolitan, which, prior to mutualization in 1915, had insurance on both participating and nonpartici-pating plans and, since its mutualization, has sold its contracts (except some individual Annuities) on the participating plan. In a company the size of the Metropolitan the total dividends paid are substantial. Thus in 1942 the Company returned in dividends well in excess of $110,000,000.

Mortality, which is an important factor in Life insurance costs, has been consistently decreasing during the 75 years under observation. It has therefore been a potent element in the reduction of such costs. The earliest records available for the Ordinary Department covering the years 1874 to 1884 indicate that the mortality then prevailing was in the aggregate very close to that shown in the American Experience Table. By 1915, when the Metropolitan became a mutual company, the mortality on Ordinary business had decreased to about 80 percent of this table, the greatest relative improvement being registered at ages under 50. These declines were reflected in reductions in premiums and in the first dividends paid on Standard Ordinary insurance in 1916.

The mortality experienced among the Industrial policy-holders has likewise been very favorable. The earliest Industrial records covering the years 1879–1889 indicate a mortality of about 145 percent of the Standard Industrial Table prepared in 1907. By 1915 the mortality had decreased to about 75 percent of this table. This improvement among Industrial policyholders made possible the payment of bonuses to them beginning as early as 1897, while the Metropolitan was still a stock company. In the period of 18 years up to 1915, a total of $49,000,000 was paid in such bonuses, bringing down the policyholders' payments more in line with the actual cost of providing protection. This voluntary distribution on the part of a stock company had few parallels in American Life insurance history.

Our greatest interest, of course, lies in the period since mutualization. Between 1915 and 1942 mortality rates on Standard Ordinary insurance have declined in every age group. The greatest relative decline, amounting to almost 70 percent, occurred at ages under 30; the decline has been 45 percent at ages 30 to 49 and 20 percent at ages 50 and over. The general downward trend was first interrupted by the influenza epidemic of 1918–1919, which took its heaviest toll in early and middle adult life. Following the epidemic, the decrease in mortality was resumed at a more rapid pace, particularly in the ages which had been hit hardest. Except for a few years after 1929 the downward trend has continued.

Inasmuch as mortality rates are normally low at the ages where the greatest relative reductions have occurred, the financial savings have not been as great as might be supposed. For instance, in 1941 the Company had a saving on Ordinary death claims of about $11,000,000 (on the $65,000,000 paid), as compared with what it would have had to pay had the death rate in 1941 been the same as 10 years earlier.

The other branches of the Ordinary Department show similar mortality trends. Because of the stricter standards used in selecting the applicants qualifying for the $5,000 Whole Life contracts, the mortality in this group over the years has averaged somewhat less than 90 percent of that on Standard Ordinary policies.

The death rates on Intermediate and Special Class policies have improved to a slightly greater extent than those for Standard Ordinary policies, particularly at the younger ages. This experience reflects several factors: first, there was more room for improvement among persons in lower income brackets who comprise a large proportion of the lives insured under these policies; second, the general standards of living and working conditions of these people have been raised appreciably, with consequent favorable effect on mortality; and third, the Company's welfare program for Intermediate policyholders has been effective. These factors are discussed more fully in Chapters 20 and 21.

Practically the same reasons can be assigned for the decline in mortality among Weekly Industrial policyholders, which has been about 40 percent between 1915 and 1942. At ages under 30 the decline has been about 70 percent; at 30 to 49 years it has amounted to almost 60 percent; while at ages 50 and over the reduction has amounted to 35 percent. As in the case of Standard Ordinary insurance, the influenza epidemic of 1918–1919 had its most adverse effect at ages under 30, where the mortality rates were about doubled; at ages 30 to 49 the mortality was increased by about 50 percent. Beyond this age the total mortality appeared to be unaffected. Unlike the experience in the Ordinary Department, the mortality among Industrial policyholders continued downward during the economic depression of the 1930's.

As has already been indicated, interest on accumulated funds is the second important item entering into the calculation of a premium. Since the Company's incorporation in 1868 there have been three long-time movements or trends in interest rates. During the period from the close of the Civil War until about 1900 the trend of interest rates was generally downward; from about 1900 to the early 1920's, the trend was on the whole upward, while since about 1925 to the present day, interest rates have again moved downward. These broad trends have not been confined to the interest rates on high-grade securities suitable for investment by Life insurance companies, but have prevailed on all types of invest-ments. In other words, the trend of the interest rates earned on Life insurance company assets has been primarily influenced by economic and social forces beyond the control of corporate or individual investors. Nevertheless, the Metropolitan has always made every effort to secure the best possible yield consistent with the safety of its investments. In addition to the long-time movements in interest rates mentioned above, there have been numerous temporary but marked intermediate fluctuations. Life insurance companies, however, in regard to the interest rate assumed for premiums and reserves, and to a lesser extent in regard to dividends, have been governed largely by the long-time trends and have been relatively unaffected by temporary changes.

In the post-Civil War years high interest rates prevailed and many companies, including the Metropolitan, earned in excess of 5½ percent gross interest on their assets. In fact, between 1866 and 1868 a 5 percent rate was permitted in New York for the valuation of Life insurance policies. In 1868, the year that the Company was incorporated, the New York law was changed to provide for valuation of policies at an interest rate not greater than 4½ percent. As the interest earnings of Life insurance companies declined in the late '70's, the New York law was again amended in 1884 to require valuation of policies at a rate not higher than 4 percent. The rates earned by Life insurance companies continued to decline, and in 1901, just about when they reached their lowest point for this period, the laws of both New York and Massachusetts were again changed to provide for valuation of policies at a rate of interest not exceeding 3½ percent. Accordingly, the Metropolitan, as well as many other companies, then changed to 3½ percent for the calculation of premiums and reserves on new business. Some mutual companies actually changed to a 3 percent rate at that time.

The rate of interest earned by the Metropolitan has fol-lowed the general trend of the rate earned by all Life insurance companies. Thus in 1900 the net interest rate (3.91 percent)

212

earned by the Metropolitan touched what was probably its lowest point up to that time. About 1905, interest rates began to rise, for some years rapidly and then more slowly. In 1920 the net interest rate earned by the Company rose to 5 percent and continued upward until 1924, when it reached a new peak of 5.44 percent. This comparatively high rate, well in excess of reserve requirements, produced a sizable surplus which made possible many liberalizations of the contracts of the Company and substantial increases in the dividend scales. From 1924 through 1929 the interest rate earned by Life insurance companies declined slightly. With the onset of the depression the earnings began to drop rapidly. In 1935 the Metropolitan's net interest rate fell to 3.66 percent, which was below the previous low point reached in 1900.

Because of this precipitate decline in the interest rate the Metropolitan, as well as other companies, decided to adopt more conservative premium and reserve bases for new Ordinary issues. The Company changed to a 3 percent interest basis for Ordinary insurance in 1935. The effect of the decline in interest earnings had been, of course, reflected earlier in dividends. On the other hand, because of the relatively higher surplus which had been accumulated on Industrial business, it was not felt necessary at that time to reduce dividends on Industrial insurance or to increase premiums. Since 1935 the decline in the interest rate has continued unabated and, as a consequence, dividends on both Ordinary and Industrial policies have been reduced almost annually since 1936. On January 1, 1942, the reserve bases for new Ordinary and Industrial insurance were changed to 2¾ percent interest, and an additional margin for an even lower interest rate was provided in computing premiums.

The decline in the interest rate during the past 15 years has, in fact, been without parallel in Life insurance history. Its financial effect is measured by the fact that if the Metropolitan had earned the same interest rate in 1941 as it had in 1931, there would have been available $27,000,000 more for dividends and contingencies on Standard Ordinary insurance, and also $27,000,000 more for dividends and contingencies on Weekly Premium Industrial insurance. The corresponding gains from mortality on these two types of policies during the same period were only $11,000,000 and $9,000,000, respectively—that is, the increase in cost due to decline in interest rate has been 2½ and 3 times as important as the effect of improved mortality during the last 10 years. Few policyholders indeed realize how important the interest factor is in determining the cost of Life insurance, particularly on such policies as Endowments, on which the amount of the reserve fund is highest.

The third factor in Life insurance costs—expense of operation—is unlike the other two in that it is much more subject to administrative control. It has, therefore, received the constant consideration of the Executives from the beginning. In a history of the Metropolitan published in 1924, attention was called to the Company's success in reducing expenses. There it was pointed out that the expense ratio on Ordinary business had been reduced by more than 60 percent from 1892 to 1924. On Industrial business, expenses had been reduced by about 24 percent over the same period. On a somewhat similar basis, the reduction in expense ratios (excluding taxes) from 1924 through 1941 has been more than 37 percent on Ordinary business and about 29 percent on Industrial business. And this reduction has occurred despite substantial increases in the compensation of the employees and Agents.

Because of the immediate expenses incident to the issuance of Life insurance policies, the expense rate during the first year is several times higher than that in later years. Comparisons between aggregate expense ratios may, therefore, be misleading to the extent that they may reflect different proportions of new business rather than different levels of expense. For instance, in recent years there has been a decline in the proportion of new business in the Metropolitan as compared with the 1920's, and this of itself has tended to reduce the Company's aggregate expense ratio. If new business is eliminated from consideration, by limiting the comparison to the expense rate per $1,000 of insurance after the first year, it appears that the reduction in the expense ratio on Ordinary business from 1924 to 1941 has been only slightly more than 9 percent, and that the corresponding reduction in the expense ratio on Industrial insurance has been about 13 percent. But these figures do not tell the entire story on expense rates, because the character of both Industrial and Ordinary business has changed over the years as a result of the introduction of Monthly Premium business. This has had the effect of reducing the average rate of expenses on Industrial policies, and of increasing the expense ratio on Ordinary policies to the extent that the costs incurred on Monthly Premium policies are higher than on those with premiums payable quarterly, semiannually, or annually.

While the Metropolitan has constantly striven to exercise every possible control over expenses, the march of time has brought with it demands for numerous additional services to policyholders as well as higher standards of compensation for employees. That the Metropolitan has succeeded in reducing its expense ratios, notwithstanding these tendencies, is largely due to the tremendous growth of the business, which has enabled the management to develop economies of operation which would not be possible except in a business of such volume. Independent studies have shown that the size of a company has an important bearing on the expense rate, and that, in general, larger companies tend to have lower expense rates.

In considering the changes in expense rates over a long period of time, it is essential to keep in mind that the Life insurance business has changed considerably over the years. For one thing, the Company today offers to policyholders a much wider variety of policies and services. To enable policy-holders to make the best possible use of the various benefits and services, the Metropolitan Field Force at the present time (as is pointed out in Chapter 12) undergoes a very rigorous training as compared with that given in the past. The additional cost of this training is slightly more than 3 percent of present Home Office expenses.

Because of rapidly changing conditions and a better appreciation by the public of the uses of insurance, the Company is today called upon to advise policyholders in a variety of matters. To do this efficiently it must employ qualified persons and this entails additional expense. A few examples of the Metropolitan's present services to policyholders for which the Company was not called upon 30 years ago, will indicate how difficult it is to compare expense rates over a long period of years.

Thirty years ago it was very rare for policy proceeds to be paid to beneficiaries in instalments; today the practice is very common on Ordinary insurance, and the expenses incident to the administration of this service are growing from year to year. In 1941 they amounted to about 3 percent of the Home Office expenses on Ordinary policies. Three decades ago the Metropolitan was asked only very infrequently to make adjustments in insurance policies after issue; today, as the result of drastic changes in the circumstances of many policyholders, the Company has expanded its advisory services and set up machinery for making proper adjustments in the insurance of thousands of policyholders. The cost of providing these services in 1941 amounted to about 5½ percent of the Home Office expenses on Ordinary policies and to about 1 percent on Industrial policies.

In 1910 all Ordinary policies issued by the Metropolitan were nonparticipating, and while the Company did pay "bonuses" on Industrial insurance, it did so of its own volition and on the basis of simple dividend scales. Upon mutualization in 1915 the Company not only had to face the added expense of making an equitable distribution of dividends on all Ordinary policies (as well as to provide for the payment of dividends in different ways), but also felt it necessary to use more refined schedules of dividends on Industrial policies.

During the past 30 years the compensation of the Clerical Staff has more than doubled, while that of the Agents has about trebled. Furthermore, all Metropolitan employees and Agents now enjoy a comprehensive Group Insurance and

Retirement Program. These facts reflect not merely the rising American standard of living, but also the high standards of accomplishment by the Company's employees and Agents. The Metropolitan has thus achieved lower aggregate expense rates per $1,000 of insurance than it had in the past, despite a larger number and variety of services to policyholders and higher compensation to employees.

The varying trends in mortality, interest rates, and expenses which have affected the cost of Life insurance have been outlined in the preceding pages. The combined effect of these three elements is reflected in the broad trends of the cost of Ordinary and Industrial insurance in the Metropolitan. When the trend of mortality or of expenses is upward or the course of the interest rate is downward, the cost of the insurance is increased; and the reverse is, of course, true when mortality or expenses decline or the interest rate rises. It should also be borne in mind that changes in the trend of these factors affect different types of policies to different degrees. For example, changes in the interest rate have a much greater effect upon the cost of Endowment policies than upon the cost of Whole Life policies, because of the higher reserve funds which must be accumulated on the former. On the other hand, changes in mortality have a greater effect on the cost of Whole Life policies than upon Endowments.

The Company began writing Ordinary insurance in 1868 on a participating annual dividend basis, and continued to do this until 1892. The first Ordinary participating premium rates were based on the Carlisle Mortality Table and 4 percent interest. Rates were increased slightly in 1870 and again, about 10 percent, in 1888. Unfortunately there is no detailed record available of the dividends actually paid on these participating policies over this period of years. The successive increases in premium rates would, however, indicate that the cost of Ordinary insurance prior to 1892 was rising. This was in part due to the downward trend in the interest rate and in part to the increase in the expense rate, reflecting the small volume of business written after 1879.

217

In 1892 the Metropolitan reorganized its Ordinary Department and began to issue nonparticipating Ordinary insurance at low premium rates, which constituted a reduction of more than 20 percent from the participating rates previously in effect. At that time most companies were issuing Ordinary insurance on a participating basis with substantially higher premiums and a provision for deferred dividends. Because of the continued decline in the rate of interest and a change in the New York and Massachusetts laws requiring new Life insurance policies to be valued at a rate of interest not exceeding 3½ percent, the Company in 1901 found it necessary to increase its nonparticipating premiums slightly. However, by 1907 a reversal in the trend of the interest rate became manifest, and with other favorable developments made it possible for the Metropolitan to reduce its premiums to about the level effective prior to 1901. In 1909 premium rates were again reduced.

In 1909 the Company also launched the $5,000 Whole Life policy, which turned out to be the most successful experiment ever undertaken in insurance for select risks. By restricting the issuance of this policy to professional persons, businessmen, and others in similar occupations, and only to those whose build and physical condition were distinctly better than average, the Company, in effect, restricted the policy to superstandard risks. The low mortality of such persons and the saving in expense due to the high average amount of these policies, enabled the Metropolitan to offer them at a cost which was lower than ever before offered by any other private Life insurance company.

Because of the increasing rate of interest and improved mortality, the Company was able, upon mutualization in 1915, to retain the premium rates it had charged on nonparticipating insurance, except that on account of certain legal requirements it was forced to increase slightly the premium rates for the $5,000 Whole Life policy. The 1918–19 influenza epidemic led to a virtual omission of dividends in 1919 and 1920 on Ordinary policies. It should be borne in mind, however, that practically all Ordinary policies in force at that time had been issued at low nonparticipating rates. As a result of the epidemic the Company decided in July 1919 to increase its Ordinary premiums moderately, except in the case of $5,000 Whole Life policies, the premiums for which had already been increased shortly before. With a continued rise in the interest rate and decline in mortality, it became possible to restore previous dividend scales, so that by 1924 the cost of insurance was back at the pre-influenza level. Substantial increases in dividends were made in 1925 and again in 1927. The dividend scale adopted in 1927 was maintained unchanged until May 1, 1933. Thus, except for the repercussions of the influenza epidemic, it may be said that the trend of the cost of Ordinary insurance in the Metropolitan was downward from 1901 until 1933. Thus, irrespective of the mortality tables and rate of interest used in the calculation of premiums and reserves, policyholders received their insurance at its actual cost based on recent mortality and interest earnings.

In the early 1930's the rate of interest began to fall sharply, and its financial effect soon overshadowed the effects of improved mortality. As a result, successive reductions in dividend scales were made in 1933, in 1935, in 1936, in 1938, in 1940, and in 1942. All other mutual companies found it necessary to make like decreases in dividends during this period.

Effective January 1, 1942, the Company adopted new and increased premium rates for Ordinary insurance based on the American Men Ultimate Table, 2¾ percent interest, and a loading which included a further margin for an even lower interest rate. It may be noted in passing that these gross rates are, if anything, somewhat higher than those adopted in 1870 but, for the lack of authentic dividend figures for this early period, no reliable comparison of costs for the two periods can be made. As a result of the unparalleled decline in the rate of interest during the past 15 years, the cost of Ordinary insurance in the Metropolitan is at present somewhat higher than it was subsequent to the Company's mutualization in 1915, but nevertheless remains definitely lower than on Ordinary nonparticipating insurance sold prior to that date. Since the Company's mutualization the cost of Ordinary insurance in the Metropolitan has been the lowest, or nearly so, among private Life insurance companies.

Unlike the Ordinary, the Industrial business, at its inception in 1879, was sold on a nonparticipating basis. It was found advisable to increase Industrial premium rates in 1887. In 1896 the basis of the Industrial rates was changed to the Metropolitan's own 1890–94 mortality experience and 3½ percent interest, with the result that increased benefits were granted on children's policies and somewhat decreased benefits at ages 13–37 on the Whole Life plan. A further increase in the benefits on children's policies was made the following year. In 1897 the Company also made a generous concession by paying quinquennial "bonuses" on Industrial policies, despite the fact that these contracts had been originally issued on a nonparticipating basis.

Because of the constantly improving mortality among Industrial policyholders and a rapidly decreasing expense rate (arising out of economies in management made possible by the growing volume of business), Industrial premium rates were reduced substantially in 1907 to the basis of the Standard Industrial Table and 3½ percent interest. At the same time bonuses were made payable annually. In 1909 the cost was reduced by increasing the benefits on the principal plans of insurance by 10 percent, and these increased benefits were made retroactive to policies written since 1907. The following year the scale of annual bonuses was greatly increased. In 1911 the Company adopted still another method of reducing the cost of Industrial insurance by granting a 10 percent refund of premiums to policyholders who paid directly to one of the Company's Offices. Thus the trend in the cost of Industrial insurance from 1897 on was definitely downward.

After the Company was mutualized it could not be expected that the dividends paid on Industrial policies would be materially larger than the "bonuses" previously allowed. The Company, after payment of nominal dividends to stockholders, had returned to Industrial policyholders in the form of bonuses the maximum amount consistent with the Company's needs for a contingency reserve. In 1916 the basis of the premium rates for the Life Paid Up at Age 75 plan was changed to the Metropolitan's own 1907-13 mortality experience and 3½ percent interest. As a result, the benefits were increased at the middle and especially at the younger ages, where the improvement in mortality had been most pronounced. At about this time also the Company introduced the loss of eyesight or limbs benefit in new policies without additional premium, and extended it retroactively to old policies on the same basis.

Following the influenza epidemic it was found necessary to reduce dividends on Industrial policies substantially, and it was not until 1925 that the dividend scale was restored to a level as high as that in effect in 1916 and 1917. In the later 1920's favorable mortality and a high interest rate made it possible for the Company to increase dividends substantially. At the beginning of 1928 the Company also adopted a program of equalizing the benefits provided under policies issued prior to 1916. To accomplish this end permanent increases in benefits were made from time to time and, in addition, so-called "equalization" dividends were paid at death or maturity sufficient to equalize the benefits payable with those provided under later premium rates.

In furtherance of its general objective of furnishing the most appropriate form of insurance at low cost, the Company in 1927 began to issue Monthly Premium Industrial policies. These policies reduced the cost of Industrial insurance to persons who could afford to pay premiums on a monthly rather than on a weekly basis. At some ages the gross premiums for Monthly Industrial policies compared favorably with Ordinary rates in some other companies. In 1928 the double indemnity benefit was added to all Industrial policies without any additional premium.

Because of the substantial surplus built up on Industrial business and the favorable mortality trend among Industrial

221

policyholders during the depression years, it was not deemed necessary during the early 1930's to decrease dividends on Weekly Premium Industrial policies, even though the interest rate was falling sharply. With the continued decline in the rate, however, the scale of dividends on Weekly Premium Industrial policies was decreased in 1935 and then again in each of the years 1936 through 1943.

It is interesting to observe that the Metropolitan has for many years paid extra dividends designed to return to the policyholder a portion of his contribution to the Company's contingency reserve. After a policy has been in force for a number of years and has contributed to the Company's surplus, an added dividend is paid when the policy terminates by death, by maturity as an Endowment, or in some cases by surrender. The amounts so paid are called mortuary, maturity, or settlement dividends, respectively. Mortuary and maturity dividends were first paid on Industrial policies in 1906, when the Metropolitan was still operating as a stock company. It began to make provision for such payments on Ordinary policies in its first dividend distribution (1916) following mutualization, and has since continued and expanded the practice. According to the scales adopted for 1943, the Company pays mortuary dividends ranging from 1 percent of the amount of claim on Industrial policies eight years in force to 7½ percent on policies of 21 or more years duration. On Standard Ordinary policies the 1943 scale provides for mortuary dividends of from 1/10 of 1 percent to 6 percent. In both Departments these additional dividends in 1943 will amount to more than $10,000,000, and since the beginning of this practice the total paid out has approximated $210,000,000. It was indeed gratifying to the Company that in the recodification of the New York Insurance Law, which became effective on January 1, 1940, the practice of paying mortuary, maturity, and settlement dividends was explicitly recognized by statute.

In addition to the three basic elements of mortality, interest, and expenses, the cost of insurance includes also an amount needed for the maintenance of an adequate contingency reserve. This assures the payment of benefits even in the event of a long-continued decline in the interest rate or in the event of other contingencies such as epidemics, war deaths, financial losses, etc., which occur at long or irregular intervals. Variations in the cost of insurance from one period to another depend to some extent on the policy adopted in regard to retentions for contingencies. While at the present trying period the Metropolitan has considered it advisable to take a more conservative view in regard to the accumulation of a contingency reserve to meet whatever emergencies the future may bring, its unique practice of paying mortuary, maturity, and settlement dividends makes possible the return to policyholders of such amounts contributed to the contingency reserve as will not otherwise be needed.

Metropolitan policyholders have long enjoyed a favored position with regard to cost, because safe and profitable investments have yielded a very favorable interest return, and sound underwriting practices have kept the mortality among the Company's policyholders at a relatively low level. At the same time the tremendous growth of the Company's business has led to decreased overhead costs. Careful management and greater efficiency, made possible through the writing of both Ordinary and Industrial business by the same Agency Force, have been reflected in the Company's low expense rates. Of course, variations between companies in the cost of insurance at any given time are largely influenced by the policy adopted by any particular company in regard to contributions needed for the contingency reserve. Under present circumstances the Metropolitan has felt it necessary to make such contributions somewhat higher than in normal times, but the policy of the Company at all times is to keep policyholders' dividends as high as is consistent with the sound and conservative conduct of the business. This is well demonstrated by the way the Metropolitan has weathered the worst depression in our history. Over the 12-year period ending in 1941 the Metropolitan has not only fulfilled every contractual obligation but, in addition, in the interest of still greater safety has strengthened the basis of its reserves to the extent of more than $50,000,000, has increased its contingency reserve or surplus by more than $170,000,000, and has paid or credited to its policyholders more than $1,200,000,000 in dividends.

On the score of costs, the history of the Metropolitan records a continuing and gratifying effort to serve the American and Canadian people economically and effectively.

A Family
of Thirty
Million

‹‹❙ *Part* III ❙››

CHAPTER 11

1 Madison Avenue

TO THE GENERAL PUBLIC, the Home Office of the Metropolitan Life Insurance Company at 1 Madison Avenue represents a striking architectural landmark of New York and the headquarters of a leading public service institution. But to those within the organization the Home Office has significance greater than this. It is the very nerve center of the Company, where more than 15,000 men and women come to work each day. It is the focus of a network which embraces 1,100 District and local Offices in all parts of the United States and Canada, and nearly 28,000 Agents and office workers. At its center are the Chief Executives, under whose broad guidance function a variety of skills: administrative, medical, actuarial, legal, financial, architectural, sales directional, and an army of clerical and maintenance personnel. From this vast human switchboard run impulses which touch intimately the lives of 30,000,000 policyholders, who own 43,000,000 policies for $27,000,000,000 of insurance. Mighty figures these; figures to be read in terms of the human energy needed to keep in accurate and effective operation Life insurance on more than one fifth of the people of two great nations.

It is doubtful whether the early Officers even dreamed of anything remotely resembling such development. Certainly they were modest in their choice of the first Home Office in 1868. The Metropolitan had its first headquarters at 243 Broadway in a small office building, the kind you can see any time on any small-town Main Street. It boasted two offices on the second floor, a small rear room for President Dow, and a front room which housed the remainder of the Staff—Vice-President, Secretary, Cashier, Policy Clerk, and Office

Boy. Two years later a desire for better quarters led to a move to more spacious third-floor offices at 319 Broadway. Here were found modest accommodations for the few Officers and a clerical force which still numbered less than a dozen. A couple of desk drawers held all the files, and the complete assets fitted easily into a small leather dispatch case.

In 1876 the Company moved to its third home, a white marble building at Park Place and Church Street which towered seven stories high and had in addition a basement and subcellar. It already owned a leasehold on this building, and Vice-President Hegeman proudly noted that the Metropolitan "had given up boarding and gone into housekeeping of its own." Here, it was believed, the organization had found a permanent home. Definitely, the elegant proportions of the pillars and the fine plate-glass partitions, etched with the Company monogram, MLICO, seemed made for eternity. There were such modern improvements as steam heating, and a dignified elevator ran up and down a central shaft surrounded by a staircase. The elevator increased the grandeur of the place, but when the lively Home Office messenger boys were in a hurry they always walked up and down. The building included some 65 offices for rental in addition to the part reserved for the Company's own use. One of the distinguished tenants was the future President of the United States, Chester A. Arthur, who, as Collector of the Port of New York, paid a rent of $40 a month for his office. The first woman employee, Carrie Foster, started work here in 1877, to remain in the service of the Company for 52 years. Like so many other employees whom Mr. Knapp had imported from his Brooklyn Sunday School group, Miss Foster traveled by ferry across the East River and thence by horsecar to work. She took her place in the Record Division of the Ordinary Department with the male Bookkeepers, working at their high desks in alpaca coats and green eyeshades. Letters were handwritten and file copies were duplicated on a hand press. Carrie Foster's fine longhand was soon replaced, however, by the Company's first typewriter purchased in October 1877,

228

forerunner of the many thousands of time-saving office machines now owned by the Metropolitan.

Before it could enjoy its magnificence in the Park Place Building, the Company was first to pass through critical days. Its primary source of business, the Hildise Bund, was rapidly dwindling, and there was no other major source of replacement of its clientele. In the beginning of 1879 the Metropolitan was limping along with only 145 employees, including Clerks in the Office and men in the Field, and with no more than 10,000 policies in force. The hard-pressed young Company was barely holding its own.

But the launching of the Industrial business by Mr. Knapp was the decisive step which saved the Metropolitan and set it on the path of success. The floodgates opened to a huge rush of business. The number of employees increased so rapidly that by 1883, when young Fred Ecker entered the Company's employ at a salary of $4 per week, there were already more than 200 office workers in a number of separate Divisions. The few Officers, however, were still sharing many details of the work, and there was comparatively little differentiation of function. President Dow had started, and President Knapp continued, the duty of personally inspecting claims, until the later growth of the business necessitated a separate Claim Division. In the same fashion, the growth and increased demands on every Division necessitated new administrators, new files, new clerks in the Home Office. For every employee needed for the original Ordinary Department, many more were required for the Industrial, a business done in nickels and with voluminous weekly records. In 1889, ten years after its inception, the Industrial business in force amounted to $200,829,929 and the Company's assets were $8,597,468.77. These funds required careful investment, and to handle the increasing volume of mortgage loans a Real Estate Division was created. The growing Industrial Department was gradually to absorb, room by room, all the office space reserved for tenants, and before long, hundreds of its Clerks were housed in neighboring buildings.

Mr. Knapp was proudly aware that his undertaking had "arrived," that an organization of permanence and vast scope had been launched. Looking toward its future, he determined that the Company must acquire not only a larger home, but also one more fitting the position it had achieved. He urged a move to 23d Street and Madison Avenue, a residential section then considered far "uptown." At once there was an avalanche of conservative criticism. Yet his farsighted plan was carried out. The famous Philadelphia architect, Napoleon LeBrun, was engaged to design the building, and in May 1890 the Metropolitan broke ground for a seven-story structure in dignified early Renaissance style. Its next-door neighbor was the Madison Square Presbyterian Church. In a section of sober brownstone residences was soon to rise a new business center to serve an army of workers in offices and trades.

Mr. Knapp did not live to see the move to 1 Madison Avenue, the fruition of his dream, in 1893. Yet before he died in September 1891 he did know that he and his associates had launched a truly great Life Insurance Company. His dynamic business sense had laid out a general plan of Departments so effective that it has been maintained in its essence even to this day. He had likewise seen that there were competent men at the helm. As we have already pointed out, he had arranged for the appointment of Haley Fiske as Vice-President. James M. Craig was—and in fact had been almost from the beginning—the Actuary of the Company. He was the small man who made the big decisions affecting financial stability; yet he was no solitary scholar. On occasion he could speak before a body of Agents with all the ardor of a football coach and send them bubbling with zeal into the Field. Mr. Knapp had put George H. Gaston, who entered the Company in 1879, in charge of the Home Office and the Field Force as well. When the Industrial business brought over the 800 English Agents, it was Mr. Gaston's particular job to supervise their work and to acquaint them with American ways of business. As attention to Field activities absorbed more and more of Mr. Gaston's time, James S. Roberts came in to assist him and took over the supervision of the Home Office personnel, particularly that of the Industrial Audit Division.

Not only in office organization were foundations laid in this period. Seen from the perspective of the years, the spirit which was to characterize the future growth of the Company was already explicit. Mr. Knapp, the shrewd and thoroughly able executive, ran every detail of the business, signed every letter and every check, knew the capacities of every employee. Vice-President Hegeman, his kindly and understanding assistant, complemented him by stressing the human side of the Company and was responsible for the friendliness and loyalty which have always dominated the Staff. He early regarded Agents and Home Office workers as making common cause, rewarded their efforts, and established with them far more than the usual ties of business association. Together, these two men put their stamp on a Company which, while administered with efficiency, has never lost sight of the fact that its employees are human beings with a stake in the business.

So rapidly was the Company growing that the plans for the new Home Office on 23d Street, even during its construction, were changed to an 11-story office building, termed by the contemporary *Harper's Weekly* "A Mercantile Palace." The Company moved in with 650 Clerks, 400 of them women, in the spring of 1893, and by the summer the Home Office was completed. It was an imposing building, of white marble, richly and delicately carved and gracefully decorated. The main entrance led to the magnificent court and marble stairway, where the designers had lavished their finest materials. Its height and bulk of marble alone would have made it impressive; and to this the architects added a double staircase and a bronze and onyx balustrade rising in sweeping curves to a collonaded open loggia above. The Board of Directors' Room on the second floor was no less imposing—here, said a contemporary journal, was "a Rembrandt feeling, typical of conservativeness, which would invite calm deliberation on the part of its occupants." All of this was in keeping with the spirit of the times and reflected the opulence of a prosperous

FREDERICK H. ECKER

JOSEPH P. DAY

LANGDON P. MARVIN

NEWCOMB CARLTON

LEROY A. LINCOLN

THOMAS H. BECK

ROBERT V. FLEMING

WINTHROP W. ALDRICH

WILLIAM W. CROCKER

WILLIAM L. DeBOST

JEREMIAH MILBANK

D'ALTON CORRY COLEMAN

WALTER EWING HOPE

SAMUEL W. FORDYCE

GEORGE McANENY

AMORY HOUGHTON

ERNEST E. NORRIS

THOMAS H. McINNERNEY

(*Continued on next page*)

233

PHILIP D. REED

JUAN T. TRIPPE

WEBSTER B. TODD

JOHN I. DOWNEY

JAMES H. DOUGLAS, Jr.

CHARLES G. TAYLOR, Jr.

EDWARD H. BUTLER

organization. And as it was a stock company the stockholders, of course, paid the bill.

The beauty and comfort of the new home were worthy of the full-functioning organization which had emerged from the uncertainties of the early years, to a leading place in the insurance world. When the administration of President Hegeman began in 1891, Haley Fiske, then Vice-President, undertook to reorganize the Ordinary Department. His success in this branch brought in another rush of business and further expansion in the Home Office. By the end of 1894 the Company was doing business in 30 States and in Canada. It had in force 3,574,909 policies, to the amount of $441,-375,367. A contemporary report of the Insurance Superintendent of the State of New York cites some of the intricacies of the Industrial business of the Company, which "requires in its office management some four hundred different forms and blanks"—only an indication of the vast bookkeeping job. In a business which only a few years before had seen little differentiation of function, a whole new structure for the Industrial and for the Ordinary Departments had to be built up, with separate bookkeeping facilities, with underwriting units to deal with the evaluation of medical and occupational risks, and with leaders to vitalize the growing Home Office and Field Forces. In 1894 George B Woodward joined the Company as Secretary to direct this expanding force. For more than a quarter of a century Mr. Woodward managed the Home Office with skill and judgment. It was he also who devised the $5,000 Whole Life policy, which became a great factor in the growth of the Ordinary Department. Besides supervising the internal management, he was a vigorous force in building up the confidence of the Field Men in their ability to sell Ordinary insurance. The name of George B. Woodward has an honored place in the annals of the Home Office.

The new building was scarcely completed when increased business called for more space. Accordingly, in the spring of 1894, it was decided to erect a similar building on 24th Street, diagonally to the rear of the original structure. It was to be devoted entirely to Metropolitan offices—ample floor space, surely, for the needs of the Company for many years to come. Alas for their optimism, hardly were the Divisions settled in their new quarters in November 1895, when more room was needed and additional properties on the block were purchased. The increased office force necessitated by the resumption of Canadian business in 1894, by the organization of the Intermediate Branch in 1896, and of Special Class in 1899, filled the offices to overflowing. Through successive additions the Home Office soon covered all of the block, with the exception of the property at the corner of Madison Avenue and 24th Street—the home of the popular Madison Square Presbyterian Church where the celebrated Dr. Parkhurst thrilled his congregations with a vision of a righteous city. In 1906 Mr. Ecker, then Treasurer, arranged for the purchase of this plot and for the moving of the Church across the street. In April of that year the transfer was effected, and on the site of the Church the Company was able to complete its original Home Office building program. Here it was that the Metropolitan Tower, symbol of accomplishment, was erected.

The Tower Building, completed in 1909, was the tallest skyscraper of its time, a monument worthy of the Company which had grown to full stature. Designed by the Messrs. LeBrun, sons of the architect of the Main Building, the Tower stands 700 feet above the ground, one of the early experiments in the use of the steel column in skyscraper construction. In its general design and outline it resembles the famous Campanile of Saint Mark's in Venice, a beloved landmark of Mr. Hegeman. Its mammoth clock is visible far and wide over the city, and every quarter hour its four huge bells ring out a noble melody composed by Georg Friedrich Handel for the Cambridge University chimes. Above the 50th story and until the war blackout quenched it, the great electric beacon, "The Light That Never Fails," flashed for miles over New York City and the neighboring towns.

The Company was to continue to grow in the ensuing

The Home Office Today

years and further to change the landscape in Madison Square. In 1921 was completed the first building of the development on the adjoining block between 24th and 25th Streets. This building replaced the second Madison Square Church, in the erection of which Mr. Ecker had been so active. But the demands of the growing business were inexorable. Little by little the Company expanded its operations on the remainder of the block, a movement which is still in process. In 1931 it began the erection of a modern steel and glass structure, essentially a creation of our age and time, which was intended, when completed, to symbolize the Metropolitan of the future, as the Tower had expressed it in the earlier decades. The new building was designed by the distinguished architects D. Everett Waid and Harvey Wiley Corbett, and set a standard in construction for ideal working conditions, for structural permanence, and for clear beauty of design.

In December 1932 a modern fireproof building of 28 stories above, and four stories below, street level was opened to Home Office workers; and in 1940 the second unit of similar construction was completed. The construction of the final unit at the corner of 24th Street and Madison Avenue will be held in abeyance until the need develops. The first of the present units has a floor space of more than 23 acres; the second, of 11 acres. Each is lighted by more than an acre of plate-glass windows, constructed at such angles that every possible bit of sunlight strikes them. Above the ground floor are four floors of filing space for which daylight was not neces-sary and which have been treated architecturally as a mass of masonry. In these, and in the three floors below street level occupied by kitchens and dining rooms, indirect flu-orescent lighting which approximates daylight has been in-stalled. There are no interior courts, and such building services as elevators, stairways, washrooms, and locker space are massed in the center of the structure to leave the outer areas free for working space. With the special requirements of a large working staff in mind, special elevators and esca-lators and pneumatic tube communications have been devised.

The buildings are air-conditioned throughout and sound-proofed in the working areas. A gymnasium for employees occupies the top story of the first "new" unit. Practically the only wood in the buildings is the floor of the gymnasium, and even this is of fireproofed maple. Thus is being completed a building program begun 53 years ago. Who shall say what future needs are still to be met?

As we have pointed out, this present Metropolitan Home Office is the coordinating mechanism and clearing house for the multitude of Company operations. Here is performed virtually every function of the business except selling and personally servicing the multitude of insurance policies. From this headquarters, 12,000 new contracts are issued each working day, covering $8,000,000 of insurance; $2,000,000 is paid out daily to policyholders or beneficiaries, and $1,000,000 is invested. It is a highly integrated piece of machinery, vast and complex. Yet, despite its size, it has much the same basic simplicity which in earlier decades characterized the anatomy of the Home Office. Let us see something of this organization and how responsive it really is to the needs of the Company's large number of policyholders.

At the center of the Home Office administration is the Board of Directors, elected by the policyholders and representing them as the fountainhead of all authority. In them is vested the ultimate control of Company management. The Board, composed of 25 leaders of wide knowledge and high achievement in a variety of business fields, operates as a whole and in six standing committees: Finance, Real Estate, Welfare, Insurance and Agency, Home Office, and Auditing. They meet at regular intervals, some as often as once a week, and pass upon important steps in the daily management of the Company's affairs. Immediately responsible to the Board are the Officers who conduct the various branches of the business. From the Chairman of the Board, through the President, the various Vice-Presidents, and other senior and junior Officers, passes authority over a multitude of functions, which in their aggregate represent the work of the Home Office.

Obviously, it would be tedious to give an itemized review of the myriads of sections handling the detail incidental to this huge organization. Let us, rather, consider a few items which concern themselves with the Life insurance business in its essence. With no pretense of a complete tour, let us make a sample inspection of a few key spots concerned with the fundamentals of policy production and maintenance.

The applications for policies come in by thousands each week and are referred, according to their type, to either the Industrial Department, to the Ordinary, to the Group, or to the Personal Accident and Health Department. The Metropolitan is really four companies in one, since all the appropriate charges are allocated to the respective Departments. The policyholder, therefore, pays the costs only on the specific type of insurance he owns. On the other hand, the cost of the insurance is lowered through the pooling of the services of highly trained experts who supervise activities for all these Departments.

When, for example, an Ordinary application is received, it is checked in the Application Division with the Agent's and Medical Examiner's reports. It reaches next the underwriting personnel, both medical and lay, who evaluate the information received and determine whether the applicant meets the requirements of the Company as to health, occupation, moral, and financial status. The vast majority of applications—seven out of eight—are approved outright; a small proportion are declined, and others, where there are physical impairments or insurable hazards of occupation, are issued on a substandard basis. For those which meet the requirements, the Policy Division next carries on the task of examining, briefing, and serial numbering the application for purposes of identification. Records of the applications are made for the Actuarial and Auditing Divisions and for Home or District Office files; and a battery of photostat machines make a complete camera record of the application at the rate of one every nine seconds. Now the actual policy is born; personal data are typed and insurance values for the appropriate age are printed in; and after a final comparison is made with facts given in the original application, the completed policy is sent to the Agent, for delivery to the insured.

To prepare and maintain all the necessary records in the Ordinary Department requires a large organization and many contacts with the policyholder over the years. At regular intervals notices must be sent that premiums are due, and their payments recorded. The policyholder may change his beneficiary or his address. He may elect a certain type of instalment benefit for his beneficiary in the event of his death, so that funds continue to be handled by the Company; or he may wish to borrow money on his policy. Each of these functions calls for a sizable Section with a large staff of workers. The records of these activities involving many millions of people call for a large number of working Sections, countless figures, and miles of filing cases. Fifty years ago the Ordinary Department shared a single room with other Divisions. Today, it covers more than seven acres of the Home Office buildings and employs nearly 4,000 workers.

It is hardly necessary to outline the procedures in the issuance and servicing of policies by the other Divisions of the Company. Suffice it to say that similar processes are followed although, in the nature of the case, there are differences in detail in writing policies for smaller amounts.

What assurance has the policyholder that at some future date—perhaps 50 years hence—the Metropolitan will faithfully fulfill its contract? It is a vast trust he has put in the Company—yet one which has been justified by an organization which for 75 years has paid every obligation in full. His policy is essentially a long-term contract and one which requires the long-range point of view and the careful computations of the Actuarial Division. Let us take a look into this Division, the "balance wheel" of the Company, which must study, on the basis of developing experience, mortality rates, interest earnings, and other determining factors. It is here that information is gathered as to the current status of the Company, and it is here that the greatest part of the volumi nous Annual Statement is prepared, as required by the laws of the 48 States, the District of Columbia, and the Dominion of Canada. It is here also that new policies are devised, that studies are made of the actual experience which provides the yardstick for determining premium rates and figuring divisible surplus to be paid back to policyholders in the form of dividends. A tremendously important Division, this, which 70 years ago needed the services of only two people and now has a staff of more than 1,100.

Only the Government of the United States exceeds the Company in the number of its financial transactions. In the course of a year a billion dollars, more or less, is received. Every item is verified before it is entered into the financial report; every penny is recorded and accounted for. There are no loose ends in this business. The vast funds which come into the Company involve the investment of $1,000,000 a day. The broad supervision of investments is still under Mr. Ecker. Responsible to him are the Treasurer, Harry C. Hagerty, who handles all security investments; the Comptroller, William S. Norton, who is charged with the responsibility of investing in and controlling mortgages on city properties and Company-owned real estate; and Glenn E. Rogers, who controls farm mortgage loan investments. There is, furthermore, a staff under George Gove, who is charged with the responsibility of supervision and operation of the Housing Projects, of which Parkchester is the outstanding example. Each of these executives is aided by specialists of wide business and investment experience.

The protection of the Company's real estate and security investments, tax problems, claims and their occasional litigation, compliance with the insurance laws of the several States, preparation of policy forms and other Company forms, all involve a host of legal questions. In a company the size of the Metropolitan, these call for a large Law Division. This occupies almost the entire fifth floor of the Main Building, where a staff of about 50 lawyers and many other personnel guide the Company's affairs from the legal standpoint. On this floor an excellent law library has been collected which contains complete sets of reports, statutes, and legal texts. The Law Division is under the direction of General Counsel Frederic G. Dunham and General Counsel Harry Cole Bates.

The Metropolitan has always made particular efforts to have the public understand how it functions and what it is trying to accomplish. Good public relations are vital to a successful Life insurance business, whose marketing is dependent upon the confidence of prospective purchasers of policies. The Company from the first gained the respect of the community, a respect which has continued to grow, until today two nations are aware of its integrity and reputation for public service. The man on the street knows that it has served his family and friends for three generations. The public appreciates the part that the Metropolitan's health education work has played in preventing sickness and accidents and in lengthening life. This work is carried on at the Home Office by the Welfare Division and the Statistical Bureau. Besides research and practical health work described in Chapter 20, these Divisions issue health booklets, exhibits, and films. If one sailed the seven seas, one would probably find Metropolitan health booklets in the most distant ports of call.

The Company places extensive advertising in national magazines with a circulation of 40,000,000 copies. But it does not follow the usual advertising patterns—to sell something. Rather, the Metropolitan advertisements have been in the nature of reports of services rendered, including one series which informed the public how a Life insurance company operates; and another on vital aspects of welfare and public health education. This advertising program is under the direction of Third Vice-President James L. Madden. To provide its customers and the public with further information about its activities, a magazine, *The Metropolitan*, has been available since 1871. Each year the Company issues a report to its policyholders covering its operations and its financial condition. The Statistical Bureau publishes a monthly *Bulletin* of informative data growing out of the Company's mortality

JAMES L. MADDEN
Third Vice-President

and morbidity experience, a publication so extensively quoted by the press that it has been estimated that it continuously reaches a wider audience than any best seller.

With a Home Office of this size has come the responsibility for its physical upkeep and for the welfare of its huge working staff. Hence a Maintenance Force of 2,516 people, which includes such a wide range of occupations as a clock mechanic, a dietician, electricians, painters, carpenters, and even stone-masons. Hence a Supply Department which is a vast sta-tionery store, and a tailor shop where 1,898 uniforms are kept in good condition. The Metropolitan Home Office houses the biggest first-class private postoffice in the world, which re-ceives a total of more than 600,000 pieces of mail each working day; a carpentry shop, which keeps everything from staircases to file boxes in tiptop working order, and among its many jobs, repairs some 300 office chairs every week; and a Standardiza-tion Laboratory, which makes efficiency tests of all materials used by the Supply Department, the Welfare Division, and the Field Offices. The volume of the Company's publications necessitated the building of a well-equipped printing plant, first on 24th Street and later in Long Island City, where 527 people are now employed. A special storehouse for Company records which have overflowed from the Home Office files is maintained in Bronxville, New York. The manifold operations of the Home Office buildings are directed by Secretary James P. Bradley, whose services in the Company cover a span of 47 years and have embraced every phase of management both in the Field and at 1 Madison Avenue.

But more than beautiful buildings, more even than a numerically large working force, the Home Office represents a point of view in action. It is not only an effective workshop, it is a happy workshop. A friendliness permeates its every Division, where people have learned to work together with solidarity and pride in their contribution. The Home Office employees feel that they are part and parcel of the Company— a team working in joint effort with their brothers in the Field. They are conscious of their identity, and proud of their importance as a group. The spirit which guides their working hours is no chance happening. It has been nurtured through the years, reflecting the experience of thousands of men and women. The employees like it here. And from early days they have remained as closely knit and as devoted a group as ever made up a working community.

The Metropolitan early established and has gradually increased its reputation for being "a good Company to work for." It offers its employees good pay and opportunity for advancement, amid healthful conditions. It offers more than the usual job of uncertain tenure; here employees find a career which lasts for their lifetime, and security after retirement. A variety of facilities are offered for recreation and study. Employees have access to one of the most comprehensive business libraries in the world, containing 100,000 volumes, including not only books, pamphlets and reports for research, but also recreational reading for circulation. In addition there

JAMES P. BRADLEY
Secretary

is a fully equipped gymnasium; a dental clinic; free umbrellas when it rains; schools in which useful arts and business skills are taught; and a wide range of musical, athletic, and social organizations for after-hours pleasure.

The early welfare measures for employees gave evidence of unusual vision at a time when such ideas were radical indeed. As early as 1893, Home Office Clerks were furnished with a suitable place in which to eat their lunches, and hot tea and coffee were provided; and since 1908 the Company has served complete, to all employees, wholesome lunches without charge. Some idea of the job done by this largest single industrial cafeteria in America may be gleaned from the following: more than 900 twelve-inch pies are baked for one day's luncheon; six mammoth ovens each roast 1,512 pounds of beef at one time; 950,000 quarts of ice cream are served each year. But there are no statistics to tell the story of relaxed and happy lunchtimes in 18 pleasant cafeterias, of

246

palatable and nourishing food available to all employees at no cost to them.

Provision for annual medical examination of all Home Office employees was first made in 1914. These examinations and the service of the Medical Rest Rooms, of the Dental Clinic, of the Nursing Service, and of the Mount McGregor Sanatorium, have had far-reaching effects on the health and well-being of the Staff. These activities on behalf of employees will be discussed more fully in Chapter 19.

As the volume of business grew and the number of employees increased, there was created a need for a Personnel Division. In the early days Mr. Knapp, and later Mr. Gaston and Mr. Roberts, were responsible for the Home Office workers; they engaged new employees and dealt with the problems of the Staff. But later each Division more or less ran its own employment service, with the result that a Clerk in one Department might be earning less than one doing similar work in another. Kindness and good will toward the workers there was in plenty; but nobody had thought through the situation and there was definite need for an organized method of translating this good will into a system of appointment, training, compensation, and advancement. Accordingly, in 1919, the Company established its Personnel Division, with William F. Dobbins in charge. At his retirement in 1933 he was succeeded by William J. Harper. On Mr. Harper's death in December 1942, Herbert L. Rhoades was elected Personnel Officer.

This Division has devoted increasing care to the selection of better-than-average workers and to the placement of the right persons in the right jobs. The employment procedure includes, besides a friendly preliminary interview, completion of a detailed application form, a clerical aptitude test, a thorough medical examination, and a check of all school and employment references. Except for a small number of professional positions, the Company endeavors to fill its hundreds of diversified jobs by promotion from its own ranks. Hence, the Personnel Division must determine not only whether an applicant will make a good Messenger, Typist, or File Clerk; but it must also select, by the most modern techniques, an employee fitted by native intelligence, education, and personality eventually to become a good Team Head, Section Head, or Division Manager. From the very beginning, promotion on the basis of merit has been a cardinal policy. Most of the present Officers came into the Company in beginner's positions either in the Home Office or Field, and have climbed long ladders of increasing responsibility. For all employees, ascent to better jobs is possible; they are constantly encouraged to climb to the next rung. Future Officers of the Metropolitan are undoubtedly to be found today among the busy rows of record-keepers or among the Agency forces.

In order to fix equal pay for equal work and to provide lines of advancement for each employee, the Personnel Division has classified all positions according to the degree of skill required, starting with Grade 1 for routine inter-Office messenger work, and ascending to Grade 27 for certain Assistant Division Managers, and has fixed a basic salary for each. The salaries of Home Office employees compare more than favorably with those paid by other organizations for similar work. The Company's welfare work for employees is in addition to salaries, not a substitute for them. Mr. Ecker has seen the Home Office pay roll grow from a few thousand dollars when he entered the Company in 1883, to more than $500,000 a week today. The Company provides its clerical employees with vacations of from two to four weeks, depending upon length of service.

The Metropolitan's practice of promoting from within its ranks has encouraged employees to supplement "on the job training" with independent study after hours. The Company itself offers courses to increase business skills, including one in the fundamental principles and practices of Life insurance, which hundreds of employees have completed. A two-year course in business English, and others in stenography, typewriting, dictaphone, comptometer, and key-punch machine operation are offered to those who show aptitude in these fields. Outside the Company, the most important Life insurance course available to Metropolitan employees is the two-year study sponsored by the Insurance Society of New York, which has been taken by more than 1,000 Home Office employees in the past 15 years. Another offered by the Life Office Management Association Institute covers advanced principles and practices of Life insurance, and since 1936 more than 200 Home Office employees sat for one or more of these examinations. Special courses in real estate, accounting, statistics, and business economics have been sponsored by the Company at Columbia University, New York University, City College, and other accredited colleges in New York for employees who show special abilities. It is significant that many young men who have become leaders of their Sections and eventually Officers of the Company have been enabled to rise through the ranks because of the training which the Company has afforded them.

The Company also takes pride in training technicians for its own highly specialized positions. Classes are held each year from October to May to prepare for the difficult examinations in nine parts given jointly by the Actuarial Society of America and the American Institute of Actuaries. Final acceptance in these societies grants an honored professional status—for these actuaries are the scientists of the insurance business. Of the total national membership of about 800 in the Actuarial Society, the Metropolitan alone accounts for one ninth of the entire group. There are 39 who have attained the status of Associate, and 52 (of whom 19 are Officers of the Company) who have attained Fellowship in one or more of the recognized actuarial bodies.

The Company has always stressed the fact that its employees were more than workers—that they were active citizens, with minds and interests of their own. These interests have been reflected in the formation of recreational clubs which develop latent talents and put leisure hours to happy uses. Of these groups, the Athletic Association, with a membership of 2,100, is the oldest and most popular. A Men's

Glee Club and Women's Choral Society and the Metropolitan Life Insurance Company Band, trained by a professional director and accompanist paid for by the Company, give excellent concerts in the Home Office, and at Mount McGregor for patients at the Company Sanatorium. Employees have likewise shown their interest in amateur theatricals, in photography, engineering, and stamp collecting, through the formation of clubs devoted to these activities. The Metropolitan Post of the American Legion, with a membership of 430, does welfare work for disabled veterans, both in and outside of Government hospitals. Metropolitan workers are congenial people, who enjoy being together in work hours and in leisure hours as well. Thus there are frequent dinners and celebrations given by these groups; all are marked by the idiom of good fellowship, by the democratic point of view, by something intangible yet real, known as the spirit of the Home Office. Here Officers and Clerks constitute one fraternity.

In its complexity the Home Office represents a small city and like a city, it has its daily and monthly "Press." The *Daily Bulletin*, a one-sheet paper published since 1905, contains announcements of Field changes and of Home Office activities. A monthly magazine, *The Home Office*, with a circulation today well in excess of 19,000, is a more human document, profusely illustrated with photos and drawings of people, and with plenty of pleasant local news about the activities of Metropolitan "citizens." Similar monthly magazines, *The Pacific Coaster* and *The Northern Star*, are issued by the Pacific Coast and Canadian Head Offices.

Nor does the Metropolitan's care of its employees cease when old age necessitates their retirement. From the paternalistic allowance of the early days has come the well-rounded cooperative Insurance and Retirement Program of today. In a recent speech, Mr. Ecker made the following comment: "The retirement program takes care of all hazards of life except unemployment—and once with the Metropolitan, there is no unemployment." And indeed, through the worker's own provision on the one hand and the Company's cooperative assistance on the other, every permanent employee is assured a good measure of economic security for his old age. A Group insurance contract, as we have seen, provides a complete circle of protection in one "package," making available Life insurance benefits, temporary and permanent disability benefits, hospital and surgical benefits (available also to employees' dependents), and definitely established retirement annuities that accrue during the period of service to provide, after retirement, a life income proportionate to earnings and length of service. Along with the certainty of employment which capable performance assures, the Metropolitan employee has real security during working days and after retirement.

These Metropolitan "citizens" are highly conscious of their responsibilities to the Nation at war. Home Office employees have pledged more than 10 percent of their earnings to buy United States War Bonds—a heartening demonstration of the patriotism of this body of Metropolitan men and women. Home Office men have helped form a Company in the New York City Patrol Corps which will guard against wartime destruction. More than a thousand Home Office employees have passed the Red Cross first-aid examinations. In fact, in case of an air raid, the Metropolitan's two square blocks of buildings are well defended, both from the human and material standpoint. More than 3,000 Home Office employees have been trained to special air-raid emergency roles. Safety devices have been installed literally from top to bottom to safeguard the buildings and records, and sandbags, steel, and cement have been used freely to reinforce valuable files and safes, and to create designed areas of safety. Most significant in the Company's war effort is the fact that there are well over 3,000 names of men and women on the "Roll of Honor." This stands in the Arcade of the Main Building for those in the Home Office and Field who have joined the country's armed forces.

The employee welfare activities have resulted in increased efficiency of administration, proving the greater effectiveness of an organization of well-adjusted people. The increase in

The Honor Roll

the number of employees and of the pay roll through the years falls far short of paralleling the tremendous increase in business. There is definite correlation between the size of a company and its economy of operation. While the number of Clerks increased about 300 percent during the past quarter of a century, the amount of insurance in force has increased by more than 700 percent. Thus, due to an increasingly effective division of the work and standardization of methods in management, and due to coordination of functions on a large scale, the cost of Home Office administration to the policyholder has greatly decreased. An important feature has been the close cooperation of the various Officers in Home Office management. A monthly meeting of the President and the Senior Officers has served to acquaint each with the other's problems and to bring the operations of the Home Office and Field into closer alignment.

Technology has played its part in improving Home Office operations. From the beginning the Metropolitan has been receptive to new ideas and anxious to use the labor-saving machines which science has produced. In 1907 the Company retained a distinguished inventor, who right in the Home Office designed and built the first alphabetical tabulator. Today hundreds of humanlike machines in the Home Office do many jobs which, if performed by hand, would entail endless clerical effort and expense. Such "robots" as the electric bookkeeping and accounting machines work at the rate of 150 cards per minute, others sort any group of information desired, and do accurate addition, subtraction, and multiplication—"mechanical men" who help living men to do a better job. But every consideration has been given to introducing mechanical aids at an orderly pace, and thus avoiding technological displacement of the Company's workers.

A progressive and efficient approach to the problem of management, and a point of view toward employees which the Appellate Division of the Supreme Court of New York, Third Department, has seen fit to call "enlightened," have resulted in great benefits to the policyholders themselves. For let us make no mistake: the Metropolitan is first and foremost a successful and intelligently managed business, responsible to its owners, the policyholders. Its activities for the well-being of employees have had practical results in terms of low turnover, of workers who learn to do their jobs thoroughly, of growing efficiency, and of development of specialized skills. In its essentials, Life insurance deals with security, with the health and well-being of citizens—and it has seemed logical to the Company to begin with its own citizens.

The friendliness which permeates the shop is reflected in the large number of people who have made Home Office work a life career. The dismissal of an employee is very rare, and in the stormy decade of the depression years the Company not only let no one go for want of work, but actually increased its staff. Still in the employ of the Company in 1942 were more than 100 men and women who were working there at the opening of the century. Of the present personnel of the Home Office more than 6,000 have been with the

Company over 10 years and more than 2,300 over 20 years. The Home Office Veterans, whose membership of today includes all employees who have seen 20 years of active service with the Company, is a visible symbol of the fellow-ship which has always existed. This organization makes no distinction between Officers and Clerks, between simple abilities and high skills; it is a group of men and women who feel solidarity because they have grown up together and worked in a common project. Their spontaneous devotion has significance in summing up the fairness and the humanity which has made 1 Madison Avenue a good place in which to work.

The 75 years since President James Richardson Dow and his associates founded the Metropolitan have brought change to the Home Office. The Company has progressed from two dingy rooms to impressive buildings which take up two entire city blocks. The five original employees have grown to more than 15,000 men and women. From a small stock company, it has become the largest financial corporation in the world, mutually owned by 30,000,000 persons — its policyholders. Yet certain fundamentals have survived: a sound business organization and an integrity of operation; a desire to serve the security and the health needs of the community; a congenial and kindly point of view toward the successive generations of employees; a pride, on their part, in the work of their hands, in the living organism which they have helped to build. For through the contribution of each, in the vast sequence of operations, a great insurance company has emerged.

CHAPTER 12

The Field Force

IF THE AMERICAN PEOPLE have enjoyed a greater measure of security through Life insurance than have the people of other countries, it is largely because of the agency system of operation, which had its origin and development in this country. The agent is the key figure in the American Life insurance business. It is through his efforts that the companies come in contact with their policyholders and serve them. Through his activities one half of our population has acquired the security of insurance, and an even greater proportion are its beneficiaries. A century of experience has repeatedly demonstrated that the services of the agent are indispensable; that wherever the business has attempted to operate without this personal intermediary between public and company, the result has been either a very small amount of protection sold, or outright failure. The American Life insurance agent has carried the gospel of thrift to every corner of our land. He has been the greatest single educational force in the business. In canvassing and in advising, he instructs huge numbers of people regarding the variety of insurance plans and programs available and their many uses. The $140,000,000,000 of Life insurance now in force in the United States and Canada are a monument to the American Life insurance agent, and a fine tribute to his effective ministration.

This is particularly true of the Metropolitan Agent. Throughout the history of the Company he has devoted the bulk of his efforts to the great mass of the American population —the wage-earners whose Life insurance needs were long neglected. Pioneering has become a tradition with him. Two generations ago he blazed a trail to bring the benefits of Indus-

255

trial insurance to large sections of our people. A decade later he became one of the first to open the door of Ordinary insurance to wage-earners, and later pioneered in making this form of protection available to those who could afford as little as $500 of Life insurance, to those whose health was impaired, and to those who worked at hazardous occupations—in other words, to the people who needed it most. It can truly be said that the Metropolitan Agent is as popular in the town as the family doctor.

He calls regularly at the homes of his families to receive premiums, and among his many services, credits annual dividends on Industrial policies, completes claim forms, delivers checks, advises. These frequent visits and his knowledge of family affairs bring him into a warm, personal relationship with his policyholders and make it easy for him to sense their needs and to advise changes in the insurance program as circumstances require, as well as to stimulate interest in additional Life insurance. But the Metropolitan Agent certainly does not conceive of his job as limited to selling and servicing Life insurance; he has assumed some of the duties of the social worker in the broadest sense of the term. For the past third of a century, since the inauguration of the Company's welfare program, he has actively participated in furthering the health and well-being of his policyholders and of the community in general. The conception of Life insurance not merely as a business but as a social institution has become firmly rooted in the entire Field Force.

We have already given sufficient consideration in Chapter 2 to the organization of the Field Force prior to 1879, when the Company was engaged exclusively in writing Ordinary business. It is clear from the old records that President Knapp and Vice-President Hegeman had constructive and progressive ideas with regard to sales promotion and the responsibilities and services of Agents. The Executives were aware that much of the success and the character of the business depended upon their sending out intelligent, earnest representatives. The fact is, however, that because of the keen competition and the prevailing high rates of commission, the desire to build an adequate and competent Field Force remained a pious hope rather than a reality. Such Agents as were connected with the Company during this period were mostly part-time men who sold Life insurance as a side line. The bulk of the business written in the first 11 years of the Company's existence, as we have noted in earlier chapters, was on the lives of the members of a German-speaking society. When the economic depression of the 70's caused this group to disintegrate, the business of the Metropolitan rapidly diminished, and by 1879 the Company was on the brink of disaster. It was then that the decision was finally made to break with tradition and to enter the field of Industrial insurance. On November 17, 1879, the first Industrial policy was issued on the life of President Knapp, and the second on the life of his associate, Mr. Hegeman.

The history of the present Metropolitan Field Force begins essentially with the establishment of the Industrial Department and, perhaps better than any other single item, it tells the story of the Company itself. There is not much information available from existing records with regard to the first Industrial Agents—who they were; where they came from. We do know, however, that within a few weeks after the issue of its first Industrial policy—i.e., by the end of 1879—the Company had 124 Agents and seven District Superintendents in the Field. Some of these men had been with the Company in the earlier days. We can trace, for example, the career of John A. Megargee, who had been an Ordinary Agent in 1875, and was transferred to the Industrial Department in November 1879. Four years later we find him Superintendent in a new District in New York City. A number of new Agents were recruited through newspaper advertisements which offered "Steady employment to industrious men; previous experience not necessary. Intelligence and energy all that is essential." In the main, the men employed were inexperienced and did not understand the intricacies of the business they were employed in. In the first week only five

Agents were successful in turning in any applications for Industrial insurance.

It was clear that the new business could progress only on the basis of a sizable and effective Agency Force. The Officers had learned that lesson thoroughly in their study of the operations of the Prudential of London. There was no doubt that the door-to-door canvassing for insurance and the receipt of premiums in the homes of policyholders necessitated an elaborate system of organization as well as the services of a large number of men. The contract made with Brice Collard provided that supply of experienced Industrial Agents. The first group sailed from England on April 3, 1880. For the next few years Mr. Collard traveled back and forth across the Atlantic, continuing his recruiting. By the middle of 1885 about 800 men had been transferred to the United States with some 1,200 of their dependents, making a total migration of 2,000 people. The British contingent gave immediate impetus to the business. They were put to work opening new offices, recruiting new Agents and training them in the technique of canvassing and servicing Industrial insurance. A considerable proportion of those who ventured across the ocean served as Deputy Superintendents, some became Superintendents, and a few served as Agents.

Once the business got under way the Company moved with vigor, and the result was prodigious growth in the Field organization. Several of the pioneers established remarkable records as producers and as trainers of men. In little more than a year, at the end of 1880, the Field Force numbered 750, and only two years later there were 1,167 men to push the new enterprise. The first District Offices were located in the industrial centers of population. Within the next five years offices had been opened at key points in 17 States and the District of Columbia. In November 1885, operations were extended to the Dominion of Canada with the establishment of what was called the Toronto East Office. The momentum of these Field operations naturally carried with it mounting new business. Thus, in the newly established District in

Detroit, at the end of two months Superintendent Wyatt had five Assistants and 29 Agents. In little more than three years the Agents were receiving weekly premiums on Industrial insurance with a face value of close to $35,000,000. During the early months of 1886 the $100,000,000 mark of insurance in force was passed. These figures bear testimony to the wisdom of the decision to pioneer in the field of Industrial insurance and to set the business in motion with experienced men brought from England.

The organization of the Field was broadly patterned after that of the Prudential of London. The country was divided into Territories, which in turn were subdivided into Districts. The Districts were broken down into subsections of concentrated city blocks known as debits, each of which was assigned to an Agent. With the importation of the debit system into Life insurance, a new and revolutionary mechanism of service to the public was introduced. This was the concept of continuous contact, as against the older practice of Ordinary Agents, whose service usually ended with the placing of the policy. According to the new pattern of operation, the Agent personally received premiums each week and served the insured throughout the life of the contract. This debit system in time proved to be of real usefulness and efficiency in carrying Life insurance to the many millions who had never before had access to its benefits.

The new plan was likewise a boon to the man in the Field. His debit provided him with what amounted to an automatic prospecting system, through which he came in contact with all members of the family and with their friends and neighbors. Moreover, commission on collections assured the Agent some income from the very beginning. Of lasting importance was the fact that this setup required Agents to devote full time to their business. A greater responsibility to policyholders was felt—interest not only to write business but to keep existing insurance in force. There is little doubt that bringing over the debit system and adapting it to American conditions was fundamental to the success of the Industrial business.

The progressive growth of the Metropolitan in the Field was basically the multiplication and expansion of individual debits.

Although the blueprint for the new Agency organization was imported from England, the building of a functioning Field Force suited to the American people was a task of great magnitude. The first years were turbulent ones, marked by considerable experimentation, and trial and error. At the beginning many Agents, instead of working their own debits intensively, canvassed for business wherever they thought it was to be had. This scattered effort consumed unnecessary time and energy, caused considerable friction, and was con-trary to the first principle of the debit system: concentration. To obviate this difficulty, Agents were instructed to work within the area assigned to them. Major stress was also placed on canvassing as the most important method of building the business. An experiment was tried with traveling Agents, who were exclusively canvassers. These experienced men moved quickly through a new District, placing policies where they could; and the business they built up served as a nucleus for a new debit which was turned over to a regular Agent. Results from this method were unsatisfactory, however, and it was soon discontinued.

The system of compensating the men in the Field followed to the letter the practice of the Prudential of London. It is interesting to note that when the Prudential Insurance Com-pany of America began business, it experimented with a com-mission schedule patterned after that used in Ordinary insur-ance—the first-year commission 15 percent, and renewals 10 percent. Within a month this plan gave way to a variation of the system used by the Prudential of London, but at the end of one year even this scheme was abandoned, and com-pensation was arranged on exactly the same basis as in the London company.

The Metropolitan followed the English practice from the. beginning. In addition to a percentage of the amount of Industrial premiums collected each week, the Company's Agents received a special salary computed on the amount of the weekly premium on policies written. Deputy Superintendents received a weekly salary of $15 and an additional amount based upon the increase in the business of their District. Although Superintendents received a somewhat smaller salary than the Deputies—$11.54 a week—their special salary based on increase in business was considerably higher. Detailed information regarding the compensation of the Field Force in the early 80's is meager, but we do know that the earnings of the average Agent were very modest. Of course, the whole scale of living at that time was based on lower costs than at present, yet most of the men were earning less than $10 a week. There were, however, a few notable exceptions. In 1885 the Company issued a recruiting poster showing that four leading Agents had earned from $15.85 to $25.89 a week in their very first year. After four years these men averaged about $65 a week. They were, however, outstanding Agents, and very few men even approached these earnings.

The average remuneration was hardly enough to win men of high caliber. Moreover, selling Life insurance was not considered much of a career at that time, and was used by many as a stopgap until they found other employment. As a result, the Agency Force was in constant flux. The turnover of men in the Field in the early 80's ran to about 300 percent, which meant that the average Agent remained on his job only about four months. This short tenure at best permitted most of the men to absorb only a few rudiments. The common practice was to engage as many Agents as possible, give them a few demonstrations in canvassing, and hope that they would pick up the rest by experience. There were, of course, men of exceptional ability who persevered and made their mark in the Company's history. But, for the most part, the men were of very limited education and ability. The Superintendent exercised little if any selection in picking his Staff, and almost anybody who applied was set to work with but a smattering of instruction. Obviously, such Agents could render little more than perfunctory service. It is true that Mr. Knapp repeatedly urged Superintendents to remedy this situation, to get qualified men and give them more adequate training. But it was many years before this wish was translated into practice.

Despite these difficulties, the Agency Force continued to grow rapidly, as did the amount of insurance it wrote. By the end of 1891 the Metropolitan had the largest Field Force of any Life insurance company in the United States, consisting of more than 4,200 Agents, working under the guidance and direction of about 100 District Superintendents and almost 600 Deputy Superintendents. Only 12 years after the beginning of the business, a network of offices had been opened in all the principal centers of population east of the Mississippi and north of the Mason-Dixon line. The Metropolitan Agent, Collection Book in hand, had become a familiar figure to millions of people in the United States and Canada. When the year 1891 came to a close, there were in force more than 2,250,000 Industrial policies for insurance totaling more than $250,000,000. The Industrial Department had arrived.

Once this branch had become established and the machinery for its operation was well in motion, Mr. Fiske decided to reenter the field of Ordinary insurance. The decision to utilize the Industrial Agents for this venture reflected the faith of the Company's Executives in the potential capabilities of their Field Force. This was a bold and courageous step. As Mr. James M. Craig, in an earlier history of the Company, put it, "The great bulk of the Field Force was like an undrilled army in the Ordinary Department." The prevailing opinion of the insurance world was that the experiment was predestined for disaster, although the Prudential of London had for some years been claiming success in the development of its Ordinary business with Industrial Agents. Mr. Fiske's enterprise in 1892 was as great a departure for the Metropolitan as had been the Industrial experiment some 12 years earlier. The Company was again blazing a trail in bringing Ordinary insurance to families of middle and lower incomes. The Agents this time, however, enjoyed the advantage of having a debit in which they already knew their clientele.

The major problem was how to equip this "undrilled army" for its new tasks. It had become obvious that selling Life insurance was a skill which could and should be taught. With the revitalizing of the Ordinary Department, the Home Office for the first time shared with Superintendents the responsibility for such teaching. One of the first steps was the organization, in the latter part of 1893, of a staff of Special Agents whose function it was to instruct the Industrial Agents in the principles and practices of Ordinary business. Even earlier, Major B. R. Corwin had anticipated the work of these Special Agents, and after the Ordinary Department had been revived he continued the training of the Field Force. He and the other Special Agents taught the Field-Men how to canvass effectively, how to conduct a sales interview, how to meet competition, and through this knowledge built up in the men a new spirit of self-reliance. The Special Agents were essentially salesmen-demonstrators, carrying on their training program largely by personal assistance and daily help in the Field. No text or course of study was provided, and nothing akin to an organized educational program was available. The work of the Special Agents was nevertheless productive. Although the years 1892 and 1893 yielded little Ordinary business, in the following year the Agents began to show the effect of these efforts to improve their knowledge and technique. Business continued to improve, and by 1896 the Ordinary writings averaged about $1,800 annually per man, and by 1900 the Agents were producing $4,666 annually per man. From that date onward the story has been one of continuous and rapid increase. It took some time for Agents to catch on, but once they did, the fertile field of their debit, when properly worked, served to produce a sizable amount of good Ordinary business.

The recognition by the Home Office that Field training was in part a function of its Agency management, in no wise diminished the responsibilities of individual Superintendents and their Deputies, who continued their efforts to increase the proficiency of their own Staffs. It took 14 years, however, before the rank and file of Field-Men were given direct contractual recognition in Ordinary business by the Company. At the beginning the Superintendent in each Branch Office was the only Ordinary representative recognized by the Company. While the men under his jurisdiction were encouraged to sell Ordinary insurance, only the Superintendent submitted applications and received commissions. He, in turn, compensated the men who wrote the business. On January 1, 1906, this method was discontinued and a completely new system instituted, which in its essentials is in operation to this day. The only barrier that had stood between the Agent and the Company was broken down. Under the new arrangement each Agent had transferred to his account, as his Ordinary debit, all Ordinary policies which at any time had been issued to his credit and which were still in force in his District. Thenceforth Agents serviced the Ordinary business as well as the Industrial, and the foundation was laid for building a rounded and qualified Field Force.

At the same time that the activities in the Field were increasing, corresponding developments were taking place in the organization of the Agency Division at the Home Office. The first Superintendent of Agencies, James Stevenson, was appointed in 1892. He was succeeded in 1896 by Ellis J. Thomas, who was given the title of Manager of Agencies, with John R. Hegeman, Jr., as Assistant Manager. The Agency Division was completely reorganized in 1899 by Second Vice-President George H. Gaston along the lines in which it has continued to operate to the present day. Thus, Mr. Gaston, a born leader, was not only the guiding spirit of the Agency Force in the critical formative period, but he was also architect of the Agency management organization. According to the new setup, the United States and Canada were divided into seven Territories, and five new Superintendents of Agencies were appointed—George B. Scott, John Wilson, Harry A. Young, Thomas W. Dwyer, and Frederick F. Taylor—while George A. Weigel and William M. Killington, who had been appointed earlier, continued in their positions. The Superintendents of Agencies were responsible for the effective functioning of the Field Force in their respective Territories. They spent most of their time in the Field instructing and directing, as well as observing where improvements in methods and management could be effected. This key position in the Agency organization of the Company has contributed many outstanding figures in subsequent Metropolitan history.

When Mr. Fiske revitalized the Ordinary Department, he likewise widened the insurance market for the Field Force. He realized how important it was for the Agent to offer a wide variety of policies. Up to 1892, when Mr. Fiske came into office as Vice-President, the Agent's stock in trade had consisted solely of Industrial contracts on the Whole Life plan. With characteristic translation of idea into action, he arranged for the Company to issue a complete line of Ordinary contracts, as well as a series of Endowments in the Industrial Department. As time went on the policy contracts, irrespective of plan, were repeatedly modified, benefits were liberalized, and additional features introduced. New fields of operation were opened—the Intermediate Branch was inaugurated in 1896, Special Class in 1899. Later, Group insurance, Accident and Health insurance, and Monthly Premium plans were added. There has been more and more for the Agent to service and sell, and more for him to know.

To keep abreast of these advances the Agent has had to be prepared thoroughly. To this end the Company has put greater and greater emphasis on the selection of men and on their education and training. The formal instruction of the Agency Staff began in 1912 with a Correspondence Course in the Principles of Life Insurance, consisting of 12 lessons prepared by Louis I. Dublin, the Company's Statistician, then but recently appointed. The course was received enthusiastically, and soon 10,000 Field-Men and Home Office people were reading the lessons and submitting written papers. For many years the course was required of all new Agents, until it was supplanted by more comprehensive instruction. In

A Typical District Office

The Public Lobby

The Agents' Room

266

1912 there also appeared the first Metropolitan textbook entitled "Policies and Plans," written by Horace M. Walton, an experienced insurance man and a gifted teacher. This volume has been revised from time to time, and is still a standard text among the Company's Field-Men. These ventures in education proved very helpful to the Agent, but in large measure he still continued to be dependent on the Superintendent and Assistant Superintendent for his training —and, in the long run, upon his own experience.

A milestone in Field training came 11 years later, in 1923, when the Metropolitan opened, in Boston, its first school for new Agents. This pioneer effort was under the direction of Henry E. North, then Superintendent of Agencies of New England Territory, who selected Max C. Fisher, an Assistant Manager in Cambridge, Mass., District, to organize the school. Newly appointed Agents were given one week's instruction to familiarize them with debit routine, policy forms, and the essentials of Life insurance salesmanship. At first there was skepticism as to whether such formal schooling was practicable or desirable, but this attitude was soon dispelled by the results of the experiment. A close check was kept on the subsequent accomplishments of the men who had attended the school; when a comparison was made with the records of untutored Agents, its value was clearly established. Encouraged by these significant results the Company transferred Mr. Fisher to the Home Office, and under his direction similar schools were opened in Philadelphia, Syracuse, St. Louis, Chicago, Pittsburgh, Columbus (Ohio), and Baltimore.

By 1930 the Field-Men of the Metropolitan were well equipped with all the prerequisites for broad training. The Instruction Book for Agents had become a volume of 157 pages. The Agents possessed a comprehensive Rate Book of some 730 pages. The Correspondence Course had been increased to 26 lessons, and most Agents had completed it. A large proportion of new men were receiving an initial week's training in Agency schools. The Home Office was providing additional instruction through *The Metropolitan*

Underwriter and other educational literature. Some training was being given through the Special Agents. In principle, responsibility for training in the District Office had become fixed on the Manager and Assistant Manager (prior to 1920 these titles were Superintendent and Deputy Superintendent), yet there was considerable variation in practice. Almost all the ingredients for an instructional program were present—but there was a lack of central direction and coordination.

The founding of the Field Training Division in 1931 under the executive direction of Henry E. North brought to Agents, Assistant Managers, and Managers the most comprehensive program of instruction and training yet offered by any Life insurance company to the members of its Field Force. The objectives were: to develop improved methods and "tools" for use by the Field Force; to foster the practice of the principles and methods advocated by the Company for continued improvement of service to policyholders and to the public; and to concentrate training as far as possible in the District Offices and in the hands of Managers and Assistant Managers, who were to be prepared for this responsibility.

The work began modestly, but soon gained momentum. In 1931 there were seven men in the Field Training Division. By 1942 there were 129 in Territories reporting to the Home Office, 14 in Pacific Coast Territory, and 15 in Canada—a total Staff of 158 men devoting full time to instruction and training among Metropolitan representatives in the Field.

To determine the most pressing Field needs, an intensive exploration of sales and service methods was conducted. In the course of this search, upward of 4,000 Agents' calls were observed and analyzed. Methods of Managers and Assistant Managers were similarly studied—a research project which required some three years to complete.

This information served as a foundation for building the training program. Agents were first coached in a few basic sales and service plans, designed to meet the common needs of most prospects and policyholders. Then followed more comprehensive plans to assist Agents in the management of their debits, and in the use of time. The up-to-then one week of training provided in the schools for new Agents was increased to two weeks, and this training and the texts and the correspondence courses for Agents and Assistant Managers were improved and enlarged.

This many-sided training through schools and study courses was supplemented by practical demonstration with Assistant Managers and Agents in the Field; instructors went to District Offices and worked directly with men needing or wanting training. For example, with the enactment of the United States Social Security legislation, members of the Field Force were schooled to assist policyholders in fitting their existing Life insurance to their new Social Security. In two Territories—and the work is expanding—continuation schools were established for "refresher" courses. Agents attend one day a week through 17 weeks. To further assist new Agents, an instructor from the Field Training Division gives a full week to each new Agent just prior to the completion of his first six months of service; this is a "follow-up" assignment to observe progress and determine what further training the new Agent should have.

Since individuals vary in their ability to absorb and use training, a procedure was developed, with the assistance of the Psychological Corporation of America, to help Managers in the selection of Agents. By 1942 this procedure had been introduced in all Districts, and had produced perceptible improvement in the already high character of Field personnel.

Supplementing all this work, which had to do directly with the Agent, a parallel program was developed for the benefit of Managers and Assistant Managers. This is a management course in three parts, each of which requires three full weeks in school. For this instruction Managers and Assistant Managers are brought together, a week at a time, at central points in the Territories in which their Districts are located. By the end of December 1941, 619 Managers and 902 Assistant Managers had completed Part I; 288 Managers and 331 Assistant Managers had completed Part II.

The objective in all these courses is further to equip Managers and Assistant Managers for the instruction of Agents.

Collateral with other phases of its Field training program, the Company in 1938 extended aid to members of the Field Force who desired to take the collegiate course for Chartered Life Underwriters. Under this plan textbooks for the courses were distributed free to District Offices, and a refund of examination fees was offered to individuals who successfully completed the C.L.U. examinations. By 1942, 197 representatives of the Metropolitan had completed all examinations, and had received from the American College of Chartered Life Underwriters either its Certificate of Proficiency or the professional designation, C.L.U. Over 500 more had completed one or more examinations and, altogether, approximately 1,000 representatives of the Metropolitan in the United States and Canada were enrolled in, had been enrolled in, or had completed the course for Chartered Life Underwriters—a greater number of candidates by far than from any other company.

In the light of this continuous effort, it is not surprising to find that a virtual revolution has been effected over the years in the character of the Agency Force. Not only is each Agent better trained, but he believes in the work he is doing and takes a more professional attitude toward it. His objective is to help prospects think through their family needs and ambitions, then to draw up an insurance program which attempts to meet these within their economic capacity. He is an advisor first, a salesman last. He may advise an Income policy which will produce a definite amount each month for a specified number of years, supplementing the prospective benefits which the widow may receive from Social Security or other sources. Or he may offer a policy of benefits accruing at age 60 or 65 to supplement other income to provide protection for old age. He may suggest the purchase of a Mortgage Redemption policy for the home owner who wishes to leave his house free and clear in the event of his death. The Agent thus employs specially designed insurance plans to meet special individual needs. To an ever-increasing degree, he has encouraged the policyholder to use the various settle-ment options which are part of the modern Life insurance contract, and which help to conserve the insurance estate for the beneficiary. In this way the Agent not only safeguards the interest of the policyholder during his lifetime, but also continues to serve the family after the insured dies. More and more, policy proceeds are left with the Company under settlement options, to be paid to beneficiaries in periodic instalments, either for life or for a specified number of years.

Just as important as selling and servicing contracts, is the Agent's effort in keeping them in force. Over the years the Field Force has worked persistently to reduce lapses because neither the policyholder, the Company, nor the Agent bene-fits when a policy is bought and is dropped soon thereafter. That success has marked these efforts is obvious from the fact that the lapse and surrender of policies at present are at the lowest point in the Company's history, in both the Ordinary and Industrial Departments. Much of this improvement is due to the constant desire to write business which adequately meets the needs of the policyholder and, therefore, remains on the books—an advantage to all concerned.

As Agents have been more carefully selected and better qualified for their duties, their earnings have improved con-siderably; and these increased financial rewards have in turn attracted men of better type and better education. The average weekly earnings for Agents during 1942 were more than $60, the highest in the history of the Company, and undoubtedly the highest for any comparable group in the Life insurance business. This is a far cry from the $10 a week average compensation for Agents which still prevailed at the turn of the century.

The better service which Agents have rendered has also been stimulated by the activities of the Company to further their security and well-being. The Agent is paid during his initial educational period and is assured of a dependable income from the day he takes a debit. The Company makes available to its Agency Staff a wide range of benefits, including

Group Life insurance, provision for retirement annuity, temporary disability benefits, total and permanent disability benefits, hospital and surgical operation benefits (which the Agent may elect for members of his family as well as for himself). Both the employees and the Company share in the cost of this well-rounded program of security. At the end of 1941, 1,343 Managers, Assistant Managers, and Agents were receiving retirement annuity payments, and 711 were receiving total and permanent disability benefits. More than 4,000 Agents have been treated at the Company's Sanatorium at Mount McGregor since its opening in 1913. The manifold Company activities for the well-being of the Force have contributed to its health and its morale, and have created a stability unsurpassed among organizations operating on the commission system of compensation.

In the Metropolitan, insurance salesmanship has become a life career. Agency turnover has steadily declined, until at present it is at a remarkably low level. In 1942 the ratio of Agents whose service terminated during the year to the average number employed, excluding deaths, retirement, and those entering military service, was about 9 percent. This is one fifth the figure of turnover only two decades ago. The increasing tendency of Agents to find a permanent career in their work for Metropolitan policyholders is strikingly revealed by the fact that there are now about 2,000 Veterans in the Field organization, men who began their Metropolitan service 20 or more years ago. More than 9,000 men have served 10 or more years. This is a splendid testimonial to the character of the Field-Men and the loyalty which the Company has inspired in its Agents. It is a real gain for policyholders, since it means a more experienced and stable body of Agents to serve them.

In the light of these changes, it will be of interest to consider the typical Agent of the Metropolitan. What is he actually like? What does he accomplish in the course of a year? Much of his effort necessarily goes unheralded, since its fulfillment lies in the future. Yet certain accomplishments emerge from yearly tabulations. Thus, during 1941 the average Agent placed $48,012 of Ordinary insurance; he sold 118 Industrial policies, on the Weekly or Monthly Premium plan, and a fraction more than two Accident and Health policies. His debit comprised about 400 families, upon whom he made 225 calls a week. And from these families during the course of the year he received premiums on more than 1,000 Industrial policies on the Weekly plan, and on more than 200 Monthly policies, at the same time providing the necessary services on 200 Ordinary policies. He was also instrumental in doing some of the spade work in developing prospects for Group insurance. There are, of course, many Agents today to whom such "average" figures are only a milestone toward a larger total, and whose exceptional sales bring their writings and earnings much higher. In the year 1941, for example, the leading Agent of the Company placed $518,541 of Ordinary insurance, and 13 of his fellow Agents achieved more than $250,000. Eight representatives, one a Manager and the others Group Supervisors, in 1941 earned membership in the $5,000,000 Club of the Group Division, and four additional Field-Men qualified as members of the Million Dollar Club.

But average or exceptional, the Metropolitan Agent must now be a well-rounded man; in fact, he must be a number of men rolled into one. As a salesman, he has continuous contact with his fellow citizens, counsels on their insurance programs, receives premiums, pays claims, renders the thousand and one services incidental to his business. But he is, as we have said before, something of a social worker too. To say that he is required to give full time to his work is an understatement; a major part of his 24 hours is devoted to the lives and the problems of the families for whom he is responsible. Through his weekly visits, he knows the financial and social ins and outs of his families, and is often able to offer useful advice. He brings the Metropolitan Nurse during illness; distributes health pamphlets—some 800 a year; sells Government Stamps in wartime; acts generally as a good citizen in his community. No wonder his career has become one to fire the enthusiasm of good men, and to give infinite satisfaction to the Company which has helped to create this type of public servant. For, among the families on the debit, the Agent is the Company.

No history of the Field Force would be adequate without a word about the work of the District Office clerical personnel, of whom there are more than 6,000 in local offices throughout the United States and Canada. These Clerks serve millions of policyholders who call at the District Offices to pay premiums or to obtain information. Each year vast sums of money pass through their hands, with rarely any shortages. In 1941, for example, they handled nearly $700,000,000, and yet there were only eight cases of intentional shortage, which amounted to approximately $5,500. In August 1941 the President, realizing the important part played by the District Office Clerical Force, was instrumental in having created a Division of Field Personnel, and in appointing Glen J. Spahn as Field Personnel Officer. This Division serves to complement the work done by the Field Training Division and the Agency Divisions. Although it has been in existence only a short time, it has already contributed much to bring about a better understanding between the Field Force and the Home Office. A new method of rating District Office Clerks has been developed, new clerical salary maximums have been established, and there has been a general revision of District Office clerical titles. As time passes, this Division will be responsible for other changes which will be of benefit to the entire Field Force.

Throughout the history of the Metropolitan, the importance of the Field-Man has been recognized in the Company's methods of advancement; promotion in the organization has traditionally been the reward of ability and achievement. From the earliest years, the men at the top have risen rung by rung from the men in the ranks—moving from Agent to Assistant Manager to Manager to Superintendent of Agencies, and to a place among the Company's Officers. This tradition has had much to do with the closeness of the ties binding Home Office and Field together. Mr. Gaston, who started

274

A. F. C. FISKE

work as a Clerk in 1879, and who directed the Field Force for at least a third of a century, was instrumental in creating the mechanism of advancement by merit. When he first set up the Territorial system headed by Superintendents of Agencies, the positions were filled by men who had made their mark in the Field. With Mr. Gaston's passing in 1922, leadership fell logically to Harry J. Miller, who had worked his way up from an Agency debit. Illness forced Mr. Miller to yield his position in 1928, at which time the Field management was divided between A. F. C. Fiske and Ernest H. Wilkes, both of whom had shown extraordinary capacity in all the positions they filled from Agent to Superintendent of Agencies and then to Vice-President. With Mr. Fiske's death in 1931, Mr. Wilkes took full command for a decade, and after the latter's passing in July 1941, Third Vice-President Cecil J. North, who, like his predecessor, had graduated from a debit, was appointed a Second Vice-President and placed in charge of the Field Force. These leaders, with their fund of first-hand experience won on the firing line, have always viewed the problems of the Field with sympathy and understanding.

Through 75 years, the close and cordial ties between the men at the Home Office and those in the Field have built a relationship which has contributed materially to the success of the Company. The Chief Executives from the days of Mr. Knapp and Mr. Hegeman have always shown keen concern for the welfare of the Field. Haley Fiske traveled thousands of miles to meet every man in the Agency Force at least once every three years. His successor, Mr. Ecker, continued this tradition, and through his warm personality humanized the relationship. More recently, Mr. Lincoln, since he became President in 1936, has made three Field tours and has traveled more than 75,000 miles. On his first and second tours he met every Agent, Assistant Manager, and Manager throughout the length and breadth of this country and Canada. During the third tour he met some 6,000 Field-Men. On these tours the President held open forum meetings.

ERNEST H WILKES

CECIL J. NORTH
Second Vice-President

Agents were free to bring up whatever topic they wished to discuss with the President; and no other Company Officials were present. Similar meetings were held with Assistant Managers and Managers, although these meetings were attended by other Company Executives. Probably nothing quite comparable has ever been attempted. The demands on the President were enormous, but the results were commensurate with the effort; and today the loyalty and devotion of the Metropolitan Field-Men to both the Company and to the policyholders are at an unprecedentedly high level.

The Field-Men have also a sense of obligation to the community in which they work, and this has become a powerful force for good in the two countries. Over the years, they have become leaders in civic improvement and health activities. Many have taken part in philanthropic work as officers of hospitals, of social work organizations, particularly of Visiting Nurse Associations. On their own initiative, they have worked with local voluntary health agencies and with their health departments to secure better and more adequate services. Since 1929 the Metropolitan has each year cooperated with the American Public Health Association and the United States Chamber of Commerce in a National Health Conservation Contest among communities. Many a District Manager and his Staff have helped to organize businessmen behind this job of community life-saving.

Cities throughout the United States and Canada have thus come to expect Metropolitan Managers, Assistant Managers, and their Agents to be among their most enlightened citizens, and have appointed them to carry on strategic services. Their war activities have been varied and useful, both in 1918 and at the present. Many are now serving on draft and rationing boards, and are leading local activities in cooperation with the national war effort. A total of 20,000 members of the Field organization at the end of 1942 were purchasing War Bonds through pay-roll deductions, and every Agent was selling War Stamps to the families on his debit. By the end of 1942 a total of more than 1,200 men from the Field, out of the Metropolitan's total of more than 21,000, had joined the armed forces of the United States and Canada. The high standing which Managers, Assistant Managers, and Agents have attained in their respective communities has contributed to the esteem in which the Metropolitan is held in the public mind, in wartime no less than in peace.

CHAPTER 13

The Company in Canada

LIFE INSURANCE plays a big part in the economy of the people of Canada. In this regard, as in so many others, Canadians and their neighbors across the friendly border follow a similar pattern of thrift and family protection. The most recent figures show that Canada, with an average of nearly $700 of Life insurance per capita, is second only to the United States, whose people own an average of just under $1,000 per capita. Canada is considerably ahead of the next ranking country, Great Britain, in the extent to which its people have provided themselves with Life insurance.

The Metropolitan has played an important role in this development. It entered Canada in 1872, only five years after the founding of the Dominion. Its growth has thus paralleled that of the country itself. The history of both reflects the vigor of the people, their intelligent initiative, their love of family life, and their devotion to democratic ideals. Today, more than 2,000,000 Canadians, or close to 17 percent of the total population, are policyholders of the Metropolitan. In Canada the Company has more than $1,300,000,000 of Life insurance in force. It is, therefore, the largest Life insurance organization there. It has $300,000,000 invested in the Dominion, and has operated a separate Head Office for its Canadian business since 1924.

The progress of the Company in Canada is all the more extraordinary, because there it is a "foreign" company. Canadians are very conscious of their nationality, and if they have taken the Metropolitan to their hearts it is in large measure due to the policy launched by Haley Fiske and followed by succeeding administrations. He felt that the Company's operations in the Dominion should reflect the national aspirations of the country and conform to the pattern of life followed by the Canadian people. Thus, the Officials of the Company early recognized the ideals of the Dominion, and have continued to respect them not only in word but in substantial deeds. It has been the Company's policy that practically the entire personnel should be composed of Canadians; that the business be administered from the Head Office in Canada's capital; that funds held in Canada to cover the Company's liabilities there should be invested in Canadian securities; that all activities of the Company should take cognizance of the two tongues spoken in the country; that the Company should stand side by side with the Canadian Life companies in facing the problems and difficulties of the business; that it should play its part in the solution of Canada's problems of public health and industrial hygiene; and that in war it should take its place with the rest of Canada in that country's effort to fight aggression and tyranny.

It is not surprising, therefore, that the Canadian people have responded warmly to this program and have entrusted to the Metropolitan a large share of their insurance protection. Today, the Company is one of the leading public service institutions of the Dominion, and if it has succeeded in expressing its own international status as a Life insurance company, it has at the same time helped materially to increase the mutual respect and harmonious and profitable relations existing between the two neighboring peoples.

The 70 years of Metropolitan history in Canada divide naturally into four periods. From 1872 until 1894 the Company did very little business and gave little promise of the prominent position it was later to occupy. In 1894, under the impetus of Haley Fiske's initiative, a vigorous development was begun which continued fairly steadily until 1917, when Canada was established as a separate administrative territory of the Company. The Canadian Head Office was established in 1924, since which date the growth has been accelerated and a truly national organization has been developed.

During the first period Canada, with a population of just a little more than 4,000,000, was facing the many problems that followed Confederation in 1867. Life insurance was then in its pioneer stages. British and American companies conducted the main business through their branches established in Canada, and carried about three quarters of the total Life insurance in force. It was during this period, however, that many of the Canadian companies whose names are now household words were organized.

The Metropolitan's earliest license in Canada is dated October 24, 1872, and its first operations were confined to the writing of Ordinary business in the Maritime Provinces. William A. Temple, head of a prominent insurance firm in Saint John, New Brunswick, was the first Agent appointed. The Canadian Government required a deposit of $50,000, which was taken to Canada in United States Government bonds by Major R. B. Corwin. Thus was started a fund for the protection of Canadian policyholders that was to grow to more than $260,000,000. In 1875 this deposit was increased to $100,000, and in 1890 Canadian bonds were substituted for the United States securities; since that time the deposit has been entirely in Canadian securities.

The Dominion Government records show a total amount of Metropolitan Life insurance in force at the end of 1872 of $554,000, with a premium income of $16,654. By the end of 1874 there was $2,129,500 of Life insurance in force, but this amount gradually declined. The Canadian Agency was discontinued, and for a period of 10 years little new business was written. In 1885 interest in the Canadian field was revived by the Company. A District Office in Toronto was opened for the sale of Industrial insurance. But again little attention was given to Canada, and by the end of the first period the Company had only 14,136 policies in force for about $1,800,000—the largest part being on the Industrial insurance plan.

The second period of our Canadian history opened in 1894, when Vice-President Fiske, who had already acquired the

habit of pioneering, became impressed with the business possibilities in the Dominion and decided upon an aggressive
development there. He came to Montreal to open a new
District Office. Other offices were opened later in Ottawa,
Hamilton, and London. Only Industrial insurance was sold,
and the total amount of insurance increased to nearly $4,500,000
by the end of that year.

Mr. Fiske's new program was well timed, because the next
23 years, to 1917, marked a new era in Canadian affairs.
Canada's population grew from slightly less than 5,000,000
to more than 8,000,000 during this period, and business expanded as the country developed. The Western Provinces
grew by leaps and bounds. Canada began to assume her place
as the senior Dominion in the Empire. Important agreements
were made with the United States respecting fisheries and
boundaries—agreements that greatly contributed to the friend-
ship of the two countries. The most important and far-
reaching event of these years was the first World War, which
Canada entered on August 4, 1914. Before the Armistice was
signed in November 1918, the country was to supply 600,000
Canadians to the armed forces and great quantities of munitions and grain to the Empire—and Canada was to assume
nationhood and, as such, was to sign the Treaty of Versailles
on her own behalf.

During these years, Life insurance expansion more than
kept pace with the growth of the country. By 1917 the
average coverage per capita had increased to $194, from the
small average of $63 in 1894. The Metropolitan got a con-
siderable part of this increase because, as the country expanded,
District Offices were opened in Ontario and Quebec, and by
1898 it had offices in Chatham, Hamilton, Berlin (now
Kitchener), Brantford, Galt, Kingston, Brockville, Cornwall,
London, Stratford, St. Thomas, Woodstock, Montreal, St.
Catharines, Ottawa, Carleton Place, Hull, Quebec City,
Toronto, and Peterborough. In 1899, offices in the Maritime
Provinces were again opened, this time by the man who was
destined to be an important factor in the Canadian business

of the Company during this second period of its history—
James E. Kavanagh.

Born in Ontario, Canada, Mr. Kavanagh came to the
Metropolitan in 1897 as an Agent in Toronto, and his progress
thereafter was extraordinarily rapid. He was soon promoted
to Deputy Superintendent, and within two years he was
made Superintendent of Saint John, New Brunswick, District.

Only five years later he became Superintendent of Agencies of Great Northern Territory, and from 1905 until 1917
he was in charge of the Canadian operations of the Company
as a part of this Territory, which included part of New York
State. His was the understanding hand that guided Metropolitan affairs when the real foundation of its future position
in the Dominion was being laid. The Company's business
in Canada during these years grew apace. In 1901, offices
were established in the Western Provinces of Manitoba and
British Columbia, and in 1907 the Company entered Saskatch-
ewan and Alberta, thus completing the coast-to-coast organization. At that time the Life insurance in force in the
Company in Canada reached a total of $48,000,000, more than
two-thirds of which was in the Industrial Department.

Two outstanding activities marked this second period.
The first was the rapid extension of the welfare services
throughout the Dominion. Dr. Lee K. Frankel had begun his
welfare work with the Company in 1909, and one of his first
projects was the establishment of a nursing service in Canada.
Under his direction Metropolitan nursing of policyholders
began in Canada in 1910, only a few months after it was
established in the United States. Montreal was the first
Canadian city to have this service, and because of the bilingual
character of the population it was necessary to employ both
English and French nursing organizations. Accordingly, on
January 12th, an affiliation was made with the Victorian Order
of Nurses for English policyholders, and a few days later a
similar arrangement was made with the Sisters of Hope for
French policyholders. It is notable also that the first Metropolitan health booklet was published in Canada in 1898.

This publication, entitled *A Friend in Need Is a Friend Indeed: Health Hints for the Home*, was written by Dr. Thomas Simpson, the Company's Medical Supervisor in Canada.

The second important activity was in relation to Canada's participation in the first World War. The Metropolitan, immediately on the declaration of hostilities, took its place along with other business organizations of the Dominion in lending all possible assistance to the Government. The Company adopted a liberal policy in both its Industrial and Ordinary Departments toward enlisted men, or those likely to enlist. A large number of the first Canadian contingent of 33,000 men for overseas service, the famous "Princess Pat" Regiment, were insured by the Company at a comparatively low extra premium. President Fiske made the trip to Canada especially to expedite the insurance before embarkation. As the war increased in severity beyond all expectation, however, it became necessary, for the protection of policyholders generally, to place additional limitations on such insurance of war risks. But this generous action of the Metropolitan still stands as one of the milestones of its service to the Canadian people. The Company also played its part in war finance through the investment of $24,225,000 in Victory Bonds, and the District Staffs were active in Victory Loan campaigns.

The Metropolitan was able to render service to the institution of Life Insurance in Canada when, at the request of the Dominion Government, it took over the financially pressed Union Life Insurance Company in 1913. Through this assumption 100,000 policyholders of that company, insured for $17,500,000, came into the Metropolitan and were able to retain without loss the benefits of their insurance. During the early years, in 1901, a Quebec company, La Canadienne Life Insurance Company of Montreal, had also been assumed, and nearly 35,000 people were thus reinsured in the Metropolitan.

At the end of 1917, Metropolitan business in force in the Dominion had risen to $222,000,000—a vast increase when compared with the 1894 total of only $4,500,000. This represented approximately 14 percent of the total business in force in Canada, and was a striking indication of the position the Company had attained in the field of Life insurance. As a matter of fact, in 1912 the Metropolitan had already achieved more business in force in Canada than any other company— a leadership it has continued to maintain. At the end of this second period of our history the Industrial in force was a little more than half the total, but more and more attention was being given to the Ordinary Department. Thus was Haley Fiske's prophetic vision of the 90's realized, and with the creation of Canada as a separate Metropolitan administra- tive division in 1917 this second period ends.

The first Superintendent of Agencies of the newly created Canadian Territory was Harry H. Kay, who succeeded Mr. Kavanagh when the latter was put in charge of the Company's new Group Division. Under Mr. Kay's leadership the Field Staff throughout Canada, fired with enthusiasm at their recog- nition as a separate entity of the Company, produced a volume of business that grew by leaps and bounds.

The years between 1917 and 1924, which constitute the third period in Canada, were both eventful and productive. The Armistice in November 1918, the return of the men in the Canadian Expeditionary Force, the influenza epidemic in 1918 and 1919, the business recession in 1921—all played a part in molding the character of the nation that was growing up so rapidly. Life insurance, too, was keeping pace. The per capita amount more than doubled in these seven years, rising from $194 at the end of 1917 to $407 at the end of 1924. The total in force in the Metropolitan increased even more rapidly—from $222,000,000 to $566,000,000. Of this latter total $302,000,000 was in the Ordinary Department, an indi- cation of the growing attention that was being given to this branch of the business. The premium income of the Com- pany at the end of 1924 was nearly $21,000,000 annually, and the Canadian investments had grown to the amazing total of $116,000,000—a substantial stake in the Dominion.

February 26, 1924, marked the commencement of the cur- rent period in Metropolitan history in Canada. On that day the Board of Directors authorized the establishment of a Canadian Head Office in Ottawa. A. F. C. Fiske, until that time Superintendent of Agencies for Empire State Territory, was named a Third Vice-President and was delegated to take charge of the new Head Office, as well as of Canadian Territory. That part of the Dominion lying west of the Rocky Mountains continued under the supervision of the Pacific Coast Head Office until January 1927, when the business came under the Canadian Head Office. Thus was constituted a Territory which for extent exceeded any other in the Company and which on that account alone presented administrative problems more complicated than those in other Territories.

Two months to the day after the authorization for a Canadian Head Office, on April 26th, a temporary Head Office covering two floors in the Jackson Building in Ottawa was in operation, complete with the necessary records—some 2,000,000 applications, accounts, correspondence, manuscripts, the essential office equipment, and a personnel of 400. At its very inception it was the second largest Life insurance company operating in Canada. The story of the establishment of this office has unique business and human interest.

Before it had been authorized, more than $500,000,000 of insurance was already in force in Canada, 1,500,000 policyholders were being served, and a Field Force of nearly 1,600 was at work. Though from the beginning it had been the intention to make the Ottawa office as nearly "A Canadian Office for Canadians" as possible, it was obviously impossible to recruit an executive and clerical force immediately from the personnel of the Dominion, and expect it to function within any reasonable length of time. The only solution was to select the experienced staff from the Home Office; to transfer it to Ottawa so that the Canadian business might be carried on uninterrupted, and to replace these people with native Canadians as rapidly as possible.

The selection of the human organization was, perhaps, the simpler part of the problem. The more difficult task was that of lifting Canadian records from the files of 61 different Divisions, where for years they had been intermingled with the other records at the Home Office; of preparing them for shipment without loss or confusion, and without interfering with the transaction of business in the Territory. When it is realized that a great part of these records are necessarily in daily use, some idea of the job at hand may be visualized.

Yet it was accomplished within a brief two days, through a "dress rehearsal" in New York and through a moving scheme which worked like the proverbial clockwork. Before the employees left their tasks in New York, a floor plan of the Ottawa office had been laid out on corresponding floors of the Home Office, and each worker had been assigned his place in the new office. The Industrial Department was moved first. Until 12 o'clock noon on Thursday, April 24th, the working day in New York was no different from any other. But when the noon bell sounded, forces of porters fell upon the office equipment and the records, which were sent on by special express. Hundreds of employees were dined, escorted to the station, put on a special Ottawa train, and awoke the next morning to find nothing changed about their office except the locale, which happened to be in a new country. There were the old Divisions, arranged in the usual way. There were the familiar records, filed just as they had been filed back in the New York office. All that was left to do was to sit down at one's own desk and take up the job which had been left off the night before in a city some 500 miles away.

On the following day the same scene was enacted for the Ordinary Department in New York—and by Saturday, April 26th, all major details of the move were complete, and the Canadian Head Office was in full swing. In the months following, a Canadian personnel gradually replaced the Home Office Clerks, and the temporary staff returned to New York. The establishment of the Head Office in Ottawa was welcomed by the people of Canada, and every help was given by Government and insurance officials. The new Canadian Staff quickly became members of the Metropolitan family. Today it has an *esprit de corps* which is immediately recognizable, a comrade-

287

The Canadian Head Office

ship and friendliness which have made for a happy and harmonious organization.

Once the decision was made to establish a Head Office in Canada, plans went forward to find a suitable site for a perma- nent and representative building to house the growing needs of the Canadian business. The corner of Wellington and Bank Streets, facing the Dominion Parliament Buildings, a spot rich with memories of early Canadian life, was obtained, and excavation work was begun in April 1925. On November 4, 1925, the cornerstone of the beautiful new building was laid by President Fiske, in the presence of a large gathering of people prominent in the official, professional, and insurance life of Canada, and a large delegation from 1 Madison Avenue. The Head Office was soon to rise as an impressive landmark, with the story of Metropolitan service to Canada symbol- ically expressed in its vaulted lobby mosaics: Mother Metro- politan protecting the weak, fighting the serpent of disease, aiding those who are rebuilding their homes after a disaster.

At the impressive ceremonies, President Fiske sketched the history and development of the Metropolitan in Canada. He stressed the point that it was a Canadian Company for Canadians, and stated that it had invested and spent in the

Dominion more than $53,000,000 above the amount it had collected in premiums. He reviewed in detail the welfare work and Nursing Service in Canada, holding it to be equal to the work of selling insurance, and prophesied that the new Head Office would come to be known as "not a Temple of Insurance, but as a Temple of Health and Welfare for the benefit of the Canadian people."

And indeed the welfare activities of the Company had already borne encouraging dividends in terms of human lives saved. The Nursing Service founded in 1910 had taken on new branches in cities all over Canada, as the result of affilia-tions with the French Sisters of Hope, with the Victorian Order of Nurses, and with individual nurses. In 1921 the affiliation with the French nursing group was discontinued and a staff of full-time Metropolitan Nurses appointed. Three of these were sent to the Province of Quebec, and assisted in a health demonstration in Thetford Mines which was to have far-reaching results for the French-Canadian people in terms of maternal, infant, and child welfare.

By the early 20's, "La Metropolitaine," as it was known, had become deeply rooted in the community life of French-speaking Canada and had placed a considerable volume of Industrial Life insurance among this section of the population. Today, 40 percent of the Canadian business is in the Province of Quebec. From the beginning the Districts operating in Quebec have employed French-speaking personnel, and have issued policy contracts, business forms, and welfare literature in French.

The infant mortality in the Province of Quebec was dis-tressingly high. In 1921 Dr. Frankel determined to show that this waste in child life was needless and could be reduced by proper public health methods. With characteristic force and persuasiveness, he journeyed straight to headquarters: to Monseigneur Roy, the Roman Catholic Auxiliary Bishop of Quebec. It was a tribute to Dr. Frankel's own conviction and to the Bishop's immediate understanding that the Com-pany secured the complete cooperation of Monseigneur Roy and of the local Catholic clergy. These churchmen were to prove an important factor in the success of this and other health projects in French Canada.

Thetford Mines, an asbestos mining town with a population of 9,000, practically 100 percent French-Canadians, was selected by the Bishop for the demonstration. The experiment began with special training in New York of three French-speaking Nurses in the most advanced methods of prenatal and postnatal care. They then opened classes and clinics for mothers, went into homes in the little town, and soon won many converts to their health work. The Mayor, M. Rousseau, was very helpful throughout the entire period. Largely through his interest the town voted a sum of money to assist in furnishing the maternity center. With the leading citizens of the community, he organized a Public Health Committee which later carried on the work that the Company had started. A local physician, Dr. Sirois, the first Public Health Officer of the community, was later to become an authority on prenatal and infant welfare, and the Nurse in charge, Miss Alice Ahern, was to become the Company's Assistant Superintendent of Nursing in Canadian Territory.

At the end of about three years the infant mortality rate, which had been 300 per thousand live births when the Metropolitan started the experiment, had been reduced to 96 per thousand in December 1923, when the Company withdrew— a reduction of 68 percent. These heartening results had repercussions far beyond the confines of the little mining community. While the demonstration was still operating, the Premier of the Province of Quebec had asked for a report, which was published in a leading Quebec paper, Le Soleil. During the course of the next session of the Provincial Legislature he asked the Government for an appropriation of $500,000 to carry on a similar five-year campaign against infant mortality and tuberculosis. All members of the Government and of the opposition voted the money without a dissenting vote. The Government did not hesitate to say that the demonstration in Thetford Mines and the tuberculosis demonstration of the

Company in Framingham, Mass., had given the original impetus to their action.

When public health authorities became aware of the effectiveness of the procedures used in the demonstrations, they launched reforms on a wide scale. In the Province of Quebec the rapid spread of nursing service, both Government and Metropolitan, brought into focus another problem: the insufficient training in public health of the French-Canadian nurse. In 1925 the Metropolitan was instrumental in bringing about the establishment of the world's first university school for the training of French-speaking nurses at the University of Montreal. Early in 1926 the Company helped to establish a Chair of Industrial Hygiene at McGill University. This project, established in affiliation with the industrial clinic at the Montreal General Hospital, had as its object the training of industrial physicians and public health officers in treating occupational diseases. The Metropolitan financed the department in its early years, and withdrew when the success of the project assured the provision of funds for its continuance.

All these life-saving efforts had results in helping to lower Canada's general mortality figures. The improvement has been even more encouraging in the case of Metropolitan Industrial policyholders, who have enjoyed the Company's welfare program. Thus, the crude death rate of the Weekly Premium-paying Industrial policyholders in Canada has declined approximately 25 percent during the past 15 years. The improvement in mortality from the principal communicable diseases of childhood and from diarrhea and enteritis has been even greater. For influenza and pneumonia combined, and for tuberculosis the rates have been reduced to one half.

From these welfare activities we turn our attention again to the Head Office, where administrative changes were taking place. On January 1, 1928, A. F. C. Fiske was recalled to the New York Home Office to become a Second Vice-President in joint charge with Harry Miller of the entire Field operations of the Company. His term of office in Canada had marked the firm establishment of the Head Office in the Life insurance business of the Dominion. Under the roof of 180 Wellington Street, more than 500 Canadian members of the Metropolitan family were effectively and efficiently handling the work in the spirit characteristic of the Company.

On A. F. C. Fiske's return to the Home Office, his position was taken by Henry E. North, who since 1925 had been Superintendent of Agencies in Canada, and who was now made Third Vice-President and Manager for Canada. Mr. North's interest in the training of the Field-Men, which was later to result in his promotion to head of the Field Training Division for the whole Company, had ample scope during his years in Canada. His talks to Managers and to Assistant Managers constitute the basis of much of the educational work of the Company today. Of great value, likewise, were the triennial meetings with the Field Force inaugurated by Haley Fiske. Mr. Ecker and Mr. Lincoln have continued these visits to the Field-Men and have thus cemented the ties between the peoples of the two countries. These visits have helped bring about a better understanding of, and a clearer insight into, each other's work.

At the 1928 annual meeting of the Canadian Life Insurance Officers Association, Mr. North was elected a member of the executive committee, on which he served continuously while he was in charge of Canada. The Metropolitan had been a member of this organization since 1906; and from 1912 to 1919 Mr. Kavanagh had served on the executive committee. The principles of cooperation inherent in Life insurance had been given practical application by this Association since its organization in 1893, and through it the companies as a group made many worth-while contributions. Two Metropolitan men have been presidents of the Life Underwriters Association of Canada, and Field-Men of the Company are represented on practically every local board of the Association. Each year an increasing number of Field-Men take examinations given by the Institute of Chartered Life Underwriters of Canada, and a number of Metropolitan men have been awarded its coveted designation.

In September 1931 Mr. North returned to the Home Office as Third Vice-President in charge of Field Training, and was succeeded by Harry D. Wright. At that time Canada was passing through a severe depression, but Life insurance passed this critical test with flying colors. There were no company failures, and the heavy demands placed upon the business were all met. This fact brought into focus the unique record of insurance in Canada—that for more than 100 years it had met depressions, wars, epidemics, and panics, and that legal reserve companies operating under Dominion jurisdiction had not failed in a single instance to pay all obligations "100 cents on the dollar." Probably in no other country in the world has the business so unblemished a record.

In spite of depression years, the Metropolitan in 1931 passed the billion dollar mark of Life insurance in force in Canada, the first company to achieve such record. The next year, 1932, marked 60 years of Metropolitan service to the people of Canada; and the Company's position in the life of the Dominion justified, beyond wildest hopes, the faith that earlier administrations had in the country. In celebrating the Company's 60th anniversary in 1932, it was realized how closely the Metropolitan's growth had paralleled that of the country which only five years earlier, in 1927, had observed a similar national anniversary—the Diamond Jubilee of the Confederation of Canada.

A further expression of the mutual regard between the Metropolitan and Canada has been the inclusion of distinguished Canadians on the Company's Board of Directors. One of these, the Honorable Richard B. Bennett, now Viscount Bennett, became a member of the Board in 1917, and continued to serve until 1928. In 1930 he became Prime Minister of Canada. Before his appointment as Director he had acted as Counsel for the Company and had always displayed the greatest enthusiasm for its activities, especially for its Industrial Department and welfare work. Mr. D'Alton Corry Coleman was appointed to the Board of Directors to succeed Mr. Bennett. Mr. Coleman's intimate knowledge of Canada and his excellent judgment have made him a valued member of the Board. He became President of the Canadian Pacific Railroad in May 1942. In 1922 another well-known Canadian was added in the person of L. A. Taschereau, then Premier of the Province of Quebec. Mr. Taschereau, while he was a member of the Board, represented an important sector in Canadian life—the French-speaking group mainly concentrated in Quebec Province. Another valued Director from Canada was Louis St-Laurent, a prominent Quebec lawyer appointed to the Board in 1939, who resigned in June 1942 to become Minister of Justice in the Dominion Cabinet.

Distinguished Canadians have also functioned on the Metropolitan Staff. In 1926 a former Dominion Minister of Health, Senator Henri S. Beland, joined the Welfare Division and made a valuable contribution to the Company's health program until his death in 1935. In 1925 the Metropolitan was honored by assistance from Dr. Frederick G. Banting (later Sir Frederick), the co-discoverer of insulin and co-winner of the Nobel Prize in medicine in 1923, in the preparation of its first booklet on "Diabetes." In recognition of the Metropolitan's contribution to the field of public health in the Dominion and as a personal tribute to Norman L. Burnette, head of the Canada Welfare Division since 1924, the University of Montreal in 1932 conferred on him the degree of Doctor of Social Science.

The year 1939 brought the presentation of 15-year service anniversary bars to 142 members of the Head Office Staff, but plans for a gala anniversary dinner to be presided over by President Lincoln were halted by Canada's declaration of war against Germany on September 10th of that year. From this time, war and its resultant calls for aid to the fighting forces have dominated the thoughts and actions of people in Canada. The Company, as an institution, took its place with the Canadian companies and prepared to make the greatest contribution of which it was capable.

Voluntary work of all types was launched at the Head Office and in the Field. A Metropolitan Life Red Cross Unit was organized, and is producing a vast amount of knitting and sewing for the armed forces and is collecting clothes for distribution in bombed areas.

In June 1940 the Government placed War Savings Stamps and Certificates on sale, and the entire Metropolitan organization went to work with enthusiasm to sell them. In two years more than $300,000 of War Savings Stamps were sold on the debits and in District Offices. In February 1941 a national drive for War Savings Certificates was launched, and the Head Office was one of the first organizations in Canada to achieve 100 percent in pledges among employees. In the same year the Metropolitan subscribed $15,000,000—the largest subscription (later to be equaled by another company) to the first large Victory Loan Campaign. The Company later subscribed $20,000,000 to each of the succeeding Victory Loans, bringing its total purchases in these issues to $68,000,-000. There are 215 Company employees in the armed forces of Canada.

Mr. Wright, who had made notable contributions to the Company's progress in Canada, retired on December 31, 1940, and was succeeded by Mr. Edwin C. McDonald. The latter quickly took his place in the life of the Dominion, was made a member of the National War Finance Committee, and has worked actively in the Victory Loan Campaigns. Under Mr. McDonald's direction the Canadian Home Office and Field Force accepted a greatly increased quota for the third Victory Loan and then exceeded that quota by more than 100 percent. At the close of 1942 George V. Brady was advanced to the position of Associate Actuary and Assistant General Manager of the Canadian Head Office, where he has served with distinction since 1930.

On July 1, 1942, the Dominion celebrated 75 years since the British North America Act established the Confederation of Canada. The young Dominion has rounded out three quarters of a century of courageous struggle, of high hopes and ambitions realized in terms of great cities, of abundant farms, of happy and healthy citizens. The Metropolitan this

EDWIN C. McDONALD
Vice-President in Charge of Canadian Head Office

year celebrates its own 75th anniversary. It has had a development in many ways parallel to the country itself, prospered
with its prosperity, enjoyed its resources and the good will
of its citizens. A company which carries one sixth of the Life
insurance of a nation has certainly found its place in the hearts
of the people. Today the Canadian Head Office has insurance
in force of $1,300,000,000, and employs more than 1,000
people in Ottawa and more than 2,000 Field-Men and Clerks.
With Canada now in its fourth year of war, with nearly 50
percent of its national income expended upon defense and
armament, with many hundreds of thousands of its sons and
daughters in uniform, the whole country is geared to a war
economy in partnership with its powerful neighbor, the United
States. Through a loyal Staff and through its great resources,
our Company is enabled to make its contribution. No other
course could have matched the rich panorama of events and
accomplishments which we have here described.

CHAPTER 14

The Company on the Pacific Coast

THE DECISION of the Company in 1901 to open the business on the Pacific Coast was based upon the same principle which guided the establishment of the business in Canada. The Company recognized in the Pacific Coast region a distinct segment of our country which, like Canada, had its special geographic and cultural boundaries. It realized the effectiveness of a unit which would reflect the life and special interests of the West, deal directly with its policyholders, and employ men and women from its own broad area.

So, as later in Canada, the Company set up in San Francisco a Head Office which was, in reality, a fully functioning insurance company although all fundamental decisions and the investment of funds, of course, continued to be made at 1 Madison Avenue. In both Head Offices the type of policies sold and the general mechanism of business were identical with those of the Home Office in New York. In both, a pioneer public was eager for the type of service offered by the Metropolitan. Frontier days had passed, and by the turn of the century a new era had begun in the West—an era of rapid development in agricultural production and in manufacturing. The population was finding employment in the swiftly growing cities. An aggressive and hopeful democracy on the Coast was establishing its own industries and was thus dissolving some of its economic ties with the East.

In the late spring of 1901, like Argonauts of the Western World, a group of representative Field-Men and Home Office people, including George H. Gaston and James S. Roberts, journeyed westward to found a community of Metropolitan policyholders. They were to make preliminary arrangements for suitable quarters in which to conduct the business. These "pioneers" were followed in August by Haley Fiske, George B. Woodward, and Dr. Augustus S. Knight.

The first action of these Metropolitan Officers, in September 1901, was to close the negotiations for the purchase of the Industrial business of the Pacific Mutual Life Insurance Company, the only company then writing Industrial insurance in the West. Through this purchase the Company acquired an Industrial weekly debit of approximately $14,000, composed of more than 106,000 policyholders. "Quite a substantial weekly increase," commented Second Vice-President Gaston.

A temporary Head Office was obtained at 439 California Street, in a truly pioneer building heated only by open fireplaces. The Field Force was composed of 15 Superintendents, 110 Assistant Superintendents, and 413 Agents, most of whom had been taken over from the Pacific Mutual. The office personnel numbered 53. They approved applications, issued policies, collected premiums, paid death claims and surrender values, and attended in general to all policyholder transactions. It is of interest that the first death claim was presented on September 17, 1901, the day after the assumption of the business of the Pacific Mutual, and was paid three days later, indicating that the office was already in good running order.

Shortly afterward more convenient quarters were secured in the fine Hayward Building, known as "the first skyscraper in San Francisco," to which the Head Office moved on January 1, 1902. The pioneering work accomplished, Mr. Gaston, who had remained in charge, followed the other Officers back to New York. Upon occupation of the new quarters, Thornton R. Richardson, Assistant Secretary, was made Manager of the Pacific Coast Head Office and remained in charge until January 1904, when he was called to other duties at the Home Office, and was succeeded by Assistant Secretary Frederick F. Taylor as Manager.

The growth of business necessitated additional space, and in 1905 the Head Office moved to the Wells Fargo Building. The records of that year showed a total of approximately $10,000,000 of Ordinary insurance in force, built up from nothing four years before, and $30,000,000 of Industrial, built up from the $16,000,000 acquired from the Pacific Mutual. The Company remained in this location until April 18, 1906, the fateful date of the earthquake and fire which were completely to gut the office building and to destroy a large portion of its valuable records.

The earthquake occurred on Wednesday. For days the fires raged violently. But even before they were brought under control, Mr. Taylor had leased for the Company the entire second floor of the Jefferson Square Building. There, on Saturday, April 21st, a primitive office was opened to render service to the insured, thousands of whom had suffered in the disaster. The following Monday 32 Head Office Clerks and 55 Field-Men reported for duty, and policyholders streamed in for assistance. On Wednesday, April 25th, the first death claim was paid. Just seven days after the earthquake the Metropolitan's employees had the office in operation.

The new quarters did not offer too many conveniences. The space secured for the Head Office had previously served as a bowling alley and billiard parlor, and there were no desks, chairs, or tables available in all San Francisco. The Clerks, undismayed by such difficulties as the installation of false floors while they worked, made use of the reverse sides of the bowling score sheets for the recording of their daily transactions. They were kept busy every minute of the day, for policyholders called continuously to report missing relatives and to bring word of the loss of policies and Premium Receipt Books. Through the efforts of Agents and the Office personnel, many families were reunited and needful relief was given. Just two weeks and a day after the earthquake, the Head Office was completely reestablished with new desks, chairs, typewriters, and printed forms received by express from the Home Office. The devastating experience had tested the courage and the devotion of the Metropolitan Staff and found them ready.

It is appropriate to note that at this time the Company, observing the growing importance of the Pacific Coast business decided to add a native representative of the West to its Board of Directors. Therefore, still in that fateful month of April 1906, William H. Crocker, an eminent banker, philanthropist, and civic leader, was invited to serve, and did so with distinction for the subsequent 31 years of his life. One of the leading figures in the rebuilding of San Francisco after the disaster, he commented, some years later, on the prompt response of the Metropolitan to appeals to help reconstruct the shattered city: "Those of you who were here at the time of our great disaster will remember how wonderfully the Company came to our rescue and loaned its money freely in our midst. It thereby gave us needed courage, and . . . in large measure restored the city so rapidly to its present grandeur." When Mr. Crocker died in 1937, his son, William W. Crocker, was chosen to succeed him on the Board of Directors, where he still serves.

The Office remained in the Jefferson Square Building over a year, and in 1907 moved to more adequate quarters in the Hooker and Lent Building. Yet even there the rapid growth of the business and memories of the destruction of Office records in the disaster soon brought a realization that a permanent fireproof Head Office building was needed. Accordingly, the Company purchased a magnificent hilltop property at the corner of Pine and Stockton Streets, overlooking the bay and a large portion of the city, and started to erect its own home. On July 10, 1909, the Staff formally took possession of the first unit of the present structure—a modern Parthenon, one of the architectural landmarks of San Francisco. This fine building was designed by the Brothers LeBrun, who had created the Home Office in New York. It is severely classical in style, of white semiglazed terra cotta, faced on each side with six magnificent Ionic columns. If "a man's character is expressed by his clothes," the Pacific Coast Head Office Building expresses the alertness, the strength, and spirit of public service which the Metropolitan has come to mean to the people of the Western States.

At the time of the opening of the new building in 1909, Agents were operating in virtually every urban area in the Territory. The Life insurance in force there had reached a total of more than $58,000,000, of which $40,000,000 was Industrial. By the end of 1913, on the basis of the amount of insurance in force, the Pacific Coast unit, considered as a separate organization, would have stood 27th in the list of the 239 American Life insurance companies. The Coast Office then had in force 382,199 Industrial and 44,043 Ordinary policies for a combined total of more than $103,000,000 of Life insurance. In the same year it paid death claims amounting to almost $750,000 and distributed $72,025 in bonuses to Industrial policyholders. The premium income of the Pacific Coast Head Office in 1913 exceeded $3,250,000.

Because of such growth, in 1914, just five years after the erection of the first Head Office unit, two end wings had to be added, more than doubling the original floor space. Yet time was to prove even this additional space inadequate. By 1916 the Industrial business had increased to $78,000,000; the Ordinary to $66,000,000. The average amount of insurance per Ordinary policy was $935; for the Industrial policy it was $143. There were 212 employees in the Head Office, of whom 67 were men and 145 women; and the Field Force numbered 909. In 1920 the adjoining property was purchased, which again more than doubled the floor space. Yet in 1929— shortly after the Territory achieved its first billion dollars of insurance in force—additional property had to be acquired and the construction of the third addition was commenced. It was formally dedicated by President Ecker on May 29, 1930. This addition joins the southerly end of the Pine Street side of the old building, is eight stories high and, by reason of the incline of the street, its fifth floor is level with what was known as the main floor of the original building. The building program, which had taken more than two decades, was completed.

First Unit—1909

The completed Head Office

The area of the Territory under the jurisdiction of the Pacific Coast Head Office is more than a third of the total area of the United States, and embraces a population of more than 13,000,000 people. Within this vast Territory, Agencies are maintained in California, Washington, Oregon, Montana, Utah, Idaho, and Colorado. In servicing policyholders, Western Agents deal with debits different in composition and in geography from those in other parts of the country. Great distances and sparse population characterize the West as a whole, and the debits are often large in area. Some Western States have less population than a moderate-sized New England factory town. Colorado, for instance, has only 11 persons per square mile, California 44 per square mile, and Montana a sparse four; whereas in New York State the population is concentrated—281 per square mile, and in Rhode Island it is 674 per square mile. The West is young and the pioneer mood is still reflected in its people and their traditions. They are the descendants of Spanish conquistadores, American fur traders, pioneer land settlers, gold seekers, and equally vigorous recent immigrants.

The Head Office has been run, throughout the period of 42 years, with understanding of local problems. Despite the great distances within the Territory, the Field personnel has been small enough for the maintenance of personal contact with the Executives. The direction has always been in capable hands. When in 1910 Mr. Taylor was recalled to other duties at the Home Office in New York, he was succeeded by Assistant Secretary George B. Scott. It was in 1914, during Mr. Scott's management of the Head Office, that the Company assumed the Industrial business of the Beneficial Life Insurance Company of Salt Lake City, and four years later the Industrial business of the West Coast Life Insurance Company. Since the activities of these two companies were largely centered in the West, the Metropolitan was able to reach an increasingly large number of the wage-earning population on the Coast. After 10 years—in 1920—Mr. Scott was called back to the Home Office and was succeeded by Ernest H.

Wilkes. When he assumed office, the Metropolitan business in force on the Pacific Coast totaled more than $335,000,000. By this time the Ordinary had forged ahead of the Industrial business, and increased its lead as time went on.

Under Mr. Wilkes' administration the Company maintained its progressive business practices and continued to be responsive to the welfare needs of its policyholders, especially in times of disaster. In June 1921, for example, when the Arkansas River floods swept away a large portion of the city of Pueblo, Colo., urgent relief was brought to destitute policyholders. In July 1923 the people of Burke, Idaho, welcomed the Metropolitan Nurses following a fire which practically wiped out the town, leaving the residents without food or adequate clothing. In the same year, following the devastating floods in Utah, Brigham City was stricken with an epidemic of typhoid fever. The Metropolitan immediately dispatched Nurses to that community, and their visits and preventive measures materially assisted in stemming the tide of the disease. In addition to this service the Field-Men distributed food and blankets to destitute policyholders. In and near Santa Paula, Calif., more than 300 were left homeless in March 1928 by the collapse of the Saint Francis Dam, which flooded the town. At great personal risk to himself one of the Company's Agents went from house to house inducing families to flee for their lives. Claims in all these disasters were paid promptly, some without the presentation of policies or Premium Receipt Books. In such times of tragedy the Company has always given prompt financial aid to its policyholders, and through its Visiting Nursing Service has brought much desired relief to stricken people.

Even in tranquil times there have been special health problems in this Territory. Smallpox, typhoid fever, and tuberculosis are more prevalent there than in the East. There are policyholders living above the timberline in Colorado where pneumonia is common, and below sea level in Imperial Valley, where infant death rates are among the Nation's highest. A seacoast harboring vessels from Siberia, China, and the East Indies presents dangers from bubonic plague and black smallpox. The hasty exploitation of vast natural resources has created unusual hazards to life and health in mine, factory, and forest.

In many Western cities and towns the salaried Metropolitan Nurse is still the only effective public health influence. Health departments are often lacking or are poorly organized, clinics are unavailable, hospitals small and distant. Rain or shine, the Metropolitan Nurse ministers to the ill. One of them reported from a post near the crest of the Continental Divide: "Today was too cold for anyone to be outside except the milkman and the Metropolitan Nurse." Two thirds of all visits to policyholders in the West are still made by Metropolitan salaried Nurses. On the other hand, in the Eastern Territories, two thirds of the total visits are made by outside Visiting Nurse Associations. The Nursing Service of the Metropolitan in the West reported more than 142,000 visits during 1942, and an average of 43 cases for every thousand Industrial policies.

In matters pertaining to the health and well-being of the Coast population, Dr. William P. Shepard, who has directed the Company's Pacific Coast welfare activities since 1926, has been an active force. Legislators, health officers, educators, and citizens—all turn to him for guidance. Inasmuch as he is responsible for only one Territory, Dr. Shepard has been able to keep in close touch with the individual Managers and Agents, and has, therefore, been better able to enlist their cooperation in various health ventures. Indeed, because of this intensive supervision, the Welfare Division of the Company has often used the Pacific Coast area as a proving ground to try out experiments, results of which have served as a guide for the country as a whole. When an epidemic threatens, the Welfare Division instructs the Manager and his Agents how best to assist the local health officer; and similarly, when a Western health department plans a special immunization or nutrition campaign, the local Metropolitan organization receives a plan and literature for cooperation in its efforts. Under

Dr. Shepard's direction, it has often been possible for the Manager in an undeveloped town to pave the way for a full-time health department. Health officers and school directors in the West have good reason to consider the Metropolitan a friend in need.

The Company, in distributing its health literature, has concentrated on those diseases which showed the greatest prevalence. Currently, 2,000,000 health pamphlets a year are distributed by the Field Force. The Metropolitan literature and exhibits are often the only educational material available to health departments, and many a schoolroom depends upon them for the study of hygiene and safety.

It is hard to prove results, hard to appraise the value of the civic enterprise of a Metropolitan Manager and his associates. There is no exact measuring rod to prove that a community is healthier because many of its citizens learned some simple rules of nutrition from a Metropolitan booklet. Yet the data for the present 1,500,000 Industrial policyholders in the West furnish ample evidence that Company welfare activities have resulted in raising health standards. The death rates from pneumonia and from appendicitis have fallen to under one half those of 1937. The first eight months of 1941 made history when not a single death from diphtheria was reported among the policyholders in this group of States; and only three diphtheria deaths occurred during the entire year. Only 16 years ago the death rate from this disease was 70 times higher than it is today. Many other preventable diseases have also been brought under control. There are indications that the Pacific Coast States now constitute one of the most favored health areas of the country. The adjusted death rate among Industrial policyholders in this Territory was 577.3 per 100,000 in 1941, as compared with a rate of 595.0 per 100,000 for the Company's policyholders in the remaining areas of the United States.

These welfare activities have been aided by the various men in charge of the Head Office. For eight years, Vice-President Wilkes' watchful care over the Company's activities

Left to right—Frederick J. Williams, George B. Scott, Thornton R. Richardson, Frederick F. Taylor, Ernest H. Wilkes.

brought about progressive steps. On August 1, 1928, he was called to the Home Office to share, with A. F. C. Fiske, the direction of the Field Force, and was followed by Frederick J. Williams, who was in charge of the Territory until his death in June 1937. His successor, Vice-President Henry E. North, assumed charge in July 1937, with James A. Smithies as Superintendent of Agencies. Mr. North has continued in his executive capacity to the present. Under his direction special progress has been made in Field management and in the application of modern methods of Agency instruction which he had introduced as director of the Company's Field Training Division.

In the course of its development, the Pacific Coast Head Office has steadily expanded its services, in part through the establishment of Divisions corresponding to those in the Home Office. Thus, while originally only Industrial death claims were paid by the Head Office, the authority of its Claim Division has been extended from time to time. In July 1930 it was authorized to pass upon and pay total and permanent disability claims. Today it handles claims, in all amounts, on Industrial, Ordinary, Group, and Accident and Health. Similarly, through the years the Pacific Coast Ordinary Department has been authorized to pass upon applications of increasingly large amounts of insurance. These extensions of responsibility have resulted in saving time formerly consumed in referring such claims and applications to the Home Office, and thereby have fulfilled one of the prime purposes of the separate Head Office—a greater usefulness to the policyholders in the West. Since 1920 other service units have been added to the Pacific Coast Head Office, including the Group Clerical Section, the Policyholders Service Bureau (December 1923), the Publication Division (February 1929), the Insurance Advisory Bureau (1930), the Field Training Division (April 1934), and the Accident and Health Division (January 1941). In July 1937 Assistant Actuary Arnold B. Brown was assigned to the Coast, and shortly afterward was given the added title of Assistant Manager.

The Head Office has been an active force in many civic and community projects on the Coast and has taken a leading role in civilian war work. While the thunder of Japanese bombs was still echoing over the waters of Hawaii, Mr. North set protective measures in motion, and the Metropolitan was the first large Company in San Francisco to complete an efficient system of air-raid security. This includes underground safety areas, equipped with a kitchen which could feed the entire personnel, and an emergency hospital. Employees have been trained in first aid and fire fighting, and in the procedure for air alarm drills. They are subscribing approximately 11 percent of their earnings to the purchase of War Bonds under the salary deduction plan. One hundred percent of the employees subscribed nearly $5,000 to the Red Cross Emergency Fund in a recent 24-hour drive. Metropolitan women employees have organized their own canteen to distribute food to men of the armed forces on guard at night. The Head Office has responded with similar promptness to countless other war emergency appeals, such as the donation of

HENRY E. NORTH
Vice-President in Charge of Pacific Coast Head Office

scrap metal and rubber, typewriters, and fats from its kitchens for the manufacture of munitions.

In the 42 years during which the Company has functioned on the Coast, the population of the region has almost tripled. The urban group among whom the Metropolitan has been particularly active is now five times its size in 1901. At the beginning of the century about 1,500,000 people were engaged in gainful work; today this figure has grown to more than 5,000,000. This active labor force, the Metropolitan's chosen market, engages in a variety of occupations. Normally, 20 percent are in trade, predominantly retail; 16 percent are in manufacturing, and 15 percent are engaged in agriculture. However, current shifts in the population and growth in certain industries due to the second World War have undoubtedly made for considerable change in these distributions.

Forty-two years is a short time indeed in the life of a great business. Yet these years have established the Pacific Coast

Head Office as one of the country's leading insurance organizations. Figures which seem best to illustrate its growth list increases in every branch. The number of the Head Office's employees has expanded from 53 in 1901 to more than 1,200 today, and the Field Force has grown from 538 to more than 1,200. The amount of Industrial business in force has grown from around $16,000,000 to more than $500,000,000. Whereas there was a little more than $850,000 in Ordinary in force at the end of the year of the Territory's founding, at the end of 1942 it amounted to more than $930,000,000. The 1942 income of the Head Office ($54,000,000) was 43 percent greater than that for the entire Company when the Head Office was established in 1901.

Yet figures alone cannot describe the position which the Company has achieved in its Coast Territory. In spite of the handicaps of great distances, peculiar health hazards, and sparse population, the Territory has been benefitted in numerous ways through the influence of the Metropolitan. That the original party which left New York in 1901 to found the Western Office built well, is attested by the 1,500,000 policyholders on the Coast to whom the Company is more than a financial institution. It is to them, rather, a constructive and benevolent factor in the affairs of this broad area. As its beautiful building is a landmark on the hills of San Francisco, so its accomplishments in protection, in health education, and in assistance to the community as a whole are landmarks in the scheme of social and economic progress.

❧❨ *Part* IV ❩❧

CHAPTER 15

Six Billion Dollars at Work

AT THE CLOSE OF 1942 the Life insurance companies of the United States and the Dominion of Canada held $37,000,000,000 in trust for the security of 70,000,000 policyholders and their families. This capital, accumulated to meet future policy obligations, constitutes a mighty reservoir of private funds. The investment of these sums safely and productively is the very hub of the institution of Life Insurance. The development of the investment program in the past three quarters of a century constitutes a basic phase, not only of Life insurance history but also of the economic growth of the Nation. Special interest attaches to the investment history of the Metropolitan Life Insurance Company because of the leading position it has occupied for many years among the financial institutions of the world.

It is inherent in the conduct of modern Life insurance companies that they are custodians of large aggregations of capital. This results from the level premium plan of operation, which is the foundation stone of the business. Under this plan the premium charged remains constant for the duration of the policy, and is so fixed that it is more than sufficient to meet the mortality cost in the early policy years, thus providing a reserve which, with interest earnings, enables the companies to pay the claims of later years, when the premium is smaller than the mortality cost. These reserves, required and regulated by law, are held for the benefit of the policyholders and guarantee that the contracts will be honored in full when they become due and payable. The income earned by the investment of these funds is an appreciable sum year after year, and reduces the cost of the insurance to the policy-

313

holder. In 1942 alone the American Life insurance companies received well in excess of $1,000,000,000 in interest on their invested assets. The huge sums thus earned are reflected in the premium rates and dividends. If the annual premium for a Whole Life policy for $1,000 at age 20, assuming no interest earnings, is $24.02, interest earned at 2½ percent reduces the premium to $15.02. An even more striking reduction is apparent for a 20-Payment Life policy, where the corresponding reduction in premium rates per $1,000 would be from $61.01 to $27.03. Interest earnings under this form of policy thus cut the annual premium to less than half.

In the early days of the Metropolitan, investing the limited funds of the Company was a relatively minor matter. President Knapp, in addition to attending to the other details of management, found ample time to make all the investments. The portfolio, needless to say, was very limited in character. Loans on real estate secured by mortgages were by far the most important single class of investment, accounting for almost one third of the Company's assets at the middle of the 1870's. Mr. Knapp personally examined the properties and negotiated with the borrowers to secure a satisfactory interest return. When a particularly difficult situation arose, he sought expert advice from builders or real estate dealers, but the final decision was always his own. Inasmuch as President Knapp's duties kept him busy in the city, most applications for loans on out-of-town real estate were rejected. The other investment items of consequence at that time were United States and municipal bonds. Large amounts of Federal securities had been issued during the Civil War and offered attractive rates of interest, even as high as 7 percent. The municipal securities owned by the Company were mostly bonds of the City of Brooklyn, reflecting the ties of residence and business of the Officers and a number of the Directors.

The Company prospered in the 1880's, after the introduction of Industrial insurance, and its assets began to mount rapidly. As the investment operations increased in volume and in complexity, Mr. Knapp and his associate, Mr. Hegeman, who was taking an increasing interest in the investment side of the business, sought the advice of such organizations as Vermilyea & Co. and later of William A. Read. By 1882 the Company was venturing into new fields. In that year the Metropolitan had almost $44,000 in Brooklyn Bridge bonds. In the same year the Company made its first purchase of railroad securities. Beginning on a small scale the Metropolitan soon accelerated its purchases in response to the expanding needs of the transportation industry, and by 1890 about one fourth of its assets were invested in high-grade railroad bonds. Loans on real estate, nevertheless, continued to form a large and increasing part of the investment portfolio.

In consequence, near the end of the decade a Real Estate Section, with Anthony H. Creagh in charge, was created in the Home Office. Young Ecker, whose bent for business had attracted the attention of President Knapp, was promoted to be Assistant Manager of the new Section. Mr. Ecker achieved a first-hand knowledge of real estate values through the inspection of properties on which loans were being considered. He devoted himself so intensively to his job, that he could walk through New York City and point out practically every one of the 600 properties on which the Company held a mortgage.

This knowledge stood him in good stead. In 1893 came the severe panic and depression which had serious repercussions on the investment market. In the critical period that followed, the Company acquired many properties through foreclosure, and the record shows that these came to be 7 percent of the Company's total assets. Mr. Ecker, at the age of 26, was faced with the task of handling the properties, many of them in Brooklyn. He applied himself to rehabilitating them, and soon the buildings were filled with tenants, were producing an income, and there was little trouble later in disposing of them satisfactorily.

As the funds available for investment continued to increase, the work of the Real Estate Division grew in proportion. This small group was faced with a multitude of tasks, including the examination of titles, the checking of the accuracy and renewal of fire insurance policies, the payment of taxes and assessments, the annual search of records for unpaid taxes, and the periodical examination of properties and their valuation in order to determine whether loans were secure. To expedite the handling of real estate transactions, the Bond and Mortgage Division was created in the summer of 1898. Having already demonstrated his ability, Mr. Ecker, at the age of 31, was chosen to be Manager of the new Division, and to take immediate charge of all loans on real estate.

Mr. Ecker soon took over a good deal of the responsibility for purchasing securities as well. With the continued financial growth of the Company and the expansion of the investment portfolio, corporate securities played an increasingly important role. By 1905, investments in bonds and stocks grew to more than half the Company's total assets, which at the end of that year amounted to $151,663,477. By far the most important item in the portfolio were railroad securities, totaling more than $52,000,000 and comprising more than one third of the Company's total investments. A sizable amount of money was also invested in governmental securities and in the bonds of public utility companies, a major part of which were street railway bonds. Of lesser importance were loans on collateral and loans to policyholders. Real estate continued to be a prominent item, although relatively less so than in the previous decade. Mortgage loans on real estate amounted to $38,000,000, and real estate owned came to $17,500,000. It is significant that the Metropolitan had only a small percentage of its assets invested in stocks, although prior to the passage of the Armstrong legislation in 1906 the New York Insurance Law did not prohibit Life insurance companies from purchasing such securities.

The investment duties and responsibilities of the Company were gradually multiplied to the point where they constituted a business in themselves. In due course the growing diversity of the portfolio demanded a corps of specialists as varied and extensive as that found in any investment banking house. To

316

evaluate railroad securities, for example, it was necessary to have detailed information regarding the operation and financing of the various roads, and the relative merits of the various issues. County and municipal investments called for familiarity with the local tax laws, with the per capita debt of the various communities, and with the major facts concerning their development. Investing in the obligations of public utility companies required the ability to analyze the complicated financial structure of the organizations, as well as knowledge of conditions in the sections served by these utilities. There was the need to train men to analyze and evaluate balance sheets of all corporate enterprises.

The mere routine of handling the investments had become a voluminous job. There were the elementary problems of safely storing the securities, cataloging them, filing them so that they would be accessible, cutting coupons, and a hundred other tasks which are indispensable for the smooth and effective functioning of an investment department. Expansion of the Home Office facilities became a necessity. Accordingly, in 1905, the office of Comptroller was established and Mr. Ecker, who had become an expert on all phases of investment, was its first incumbent. One year later the office of Treasurer was created, and again Mr. Ecker was promoted to be the first to fill that position. Thus, at the age of 39, he became chief financial officer of a rapidly expanding institution with assets exceeding $175,000,000. The subsequent financial development of the Company has been continuously under his immediate direction.

In the next 10 years the investments of the Metropolitan continued to grow essentially along the lines already established. However, during the period of the first World War and in the feverish decade that followed, there arose a number of striking developments and innovations. In response to the need for financing the war, the Metropolitan bought large blocks of United States Liberty Bonds and Canadian War and Victory Bonds, these purchases coming to a total of more than $120,000,000. Whereas during the period from 1907 through

317

1914, Government bonds constituted less than 1/10 of 1 percent of all assets owned by the Company, by 1919 this ratio
had risen to 16 percent. During and after the war there was an
accelerated growth in American industry and extensive development of power, light, telephone, and other public utilities,
and the securities of these enterprises began to play a more
prominent role in the Company's portfolio.

This period also witnessed an important innovation in the
investment program—the granting of loans on farms, the
development of which will be described in detail in the next
chapter. But overshadowing by far any other investment item
in the 1920's were mortgage loans on urban real estate. To
relieve the serious housing shortage, new construction activities were undertaken at a feverish pace in the postwar decade
and provided a considerable outlet for Life insurance investment. In the Metropolitan portfolio, urban mortgage loans
increased from 31.3 percent of the assets in 1920 to nearly
38 percent in 1928, in which year the actual amount in such
loans came to $1,019,052,553. This category of investment
dominated the portfolio, repeating the experience of an earlier
period of the Company's history. Moreover, to meet the
serious housing shortage which existed on a national scale the
Company, on the suggestion of a legislative committee and as
a demonstration in housing developments, took the unprecedented step of building low-cost model apartments under its
own management and ownership.

Despite the fact that the postwar decade, especially toward
the close, was characterized by frenzied speculation, the
Metropolitan, as well as other Life insurance companies, remained aloof from the current enthusiasms. Stock prices in
those years rose like inflated bubbles, with the result that in
the autumn of 1929 came the most serious financial upset in
American history. In a short time values dropped by billions
of dollars, and panic reigned in the financial world. Hundreds
of thousands of people, lured into the market by the desire
for speculative gain, saw their life savings swept away. But
during that critical period, when the financial structure of the

318

CHART V

Amount of Assets
Metropolitan Life Insurance Company, 1868–1942

Billions of Dollars

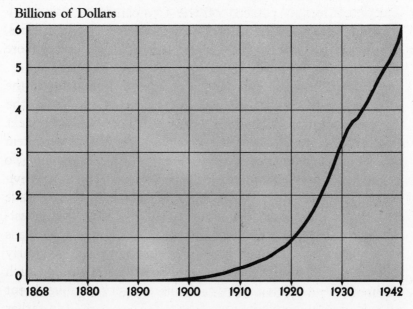

country seemed shaken to its foundations, Life insurance investments remained fundamentally sound. This stability reflected the high character of the holdings and was a tribute to the judgment of the investment officials of the companies, who, over the years, had avoided the siren calls of quick profits held out by the rising market in speculative securities.

There was need, nevertheless, for the rapid readjustment of the investment portfolio in accordance with conditions then prevailing. Mr. Ecker, with the assistance of Mr. George and the younger Ecker, handled this difficult task with rare skill. The percentage of the Company's assets in urban mortgage loans was reduced steadily from 39 in 1929 to 25 in 1935, and to 14 in 1942; farm loans, which had been decreasing since 1925, declined still further, until they amounted to only 1½ percent of the Company's assets. Railroad securities dropped from a little more than 20 percent of the portfolio prior to the depression, to about 10 percent a decade later. On the other

319

hand, Government bonds, which represented a very nominal amount in 1929, rose steadily in prominence among the Company's holdings during the 1930's; by 1942 these securities accounted for 30 percent of the Company's total assets. Readiness to cooperate in necessary Government financing, a desire for safety, and the general lack of other investment opportunities, were all factors in this rise. Public utilities took on an increasing prominence, advancing steadily year after year until, in 1942, they occupied second rank among the bond classifications. Similarly, industrial holdings rose rapidly in the last decade.

As invariably happens during periods of economic depression, loans to policyholders on the security of their contracts increased rather sharply. In the decade following 1929 the amount of new loans made to Metropolitan policyholders totalled more than $1,000,000,000, much of which was repaid. Policy loans rose from 8.2 percent of the Company's assets in 1928, reached a peak of 13.0 percent in 1933, then steadily declined to 7.6 percent of the assets in 1942. Large numbers of policyholders looked to their Life insurance funds to tide them over the period of stress. Then, as seldom before, they came to understand the solid character and value of their investment in Life insurance.

It was inevitable under the conditions prevailing in the 30's that many of those to whom money had been loaned on the security of city real estate and on farms should find themselves unable to meet their obligations. The Company invariably attempted to work out a satisfactory adjustment with such borrowers, and to resort to foreclosure only as a necessary last step to protect the interest of policyholders. Nevertheless, such foreclosed properties reached a total of more than $350,000,000, or 7.1 percent of the Company's assets in 1938. This ratio was not excessive as compared with some earlier depressions. Moreover, as economic recovery began to make itself felt, the foreclosure rate declined rapidly while the sale of acquired properties increased. During 1941 alone, foreclosed properties dropped from 6.3 percent of the Company's assets to 5.3 percent, representing a decrease of nearly $40,000,000, for the year. It is significant that the total sale price of foreclosed farm and city real estate for the decade of the 30's as a whole was greater than the amount at which these properties were acquired. In every respect, Mr. Ecker and his associates were successful in guiding the Company through the depression hazards. Its financial condition today appears more solid than ever before.

In view of the many changes in the investment portfolio during the period of readjustment, it is of interest to analyze the current distribution of the Company's assets, totaling just short of $6,000,000,000. On pages 322 and 323 appear the list of assets, together with the liabilities of the Company, as of December 31, 1942.

Defense preparations prior to the second World War and the actual outbreak of that war brought United States and Dominion Government securities into sharp focus. During 1941, for example, the Company increased its holdings of United States Government securities by $150,000,000, equivalent to fully one half its total increase in assets in that year. Since the attack on Pearl Harbor, December 7, 1941, assistance to Treasury financing has become the cardinal objective of the Metropolitan's investment operations. In 1942 the Company added about $425,000,000 to its portfolio of United States Government securities. This was larger even than the increase in total assets for that year, and raised the percentage of these bonds to over 27 percent of total assets at the year end— more than double the similar percent of total at the end of the first World War.

In the decade ending 1941 the Company's investments in Dominion Government obligations rose from 17 percent of total Canadian assets to about 35 percent, and since the Dominion of Canada entered the war on September 9, 1939, all funds invested by the Metropolitan in Canadian bonds have been placed in Dominion, or Dominionguaranteed, obligations, with the exception of $2,000,000, which was invested in bonds of the Province of Quebec.

Metropolitan Life

ASSETS

National Government Securities		$1,772,834,288.52
U. S. Government	$1,640,023,863.53	
Canadian Government	132,810,424.99	
Other Bonds		2,034,305,897.93
U. S. State and Municipal	$86,482,597.79	
Canadian Provincial and Municipal . .	92,268,974.32	
Railroad	527,015,597.35	
Public Utilities	818,347,218.79	
Industrial and Miscellaneous	510,191,509.68	
Stocks		81,805,186.00
All but $320,750.00 are preferred or guaranteed.		
First Mortgage Loans on Real Estate		952,431,702.03
Farms	$89,380,287.45	
Other Property	863,051,414.58	
Loans on Policies		453,940,104.42
Made to policyholders on the security of their policies.		
Real Estate		383,026,409.36
Includes housing projects, and real estate for Company use.		
Cash		158,765,194.49
Premiums, Deferred and in Course of Collection, net .		95,913,691.33
Interest and Rents Due and Accrued, etc.		61,893,102.50
Total Assets		$5,994,915,576.58

NOTE—*Assets carried at $271,804,055.40 in the above state of law or regulatory authority. Canadian business embraced*

Insurance Company

the State Insurance Departments of the United States.)

LIABILITIES

Policy Reserves Required by Law	$5,188,714,637.87
Dividends to Policyholders	102,733,947.00
Funds for Future Payment Under Supplementary Contracts	189,169,000.07
Dividends Left with the Company	30,301,837.94
Policy Claims Currently Outstanding	30,307,563.89
Other Policy Obligations	18,993,606.98
Taxes Due or Accrued	17,542,243.00
Reserve for Mortgage Loans	17,000,000.00
Miscellaneous Liabilities	18,083,549.37
Special Surplus Funds	12,300,000.00
Unassigned Funds (Surplus)	369,769,190.46
TOTAL	$5,994,915,576.58

ment are deposited with various officials under requirements
in this statement is reported on the basis of par of exchange.

At the end of 1942, obligations of the United States and Canadian National Governments comprised the largest single category of the Company's assets, representing $1,772,000,000 or 30 percent of its total assets. In addition, the Company holds more than $178,000,000 in bonds of the States of the Union and the Provinces of Canada, and of the Municipalities of both Nations.

Although mortgage loans on real estate are now second in importance in the Metropolitan portfolio, the proportion of assets in this type of investment is the lowest in the history of the Company. Such loans account for 16 percent of the Company's total assets. Of this amount, by far the largest part is on urban property. Ranking third in importance at the end of 1942 are the bonds of public utility companies which supply light, power, water, and heat to homes and factories in the United States and Canada. These securities are almost entirely those of operating companies, and experience has shown them to be sound and well suited for Life insurance purposes. Investments in public utilities currently come to $818,000,000, or 14 percent of Metropolitan assets.

The Company still holds more than $500,000,000 in railroad securities. It should be noted, however, that this class of investment currently comprises a smaller proportion of the Metropolitan's assets than at any time since the middle of the 1880's. In recent years substantially all the Company's new investments in the railroad field have been limited to two types of bonds which afford a high degree of safety, namely, securities issued to finance the acquisition of equipment, and bonds secured by terminal property, where the property is leased to, or the bonds are guaranteed by, the leading railroad systems.

The securities of industrial corporations now form as large a part of our investment portfolio as do railroad bonds, adding up to a total of $510,000,000. These corporations have had a long and favorable record of earnings and are engaged in the production or manufacture of such commodities as steel, oil, rubber, chemicals, nonferrous metals, and foodstuffs for which there is a sustained demand. A number of these industries are now putting their major effort into war production. The selling of bonds by an issuer directly to the Metropolitan and other Life insurance companies has become an advantageous and an accepted method of corporate financing. From 1935 to 1942 the Company invested well in excess of $1,000,000,000 through the private or direct placement method.

Loans to policyholders at present amount to $453,000,000, or 7.6 percent of the total assets. This item is, of course, not part of the investment design, but enters the portfolio as a phase of the Life insurance business in accordance with a clause in the policy contract. The Company has constantly urged that policy loans be used only to tide over emergencies, and be resorted to only when no other source of funds is available.

The Company's real estate holdings at the end of 1942 amounted to $383,000,000. This included the Home Office in New York City; the Head Offices at San Francisco and Ottawa; Parkchester and other Company housing developments; and properties acquired by foreclosure. The Company does not seek the ownership of real estate outside of such housing developments and the properties necessary to carry on its business, nor does the law permit long-continued direct ownership of business properties, apartment houses, and other real property acquired by foreclosure without the consent of supervisory officials.

Inasmuch as the Metropolitan and other Life insurance companies constantly utilize their funds productively, they keep only a very small proportion of their assets in cash. Currently, about 2½ percent of the Company's assets are in cash on hand or in banks. This amount is adequate, even allowing for the demands for loans in emergency situations.

Stocks of all kinds comprise a very small proportion of the Company's investment portfolio, amounting only to 1½ percent of the total assets. Of the $81,000,000 so invested, 99.6 percent is in preferred or guaranteed stocks. Almost all these securities have been purchased after 1928, when the New York State Legislature permitted Life insurance companies to buy guaranteed and preferred stocks under specified restrictions. The trifling proportion of common stocks held by the Company has come into the portfolio through reorganizations, and represents values that were for the most part originally bond investments. Moreover, stocks so acquired must be sold within a specified time.

It is significant that the Metropolitan, as well as the entire institution of Life Insurance, has carried on over the decades with never a question as to the fundamental safety of the invested funds. Periods of depression and periods of prosperity have come and gone, but the financial structure of the Life insurance companies has remained intact. They have always been ready to meet every obligation. It will be of interest to consider the factors which account for this extraordinary achievement.

Safety has always been the first principle guiding the investment of Metropolitan funds. It is, of course, essential that the invested funds earn as high a rate of interest as is feasible, so as to reduce the cost of insurance to policyholders as far as possible. But the first consideration has always been safety, attained through the protective measures set up by statute and supplemented by the voluntary rules and procedures which the companies themselves have formulated. The laws of the various States define the character of the securities which companies may buy, and specify certain conditions under which investments may be made. In New York State, for example, investments must be properly authorized by the Board of Directors or one of its Committees. Companies are forbidden to purchase common stocks, or to participate in underwriting syndicates; officials may not profit personally by investment transactions.

It is wise, however, that the statutory requirements, stringent as they are, allow Life insurance management discretion and initiative in exercising the investment function. Laws, however valuable, can never substitute for judgment. Actually, the investment policy of the Metropolitan and other Life insurance companies has in many ways been more rigid than the requirements of the laws which govern them. Each proposed investment is thoroughly investigated by a specialist in the particular field. In the case of corporate securities, the history and stability of the enterprise, the character of its management, and its competitive record are studied. Its financial statements over a series of years are subjected to established tests and standards involving such considerations as ratios between net earnings and fixed charges, between assets and liabilities. The terms of the issue are scrutinized with regard to provisions for sinking funds, and protective covenants relating to such matters as maintenance, depreciation, the incurring of additional debt, and the payment of dividends. These protective provisions are particularly important in the case of preferred stocks and debentures, which were made eligible for investment by the amendment of the New York Insurance Law in 1928. If, upon thorough analysis, the security promises safety of principal and a satisfactory return, it is recommended to the Finance Committee of the Board of Directors for approval.

Those charged with the duty of investing Life insurance funds cannot relax their vigilance even after the policyholders' money is invested. Even the best investments are not without some risk. The Company, accordingly, has a staff of specialists whose function it is to study and analyze all the facts—business, financial, and otherwise—which will aid the investment Officers to arrive at sound conclusions, not only with respect to the investment when made, but also as to the wisdom of retaining or disposing of it in later years, when changed conditions warrant reconsideration. These specialists are familiar with particular industries, such as railroads, power and light, telephone, steel, and chemical, as well as finances of governmental bodies. Through periodic financial reports and other sources the experts continue to follow the progress of each corporation in which the Metropolitan has investments, and to study the changes in the industry as a whole.

Through the years the Company has taken the position that the character of the Life insurance business does not allow of investments with a speculative element. Even during the financial fever that raged prior to the stock market debacle of 1929, when many people advocated the purchase of common stocks for trustee funds, Mr. Ecker took every opportunity to caution against departures from the established standards of investment. When attempts were made to modify investment laws to allow common stocks in Life insurance company portfolios, he repeatedly and tenaciously opposed the weakening of the legal standards.

With serious misgivings as to the trend of the times, Mr. Ecker, on September 26, 1929, spoke before the National Association of Life Underwriters in Washington, D. C., and again emphasized that Life insurance investments were held to insure the faithful performance of the policy contract. He took the uncompromising position that even the best common stocks should have no place in the investment program of Life insurance companies. "Common stocks," he said, "are inherently speculative. Profits are large if the enterprise is eminently successful; but, in the event of failure, losses may be correspondingly large, or even larger, since the entire value may be wiped out. Of a given number of enterprises started each year, a certain number fail. We are today riding on a high wave of prosperity. We want to foster it and to have it roll on, but we do not entirely forget that there will always be an ebb and flow of the business tides. The curve of advancing prices has, in the past, invariably been offset by cycles of declines of equal degree." Within a month these words proved prophetic.

In 1931 Mr. Ecker, in studying the immediate effects of the stock market crash, reviewed the experience of about 50 common stocks that had been urged for Life insurance investments. Prior to October 1929, experienced financiers would have characterized the list as a very select one. They were the stocks of outstanding business organizations in the United States which had either no bonds or practically no funded debt ahead of them. Nevertheless, between December 31, 1929, and June 30, 1931, the average depreciation in market value of these common stocks amounted to more than

30 percent. During that very period, the investment account of the Metropolitan showed a profit. On December 31, 1929, the Company had in its portfolio about 1,300 separate items of bonds and preferred and guaranteed stocks, the market value of which was approximately $1,200,000,000. Between the end of 1929 and the middle of 1931, there matured or were sold out of that portfolio securities of market value of about $74,000,000, from which the net profit amounted to something in excess of $1,000,000. The securities remaining unmatured and unsold on June 30, 1931, had then a market value of $1,139,000,000, which sum, taken with the amount matured or sold, showed a total of $1,213,000,000. Thus, in market value of securities still owned, plus market value of securities sold in the interim, the Company had a profit between December 31, 1929, and June 30, 1931, of $13,000,000.

The second cardinal principle of the Company's investment policy is to obtain as high a return as possible commensurate with safety. It has already been pointed out that the insurance contract is predicated upon the earning of adequate interest. The actual investment yield, if it exceeds the rate assumed in calculating the premium, is one of the three principal sources from which dividends are paid. Therefore, the rise and fall in interest rates necessarily affect the cost of insurance to the policyholder.

In the past three quarters of a century, interest rates in the United States have tended to move in cycles. There have been three major movements—a downward trend from 1870 to the turn of the century, an upward movement from about 1900 to 1924, followed by another down swing which has continued to the present time. The rate of interest earned by the Metropolitan has passed through the same three periods of rise and fall. In the first few decades of the Company's history the amounts available for investment were relatively small, with the result that the earnings fluctuated rather widely from year to year. Yet it is clear from the data available that the general tendency was toward a decreasing yield. With the reversal of the trend, the net interest earnings by the Company increased quite steadily from 4 percent about 1900 to nearly 5½ percent in 1924. Thereafter, however, the return on investments has tended to drop. During the latter half of the 1920's the fall was gradual, declining from 5.4 percent in 1924 to 5.2 percent in 1929 and 1930. During the early years of the depression there was a greatly accelerated drop, and by 1935 the net income on Metropolitan investments was slightly less than 3.7 percent. Since then, the decline has leveled off and in 1941 the interest earned was 3.4 percent.

The interest rates for each of the major classes of investment have, in general, followed the same course as that for all types combined. Their respective net returns, however, have differed. Considering the two major classifications of Life insurance investment, we find that mortgage loans on city and farm property have yielded a higher return than has the bond portfolio. For 10 years prior to 1929 the interest earned on mortgage loans, deducting investment expenses and asset losses, was 5½ percent, as against 5 percent for bonds and stocks. However, at least a portion of the higher yield on mortgage loans represents a risk element for possible future losses and reduced return on real estate acquired through foreclosure. During the period from 1929 to 1941, inclusive, the corresponding net yield on mortgage loans and foreclosed real estate combined was 3.4 percent, as against 3½ percent for bonds and stocks. The marked increase in Government bonds in the Company's portfolio, coupled with the decrease in investments such as mortgage loans, has contributed toward lowering recent interest earnings. The average rate on bond purchases during 1941 and 1942, excluding short-term bonds, was only 2.7 percent. We can, therefore, realize the serious impact of economic trends and current investment conditions on the cost of Life insurance to the policyholders. This subject has been more fully considered in Chapter 10.

In addition to considerations of safety and interest yield, Life insurance company investments are made in accordance with the principle of diversification. Neither law nor careful administration can absolutely eliminate the risk of loss and, in order to minimize it, Life insurance companies spread their investments as widely as possible. The old adage not to "put all of one's eggs into one basket" is a fundamental investment policy. Metropolitan funds, invested in more than 100,000 separate items, are widely diversified in character, and are spread over many communities and enterprises throughout the United States and Canada. In fact, these investments cover every State and every Canadian Province. Wide geographic distribution minimizes the effect of adverse business or agricultural conditions in particular localities. Not only are the funds spread over a great variety of categories, but within each class as wide a distribution as possible is made. With the large sums of money held by the Company, and with the experienced staff available, the Metropolitan can and does carry the practice of diversification to an extent which is impossible for an individual investor.

The principle of diversification is also applied to maturity dates of investments. Life insurance companies can predict with a fair degree of accuracy the amounts they will be called upon to pay in future years, and, therefore, can select their investments to mature over a period so that when such funds are needed there will be a constant flow of maturities. Care is taken, too, to provide a proper balance between long- and short-term investments, so that assets will neither be frozen nor require too frequent reinvestment. A diversified portfolio with reference to maturity dates will not only bring a steady income, but in case of emergency will provide securities which can be sold in a ready market without sacrifice.

The financial soundness of Life insurance companies is, moreover, safeguarded by the conservative valuation of their assets. In its report to the public and to the Insurance Departments, the Company may claim credit only for the so-called "admitted assets," which exclude the intangible item of good will and even furniture and equipment, book value of bonds over amortized or investment value, and overdue interest and rent. The basis for the valuation of assets is provided by State laws, but in practice the rules are laid down by the National Association of Insurance Commissioners, whose membership consists of the heads of the Insurance Departments of the various States. The values are reappraised from time to time, so as to prevent overvaluation of investment items in prosperous periods, and to protect policyholders against ruinously low valuations in times of depression. The Metropolitan follows a conservative policy in valuing its assets. The securities held by the Company usually have an aggregate market value many millions of dollars in excess of that carried in the Company's statement. As a result of the depression the Company conservatively wrote down the book value of its securities and its real estate holdings. This does not always mean an ultimate loss in the case of any particular investment, because with the return of normal conditions some of the amounts written down have found their way back into the assets of the Company. Life insurance companies are in an especially strong position with regard to their security holdings, inasmuch as these are bought for long-time interest yield and not for speculative gain. As long as payments of interest and principal are made when due, and the bonds remain sound, fluctuations in market value usually have little or no effect on the stability of the Life insurance companies.

The investments of the Life insurance companies are, furthermore, directed along channels which benefit the economic life of the Nation. The vast funds accumulated by the companies, which otherwise might have been dissipated in consumers' goods, have become essential elements in the expanding national economy. It would be difficult to find any large construction program, whether it be a dam, a hydroelectric plant, a sewer system, or a public school, in which Life insurance funds have not played some part. Moreover, these funds have always flowed in the direction of meeting changing public needs. In fact, if one wished to trace the history of economic progress in the United States, one could find it nowhere better mirrored than in the investment record of the American Life insurance companies.

When the national Government, especially during times of war, required vast sums, the companies at once responded liberally to meet the situation. When railroad building was indispensable for our country's welfare; when agriculture needed financial assistance; when a housing shortage threatened the Nation; when industry required the encouragement and stimulation of capital; when policyholders could find few other sources for emergency assistance, as during the bank holiday—Life insurance funds met the need. In the early 30's, when States and municipalities experienced difficulty, due to the depression, in obtaining funds through normal investment channels, the Metropolitan proved helpful in some important instances. Such purchases have been satisfactory investments. Through the years, probably no other single important class of investment funds has been more sensitive to the sound requirements of the American people than those which have been entrusted to the management of the Life insurance companies.

This does not mean, however, that Company funds are hastily shifted from one class of investment to another. That would be neither in the public interest nor in the interest of policyholders. The spreading out of maturity dates and the growth of the assets permit an orderly redistribution without shifting. Insurance funds, because of their trust nature, obviously cannot be the first to flow into a new industry, which must first be served by "venture capital." Nor would it be in the public interest for Life insurance funds to be impulsively withdrawn from a mature industry. Because their holdings are commonly of prior lien nature, companies such as the Metropolitan can well afford to retain them temporarily even in unfavorable times, awaiting a return to more normal conditions. Similarly, when the Metropolitan becomes the involuntary owner of property through fore-closure, it functions in the interest of the community. Acting as a "good citizen," it promptly pays back taxes, rehabilitates the property, and keeps it in good condition until sold, fre-quently to its former owner.

HARRY C. HAGERTY
Treasurer

In serving the community, Metropolitan investments also serve the policyholders who comprise so large a part of the population of the United States and Canada. The insured find part of their money invested in or near their respective communities in farms, homes, stores, roads, schools, and many other local projects. Whether they are wage-earners, business or professional men, they benefit by the tendency of these investments to create a demand for goods, to sustain real estate values, give employment, and to serve other modern economic needs. One policyholder may live in Parkchester; another may live in a community which has been enabled by Metropolitan funds to build a much-needed public improvement. Most policyholders use the railroad, the telephone, electricity, and other services of which they are part investors by virtue of their Metropolitan insurance; all of them are interested in the success of the present war effort, which is being aided by the invested funds. The diversification and geographical distribution of the Metropolitan's investments are not only important safety factors, but also indicate that the Company recognizes the needs of the communities from which the premium money has come, and puts it back to work in those regions so far as appropriate investments are available.

The way in which the Company has distributed its investments in relation to the origin of the funds is well illustrated by the fact that the Company's Canadian investments are in excess of its Canadian reserves, and that the amount of investments exceeds the reserve in every State except the New England States and a few others, where the local supply of investment funds is plentiful. In considering the needs of the localities in which the policyholders reside, the Company does not, however, lose sight of the fact that the real interest of the policyholder, regardless of where he resides, is to get the best returns out of safe investments, and that his funds should be placed where the soundest opportunities arise.

WILLIAM S. NORTON
Comptroller

GLENN E. ROGERS
Third Vice-President

Throughout its investment history, the Metropolitan has had an impressive record of safety, good earnings, and public service. This achievement is closely associated with the career of one personality. For almost half a century Frederick H. Ecker, now Chairman of the Board, has skillfully and resourcefully guided the investment program of the Company, giving it continuity of policy and unity of direction. Even at the present time, at the age of 75, he still carries the major responsibility of keeping $6,000,000,000 at work. His has been an experience which has no counterpart in financial history.

The Company has been fortunate, also, in the men in charge of the various investment departments working under the guidance of Mr. Ecker. For 22 years, from 1906 to 1928, the Comptroller's Division, which handles city real estate, was under the supervision of Walter Stabler, who had had a quarter century of experience in this field before joining the Company. Since Mr. Stabler's retirement in 1928, William S.

Norton, who had been working with him since 1911, has carried the responsibility of the Division, which now has a personnel of 550 and completes well in excess of 18,000 transactions a year involving more than $200,000,000. When Frederick H. Ecker was advanced from Treasurer to Vice-President, he was succeeded by Henry W. George, who in turn was followed by Frederic W. Ecker. The latter was appointed Treasurer in 1931 and was elected to the office of Vice-President in charge of investments in 1936, which position he held until January 14, 1942, when he resigned to devote full time to the war effort as special assistant to the Lend-Lease Administrator. Harry C. Hagerty, whose service with the Company began in 1917, has been Treasurer since 1936. The Company's Farm Loan Division has been under the direction of Third Vice-President Glenn E. Rogers for more than a decade, and the housing projects have been under the management of George Gove since 1938.

GEORGE GOVE
Manager, Housing Projects

The important role played by the Company's Directors in determining its investment policy is too often overlooked. The members of the Board responsible for this phase of the business are leading figures in the world of finance, and serve the interests of policyholders with no other incentive than to render a fine public service. The Chairman has enjoyed the rare privilege of having shared with the members of the Board in safeguarding the assets of 30,000,000 policyholders and in providing for their security.

CHAPTER 16

Financing Homes and Farms

IN DISCUSSING the Company's investment program in its
broadest terms, we have already touched upon the many
ways in which the funds invested in Government bonds, in
railroad securities, and in public utility and industrial enterprises promote the social and economic welfare of individuals
and communities. In this chapter we turn our attention to
the premium dollars which are at work to provide the very
fundamentals of everyday life—homes for our families and
food for our people. Actually, the Metropolitan's investments in real estate mortgages, in large-scale housing projects,
and in farm loans have rendered services far beyond their
primary objective, a fair return on capital. In each of these
fields the Company has taken the lead in developing new
techniques to serve the general welfare of the country. Let
us examine these three classes of investment in turn.

Loans on urban real estate mortgages have always provided
an important field for the investment of Life insurance funds.
This type of security, as we have seen in the previous chapter,
constituted the largest single item in the Metropolitan's
investment portfolio during the greater part of its history.
At some periods it comprised not far from half the total
assets. The popularity of mortgage loans with lending institutions reflects the prime character of the security and its
relatively high interest return. In this way the Company
has not only invested its funds safely and profitably, but has
at the same time rendered a timely and valuable service in
providing housing and commercial structures for large sections
of the American people.

The Company's investment policy in its mortgage loans
not only meets the provisions of the New York State Insur-

ance Law, but also its own added requirements as regards safety, interest return, and maturity. Under the present Insurance Law the Metropolitan is permitted to loan on first mortgage security an amount not to exceed two thirds the value of the real property. The total mortgage loan investment of the Company must not exceed 40 percent of the admitted assets, and the maximum loan upon the security of any one property must not exceed 2 percent of the Company's assets. The law permits investments in Canada under the same provisions as those which apply in this country.

Of prime importance in assuring the safety of mortgage investments is the sound valuation of property. Although the law provides no yardstick for valuation, the Company appraises properties conservatively on the basis of normal value, discounting sharp temporary fluctuations in prices. Metropolitan mortgage loans are qualified also by such factors as the relative character of the property and its surroundings, the possibility of adverse trends, the building design, and the layout. The Company avoids mortgage loans on improvements of a specialized or restricted character, such as those in resort areas or in places depending on one or a small number of industries. In this category fall also such properties as are owned by industrial corporations, except in stable and fundamental industries.

In conformity with the principle of diversity, the Company spreads its mortgage loans over a variety of properties such as private houses, apartment buildings, stores, office and loft buildings. In each group further diversification is achieved through varying the size of loans and through wide geographic distribution.

By far the largest number of Metropolitan investments in urban mortgages—more than 50,000—are on small residential properties. These constitute 91 percent of the Company's real estate loans and average about $3,000 each. Such properties offer the safety of diversity, are readily sold if acquired through foreclosure, and provide a mortgage-lending service for large numbers of individuals throughout the country. The

Company's mortgages also cover large income properties. Loans on apartment houses, averaging about $100,000 each, number over 3,000, or 6 percent of the mortgage loans. The remaining 3 percent, some 1,600, are on business buildings which average about $225,000 each and comprise 45 percent of the sum loaned on mortgages on urban property. There is much to be said in favor of large loans. They are not subject to the same degree of competition as small loans, and at the same time are relatively less expensive to handle. The Company's experience over a period of 40 years indicates that real estate loans of more than $500,000 have a foreclosure rate 25 percent less than that for loans of smaller amounts.

Another principle guiding these investments is their service to the public and their social utility. Prior to the first World War, the rapid growth of cities throughout the United States and Canada caused a shortage of housing facilities. As cities, particularly New York, opened new residential sections, the Metropolitan, through its mortgage loans, encouraged the construction of many apartment houses and business buildings. At the same time, the Company made loans on groups of houses to employers who aided employees to purchase their own homes. The first loans of this type were made in Akron, Ohio, to employers in the rubber industry. Beginning in 1913, group housing loans aggregating $4,000,000 were placed through two companies on 1,800 homes for industrial workers. Later, similar types of loans were granted to other employers in New York, Tennessee, West Virginia, Wisconsin, and other States. The houses were built and sold by the employers on convenient terms to their workers. The mortgages ran for a term of 15 years, with provision for repayment by instalments which were remitted semiannually to the Metropolitan by the employers. These loans not only assisted in relieving local housing shortages but also contributed toward promoting better employer-employee relations.

It was in the period after the first World War that the housing problem reached its most serious proportions, partly as a result of restrictions against new construction during the war. The Metropolitan, recognizing the seriousness of the situation, decided to grant large loans for the construction of moderate-priced dwellings and apartments. Walter Stabler, then Comptroller of the Company, took leadership in this movement not only to provide adequate housing at reduced rentals and to stimulate employment in the building trades, but to encourage other institutions to finance new building as well.

To meet the emergency it was necessary to devise a practical system of operation which would make the Company's funds immediately available throughout the country. The assurance was needed that the loans would be made properly, that investments would be safeguarded adequately, and that at the same time the Company would be relieved of the prohibitive detail and expense ordinarily incident to caring for a great number of small loans in locations distant from the Home Office. In 1920 it was decided to transact the business through Loan Correspondents—namely, banks, trust companies, or mortgage guarantee companies selected because of their experience and organization for handling city mortgage loans. The plan worked out most satisfactorily, and at the end of 1923 the Company had some 66 Loan Correspondents, who in turn had appointed 165 local Correspondents for smaller locations, making a total of 231 lending institutions from which the Metropolitan bought housing loans on properties located in 37 States. In New York City and the immediate vicinity the loans were made directly to individuals and builders and were handled by the Home Office.

According to the arrangements under this plan of operation, loans are made by the Correspondents with their own funds. After the improvements are completed and the loans are approved, they are assigned to the Company. Acceptance may be had from the Company in advance of construction, provided the plans and specifications submitted are approved and the Correspondent's appraisal of the land and recommendation of the loan are satisfactory. This feature is of special importance, as it permits borrowers to arrange for permanent financing before starting to build. The Correspondent, for a fixed fee, collects the interest and instalments and looks after the payment of taxes and fire insurance.

The loans were made for a 15-year term, which was a new idea to a large number of home borrowers and distinctly to their advantage, as it eliminated uncertainty in regard to extension or renewal of the usual three- or five-year maturity obligation. To protect the Company against depreciation and to encourage thrift, the borrower was required to increase his equity by semiannual payments in reduction of principal, equivalent to 6 percent of the original loan per annum. The borrower also had the privilege of paying off a loan at any time after three years. Under this policy of requiring principal reductions, the total amount of repayments received in the period from 1922 to 1931 was almost 10 times as great as in the previous decade, whereas loans made during that period increased only 5½ times. The foresight in advocating the repayment of principal on such a wide scale made the Company's loans more secure during the depression years.

The Metropolitan has also aided in the solution of the national housing problem through cooperation with official agencies. In 1926 the New York State Housing Law was enacted, authorizing municipalities to extend tax exemption to buildings erected by publicly regulated, limited-dividend corporations, which were organized to provide housing at cost and at rentals fixed by the State Board of Housing. The 1939 report of the Board shows that of the total $22,000,000 loaned under this act on 14 projects, more than $5,000,000 was taken by the Company. This was 77 percent of the total loaned by other than United States Government agencies. The Metropolitan was the only insurance company which up to that time or since has loaned on projects built in accordance with the provisions of the act. Thus the Company assisted in the creation of modern housing totaling 6,024 rooms at moderate rentals for 1,578 families.

Through the Company's interest in investments in dwellings and apartments during the last 21 years, loans amounting

One of the Spacious and

...ped Areas at Parkchester

to $1,377,643,784 were authorized on new construction and on older buildings to accommodate 356,453 families, or well in excess of 1,000,000 people. These figures are an index of the social use to which Metropolitan funds have been put.

The Company's experience with urban mortgage loans over the years has been generally satisfactory. In addition to an excellent record of safety, the Company's real estate loans have also been a reliable source of interest return. In general, the trend of the interest yield for this type of investment has paralleled that for the interest rate in the country as a whole: a decline from the post Civil War period until the beginning of the 20th century, an upward trend through the first World War, and then another downward movement. In the early 1920's the largest proportion of loans outstanding was on a 6 percent basis. A decade later 5½ percent was the predominating rate, and in the early 1940's more than 60 percent of the city mortgage loans brought 4½ percent or less. The trend toward lower interest rates results from surplus money seeking investment and from competition by lending organizations for well-secured mortgages.

When a borrower fails to make the required payments on a mortgage loan, it has been the policy of the Company to avoid foreclosure if possible. If the property owner has been cooperative, and there appear to be good prospects, the Company tries to let him work himself out of his difficulties. The Mortgage Division, under the direction of the present Comptroller, William S. Norton, attempts to maintain a nice balance between being reasonably lenient to a conscientious property owner and not being lax to a point detrimental to the interest of policyholders. Since most of the owners have been cooperative, it has been possible to make various arrangements for them. In some cases, during periods of economic adversity, reductions in interest rate were made. This procedure has often resulted in removing the default and saving the property from foreclosure. These cases are carefully supervised to insure that income from properties is correctly applied, in keeping with the forebearance program. If subsequent review of the case indicates that foreclosure cannot be avoided and that further leniency would not be to the best interest of the policyholders, foreclosure is then made.

Whenever properties are thus acquired, the Company makes necessary repairs and modernizes the buildings, in order to dispose of them as quickly and as profitably as possible. During the period of the depression, foreclosed properties were placed under the management of highly qualified real estate organizations working under the supervision of the Comp- troller's Division. Offices were established at strategic points throughout the country, manned by personnel familiar with their respective territories and qualified to supervise the work necessary to put the acquired real estate into good condition. Well-rounded sales forces were organized and local contacts were established to assist in the rental and sale of these properties. As a result of these efforts, 88 percent of all the properties owned or acquired during the decade 1932 to 1941 have been sold.

During the depression the Metropolitan has rendered an important public service by assisting other lending institu- tions. In the decade following 1932 the Company came to the aid of building and loan associations, savings banks, and trust and title companies, when they needed cash, by making properly secured loans of more than $35,000,000. The Metropolitan has also aided in the liquidation of title com- panies and other institutions through cooperation with the New York State Mortgage Commission, the New York State Insurance Department, and the New York State Banking Department. In the years 1937 and 1938 the Company purchased 15 loans at the invitation of the Reconstruction Finance Corporation.

Currently, the Metropolitan is in a strong position with regard to its real estate loans. Many mortgages in recent years have been satisfied or their balances considerably re- duced. A large number of properties which it was compelled to take over have been sold on a satisfactory basis and the orderly liquidation of real estate holdings is being continued,

347

with due regard for the influence of the sale on neighboring properties and the community at large. The Company is continuing to make new mortgage loans, the amount of loans made during the last decade being equal to almost half the present city mortgage portfolio. With economic recovery have come improved earning power, greater security of invest- ment, and a continued decline in the foreclosure rate. These developments give the Company confidence in the future of this type of investment.

* * * *

The Metropolitan's contribution to the solution of the housing problem has by no means been limited to real estate loans. The Company itself has taken leadership in building and managing large-scale housing projects which have success- fully demonstrated that adequate housing can be provided for large sections of the population through private enterprise at moderate rentals and yet bring a fair return.

At the time of the first World War the housing shortage was particularly acute in New York State. A Legislative Investigating Committee, knowing the Metropolitan's interest in housing and community welfare, asked the Company to create a large residential development. The legal barrier was removed when the New York State law was amended in 1922 to permit Life insurance companies to invest a limited portion of their assets in new houses, renting for not more than an average of $9 a room monthly. Buildings were exempted from taxation for a period of 10 years, taxes being payable only on the land. The Company thereupon invested about $7,500,000 in the construction of three groups of apartment houses in the Borough of Queens, close to Manhattan, for 2,125 families of moderate income. The plan attracted wide attention, and *The New York Times* commented that this was the first constructive result of the housing investigation. On August 16, 1922, President Fiske turned over the first spadeful of earth for the construction at Anable Avenue and Heiser Street in what is today known as the Sunnyside section of

Queens. A new conception of housing for New York families was in the making.

The Company constructed 28 buildings on three blocks in Sunnyside, 10 on two blocks in Woodside, and 16 on a large single block in the Astoria section. All were five-story U-shaped walk-up structures of harmonious architectural line. They were designed by Andrew J. Thomas and D. Everett Waid, both distinguished architects, and set new standards in housing. The law allowed building coverage to the extent of 70 percent of the land, but these buildings covered only 50 percent. Apartments ranged in size from two to six rooms, most of them three's or four's, and contained improvements heretofore unknown at such rentals. Large, airy courts opened on inner garden areas planted with trees, shrubs, and flowers.

When the buildings were completed early in 1924, all the 2,125 apartments were rented to families of limited income, selected from a waiting list of 25,000. Between 1924 and 1930 the apartments maintained an almost unbroken record of complete occupancy and yielded a net return of about 6 percent. The net income decreased, however, when the tax-exemption period expired, but rentals were not increased. At present more than 95 percent of the apartments are occupied, at an average monthly rental of $8.60 a room. Sixty of the original families still live there, and many of the present office and maintenance staff began their employment there in 1924. The buildings remain attractive, yielding little in appearance to more modern structures. Both the community and the Company continue to profit from the effective functioning of this project.

The success of the Queens housing gave further impetus to the Company's interest to provide comfortable living quarters for families of moderate means. It remained for Mr. Ecker to create a still more advanced concept in community housing. Out of a lifetime of interest and experience in the real estate field, he conceived a planned community of broad pattern, composed of efficient buildings, delightful park and recreational areas, and store centers. It was a conception calling for both realism and imagination, and pointing the way to higher housing standards in this country. In his mind's eye Mr. Ecker could see a project which would express the aspirations of large numbers of families, and which would at the same time demonstrate the Metropolitan's constructive interest in better homes.

In 1938 the Company announced its intention to build the largest single housing project ever undertaken either by the Government or by private enterprise. A city within a city, to be known as Parkchester, was to be created in The Bronx, New York City, a half hour's ride from midtown Manhattan. The Company acquired 129 acres, virtually all of it purchased from the New York Catholic Protectory, which had owned the property for almost 80 years. The community was designed to accommodate more than 12,000 families, whose incomes ranged between $1,800 and $4,500 a year. Parkchester was a complete expression of private enterprise. Unlike Federal and municipal housing projects which called for public subvention and tax exemption to establish low rentals, the Company wanted no subsidy what-ever and paid all the required taxes. Only a reasonable return and a sound investment were sought.

The detailed plan of Parkchester was evolved by a Board of Design working in close consultation with Mr. Ecker and the general contractors, Starrett Bros. and Eken, Inc. The Board consisted of seven men of outstanding ability, each of whom brought to the conference table an extensive and specialized experience. The chairman was Richmond H. Shreve, a member of the architectural firm which designed the Empire State Building, and who in 1941 became president of the American Institute of Architects; Andrew J. Eken, president of the general contracting company, was a builder of wide repute; Gilmore D. Clarke, dean of the School of Architecture of Cornell University, was an authority on city planning; Robert W. Dowling was an expert on New York real estate values; Henry C. Meyer, Jr., possessed a wealth of engineering experience; Irwin Clavan had specialized knowledge in architectural problems; and George Gove, who had been secretary of the New York State Board of Housing and who has been retained by the Company in administrative charge of its housing projects, completed the Board. From the pooled abilities and understanding of these men, supplemented by the insight of the Company's Chairman, came Parkchester's basic plan.

A birdseye view of Parkchester suggests a square which extends for about a half a mile in each direction. Two broad parkways cross diagonally and divide the land into four large sections. Where the two parkways meet at the center of the community is a two-acre park called the "Metropolitan Oval." The community contains 51 apartment structures, 7 to 12 stories high; an unusual central heating plant; five ramp garages with a combined capacity of about 3,500 cars; and a motion picture theater seating 2,000. The apartment buildings contain 12,272 suites, of which 103 consist of two rooms; 7,181 of three; 4,245 of four; 732 of five; and 11 of six- and seven-room suites. Only 27 percent of the area is covered by buildings, making available large open spaces, supervised playgrounds for children, and recreation facilities for adults. Parkchester was designed for a community of about 40,000 people.

The buildings are a modern expression of simplicity in design. They rise in harmonious heights and masses, conform to the rolling topography and, by their position, afford light and air to a maximum degree. At no point are they closer than 60 feet to one another, the width of an ordinary street. They represent the best type of steel and concrete fireproof construction. The glass wool insulation of their exterior walls, hitherto unknown in tall buildings, preserves warmth in winter and retards heat in summer. The rooms are attractive and conveniently arranged for economical housekeeping. They have large casement windows, concealed radiators, cross-ventilation, hardwood floors, large foyers, and complete, well-equipped kitchens. More than 200 automatic elevators serve the thousands of tenants.

Parkchester is attractively and extensively landscaped. Its 4,000 trees include maples, birches, honey locusts, pines, oaks, dogwoods, and magnolias. The broad acres are filled with many thousands of plants and shrubs, in which are included azaleas, native holly, mountain laurel, lilacs, rhododendrons, and snowballs. Equally delightful are the recreation areas along the lawns and paths. There are a total of 43 courts for basketball, handball, shuffleboard, paddle tennis, horseshoe pitching, or badminton; a large softball diamond; six wading pools; eight play areas with varied equipment for youngsters; eight sandbox areas; four roller-skating ovals, and other facilities. The children can play freely and safely because through traffic is confined to the parkways, Parkchester's only public arteries. Traffic is reduced to a minimum by having all the garages placed on the outskirts of the community. As a result of these safety measures, to date not one child or adult has been struck by an automobile in Parkchester since the opening of the first building in 1940.

The community contains within itself the essential facilities for normal everyday life. Each quadrant has its own local shopping centers, planned to provide for all daily necessities. Prominent among the stores is the only New York City branch of Macy's, with a frontage of almost 700 feet on two streets. Banking facilities are available through branches of the National City Bank and the Bronx County Trust Co. In the fall of 1940 Albert Goldman, New York City's Postmaster, dedicated the new local Post Office with appropriate ceremony. The New York Public Library has opened one of the most attractive branch libraries in the city on space made available, rent free, by the Metropolitan. The community has a planned number of offices for physicians and dentists. We have already mentioned the play areas, theater, garages, and central heating plant. The whole atmosphere is one of a large, self-contained village. Considering the attractiveness of the accommodations, rents are extremely moderate.

There has been tremendous interest in Parkchester since its inception, and as soon as the facts regarding the community became public, applications for apartments began to pour in, some from as far as Texas and California. Before renting began on October 1, 1939, there was already a waiting list of more than 50,000 families. Under the direction of Frank C. Lowe, Parkchester's resident manager, rooms were rented by inspection of model apartments and floor plans. On March 1, 1940, the first buildings were opened and several hundred families moved in. Section after section was finished and inhabited, until the entire community was completed in 1941. At the end of 1942, 95 percent of the 12,272 apartments were rented and occupied.

Parkchester's tenants include school teachers, engineers, newspaper men, mechanics, owners of small businesses, civil service employees, and salesmen. A sizable number of the Company's own Clerical Staff have found homes there. About 85 percent of the families have incomes from $2,000 to $4,500 annually, slightly less than 20 percent of their income being spent for rent. Many of the families consist of newly married couples; more than one half of the adults in the community are under 35 years of age. Parkchester is a happy town and an asset to the city and to the Metropolitan.

As Parkchester neared completion, the Company began to write new chapters in the book of modern living by undertaking three other housing projects. Two of these are in ideally located sites in the cities of San Francisco and Los Angeles. The latter plot of 173 acres is in the La Brea section, one block from Wilshire Boulevard. The San Francisco location consists of about 200 acres overlooking Lake Merced and the ocean, and adjoining San Francisco State College. Each of these projects provides accommodation for about 2,500 families. The buildings are planned to cover about 18 percent of the land and to consist of two-story apartments facing patios of beautifully designed gardens, with supervised playground facilities for the young children, swimming pools in one, and tennis courts and other recreation facilities in both. Taking advantage of California climate, the buildings are planned to secure the maximum of sunshine, and the landscaped gardens make delightful places of residence for tenants of moderate income. Both of these projects are in defense housing areas and are of immediate value as a "Help Win the War" activity.

The third development, also in course of construction, was undertaken at the suggestion of the Federal authorities, to help relieve the serious housing problem now existing in the Nation's capital. It is located on 200 acres in Alexandria, Va., just outside of Washington, D. C. This development also will be of parklike character, with designed gardens, playgrounds, and recreation facilities. The two-story apartment buildings, occupying only about 12 percent of the land, will result in homes for about 1,700 families in beautiful and healthful surroundings.

The Company's activities in the housing field have combined efficient management of Life insurance funds with useful public service. The building of communities by the Metropolitan represents a practical application of the modern conception of large-scale housing for urban families. It is an important contribution to public health and public welfare. Thousands of families in the middle-income groups have been given the opportunity to enjoy residential standards and environment far above the average. The steps taken by the Company in the building of such communities have pointed the way for similar operations by other organizations. This type of housing, on an economically self-sustained basis, can proceed without any conflict whatever with Government subsidized housing for the lowest income groups. In these projects the Company is creating its own investment opportunities, which, while helping to build America, will prove at the same time to be investments sound in character and satisfactory in interest return.

*   *   *   *

The Metropolitan's interest in real estate has not been limited to loans on urban property. As we have seen in the previous chapter, the Company in the past quarter century has invested large amounts in mortgages on farm land to meet the needs of the American farmer. Agriculture was and has continued to be the country's largest single enterprise. Farmers feed the Nation, supply a substantial proportion of the raw materials used by industry, and themselves constitute a major market for industrial products. Through investment in this field, Life insurance companies have made an important contribution to a large sector of our national economy.

The Company entered the farm mortgage field in 1917 in order to aid the agricultural part of the war expansion program. To carry on this new development, the Farm Loan Division was organized under the general direction of Vice-President Robert Lynn Cox, with Frank L. Bashore as Manager. Mr. Bashore continued in this capacity for 15 years, and at his death in 1932 was succeeded by his colleague, Glenn E. Rogers, who had had wide experience in dealing with agricultural problems. Under Mr. Rogers' very capable direction the Division has brought great credit to the Company for the many services it has rendered to American agriculture.

When the Company made its first farm loan in April 1917, farmers were enjoying good incomes, reflecting the wartime need for agricultural products both here and abroad. By 1919 the number of farm loans issued by the Company had increased to 2,406, and the amounts outstanding had reached the sizable figure of $17,000,000. At the close of the war, the return of young farmers and farm laborers to their former employment, together with the increased export market for agricultural products at high prices and the large volume of easy credit available, resulted in an immense boom in farm lands. Real estate brokers, country bankers, and others in rural communities, including the farmers themselves, took part in bidding up values on farms. Occasionally individual farms would be sold several times within a few months, each time at an increased price. It was not uncommon for land in Illinois and Iowa to sell for $400 to $500 an acre; a number of good cornbelt farms in Illinois sold for as high as $700 to $800 an acre in 1920.

This period of rising prices soon reached its climax and was followed by a period of deflation. In the 12 months beginning with May 1920, the general price index for American farm products dropped from 244 to 113. Agriculture in the United States had been greatly expanded during the war period, and when the foreign demand fell off, surpluses began to accumulate and prices dropped. The economic pressure thus created on farmers and local country bankers, particularly in the Midwest and the South, increased the demand for mortgage loans from outside agencies. Authoritative sources, however, emphasized the temporary nature of the price slump. Since the loans were well secured by fertile lands and yielded a good return, the Life insurance companies increased their farm mortgage holdings appreciably. Between 1922 and 1928 the Metropolitan issued from 4,000 to nearly 6,000 loans a year to meet the demand. At the beginning of 1928 the Company's books showed a total of 25,483 farm loans amounting to more than $196,000,000.

But agricultural values failed to recover as many had optimistically predicted. As early as 1924 the farmers of the Nation began to have difficulties. Subsequently country banks failed in growing numbers. In the next few years defaults and foreclosures became definitely noticeable and, accordingly, by 1929 the Company further tightened its lending policy.

The stock market crash in October 1929 climaxed the many difficulties of the farmer. Farm commodity prices started on a downward spiral, and by 1933 had dropped to only a little more than 25 percent of their 1919–1920 level; the corresponding drop in farm exports was about 85 percent. By 1933 land value per acre in the United States as a whole had fallen to less than half the figure prevailing at the close of the first World War. As a result, many farm mortgage loans which had been made conservatively on the recognized value of the property, were now in excess of the prevailing value of the farms. The period of heavy foreclosure was thus ushered in. This calamitous experience started in the latter part of 1930, but the bottom of the farm depression was not reached until 1932 and 1933. Even with a policy of the greatest consideration to defaulting farmers, nothing could be done to avoid widespread foreclosures under the economic conditions prevailing in the early 1930's.

The problem was so acute that a special and carefully designed program was developed by the Metropolitan expressly to meet the foreclosure situation. For one thing, the Company refused to foreclose any mortgage without a personal interview with the borrower. The Metropolitan never forgot that it was dealing with good people in distress, and it recognized its obligation to help devise a way out of a difficult situation with the least amount of hardship to all concerned. It was realized that, with the best will in the world, the financial condition among borrowers was, in many cases, so bad that there was no hope of working out their situation as owners; and it was actually more sensible—and more benevolent to the farmers—to induce them to let their farms go and to start anew as tenants. This gave the Company a new opportunity for a service which has been so successful that it constitutes one of the brightest pages in its history. What was needed was to rehabilitate the farms which had been allowed to run down, and to help bring back the productive capacity of the people who had owned them. The situation which had arisen called for wise management of literally thousands of farms, with an eye not only to protect the financial interest of the Company, but to help solve a nationwide economic problem.

Realizing that such farm management was a business of its own, and that it would take several years for the acquired properties to be liquidated, the Metropolitan, beginning in 1932, developed a farm management organization as an integral part of its Farm Loan Division which, under Mr. Glenn E. Rogers' able direction, has attracted nationwide attention and commendation. The Company employed a staff of farm managers, each of whom had had sound experience in practical farming and was familiar with the latest agricultural methods. To these men was entrusted the task to rehabilitate the foreclosed farms and to infuse a new spirit of confidence in the farmers who had lost their property. Here was an opportunity to develop an intelligent, constructive, and scientific plan that should be of use not only to the farms under Metropolitan control, but to the country as a whole. Each of the Company's representatives, working directly under a Field Manager, had from 80 to 100 farms to supervise.

The first step in the rehabilitation program was to analyze the situation on each farm and to determine the type of agriculture for which it was best adapted. In each case a plan of crop rotation and soil improvement was put into effect. Hundreds of thousands of tons of fertilizer were dumped on perishing soil, erosion was stopped, and weeds were exterminated. These measures brought the land up to top productivity, and the farms under Company management have averaged a yield from 10 to 40 percent better than they did under earlier ownership. At the same time, houses and barns were modernized and improved and new buildings were erected where needed. Much of this work was done during the worst years of the depression. The employment of labor in the local communities and the improvement in the appearance of the farms gave new courage to people in farm communities and country towns. To them it reflected the Company's confidence in the future of American agriculture, and they too took on fresh vitality. The Metropolitan plan proved so successful that many other corporate holders of foreclosed farm land and the Federal Government itself have adopted a similar constructive policy. The system has worked admirably not only for the Company but also for the tenant farmers who are a part of the program.

While the farm management program was in full swing, the Company also created a farm sales organization for the purpose of liquidating the properties which had been made over. In developing this sales policy it was the Company's desire above all to sell its properties to real farmers and, wherever possible, to their former owners. Accordingly, a policy was adopted of selling the farms, often with a down payment as little as

10 percent of the purchase price, to bona fide farmers, preferably to the tenants who had lived upon and worked the land. In special cases, where careful analysis of the character and ability of the prospective purchaser indicated an unusually competent and reliable person, even less than 10 percent of the purchase price was accepted. The Metropolitan has now liquidated more than 65 percent of the properties which it had been obliged to acquire during the foreclosure period. Close to 90 percent of them have been purchased by farmers, many of whom were the former owners or members of the former owners' families.

Moreover, these people came back to farms which could be operated on a paying basis. Their buildings had been put into first-class condition, fences were in repair, and land fertility had been restored. The purchaser's overhead was thus reduced to farm operation and mortgage payments. Of prime importance was the increased knowledge of management that these farmers had acquired, which served to make their future efforts profitable. Rule of thumb gave way to planned agriculture, and the American farmer could look forward to sustaining his home and family once more out of his labor and his lands.

And the experience in the farm mortgage field has been profitable for the Company as well. It has continued to lend money to farmers on first mortgage. Farm properties continue to be sold and foreclosures have virtually ceased. Of loans made in the decade 1932–1941 totaling $52,000,000, the Company has acquired through foreclosure only one farm with a mortgage of $5,600. On the sale of farms the Company shows a small profit, after charging rehabilitation expense. But above all, the Company's constructive procedure has helped to advance the application of scientific management to the farming industry. The American farmer is the backbone of this Nation, and in assisting him to meet his problems the Company has performed a lasting national service.

CHAPTER 17

Claim Payments:
The Completion of the Contract

THE PAYMENT of a Life insurance claim represents the fulfillment of the insurance service—the keeping of a promise to the insured, often made many years before. Promises, in the form of policies, are the stock in trade of an insurance company. These promises are as varied as the type of contracts issued. The greater number call for the payment of a specified sum on the death of the policyholder; others are payable at maturity, as an endowment. Either of these policies may provide also for waiver of premiums or monthly income in case the insured becomes totally and permanently disabled. Accident and Health policies provide lump sum benefits, and weekly payments in case of disability resulting from sickness or accident. Annuities promise periodic payments to the annuitant during life, sometimes with a payment at death. The fulfillment of these promises implies a completed contract; but in many cases where the Life insurance contract is terminated before it has run to the stipulated completion, the insured may surrender his policy and receive its current value, the fulfillment of an incidental promise.

Since the contract may not be consummated for many years to come, perhaps not until after his death, the insured must have faith in the integrity and resources of his company. The legal reserve Life insurance companies of the United States and Canada have admirably justified the confidence which the people have placed in them. With inconsequential exceptions, certainly during the 75 years of the Metropolitan's

360

existence, the companies have not failed to pay claims in full, through war and peace, in prosperity and depression. During the year 1941 alone the Life insurance companies of the two countries paid out in death claims, disability claims, matured Endowments, Accident and Health claims, and annuities, about $1,900,000,000, of which beneficiaries received nearly $1,200,000,000 and living policyholders more than $700,000,-000. The Metropolitan's part in these payments has been considerable. During the same year the Company paid claims of more than $323,000,000, which was 17 percent of all claim payments by Life insurance companies. The payment of such enormous sums has gone forward promptly and in orderly fashion year after year. They have been a source of help in time of distress and a sound stabilizer to the entire economy.

In this chapter we shall, for the most part, confine our discussion to death claims, since they constitute the major item in the claim payments of the Company. The Claim Division, through which these payments are made, is an important part of the machinery of the business; by its work the policyholder measures the value of his entire insurance service. It will be of interest to see how the work of this Division has grown through the years. The Company still has among its archives a Minute Book of the meetings of its first Claim Committee, which notes that in the first years the President, Dr. Dow, attended personally to the investiga-tion of all claims. The first death claim in the earliest Mortuary Record covered Metropolitan policy number 163. This policy had been issued by the Metropolitan's predecessor, the National Travelers Insurance Company, on September 9, 1867, on the life of one Dwight G. Smith, age 25, resident of West Chesterfield, Mass. He died of "galloping consump-tion" on May 10, 1868. His beneficiary was paid $1,000 exactly one month later. In this case death occurred within one year of issue, and by reason of the cause of death an investigation presumably was held prior to the approval of the claim. Apparently satisfactory inquiries were completed within a 30-day period. In the light of the practice of those early days, there seems to have been no unusual delay in the adjustment of this claim.

The Metropolitan's Claim Committee held its first recorded meeting on November 6, 1869, and on this occasion Dr. Dow reported upon six claims. To quote from the minutes, "after his explanation of their merits" to the other Officers present, four claims were approved and ordered to be paid. Two others the President was empowered either to "resist or compromise as he may deem best." Furthermore, he was empowered personally to settle and pay any claims not exceeding $5,000 in one case. The payment of claims continued to be a not too arduous task. The Committee held no further recorded meeting until eight months later, at which time a single claim for $2,000 was examined, approved, and ordered to be paid. At the next meeting—on October 22, 1870—the Claim Committee approved 10 new claims, bringing the total which had been paid up to that time, including those settled by Dr. Dow, to 28. The 18th claim in this record shows as cause of death "Congestion of brain caused by free and full living," a medical certification which would hardly be accepted today. In general, the causes of death among Metropolitan policyholders reflected the mortality picture of the time, the respiratory diseases taking first rank.

After President Dow's death, his successor, Mr. Knapp, took on the function of approving claims. The business was growing and claim payments increased as well. More than 11,000 policies were in force when the 100th claim was paid on February 7, 1872. In that year and the next the Metropolitan continued to forge ahead. By the end of 1873 the business had increased to 18,598 policies and the amount paid out in death claims to $189,485. But the Company was to encounter difficult times. For reasons already discussed in earlier chapters, new business was harder and harder to get, until in 1879 only 510 new policies were issued and payments for death claims totaled more than $144,000. In a speech made many years later Mr. Hegeman recalled the financial hardships of the period, and described a scene when a claimant dropped into the Park Place office to collect a death claim. While Mr. Knapp consumed the time with cheerful conversation, he recalled, "I slipped down to the bank to borrow the money to take up the policy. All normal claims at that time were paid within 90 days after the filing of proofs. We often wished that the claimant was down in South Africa or otherwise engaged, so that the papers might be delayed."

Those were days of struggle, and it was evident that resolute action was necessary if the Company was to survive. Mr. Knapp's courageous launching of the Industrial Department provided the lifeline which was to carry the Company into new and smoother seas. The first Industrial death claim was paid on December 12, 1879, less than one month after the issue of the new policy in that Department. It is interesting to note that the policy had been in force only four days, yet the claim was a valid one and was paid immediately. Indeed, if one were to seek a distinguishing characteristic of the claim practice of the Metropolitan, he would undoubtedly find it to be promptness. Particularly on Industrial claims, where the need for immediate emergency funds was ordinarily great, Mr. Knapp laid emphasis on immediate payment. No effort was spared to see that every just claim was paid on the day that proofs of death were received at the Home Office. The black bordered envelope (since changed to yellow), which signified the death of a Metropolitan policyholder, always took precedence over all other mail.

As early as 1881 President Knapp wrote a Circular Letter to the Field urging prompt action on death claims, and advising District Superintendents that the forms could not be acted on at the Home Office the same day unless received by 2 p.m. or on Saturdays by 1 p.m. Four years later he again pointed out the labor involved in acting on death claims (then being paid at the rate of 70 to 100 a day), and said "doing all this on the day the claims are received renders it imperative that they be here by the first delivery in the morning." Another Circular Letter in 1885 informed Superintendents that Saturday, August 8th, the day of burial of General Grant, would be a holiday, when no claims would be paid, and urged them to get everything possible in by Friday. Later, however, holidays made no difference; a skeleton force paid claims on these days exactly as on others. In 1898 the Company began to pay claims even on Sunday to reduce delays to a minimum. The Circular Letters do not tell how long this rigorous practice continued; but payment of claims on holidays continued at least through 1909, when a skeleton force worked during the three gala days of the Hudson-Fulton celebration.

In the later Park Place days, and when the move was made to 1 Madison Avenue, the Claim Division was in charge of one Charles J. Harvey, now become somewhat legendary, as he is reputed to have been an Actuary (though there is no record of him in the Actuarial Division) and an Englishman (though there is no record of him as one of the Englishmen brought over). He is remembered, however, as a husky individual wearing muttonchop whiskers and taking snuff. A set of "Rules for the Claim Division" promulgated by Vice-President Fiske and addressed to Mr. Harvey on August 9, 1892, directed its organization into four territorial subdivisions corresponding to the Audit Divisions and gave detailed instructions as to function, including the reiteration that all claims were to be examined and passed upon the same day on which they were received. Mr. Fiske personally kept watch on claim payments, and directed that each morning by 10 o'clock a statement be placed on his desk showing how many claims had been received the previous day, how many claims had been paid, how many rejected, how many held over for investigation, and the total number of claims remaining in the Claim Division unadjusted, specified according to the respective subdivisions. Some of the practices prescribed by these "Rules for the Claim Division" are still in current use. The proofs of death now required are fundamentally the same, and the general plan of operation is very similar to that devised by the pioneers 50 years ago.

Under Mr. Harvey's management the Division handled only Industrial policy claims; Ordinary claims were handled

FREDERIC G. DUNHAM
General Counsel

in the Ordinary Department under I. J. Cahen. In 1893
Frank O. Ayres was appointed by Mr. Fiske to supervise
Industrial claim payments and to be associated with Mr.
Roberts, then Manager of the Audit Division. Two years
later the Claim Division was consolidated as one unit to
include Ordinary claims also, all in charge of Mr. Ayres. The
increase in the number of claims brought the problem of
litigation in its train, and in 1897, after David L. Buckman
became Manager of the Claim Division, its designation was
changed to the Claim and Law Division. When, in 1909, a
separate Law Division was established under the direction
of William J. Tully as General Solicitor, Mr. Buckman's Division became the Claim and Investigation Division. After
Mr. Buckman's death in 1916 Edward O. Wieters became
Manager, and three years later was advanced to be Assistant
Secretary. In 1922 a separate Investigation Division was
created under Assistant Secretary Charles C. Rose. Today

the Claim Division under John B. Northrop is charged with responsibility of payment of death and disappearance claims, and of unclaimed equities.

As the disposition of claims involves many legal questions —and in some cases litigation—a close relationship has continued between the Claim Division and the Law Division since the organization of the latter in 1909. In 1918 Leroy A. Lincoln was appointed to the Law Division as General Attorney to share the direction of the Division, and he interested himself, among other matters, in the functioning of the Claim Division. In 1927 Mr. Lincoln became the directing head of the Law Division with the title of General Counsel. On his promotion to Vice-President he retained also the title of General Counsel until he became President in 1936, when Frederic G. Dunham and Harry Cole Bates both became General Counsel. The latter has since principally supervised the Law Division functions relating to claims.

HARRY COLE BATES
General Counsel

366

Up to February 1898 all claims had been paid by mail. In that year, however, in order to expedite payments President Hegeman entered into an agreement with the Western Union Telegraph Company for payment of claims by telegraph. Such telegrams, of course, were sent only in cases where Home Office calculation of benefits agreed exactly with the sum claimed by the beneficiary. As an additional expedient in speeding payments to policyholders, authority was granted in 1905 to Superintendents of local Districts to pay smaller claims on the spot, and in 1930 this practice was extended to claims up to $500. The telegraphic authorization was discontinued about 1926, except in unusual cases, due to difficulties in computing the exact amounts payable under Industrial contracts in the District Offices.

But promptness has remained a firm tradition in this Division to the present day. Claims, when properly established, are always paid on the day that the papers are received in the Home Office. A test made in 1941 showed that 77 percent of *all* death claims had been paid by the end of the second day after receipt, and by the end of the fourth day 97 percent had been paid. The remaining 3 percent had been delayed for a variety of reasons. In a number of instances the policy had lapsed, thus necessitating a search through the records to determine its value; in other cases death occurred within the contestable period, or there was an age discrepancy requiring investigation. A large number of these claims were soon settled. Some few fraudulent ones and some made through misunderstandings and ignorance were rejected. Although the Company has always been prompt in paying claims, it is trying constantly to improve upon its own record.

The modern history of the Claim Division dates from 1912, when a new point of view began to characterize its practices. The report by the New York Insurance Department after its triennial examination of the Metropolitan in 1909 noted the Company's record of claim payments and the small percentage of rejections. But the report also suggested a modification of the system of passing on claims, by establishing a final court of review composed of certain principal Officers. In accordance with these recommendations, the Company required that all rejections be passed on by a qualified Vice-President and by the General Solicitor. This work was accordingly assigned to Third Vice-President Woodward and to General Solicitor Tully; and later Fourth Vice-President Barry shared with Mr. Tully the final consideration of rejections. It has often been said, and truly, that in the Metropolitan it takes somebody pretty important to reject a claim.

The aim of the Claim Division has always been to resolve reasonable doubts in favor of the policyholder. After all, the chief function of an insurance company is the paying, not the contesting, of just claims. General Solicitor Tully was fond of telling the story of the applicant for a position in the Claim Division who asserted he knew more ways to "beat a claim" than anybody in the business. The General Solicitor promptly told him he wasn't the man he wanted; that the Metropolitan was looking for a man who could find more reasons to pay a claim than anybody else. Hence, in choosing its claim executives the Company has always insisted on men of integrity and imagination, and above all, on men who possessed sympathy and understanding.

That justice is done is evidenced by the fact that comparatively few claims are contested, that the percent of rejections is small and grows less each year. In 1909 the report on the Metropolitan by the New York State Insurance Department disclosed that less than ½ of 1 percent of the claims received were contested. This figure has since been improved. For the six years 1935–1940 the percentages of rejections have ranged as follows: In the Ordinary Department from 0.42 percent (in 1935) to 0.30 percent (in 1939 and 1940); in the Intermediate Branch from 0.29 percent (in 1935) to 0.08 percent (in 1938); in the Industrial Department from 0.34 percent (in 1936) to 0.15 percent (in 1940). Figures for 1941 show 0.23 percent rejections in the Ordinary Department, 0.17 percent in the Intermediate Branch, and 0.16 percent in the Industrial Department, or less than ¼ of 1 percent in each. While the percentage has never been high, the recent reduction may be ascribed mainly to better underwriting by the Field Force and to improved claim administration.

But it is the ¼ of 1 percent of rejections, rather than the prompt payment of every just claim, that challenges a Company which wishes to act with humanity and with justice. Two principal considerations govern the rejection of claims. The Company cannot and should not pay fraudulent claims, and it cannot and should not (except where there has been a liberalizing action of its Directors) pay claims on losses not covered by the contract. The funds held by the Company are held for the benefit of all its policyholders. No one policyholder has a right to profit through fraud at the expense of the others, and the Company should pay only proper claims, measured by just criteria. The principles governing the Company's payments have varied little since the early days. For instance, in 1897, in a letter to the Superintendent of Insurance of Kansas, Mr. Fiske said:

> It is our custom to pay just claims, and many unjust claims, as soon as they are received. Occasionally, however, but very seldom, we have been imposed upon to such an extent that we believe it our duty to the public to defend the claims so as to prevent conspiracies to rob insurance companies. The amount of the claims in these two cases is small and our defense of them will probably cost more than the amount. The fraud attempted, however, was so aggravated that we believe it to be our duty to contest the cases in the public interest.

It is to the interest of the public, and particularly of policyholders, to prevent the successful imposition of fraud, even at an expense greater than the amount of the particular claim involved. It is quite true that the Metropolitan frequently appears as a litigant in the appellate courts. This is for two reasons: one, the volume of the Company's business is so large that even the fractional percentage of rejected claims results in a substantial number; the other, the tradition of the Metropolitan against compromise of claims believed fraudulent, once rejection is decided upon. This policy has fully justified itself in the discouragement of unwarranted litigation. The Company's percentage of victories in contested claims is excellent. But juries are not infallible and controversies are often carried to higher courts. A recent case of record dealt with a disappearance claim in which one jury decided the insured was alive, another disagreed, and a third found he was dead. The final testimony revealed that since his "death" he had married, raised a family, and at the end signed a full confession of his attempted fraud.

But these are exceptions. The great bulk of death claims received are paid almost automatically, there being no question as to their regularity and genuineness. In order to meet the policyholders' needs as fully as possible the Company has constantly liberalized its practices in claim payment. As early as 1893 the Metropolitan offered liberal terms of revival to those whose policies had lapsed because of the severe economic depression, and many claims were paid in that year on policies where death had occurred after the expiration of the grace period. Two years later the pulmonary and consumption clauses were removed from Industrial policies, and all previously issued policies were put on the same basis. In the early days when death occurred from tuberculosis or pulmonary trouble within a year after the issuance of the policy, only half of the amount was payable. Another step in granting additional benefits was the removal of "ratings" on Industrial policies which had been issued on substandard lives. Up to 1894 it was customary to "rate" Industrial policies on lives not up to the usual standard by advancing the age five or ten years and giving only the benefit provided in the tables for the advanced age. In 1913 all such policies still on the books were put on the same basis as standard risks. Another liberalization as regards claim practice was the application for many years of a one-year contestable period in Industrial, even though the policy provided for a two-year period. Thus policyholders in the Metropolitan have received not only all their insurance contracts called for, but often substantially more.

Mortuary and maturity dividends, varying in amounts, have constituted an important feature of the Company's extra-claim payments over the amount guaranteed by the policies. The first mortuary dividends were declared in 1906 on all Industrial claims where the policy at date of death had been in force more than five years. These dividends amounted to more than $1,000,000. In 1941 the Company paid $12,760,-574 in mortuary, maturity, and settlement dividends on Ordinary and Industrial policies. Since the various dates on which the Company began paying mortuary, maturity, and settlement dividends, the aggregate amount of such dividends paid through December 31, 1941, has been $191,490,084.

In time of emergency and catastrophe the Metropolitan's Claim Division has met severe tests with credit, and has rendered extra service to help suffering policyholders or their beneficiaries. It has been asserted that this Division is as accurate a disaster recorder as is the seismograph, which registers earthquakes. The Metropolitan, through its ties with all classes of the population in every geographic area, has shared in the losses which have accompanied all national disasters. Usually within a few hours after a disaster by fire or flood, the roll of Metropolitan policyholders who have suffered in the disaster has already been reported. Thus, when the news came of the St. Louis tornado of 1896, a telegram was sent to every Superintendent with orders to pay claims without waiting to send proofs to the Home Office, and a special envoy was sent to expedite these payments. Within a few days death claims had been paid on 68 policies. During the San Francisco fire of 1906 and during the Mississippi Valley floods of 1937, special Field arrangements were made not only for the payment of claims, but for keeping policies in force when the insured was unable to meet premium payments. As the result of the catastrophic fire in a well-known Boston night club on November 28, 1942, the Company paid 199 claims totaling $408,003.95.

In the first World War an extra load of claims for deaths from war causes amounting to $8,250,000 was paid on a total of more than 25,000 Metropolitan policies. In the influenza epidemic which occurred toward the close of the war the claim load went up to a peak of more than 3,600 claims in one day, as against a normal load, even today, of 1,200 to 1,500. Death claims paid in the eight-month period between October 1, 1918, and June 1, 1919, exceeded $27,000,000 on more than 83,000 policies. This sudden call for payments taxed the Claim Division far beyond its capacity, and Clerks were at their desks far into the night to insure the prompt receipt of money at a time when it meant so much. Beside the heroic overtime work of this Division during the epidemic, Superintendents were given the privilege of immediate payment of death claims on policies that called for less than $300 and which had been in force at least a year. Never is the effectiveness of Life insurance better shown nor the good work of the Claim Division more effectively proved than during such times of stress.

The effect of the second World War has not yet been seriously felt in the claim experience of the Metropolitan, and any attempt at prediction would be pure speculation. Life insurance policies issued up to September 1939 now carry no war restrictions. At that time war clauses were introduced for new Canadian policies and for a restricted class of applicants in the United States. Beginning in December 1941 war clauses were included generally in all new policies issued in the United States. Most Accidental Death and Total and Permanent Disability provisions of the Metropolitan are suspended if the insured is in the military or naval service in time of war. There arose from this fact an interesting question as to liability for accidental death payments to policyholders having such benefits who were in the Army or Navy and were killed in the Japanese attacks on the Hawaiian Islands and elsewhere on December 7, 1941. Did these deaths occur "in time of war," since declaration of war was not made by the Congress of the United States until December 8th? The legal question is close, but the doubt was resolved in favor of the claimants, and a number of such claims were paid

372

in a substantial total amount. The total claims paid on account of fatalities at Pearl Harbor alone numbered 422.

If the volume of claim payments has reflected certain events of the country's history, it has been even more an index of the developments in the Company itself. The Metropolitan ended its first year with $5,081 paid in death claims. These payments continued to grow for the next few years, until 1876, when the loss of business showed itself in a drop of more than $75,000 in death claim payments from the year before. Considerably less was paid out each year until 1880, when the introduction of Industrial insurance changed the trend to a payment of more than $200,000 in death claims—an increase of $56,000 over the previous year. By the start of the century death claim payments had jumped to more than $10,000,000, and thereafter grew by a substantial amount each year. A decade later, in 1911, more than $22,000,000 was paid out. This annual figure more than doubled in the next 10-year period; and by the end of the next decade, in 1931, the amounts paid to beneficiaries in death claims amounted to more than $152,000,000. In 30 years the death claim payments of the Metropolitan had multiplied some 14 times. The current volume of claim payments has reached very large figures. Of the $323,339,000 paid on all types of claims in 1941, $177,733,000 was in death claims, $102,512,000 was paid to owners of Endowment policies which had matured during the year, $10,694,000 was paid in disability claims, and $18,208,000 in Accident and Health claims. Annuitants received $14,191,000 in payments on their contracts. Of the death claim payments, $84,342,000 was in the Ordinary Department; $63,695,000 in the Industrial Department, and $29,696,000 under Group policies.

The Claim Division now is a far cry from that of the Park Place days, when claims were handled by Audit Clerks in their spare time. The present paymaster, W. R. Marriner, came to the Company in 1906 and his first duties consisted in writing out death claim checks in longhand. Today special pin-point machines in the Check Writing Division can write

Check Writing Division

payment checks at the rate of 28,000 a day. Another machine
signs them in sheets of six, and then cuts and stacks them in
numerical order almost faster than the eye can follow. About
90 percent of all the Company's checks represent payments
to policyholders or their beneficiaries. It is an interesting
commentary on the efficiency of the Claim Division that when
it moved across the street to the new building in 1941, there
was no interruption in its work. Over a week end the desks,
files, and other equipment were moved; telephone and dictaphone connections were ready for use in the new location,
and the first claim was handled promptly at 9 o'clock the following Monday morning.

Today the Division requires a force of more than 200
people to handle the routine of payment and to complete the
mortuary records. There are consistently some 10,000 death
claims and 2,500 disappearance cases in the active files.
Ordinary and Industrial claims are treated in substantially the
same way, nor is there the slightest difference between a large
or small claim in order of payment. However, the District
Manager has authority to make immediate payments and

advances on certain Industrial claims, but must await Home Office approval to do so for Ordinary or Group policies.

There is a dramatic story in the number of policies which become claims in less than a year's time. A substantial amount of claims has always been on short-lived policies, proof of the need for Life insurance. In 1941, $3,206,078 was paid on 9,298 policies which had been in force less than one year, of which $864,488 was paid on 3,287 policies in force less than three months. The families of these policyholders have reason indeed to be grateful to the Agent who persuaded the insured to act in time.

An increasing activity of the Life insurance business has been the management of claim funds after the death of the insured—in a real sense, insuring the insurance. The Metropolitan began this practice in 1897, about five years after the reorganization of the Ordinary Department. In that year an Optional Modes of Settlement clause was added to Ordinary policies, a feature which provided that if the insured desired, the benefits could be paid, not in one sum, but in a series of equal annual payments extending over a specified number of years. The aggregate amount paid was larger, by reason of interest, than if all payments were made immediately. This added service not only relieved the insured of anxiety as to his family's investment and management of the insurance proceeds, but also assured a regular dependable income; and the minimum rate of interest guaranteed by the Company on the Optional Modes of Settlement was very favorable. Since the beginning of 1907 practically all Ordinary policies have contained additional instalment features as possible modes of settlement. Thus today the insured or beneficiary may elect to receive payment of interest only, for a specified period or until a specified event; payment of the insurance in instalments; or payment as a life annuity. In 1941 the amount so left with the Company for payment was more than $44,400,-000. The sum held by the Company at the end of 1941 as reserves to assure payment of the elected Optional Modes of Settlement was $186,379,901, or about the total of one year's death claim payments. Today the use of Optional Modes of Settlement has become generally accepted and the Metropolitan policy is often serving for two lifetimes instead of one.

It is an interesting paradox that after premium payments have been made on a policy, the Company should have difficulty in finding the beneficiary or assignee in order to pay the claim. These situations are relatively few and arise because policyholders, overlooking or forgetting the non-forfeiture provisions of lapsed policies, assume that these contracts have no value. The Claim Division of the Metropolitan today includes, therefore, a Section—a human Lost and Found Bureau—which attempts to locate the proper payees in such cases, and also to investigate whether persons, supposed to have disappeared, are dead or alive. In 1941 alone this Section located alive 1,363 persons who, it was declared, were dead when the claims were made. In recent years the insured has been located in almost one third of the disappearance claims.

What claim payments, coming in time of need, have meant to widows and children, to the disabled, and to those incapacitated by old age, cannot be estimated merely in the number of claims or in the amounts paid. They have meant that thousands of families have been able to carry on with self-respect and with some sense of confidence after the bread-winner is no longer there. Some insight into the use made of Life insurance funds is revealed by a recent survey among representative families in 22 States to whom Industrial claims had been paid. It was found that in about 86 percent of the families these funds more than covered burial expenses; and that after these costs had been met, there remained with the average family money equivalent to almost eight months' earnings of the deceased husband. About half the families used some of the remaining money for food, rent, and other living necessities; 40 percent of them saved some of it and 32 percent used some of it to pay past debts. (The answers total more than 100 percent because several families had more than one use for the claim funds). That these claim payments have met a vital need is evident from the fact that less than one fourth of these families had any cash, savings, or assets other than their Life insurance benefits, to meet the pressing expenses after the death of the breadwinner.

The Company receives letters from such families which tell of gratitude for the foresight of the person who took out the policy and for the work of the Agent. The following from the wife of a Vermont policyholder is typical: "Accept my most sincere thanks for your kindness and thoughtfulness in providing funds at the time of my husband's death. I shall never forget how much consideration and understanding you showed my husband, ever since your first call in our home." Thousands of such letters give testimony to the writers' appreciation of the Company's prompt and helpful claim service. Millions of people throughout the United States and Canada have had reason to be grateful to their insurance Agent and to the Company behind him. In its 75 years of existence the Metropolitan has become known for the conscience behind its business. It has kept faith with its policyholders.

CHAPTER 18

The Contribution of the Actuary

THE ACTUARY is the technical advisor of the Life insurance business. Upon him depends in large measure the stability and soundness of the company. He must, from his knowledge of past experience and his judgment of present and probable future trends, determine the basis on which the company issues new policies and provides for their fulfillment. He computes the premiums, reserves, and nonforfeiture and other values. He is largely responsible for the preparation of the Annual Statement required by the various State insurance departments. In a mutual Company like the Metropolitan, the Actuary also submits recommendations and arranges for the distribution of the Company's divisible surplus in the form of dividends to policyholders. These many functions call for highly technical skills. To attain the professional status of an actuary, a difficult and highly prized accomplishment, one must meet the rigorous qualifications set by the Actuarial Society of America and of the American Institute of Actuaries.

With his comprehensive training the Actuary not only is entrusted with the mathematics of Life insurance, but also is consulted in virtually all other phases of the business. His experienced judgment benefits every field of the Company's operations. In cooperation with other Officers of the Company, the Actuary in the Metropolitan recommends new plans of insurance which will be attractive to the public, and together with the General Counsel he drafts the new contracts. In cooperation with the Underwriting Executives, the Medical Director, and the Statistician, he determines underwriting practices of the Company. He also assists the Agency

378

Executives in determining the bases of Agency compensation, and on occasion he advises the Treasurer on certain phases of the Company's investment policy. The Actuary is, thus, one of the key officials whose responsibilities require that he be familiar with every aspect of the Life insurance business. It is not surprising that actuaries are filling many executive or administrative positions in insurance companies.

The Metropolitan has been fortunate in its Actuaries. When it began business in 1868 it did not have a full-time Actuary but, like other small and new organizations, obtained the services of a consultant. Its choice fell on David Parks Fackler, who was to become a distinguished member of the actuarial profession. He had previously served the National Travelers Insurance Company, the predecessor of the Metropolitan. In that capacity he probably computed the first premium rates and other values which were continued by the Metropolitan when its business was launched. Mr. Fackler's active connection with the growing young Company continued for about five years.

In 1872 the Company employed William Peter Stewart as Actuary. James McIntosh Craig came into its employ in the same year from the National Life Insurance Company, an offshoot of the Metropolitan's progenitor, the National Union Life and Limb Insurance Company. These two men worked together for five years, until Mr. Stewart left the Company in 1877. But even during this period much of the actuarial work was performed by young Craig, as Mr. Stewart spent most of his time in selecting and training Agents and in trying to popularize certain plans of insurance which he had developed. Mr. Craig succeeded to the position in 1877. He was appointed an Officer of the Company with the title of Actuary in 1891 and a member of the Board of Directors in 1897. He continued with the Company until his death in 1922. In his 50 years of service he made an indelible impress on every branch of the business. Furthermore, he created a Craig tradition in the Actuarial Division. Three successive generations of Craigs have served the Company. In addition, a host of young men trained by the elder Craig and his son have achieved positions of great responsibility in the Actuarial and other Divisions. That continuity of administration which we noted earlier as a particularly fortunate circumstance in the history of the Company is especially true of the Actuarial Division. The Craig tradition has served the Company well throughout its history.

In the early years actuarial operations were comparatively simple. The entry of the Metropolitan into the Industrial field in 1879, however, brought with it a host of new actuarial problems. In their solution young Craig proved his resource fulness and his capacity. The rapid growth of the Industrial business, and the development and expansion of an agency system placed a serious strain upon the Company's finances. Several of the States required that Industrial policy liabilities be valued annually on the very stringent reserve bases used for Ordinary policies. Because of this and the relatively high initial expenses incidental to the extension of Industrial insurance, it soon appeared that further expansion of the business would be jeopardized if these legal requirements for valuation were maintained. Under the leadership of Mr. Craig a plan was devised for a new basis of valuation which took into account certain essential differences between Industrial and Ordinary insurance at that time. Mr. Craig showed that the reserve bases used for Ordinary insurance were actuarially unnecessary on recently issued Industrial policies, because they provided only a limited death benefit during the first year of insurance, because they contained no surrender values, and because they were sold at age next birthday rather than nearest birthday. The leading actuaries were in accord with this reasoning, and their support led to the approval of a modified valuation basis for Industrial insurance by the Insurance Department of New York State. The Company was thus able to maintain reserves at a figure which assured its financial soundness, and which at the same time permitted it to expand the business and to accumulate an adequate surplus. In this happy solution Mr. Craig overcame an obstacle which would have seriously hindered the growth of the Company. In the course of time, as the differences between Industrial and Ordinary insurance became less and less significant, the Company changed the basis of valuation for Industrial policies to conform with that for Ordinary.

Mr. Craig's work in the 80's was largely concerned with the actuarial administration of the Industrial Department and with continuous checking of the Company's financial position. It was particularly important to keep watch over the Company's mortality experience among Industrial policyholders. Inasmuch as no recognized mortality standards were available for this class of insured people, the original premium rates were based on the American Experience Table, commonly used for Ordinary policies. Through Mr. Craig's foresight, the margin provided for expenses and contingencies in the computation of the original premiums was more than enough to absorb the higher mortality prevailing among the industrial population. By 1886 the financial problems on Industrial business had been worked out and a surplus began to accumulate. Within five years the Metropolitan was in such excellent financial condition that it was able to undertake important new ventures. First came a broadening of the scope of Industrial insurance, and then followed the Company's reentry into the Ordinary field.

All through the crucial early years the only Industrial policies issued were Whole Life contracts. Now the Company was ready to issue Industrial insurance on other plans, which combined opportunities for saving as well as protection. The Actuary had to prepare new schedules of values appropriate to these policies. On January 1, 1892, new tables of benefits for Industrial Endowment policies of varied durations were ready for the Field Force. In the next few years many contracts were liberalized and provided larger benefits.

The Actuary assumed great responsibilities in helping to revitalize the Ordinary Department. In order to compete successfully in this branch of the business against the older companies, most of which were still selling high-premium

381

policies on the strength of glowing promises of future dividends, the Company had to offer something better to the public. The solution was to issue simply worded and low-priced nonparticipating contracts which the man on the street could afford. This involved for the Actuary the difficult problem of determining the lowest premium rates which the Company could safely charge on more than 15 different policy plans, including Whole Life, and Limited Life and Endowment policies of various terms. These policies contained very liberal provisions for that era, such as paid-up values after three years and no restrictions on travel or residence. Women were accepted, although the payment of an extra premium was required on some plans.

The succeeding years were again exceptionally busy ones for the Actuary. The Metropolitan added several new branches to its business. In 1896 it brought out its Intermediate policies, necessitating the computation of new premium rates and nonforfeiture values for the various plans of insurance issued in this Branch. This again was a distinctly new venture, as the mortality to be expected among these policyholders was unknown. The mortality table used for the computation of Intermediate premiums was that derived from the experience among Industrial policyholders during 1890 to 1894, but with a loading for expenses smaller than that used for Industrial insurance. Because it was anticipated that these premiums would be more than ample, provision was made to return surplus earnings in the form of dividends, and in 1901 the Company began paying dividends on these policies.

There still remained a sizable group of persons who were not eligible for either Standard or Intermediate insurance, because their occupations were too hazardous or because they had certain physical impairments, but who were insurable at higher rates. Again the Actuary successfully met the problems involved in providing insurance protection for this group of the population, and in 1899 the Company began to issue its so-called Special Class policies. Standard Ordinary and Intermediate premium rates were used for these policies, but the expected extra mortality was compensated for by a lien which reduced the amount of benefit for a period of years. Without any actual experience to guide him, the Actuary computed this lien according to an assumed mortality that he thought would prove adequate. As the Company wished to keep the actual cost of these policies as low as possible, it provided for the reduction of the lien through dividends. In the course of time the sizable dividends paid on these policies canceled all the liens. In 1907 the Company began to issue Special Class policies which provided the full amount of coverage but called for increased premium rates, which were calculated by the Actuary on the basis of the actual experience among Special Class risks. This was a significant step toward the Metropolitan's present unique method of underwriting business on substandard lives. The method involves the grouping of such risks into broad classes, each with its separate scale of premiums, reserves, and dividends based on its own experience.

During this period there were also important developments in the procedures of the Actuarial Division. As far back as the early 1880's, when the Company began to issue Industrial policies in increasing numbers, Mr. Craig had devised a new system of record keeping which facilitated the annual valuation of thousands of Industrial policies. Such an annual valuation had then been required for some years in connection with Ordinary business and was naturally extended to the Industrial, even though the size of the problem of making the valuation required entirely different procedures. In the course of time Mr. Craig's original procedure was improved by the introduction of methods whereby policies were valued in groups rather than individually, as had been done for Ordinary business. As the volume of Industrial business continued to increase, Mr. Craig, with the collaboration of Charles G. Reiter, later Assistant Actuary, developed a system whereby the Company's records could be kept up to date from card files, with considerable savings in time and expense. This system was conceived on such broad lines that today, with more than 30,000,000 Industrial policies in force, essentially the same principles are followed.

During all this time the Actuary gave constant attention to the mortality experienced in the several Branches of the Company. The Metropolitan's own experience became sufficiently large to provide the basis for new schedules of rates and benefits. The first such mortality table, developed in the Industrial Department in 1895, was largely the basis for benefits adopted in 1896 and for the paid-up values allowed to Industrial policyholders in the next year. As already noted, this mortality table was also the basis of the initial premium rates for Intermediate policies. About 10 years later several additional mortality tables were developed. These were the so-called Standard and Substandard Industrial Tables, and the Intermediate and Special Class Mortality Tables, all of which were based on the actual experience through 1905. The Industrial tables have been widely adopted as legal valuation standards for Industrial business, while the Intermediate tables are still used by many companies for valuing their small Ordinary and Substandard policies.

The studies of the mortality of Industrial policyholders were to prove of real financial benefit to the insured. Because of the increasing surplus from this business, due largely to decreasing mortality, it was decided that bonuses to Industrial policyholders might safely be granted, even though the policies were nonparticipating. It fell to the Actuarial Division to develop suitable methods of surplus distribution. As early as 1896 records were set up designed to trace the earnings of the various branches of insurance by year of issue, plan of insurance, and other essential categories. With these financial analyses as a guide, the Actuary was in a position to determine which classes of policies were contributing to the surplus and the amount of bonus which could equitably be paid to each class. The first of these Industrial bonuses was credited in 1897.

With the growth of the business through the years and with the increased variety of policies, the duties of actuaries

384

became increasingly complex. The profession was being recognized. Actuaries of the various companies began to meet informally to discuss common problems, and in 1889 organized the Actuarial Society of America. Mr. J. M. Craig was a charter member and active in its affairs. He became its President in 1914, serving for two years. Under the auspices of the Society, standards of accomplishment for entry to the profession were established, and a system of examinations was instituted. Mr. Craig was interested in helping a group of ambitious young men under his direction who were eager to get such training, and organized classes in actuarial science in his Division in 1896.

Once the Actuarial Society was organized it served as an instrument for productive research by the Life insurance companies. The Metropolitan's growing Actuarial Division took an active part in the Society's studies of mortality among various classes of policyholders. In 1901 it cooperated in the first intercompany study (known as the Specialized Mortality Investigation) which analyzed the relative mortality of Ordinary policyholders in various occupations or with certain medical impairments. Subsequently, most such investigations were made jointly by the Actuarial Society and the Association of Medical Directors, which was also organized in 1889.

In 1910 the Company contributed its records to a much more comprehensive mortality investigation conducted under the auspices of the two Societies. The results of the joint study, known as the Medico-Actuarial Mortality Investigation, proved invaluable in underwriting, since, for the first time, specific information became available as to the effect on mortality of build, and of a large number of occupational hazards and medical impairments. A few years later the Company contributed its Ordinary experience to another cooperative investigation conducted by the Actuarial Society and the American Institute of Actuaries (organized in 1909) which resulted in the construction of the American Men Mortality Table. This table has become a recognized legal valuation standard in many States and forms the basis of

JAMES D. CRAIG

reserves and surrender values on Standard Ordinary policies now being issued by the Company. The early 1920's also saw the beginning, under actuarial auspices, of intercompany investigations into disability and Group mortality experiences.

The responsibilities of the Actuary became even more arduous upon mutualization of the Company in 1915. In order to determine more accurately the earnings of different branches, plans, and benefits, a great deal of painstaking work had to be done to allocate expenses and other items properly. Such allocations have been reviewed periodically by the Insurance Departments, which have frequently commented on the care taken to assure that no one line of business, plan, or benefit is favored at the expense of another. At the same time detailed studies had to be made in regard to mortality and interest trends, and appropriate formulas had to be devised for the calculation of dividends. Much of the work in connection with Ordinary dividends was conducted by Assistant Actuary James D. Craig and Mr. Samuel Milligan (now Second Vice-President). The financial analyses, properly interpreted in accordance with the principles of surplus distribution, not only furnished a most useful guide for considering scales of annual dividends, but also provided a basis for determining mortuary, maturity, and settlement dividends. The Metropolitan's dividend formulas together with the practice of paying mortuary, maturity, and settlement dividends constitute a unique system of surplus distribution.

The extraordinary growth of the several Departments of the Company and the many special problems that arose for solution called for capable assistants to share the increased burdens of the Division. Fortunately, there were already in the Company a few men trained by J. M. Craig able and ready to accept the new responsibilities. Among these men were his son, James Douglas Craig, and Raymond V. Carpenter, both of whom had begun their careers as actuarial clerks in the late 90's and had completed their actuarial examinations together. They were both appointed Assistant Actuaries in

RAYMOND V. CARPENTER

387

1909. The achievements of these two men epitomize the developments in the Actuarial Division of the Company for a quarter of a century. Following the death of James McIntosh Craig in 1922, the direction of the Division was placed under their joint control. Both were appointed Actuaries at that time, J. D. Craig in charge of the Ordinary actuarial activities, and Mr. Carpenter in charge of the Industrial.

The task of determining suitable benefits and premium rates for newly developing forms of Group insurance and Disability or Health insurance had engaged the Metropolitan Actuaries for some years. The problems involved were difficult, because they required careful judgment as to what the experience might be. Frequently this judgment had to be made on the basis of fragmentary and not strictly relevant data. J. D. Craig had a rare understanding of the problems involved. He knew how necessary it was to define carefully the nature of these new insurances, and how essential to have adequate safeguards in order that the benefits would be within the defined limits. In addition, he took pains to study at first hand the administration of such insurance plans wherever they had been developed. For example, he went to Europe in 1912 in order to study Health insurance practices, when consideration was being given to disability benefits by the Company.

The wide range of interest of James D. Craig made itself felt in a variety of Company undertakings. He was very active in the development of Disability provisions and Personal Accident and Health insurance, for which he had adapted sickness data from the experience of the Manchester Unity of England. In the early 1920's, when many companies were vying with each other in liberalizing disability benefits, Mr. Craig adopted a conservative attitude in regard to these benefits and adjusted premium rates at the first indications of unfavorable experience. His was a steadying influence. Subsequently, as Chairman of a Committee appointed by the Superintendent of Insurance of New York State to consider the whole question of disability benefits, he helped make

388

specific recommendations for standard policy provisions, which were later put into effect in New York and in 18 other States.

The development of Group insurance in all its branches also benefited from Mr. Craig's keen understanding of insurance principles. He was a leading member of the Committee appointed by the Actuarial Society of America at the request of the National Convention of Insurance Commissioners to establish a statutory definition of Group Life insurance. His contributions helped to launch this type of business on a sound basis. He pioneered in Group Accident and Health insurance, upon which he brought to bear his ample and specialized knowledge. In fact, Mr. Craig was responsible for one of the earliest policies of this kind—that issued by the Company for its employees in 1914. In the Group field he was later assisted by H. R. Bassford, now Actuary of the Company. With the aid of Mr. Hohaus, now Associate Actuary, Mr. Craig worked out the actuarial basis of Group Annuities and then planned the comprehensive Insurance and Retirement Program first offered by the Company to its own employees. Such programs were later issued extensively to employees in other industrial establishments. The scope of Group insurance was further widened in 1928, when Mr. Craig entrusted Mr. Dunlap (then Assistant Actuary) with the computations for the issuance of what was probably the first Group Hospital and Surgical Benefit policy. Altogether, Metropolitan Actuaries were constructive forces in laying the foundations and improving every phase of Group insurance which, during the last quarter of a century, has served the wage-earners of America well and has promoted better relations between employers and employees.

Mr. Craig's work on pensions and employer and employee relations aroused his interest in social insurance. He devoted years to its study and wrote a great deal on the subject, beginning with his original paper presented before the Actuarial Society in 1923. With Dr. Frankel, he visited a number of European countries in 1931 to survey their various governmental systems. Largely as a result of this survey, the Company later issued a long series of publications dealing with the social aspects of old-age, health, and unemployment insurance. These stimulated thought on such topics and helped to channel legislative efforts along practical lines.

These and similar developments continued to tax the technical staff of the Actuarial Division. Messrs. Craig and Carpenter foresaw the many-sided expansion of the Metropolitan. They realized the necessity for attracting promising young men and training them to take responsible positions throughout the organization. To them belongs the credit for a long-range plan for educating future insurance leaders. They improved and broadened the instruction given in the actuarial classes, assisted young men in the Company's employ and those subsequently recruited from colleges to prepare themselves for the successive examinations of the actuarial societies, and saw to it that when they became Associates, and later Fellows, they were given opportunities in the Company commensurate with their training and ability.

Thus, over a long period of years, the Metropolitan's Actuarial Staff was built up, and today, in numbers and in skill, it has no counterpart in any other insurance organization. The men so trained have played an increasingly important part in the operations not only of the Actuarial Division but of other important Divisions of the Company. Among these men are Second Vice-Presidents Samuel Milligan and Francis M. Smith and Actuary Horace R. Bassford and his Associates and Assistants. Mr. Craig often presented his liberal ideas regarding the place of the Actuary in the Life insurance business to his colleagues in the profession. This was the theme of his Presidential address before the Actuarial Society of America in 1929. He had also served as President of the Casualty Actuarial Society. Mr. Craig wrote numerous papers on actuarial subjects and took a very active part in the discussions of the day.

Raymond V. Carpenter, on his part, administered the Actuarial Division in all that related to the Industrial Department. Because of the size of this business and its close relation to the Field Force, his task was a vital and complicated one. He was a major force in the continuous improvement which was being made in Industrial insurance. Each of the many steps in the liberalization of the contracts, as well as new types of policies, required careful actuarial analysis, and this was carried on under his direction. He was active in the problems relating to Field compensation and to the assumption of business of other Industrial companies. He was keenly interested in the Company's welfare program for Industrial policyholders, particularly in the Nursing Service. Mr. Carpenter was an international authority on Industrial insurance and wrote important papers on the subject which were characterized by his usual thoroughness and accuracy. Because of his foresight and ability to examine a question from all possible angles, Mr. Carpenter's advice was very much sought after on matters other than those of Industrial insurance. He was joint author with Mr. Fiske of *An Epoch in Life Insurance*, a chronicle of the history and services of the Company for the third of the century ending in 1924.

The decade beginning in 1930 brought into focus a succession of actuarial problems engendered by the prolonged economic depression and the resulting decline in the interest rate. In point of time, the first of these problems arose from an extraordinary increase in claims under disability income benefits. In order that the increased cost of such disability protection be borne by those who had this form of coverage, the dividends on policies with disability income benefits were accordingly reduced. This dividend reduction was contested in a series of suits over a period of years, but the Company's practice in this regard was completely vindicated as the only fair course that could have been taken.

For a decade prior to the depression, surplus earnings had been rising and dividends had been increased several times. But as the financial slough deepened the fall in earnings from interest became so great that adjustments in dividends had to be made. Hence, despite material savings from lower mortality during the later years of the depression, the Actuaries had the unpleasant duty of recommending successive reductions in dividends. When it became apparent that interest earnings would continue on a definitely lower level, it also became necessary for the Actuaries to revise the premium structure itself for new policies. The first such change was made in the Ordinary Department and went into effect in 1935. Basic revisions of premium rates and nonforfeiture values in both Departments were undertaken more recently and were put into effect in 1942. This required detailed studies of the trends in mortality, interest, and expenses. Due to changes in the New York Law, the State Insurance Department requested the Company to prepare new Industrial Mortality Tables under Department supervision. These tables were subsequently promulgated as legal valuation standards for new Industrial policies. The Actuary also prepared new Special Class Tables. Exhaustive consideration was given to the computation of premium rates which would contain proper margins of safety, and of nonforfeiture values which would be fair and equitable to all concerned. The Company was the first in this country to announce premium rates and nonforfeiture values based on an interest rate of less than 3 percent. These new schedules in their entirety constitute a monumental achievement in actuarial work.

The establishment of the Federal system of old-age benefits in 1935 brought into relief certain actuarial problems in connection with Group Annuities. Because of the contributions which employers and employees had to make under the Federal program, many of the companies with Metropolitan Annuity contracts asked to have them revised to take into account the pensions provided by the new law. To meet the situation, the Actuary devised schedules of benefits and contributions which would, in combination with the Federal old-age benefits, meet the same objectives as the Group Annuity plans formerly had. Most of the existing contracts of employers who came under the Federal system were thus changed and, in addition, a large volume of new business of this type has been issued.

HORACE R. BASSFORD
Actuary

The outbreak of war has always presented serious problems to the Life insurance business. Shortly after the first World War began in 1914, various restrictions were introduced on new contracts to moderate losses due to military service. Such limitations involved a reduction in the amount of benefit and additional premiums to cover the war hazard. This extra premium was considerable, but the Company obligated itself to refund part of it if military death losses were less than anticipated. All these restrictions were removed soon after the end of the war. The experience during that conflict laid the basis for actuarial recommendations regarding policy restrictions necessitated by the present war. The use of war clauses in Life insurance policies has been frequently mis-understood, not only by the general public but also in insur-ance circles, and Mr. Bassford's discussions before under-writers and in the insurance press have done much to shed light on this question.

393

During the past 15 years the Actuarial Division has carried out or participated in mortality and morbidity studies on a greatly increased scale. These investigations have been largely concerned with substandard risks and the experience under Group policies. The Division has contributed much to the work of the Joint Committee on Mortality of the Actuarial Society of America and the Association of Life Insurance Medical Directors, which, since 1929, has issued a steady stream of reports relating to the effect on longevity of various medical impairments and histories, as well as the mortality associated with various occupations. Mr. Bassford's study of blood pressure in 1932, in which the experience was considered in relation to both the systolic and diastolic readings, set the pattern for a major intercompany investigation of the effect of blood pressure on mortality in 1939. To a considerable degree these various studies have formed the basis of present underwriting rules. The experiences on recently issued standard policies, on policies for large amounts, on Ordinary policies on children, on annuities, and on settlement options have also been developed in intercompany investigations, in which the Company took a very active part. With the growth of aviation, much study was given to the effect of its hazards on Life insurance. Mr. Bassford, and later Associate Actuary Herman, represented the Company on the Aviation Committee of the Actuarial Society, which pioneered in collecting information on the subject.

In 1936, with the appointment of Mr. Craig as Vice-President of the Company in charge of Home Office operations, Mr. Carpenter became Senior Actuary in charge of Industrial insurance, and Horace R. Bassford became Actuary in charge of Ordinary insurance. Upon Mr. Carpenter's retirement in 1939 Mr. Bassford took charge of all actuarial operations, and the Division was reorganized along functional lines. In this reorganization under Mr. Bassford, Mr. Reinhard A. Hohaus was appointed Associate Actuary in charge of the Group activities in the Division. James R. Herman and Malvin E. Davis were appointed Associate Actuaries jointly in charge of the actuarial work pertaining to both Ordinary and Industrial insurance. Because the Company maintains two Head Offices in addition to the Home Office, it was deemed advisable with the increasing complexity of the business and the need for uniformity in practices to have an Actuary in each Head Office. George V. Brady, Associate Actuary, and Arnold B. Brown, Assistant Actuary, are Assistant Managers at the Canadian and the Pacific Coast Head Offices, respectively.

Mr. Hohaus directs the many and complex tasks related to Group insurance. He and his Staff develop the underwriting rules, determine and revise premium rates, conduct practically continuous investigations into mortality and morbidity experience of the business, prepare the valuations and financial analyses relating to Group contracts, and determine the amount of dividends to be paid. Mr. Hohaus has also continued the studies in social insurance which were begun by J. D. Craig. Because of his expert knowledge of the subject, Mr. Hohaus has frequently been consulted by officials in charge of the Federal program for social security. He has also been one of the best interpreters of the respective roles of private and public insurance in advancing the security of American families. Among the most notable of these interpretations were his Presidential addresses delivered in 1939 and 1940 before the American Institute of Actuaries.

Mr. Herman is responsible for the study and administration of methods whereby individual policies share equitably in the distribution of the total sum set aside for dividends. Constant research is made of the basic factors which enter into these calculations. Another important function under Mr. Herman's supervision is the preparation of the Company's policy forms, in the drafting of which it is necessary to consider statutory requirements. New forms must be approved by State Insurance Departments in advance of their use. Therefore, constant attention must be paid to changes in the law and in the regulations of the State Departments. Mr. Herman has charge also of filing statements and returns

James D. Craig and Raymond V. Carpenter
Honored by Their Associates at Retirement

Left to Right: Standing—Roy R. Benjamin, Joseph A. Christman, Joseph J. Clair, Malvin E. Davis, Douglas S. Craig, George V. Brady, Frederic P. Chapman, Edward A. Lew, Gilbert W. Fitzhugh.

Seated—Reinhard A. Hohaus, Francis M. Smith, Samuel Milligan, Raymond V. Carpenter, James D. Craig, Horace R. Bassford, Earl O. Dunlap, James R. Herman.

required by law, and the work of computing and authorizing the payment of premium and other insurance taxes. Finally, he supervises actuarial studies pertaining to the compensation of the Field Force and to underwriting rules for Industrial and Ordinary insurance.

Mr. Davis directs various administrative work in connec-tion with policy valuations, the preparation of financial analyses, and the maintenance of actuarial records. The valuations form an essential part of the Annual Statement required by State Insurance Departments, which review the methods of valuation every three years. On the basis of his annual valuation of the Company's liabilities and the valuation of its assets by the responsible Executives, the Actuary computes the surplus earned during the year. In addition, Mr. Davis is responsible for studies and computations involved in preparing Ordinary and Industrial premiums and non-forfeiture values and for research on administrative problems.

At the close of 1942 the Metropolitan's Actuarial Division totaled some 1,100 employees, of whom only about 250 were men. This number included 13 Officers at the Home and Head Offices, 24 fully qualified actuaries, and 29 associate members of the Actuarial Societies. In addition, 113 men of the Division had entered military service by the end of 1942, of whom 6 were fully qualified actuaries, 5 associate members, and 55 students who had passed one or more of the actuarial examinations. The rapidity with which so many of them have been commissioned by the various services reflects their all-around ability and the value of their training in the solution of difficult technical problems arising in the war emergency.

Impressive as is the present size of the actuarial personnel, it would be much larger were it not for the intensive use of modern mechanical devices in the routine work of the Division. These include batteries of electrically operated sorting and tabulating machines for perforated record cards, as well as numerous calculating machines. These devices make it possible to carry out large and complicated jobs with almost incredible speed. The Company was, in fact, one of the pioneers in the use of machines in office administration. It has not only availed itself of the best practical devices on the market, but has been active in perfecting them for use in insurance account-ing. Some 30 years ago the Company retained J. Royden Peirce, an experienced inventor, to adapt his devices to the special requirements of the Actuarial Division. As a result, new types of tabulating machines incorporating many vital improvements were first designed and built in the Home Office of the Company. Later, through an arrangement whereby the International Business Machines Company took over Mr. Peirce's inventions, various new types of punch card, sorting, and tabulating machines were developed which are now extensively used by the Company. Even to a greater extent than the use of up-to-date labor-saving machinery, numerous improvements in administrative practices and short-cut methods have brought the Actuarial Division to its present peak of efficiency.

In its long career, the Actuarial Division of the Metropolitan has made important contributions to the Nation's scientific and social progress. To appreciate their significance it must be realized that the actuarial field is a distinct branch of applied science, comparable to engineering or medicine. Consequently, the many improvements made in its theory and practice have in themselves constituted scientific advances. Actuarial studies, in which the Metropolitan has played an important part, have thrown a great deal of light on factors influencing health and longevity. These researches have directed attention to industrial hazards, as well as to medical defects and conditions which shorten life. Metropolitan Actuaries have also helped in the efforts to solve problems relating to the financial security of the individual and the family. Beginning with J. D. Craig's first studies of Unemployment and of Health insurance, members of the Division have contributed many significant studies which have been of value in the development of our national system of social security.

But over and above this, and as part of their day-to-day work, the greatest contribution of American actuaries to the social welfare of the Nation has been to put the institution of Life Insurance on a firm and unshakable foundation. They have enabled the business to expand safely to its present status, where fully half the people of the United States and Canada use this medium to build up voluntary programs of individual and family security. The creative abilities of American actuaries have thus made possible the development of private Life insurance in this country on a scale unrivaled anywhere else in the world. Modern actuaries recognize also their obligation to the future. Their broadly conceived and thorough program of training insures a new generation of capable men to carry on this vital work. The American public may be confident that, under the wise counsel of the actuaries, the Life insurance business will be conducted in the best interest of the policyholders and of the Nation.

CHAPTER 19

Life Insurance and Medical Science

MODERN LIFE INSURANCE, as we have seen, requires the services of many types of experts: investment analysts, actuaries, physicians, lawyers, and many other technically trained people. The physician is essential because his judgment and skill are necessary to determine the insurability of applicants for insurance. The actual procedure of accepting Life insurance risks, usually referred to as "underwriting," involves, however, not only the services of the Medical Director but also an Underwriting Executive who in cooperation with the Actuary, the Medical Director, and the Statistician determines the rules for the proper classification of risks. As has already been emphasized, policyholders are expected to pay a premium commensurate with the class of risks to which they belong.

The importance of the physician in the selection of risks was appreciated even in the earliest days of Life insurance. In England, where Life insurance on the level-premium plan began in the latter part of the 18th century, the applicant for a policy was required to appear personally before the officers of the company, who plied him with questions regarding his health, character, and financial resources. Usually this group of officers included at least one physician, upon whom the others depended to elicit and evaluate the details of the applicant's medical history and to note any outward signs of ill-health. The early applicant for insurance was not given a medical examination in the modern sense. It was not until well along in the 19th century that such examinations were instituted. Thus, while the medical aspect of selection was by no means neglected at the beginning, methods of detecting early signs of chronic disease were lacking and there was little knowledge of the effect of many medical impairments on longevity. Consequently more attention was then paid to the personal character and integrity of the applicant. If he did not live in the city where the insurance office was located and could not conveniently appear for questioning, he was required to pay an extra premium.

The first American Life insurance companies followed the medical practices of the English companies. Thus, a history of the New England Mutual Life Insurance Company, one of the first American companies, notes that at the beginning more reliance was placed upon the judgment and personal recommendation of the agent than upon the findings of the physician. The Mutual Life Insurance Company of New York, which was launched in 1843, did not require a medical examination until 1856. Both companies, however, required rather full statements from the applicant as to his previous medical history and his physical condition at the time of application. These companies, and the many others then being formed, often required also a certificate of health from the applicant's personal physician, and this custom persisted for many years even after insurance medical examinations were inaugurated. Some of the physicians associated with these early insurance companies were very prominent men. For example, Dr. Willard Parker, one of the great figures in American medicine 75 years ago, served as physician for the Equitable Life Assurance Society.

When the Metropolitan was founded in 1868 Life insurance medicine was still in a formative stage. In the Company's early days there was no separate Medical Department. In the by-laws of the Company provision was made for the medical oversight of the selection of risks. It was "the duty of the consulting and examining physician to attend daily, at stated hours, at the office of the Company to examine applicants for assurance at the office or elsewhere when requested by an officer of the Company, and to make in each case a report thereof to the officers of the Company; to give advice and counsel on all applications from abroad, and also, when requested, on all proofs and papers in support of claims, occasioned by the death of the insured." Dr. J. A. White, a Brooklyn physician, first held the official title of Medical Examiner for the Company and, as was the custom, his address and office hours were listed in the early publications for the Agency Force.

Medical selection of applicants in the Company's early days was a prime interest of the first President, Dr. Dow, who was himself a physician, and who had had experience as a medical examiner for insurance companies for many years. After his death, in 1871, direct charge of this phase of the Company's work was assumed by the Executive Officers, who arranged for the appointment of Medical Examiners and handled the medical phases of underwriting. This continued even after the Company entered the field of Industrial insurance. Medical problems kept cropping up, however, and there was lacking a good set of standards by which to handle them. As a means of getting the Company's Medical Examiners to understand the basic requirements of the Industrial business, Mr. Knapp called them together from time to time to discuss their problems. Thus they came to agree on uniform methods of handling at least the most pressing ones.

As time went on it became clear that for the efficient conduct of Industrial insurance a well-trained, full-time physician should be responsible for the medical work at the Home Office. In 1890, therefore, it was decided to put a physician in active charge of the newly formed Medical Division. In taking this step the Company made a remarkable choice for that day in appointing a woman, Dr. Isabelle M. Rankine. Career women were only then beginning to appear in the professions, and had a most difficult time making their way. Dr. Rankine, unfortunately, was no exception to this rule and was unable to get sufficient cooperation in her work from her male colleagues to establish a smoothly functioning depart-

Dr. THOMAS H. WILLARD

ment. Consequently it was necessary to put a man in charge, and on September 15, 1890, Dr. Thomas H. Willard joined the Company to take up this work. On October 27, 1891, he was made Chief Medical Examiner of the Company, and he received the official title of Medical Director in 1899. His first task with the Company was to build up the Medical Department, which Dr. Rankine, not without some success, had begun. Dr. Willard was not satisfied with the mere task of appointing and supervising the work of examining physicians. He soon made his presence felt in the active conduct of the business. He interested himself in the rules for underwriting Industrial insurance and exerted himself to improve them in various ways.

The reorganization of the Ordinary Department in 1892, and the entry of the Company into the field of substandard insurance a few years later, added greatly to the responsibility of the Medical Division in the selection of risks. At the same time its administration of the medical side of Industrial insurance remained a sizable job because of the extraordinary expansion of that Department. Seeking an able physician to share the burden with Dr. Willard, Mr. Fiske's choice fell on Dr. Augustus S. Knight, a young physician who had already shown such promise in his profession that soon after his graduation from the Harvard Medical School he had been made a member of its faculty. Dr. Knight first became associated with the Company as a Medical Examiner in Boston in 1892, and had advanced to the position of Chief Examiner for that area. The two men first met in 1895 when Mr. Fiske was fighting legislation against Industrial insurance in Massachusetts. He had been greatly impressed with the young doctor's ability and capacity. Dr. Knight was appointed Assistant Medical Director in 1899 and was made a Medical Director in 1901. Mr. Fiske's judgment of Dr. Knight was well founded. Many of the later innovations by the Company in insurance medical practice and in its medical welfare program for employees were primarily due to Dr. Knight's foresight and initiative.

The development of the Medical Division during the 1890's, largely to meet the needs of the reorganized Ordinary Department, came at a particularly opportune time. The institution of Life Insurance in the United States was beginning to mature. Cooperation between companies was being established along lines that promised to be advantageous both to the business and to the insuring public. This was evidenced by the increasing frequency with which the actuaries and the medical directors of the various companies got together and exchanged ideas. It is more than a coincidence that the year 1889 marked the organization both of the Actuarial Society of America and of the Association of Life Insurance Medical Directors of America, in both of which the Metropolitan was later to play a leading role. This was also a period in which modern scientific medicine was making tremendous advances, which were to be of great significance for Life insurance. New discoveries in bacteriology, together with the development of sanitary science and public health organization, were beginning to have a direct and beneficial effect on longevity. Other medical discoveries at about this time were to contribute to greater accuracy in diagnosis and hence lay the groundwork for better methods of medical examination for Life insurance and for better standards of medical selection. Thus, the discovery of the X-ray, which was to prove of such fundamental importance to every field of medicine, came only in 1895. Practicable and dependable methods of measuring blood pressure were also being developed about that time, and Einthoven's work on the electrocardiogram, now a fundamental aid to diagnosis of many heart conditions, came to fruition in 1902.

The joint administration of the Medical Division by Drs. Willard and Knight covered a period of more than 30 years, until Dr. Willard's retirement in December 1932 after serving the Company for 42 years. Dr. Knight then took full charge for the ensuing two years, retiring at the end of 1934, also with a record of 42 years of service, 35 of them

Dr. AUGUSTUS S. KNIGHT

Dr. CHARLES L. CHRISTIERNIN
Medical Director

in the Home Office of the Company. Since 1934 the direction of the Medical Division has been in the hands of Dr. Charles L. Christiernin. When appointed to this position he was already a veteran of 25 years of service with the Company, the first two of which had been spent as a Medical Examiner in Boston. In 1911 he was invited to join the growing Medical Staff at the Home Office. He was appointed Assistant Medical Director in 1916. In his administration the Medical Division has kept abreast of the many advances in medical science, and underwriting results have reflected this progress.

The Medical Division as now organized is relatively small as compared with some of the other operating departments, but carries on a varied and vital function. The Administrative Staff of the Division at the Home and the two Head Offices consists of the Medical Director, 16 Assistant Medical Directors, and the chiefs of the Biochemical Laboratory and of the Dental Division. The Division's primary functions are the direction of the medical phase of underwriting and the recruiting and supervision of the Staff of Examining Physicians in the Field. Its underwriting duties include the review of applications presenting difficult or unusual medical problems and those involving large amounts of insurance. The members of the Division also review medical facts on death claims whenever necessary. The Division conducts the Biochemical Laboratory, which makes annually many thousands of tests of urine and blood specimens. It takes an important part in the mortality investigations which the Company makes alone or in cooperation with other companies.

The Medical Division administers also the extensive facilities of health service for the nearly 50,000 employees and Field-Men (including the Company's Sanatorium and the Medical and Dental Clinics), and is responsible for the medical examination of applicants for employment. It participates in many of the Company's welfare activities in behalf of policyholders. Thus it was a prime mover in the offer first introduced in 1914 of free periodic health examinations to Ordinary policyholders. It advises on medical aspects of the Welfare program—national health advertising, health literature, health campaigns, and Company-supported medical research. It has encouraged the Company's Medical Examiners to participate in public health activities in their communities and to support the national health campaigns conducted by the Welfare Division and leading health organizations.

Despite the great variety of its functions, the Medical Division is a well integrated and coordinated unit. Its staff of trained and experienced physicians has made distinct contributions to medical science. They have not only aided in the development of the technical aspects of Life insurance medicine, but have also shown how certain of these methods and results could be useful in general medical practice. They have used the opportunity, afforded by periodic medical examination of the large Home Office personnel, to prosecute many original clinical studies on tuberculosis, heart impairments, and other disorders. The results of these studies have proved of great

406

value not only to Life insurance medicine but to the whole field of medical science.

The Field Staff of Medical Examiners of the Company prior to the war emergency numbered nearly 9,000 physicians, located in cities and towns throughout the United States and Canada. The number of examinations made for the Company by these men varies a great deal from year to year, primarily as a result of fluctuations in the volume of new business. In 1941 a total of 1,310,257 examinations were made. Following our entrance into the war the number of Examiners has been reduced sharply because, with nearly one third of American physicians expected to enter military service, the Company has been conscious of its obligation to lighten the burden of those physicians who are left to serve civilian needs. To meet this situation the Company has increased the amount of insurance it will issue without medical examination and has thus reduced appreciably the number of examinations of applicants for new insurance.

In cooperation with the Underwriting Executive, the Actuary, and the Statistician, the Medical Director has worked out efficient, rapid, and economic methods for the medical selection of risks. Rating manuals for medical impair- ments have been prepared so that the major part of the selec- tion can be done by carefully trained lay personnel, under the guidance of the Medical Division. The trend has been toward giving more responsibility to the lay personnel by appropriate additions to the manual which have in large part been made possible by information obtained from mortality studies. The physicians at the Home Office have thus been able to devote a greater part of their time to those cases which present the more difficult medical problems.

The development of medical underwriting is one of the most interesting phases of insurance medicine. A few examples will show how, especially at the Metropolitan, the scientific method is applied to it. Over the course of the years, medical selection of applicants has become increasingly accurate, and consequently fairer. The growing knowledge of the factors influencing human longevity, supplemented by numerous investigations of the mortality among impaired persons, has made possible the quantitative appraisal of the effects of many medical impairments on mortality. Medical selection has also tended to become more liberal. Underwriting restrictions because of an applicant's medical history have greatly decreased as a result of improved health conditions generally, and as a result of the mortality studies referred to which have shown that the original reason for certain restrictions no longer applied. Indeed, for many years now, younger male and single female applicants for moderate amounts of Ordinary insurance have been accepted without any medical examination, except when available information indicated need for such examination. Today less than 4 percent of the applicants in the Ordinary Department are rejected for medical reasons, and about the same proportion are limited to Substandard insurance. Overweight is the most common impairment causing limitation to Substandard insurance, while heart disease and high blood pressure are the leading medical causes of rejection. The increasing efficiency of medical selection has been a major factor in the highly satisfactory mortality record in the various branches of the business, especially in the Ordinary Department.

The first contributions of the Company to insurance medicine were modest. In 1909 a Committee on Mortality was created jointly by the Actuarial Society of America and the Association of Life Insurance Medical Directors. This Committee, whose research activities have been most vital in the evolution of insurance medicine, has had Metropolitan representation, both medical and actuarial, from the beginning. In the succeeding years Company representatives have played an increasingly prominent role in its activity. These cooperative investigations have been of tremendous benefit to the Life insurance business and to the policyholders because the combined experience of all the companies yields information that in many cases no one of them could obtain from its experience alone.

The first fruit of the Committee's work was the Medico-Actuarial Mortality Investigation made during 1909-1911. This study included nearly 100 groups with specific medical impairments, and also data for the construction of a standard weight table as well as for the study of the influence of body build on longevity. From this investigation is derived the table of average weights in popular use, as well as some of our knowledge of the adverse effects of overweight on health and longevity. The next comprehensive investigation of medical impairments by the Committee was made in 1929. This study covered the experience on 128 medical impairments, or combinations of them. It was supplemented immediately afterward by further investigation of the influence on longevity of body build and of a family history of tuberculosis. The activities of the Committee have increased in recent years. It has published a series of further studies dealing with a variety of medical impairments, the latest of which is a comprehensive investigation of the effect of blood pressure on mortality, the second large study of this kind.

In addition to these joint studies, the Medical Division of the Company has collaborated with the Actuarial Division and the Statistical Bureau in many studies based upon the Company's own experience. The rapid growth of the Ordinary Department, at a time when the extraordinary advances in medical science were producing a steady increase in longevity, made it desirable for the Company to make continuous investigations into the mortality of special classes of risks. For that purpose the three divisions cooperated in setting up, in 1921, a basic record system through which such investigations could easily and quickly be made, and which also would facilitate the Company's contributions to a variety of intercompany studies.

A striking example of the Medical Division's pioneering has been the development of laboratory procedures. These have become increasingly important in Life insurance medicine. Most useful have been the various urinary tests because the presence, in abnormal amounts, of certain substances in the urine, more particularly of albumin, sugar, casts, and blood cells, are often an early indication of serious disease, even before actual symptoms develop. When the Ordinary Department was reorganized in 1892 the Metropolitan followed the usual practice of having the Examining Physician himself make such tests if the amount of insurance applied for or the medical history given made it advisable. The Examiner was not limited to any particular tests, but he was expected to specify those he used. However, since all results were reported in qualitative terms and depended partly on the individual judgment of the Examiner, the reports were frequently unreliable. To overcome this difficulty the Medical Division established a central Biochemical Laboratory in the Home Office in 1905, to which Examiners were required to send specimens.

At the beginning, ratings were rather severe on applicants even with insignificant urinary abnormalities, and the rejection rate for such cases was generally quite high. A series of investigations, initiated in 1917, both of rating practices and of test procedures, eventually resulted in a number of important changes in this phase of insurance work. First of all, an investigation of the subsequent mortality among applicants rejected by the Company for supposed urinary impairments showed that a large number of them were insurable, and underwriting practices were consequently much liberalized. Quantitative standards for albuminuria, which were set by a Committee of the Association of Life Insurance Medical Directors, were introduced shortly thereafter. This investigation was significant in another direction, in that the Company's Statistician perfected a technique of follow-up study through which all but an insignificant fraction of the cases were traced and details regarding their subsequent medical history were obtained. This technique has not only proved of great value in later researches by Life insurance companies, but also in similar studies by physicians, surgeons, and other scientists. In this way the long-term results of specific methods of treatment of various diseases and of surgical and X-ray procedures have been carefully and accurately appraised.

While the mortality investigation was being made, all the procedures of the laboratory were reviewed. For this purpose the Medical Division called in the foremost experts in the field, Dr. Otto Folin and Dr. Stanley Benedict. These men devised new quantitative tests for glycosuria and albuminuria which have become standard procedure in medicine. In addition, the Laboratory has refined and improved methods of analysis of various substances in the blood. Dr. Folin developed for the Company a method of determining accurately the amount of sugar in a very small quantity of blood, and this method is now used in medical laboratories all over the world.

Another interesting development has been the use of X-ray procedures in solving medical problems of Life insurance. This revolved primarily around the use of the fluoroscope, an X-ray device through which the physician can "see" instantly the internal structures of the body. Fluoroscopy was first taken up by the Medical Division as an efficient and inexpensive method of detecting early tuberculosis in applicants for employment and in Company employees at the Home Office. Studies of various abnormalities of the lungs disclosed in these examinations helped the Company's doctors to determine their significance, and as a result some abnormalities, such as healed childhood tuberculosis, were proved to have no adverse effect on longevity. Insurance practices were consequently revised in the light of these findings.

X-ray films have also been extensively used in examinations of the heart and lungs. The determination of the nature and extent of cardiac enlargement by the usual methods of examination is, in some respects, a "rule of thumb" affair. An X-ray film of the chest, however, yields more accurate information on the size of the heart and often discloses other valuable details regarding that organ. Consequently its use, when a heart abnormality is present or suspected, results in more accurate and fairer judgment than would otherwise be possible. Here again observations on Home Office employees have expedited the development of standards for insurance and general use.

The investigation of heart impairments has had especial interest for those concerned with medical selection in the Metropolitan. In 1899 the Company began to insure persons with certain types of heart murmurs, issuing policies in the Special Class branch to these applicants. As there was no mortality experience to go by, the decision to accept such risks was made on the basis of clinical judgment. In the aggregate, the mortality experience on these heart cases proved to be within the expected limits. Periodic studies proved, however, that some types of heart murmurs were insignificant abnormalities, while others were of such seriousness that persons so impaired were not insurable at all.

New procedures for diagnosing heart disease have also been useful in insurance medicine. One of the most important of these is electrocardiography, which is of prime value in detecting diseases of the heart muscle. Prior to the use of this technique in insurance examinations little distinction could be made with respect to applicants with such disorders. The development of electrocardiography, however, has made it possible to identify some cases of serious heart disease that would not ordinarily be picked up by the usual physical examination. While the normal pattern of the electrocardiogram has been defined in broad outlines, there are numerous deviations the nature and significance of which are still obscure. In the accumulation of data for the solution of these problems the insurance companies, and particularly the Metropolitan, are laying foundations for future scientific advances which should prove of great value not only in insurance medicine but also in general practice.

The Medical Division of the Metropolitan has greatly aided the progress of industrial medicine through its work for Company employees. The story of this development is of extraordinary interest, as it illustrates how an enlightened employer can foster good health in a large employee group, while at the same time capitalizing on the excellent opportunities for clinical research afforded by the presence of a large and stable personnel. The Metropolitan's medical welfare program for employees, as has already been pointed out, was conceived, organized, and developed by the three gifted men mentioned previously—Dr. Knight, Mr. Fiske, and Dr. Frankel. In its beginnings the program was very modest. Industrial medicine for clerical and selling personnel was a virgin field. The Company's efforts were, therefore, advanced step by step. Each new procedure was carefully planned and tested, and put into general use only as it proved its worth. At all times the confidential relationship between physician and patient has been carefully observed.

The first step in the Metropolitan's medical welfare work for employees was taken in 1906, when women applying for employment in the Home Office were required to have a medical examination. This practice was extended in 1910 to male applicants for Home Office employment, and to all applicants for the Field Force. In 1908 a special room was set aside, near the offices of the Medical Division, for Clerks who became ill at work, and they were seen by one of the Staff Physicians. In 1911 the scheme was considerably expanded. The number of Home Office employees was now sufficiently large to organize a Medical Dispensary for emergency care and for examinations, and shortly afterwards a Nurse was added to the Staff to give whatever nursing care was needed to employees becoming ill during office hours. In 1913 the Company Sanatorium at Mount McGregor was opened. In 1914 the annual health examination of employees was instituted, as was also a Visiting Nursing Service for employees absent from work because of illness. In 1915 a Dental Division was established in the Home Office, where employees received a regular examination and cleansing of their teeth and, later, whatever dental X-ray examination they required. In 1922 a Psychiatrist was appointed to the Home Office Staff, one of the most forward-looking steps in the whole program.

Thus the Medical Staff and the health services available to employees have expanded gradually, and today the Company has a well-rounded industrial medical organization. Apart from periodic medical examination and emergency care, the service given to employees is necessarily limited. Employees who have been absent for illness are interviewed, and, when advisable, examined by a physician before returning to work. The volume of this medical work is extremely large. As early as 1913, visits to the Home Office dispensary exceeded 15,000 annually. At the present time the Staff of more than 15,000 Home Office employees makes nearly 75,000 visits to the Medical Division annually, or an average of about 300 per working day.

Similar though necessarily less elaborate facilities for the Office Staff are found at the Head Offices in San Francisco and Ottawa. Medical services for Field-Men cannot, of course, be organized in the same way, but each member of the Field Force, whether on the Selling, Managerial, or Clerical Staff, is examined before coming with the Company and annually thereafter at Company expense by a physician in his own community. All members of the Field Force are eligible for Sanatorium care on the same basis as Home and Head Office employees. The Company also looks out for their medical welfare in many other ways.

The outstanding feature of the medical program for employees has been the extraordinary reduction of tuberculosis among them. The concern of Company Executives over employees falling ill with tuberculosis long antedated any organized plan for their care. At first the Company paid for treatment of employees at private sanatoria. But about 35 years ago the Officers felt that the best solution of the problem of tuberculosis among employees, which was by far the most frequent cause of chronic disability, was to care for them, at Company expense, in a Sanatorium owned and operated by the Company. This plan could not be carried out until the important legal obstacle forbidding insurance companies to own real estate unless necessary for the direct use of the business, was overcome. A friendly suit instituted in the Supreme Court of New York State was decided in favor of the Company, and in a historic decision the court said "The reasonable care of its employees, according to the enlightened

414

Ward Building, Mount McGregor Sanatorium

sentiment of the age and the community, is a duty resting upon it (the Company), and the proper discharge of that duty is merely transacting the business of the corporation." The Metropolitan lost no time in picking a good site for the projected institution, at Mount McGregor, in the foothills of the Adirondack Mountains in New York State. The planning and erection of the Sanatorium were speedily carried out, and in November 1913 it was ready for its first patients. In charge of the Sanatorium from the beginning was Dr. Horace J. Howk, a physician of great skill and administrative ability, who also possessed a warm personality which endeared him to his many patients and associates. At his death in 1926 he was succeeded by his capable colleague, Dr. William H. Ordway, the present head of the Sanatorium. Since 1913 more than 3,000 Company employees and Field-Men have received treatment there for tuberculosis.

With its own Sanatorium in operation, the Company was in a position to develop a unique and thoroughgoing plan for the control of tuberculosis in its Home Office Staff. By means

415

of pre-employment examinations it was possible largely to avoid the introduction of new cases, while constant health supervision of the working force brought about early detection of cases occurring among its personnel. These cases could be given the benefit of adequate Sanatorium treatment, which was maintained until they were able to work. During this period patients received a large part of their normal income from disability benefit payments, and the resulting freedom from economic worries has helped measurably toward their recovery. The restoration of the patient to his job has also been one of the most significant parts of the program. The "graduate" of the typical sanatorium usually has the difficult task of finding suitable employment. Often the doors are closed to him because of his history of tuberculosis. The rehabilitation of the patient, the weakest link in the national program of tuberculosis control, is a vital and valuable part of the scheme at the Metropolitan.

In this program the Medical Division has taken advantage of all new facilities and methods that science has developed in the diagnosis and treatment of tuberculosis. Notable in this regard has been the routine use of fluoroscopy and X-ray in the examination of employees since 1928. It was long suspected and eventually proved that X-ray procedures were the only effective means of detecting tuberculosis in its early stages. By the time actual symptoms appear the disease is usually well advanced.

The long-term results of routine fluoroscopy at the Home Office have been extraordinarily good. Thus, while among applicants for employment the proportion with tuberculosis, active or healed, has remained constant in the period since the procedure was begun, the proportion among Home Office personnel has declined sharply—by more than 50 percent in only 10 years. Again, whereas before the inauguration of routine fluoroscopy only 30 percent of the tuberculosis cases discovered among employees were still in the early stage, this proportion has practically doubled, while far-advanced cases have declined from 22 percent to 5 percent of the total. In fact, in some recent years not a single new case of far-advanced tuberculosis was found among the many thousands of Home Office employees. Thus not only have new cases been generally less advanced, but they have been appreciably fewer in number. Since the chances of complete recovery from the disease are best when patients are brought under early treatment, a greater proportion were successfully treated and the time lost for treatment was markedly reduced. A recent study showed that, of the patients followed for at least 10 years after discharge from the Mount McGregor Sanatorium, half were at work or still able to work at the end of this period. Among patients who had been brought under treatment in the early stage of the disease, and whose condition on discharge from the Sanatorium was considered satisfactory, the proportion was nearly 80 percent. Among such ex-patients the subsequent mortality was little if any higher than that of their fellow workers, who have a very low mortality.

With a steady increase in the number and proportion of older employees, the Medical Division has been alert to their medical needs. It has instituted procedures for the detection and care of those presenting early signs of diseases, both physical and mental, which are characteristic of middle and later life. At the same time it has developed a systematic plan for the study of some of these conditions, especially of heart disease and high blood pressure. As a first step in a long range plan the Medical Division inaugurated, in 1930, a more thorough and searching medical examination for employees reaching or already past age 40. This examination, which is repeated at least every year or two, includes routine electrocardiographic and X-ray study of the heart. The individual's medical history is also reviewed. It is through careful evaluation of all this information that many instances of early or developing cardiovascular disease are disclosed. The medical observations on these men and women, now numbering more than 2,000, constitute a unique and valuable set of data, and out of their systematic study new guides to the diagnosis of early cardiovascular disease may be expected to develop.

The many activities of the Medical Division in behalf of employees are reflected in their high degree of health and efficiency. This partly accounts for their extremely low mortality, which is only about one half, and among the younger employees only one fourth, that of the general population at corresponding ages. The record for tuberculosis is exceptionally good, with a death rate nearly 70 percent less than that in the general population.

The results of the Medical Division's work in both insurance and industrial medicine have been made available to scientists through numerous papers and reports. These have appeared not only in insurance publications, but in medical and other scientific periodicals. Scientific exhibits at medical meetings and conventions have also served as a medium of disseminating information on the methods and results obtained by the Medical Division.

It is abundantly clear that the Medical Division, as it is organized and as it functions at the Metropolitan, has not only played a vital role in the conduct of the business, but has contributed much to medical science. The Division has continuously shown a capacity to adapt new medical procedures to its work and to develop original methods.

Physicians have earned their high place in Life insurance. They will continue to be an effective influence on the progress of this institution, which is so closely bound up with the public welfare.

A Family
of Thirty
Million

❧❧ *Part* V ❦❦

CHAPTER 20

A Program of Welfare

I N 1909 AN EVENT of great moment occurred, both for Life insurance and for American public health. In that year the Metropolitan organized its Welfare Division, and launched a program of life conservation as a definite part of its business. A new era for Life insurance, and more particularly for Industrial insurance, was thus inaugurated. These efforts were primarily instituted for the families of wage-earners insured in the Company. Yet the campaign against unnecessary sickness and premature death has reached far beyond these people and has been translated into terms of welfare for the whole Nation.

During the half century prior to the founding of the Welfare Division, knowledge regarding disease had been fabulously enriched and Medicine had made great advances. The establishment of the germ theory of disease in the 1870's by Pasteur was soon followed by the identification of the causes of such important diseases as anthrax, tuberculosis, typhoid fever, diphtheria, and pneumonia. Diphtheria antitoxin and vaccines against smallpox and rabies were becoming widely available. The important role of insects in the spread of diseases had been proved. Surgery was progressing rapidly. The potentialities of good public health administration had just been magnificently demonstrated by the transformation of the Panama Canal Zone from a "white man's grave" to a healthy district. Health officers all over the country were learning that it was possible to control disease, that "public health was purchasable." Knowledge of the basic principles of nutrition was increasing. Medical research was constantly adding to the store of knowledge which was to make for a richer and more abundant life.

At the same time that progress was being made in life conservation, a new concept of the value of the human factor in industry was also developing. The past 50 years had been a period of tremendous growth in American business. Mass immigration was rapidly pouring such a huge supply of labor into our cities, that it was impossible to give many of these people adequate housing and safe working places. Sweatshops, insanitary tenements, and generally low health standards were the result. Fortunately, a new attitude toward those engaged in industry was in the air, a consciousness that the working-man, no less than the working machine, should be protected against deterioration and damage. Social legislation was being passed to protect him and his family. Sanitation and safe-guards in homes and factories, child labor laws, and shorter working hours were gradually making it possible for wage-earners to have greater comforts and health advantages.

The time was indeed ripe for a large-scale attack on public health problems. But facilities for the widespread application of the new medical knowledge were only slowly being con-trived. Health departments of cities were often restricted in their activities, held a narrow view of their responsibilities, and frequently suffered from inefficiency. It is significant that the Metropolitan should have felt the propriety and urgency to contribute toward the improvement of the situation. Through its vast network of District Offices and its Agents, it had adequate facilities for reaching a great number of people. Its clientele, so large a proportion of the working population, gave it a real stake. A saving in human lives would prove advantageous in many ways.

It was fortunate also that two men were at hand to focus the current interest in medical and industrial welfare into a program for Metropolitan policyholders. One, Lee K. Frankel, as a scientist and a humanitarian, exemplified the tendencies of the day. An internationally distinguished social worker, he had already acquired knowledge of the health problems of the poor through his earlier work as director of the United Hebrew Charities of New York. He was a person of warm human sympathies, lovable and inspiring, but also a man of scientific training, with experience in business which few social workers possessed. Not only aware of difficult and pressing social problems, he could see practical solutions as well. He was a great teacher who could win others over to the wisdom of his projects and stimulate them to accomplishment.

But the chief credit for the development of the welfare program belongs to Haley Fiske. By a striking coincidence, the two men first met in December 1908, at a meeting in the Charities Building in New York City, at which Mr. Fiske spoke in defense of Industrial insurance. Dr. Frankel was then numbered among its critics and had just returned from Europe, where he had made a survey of workingmen's insurance for the Russell Sage Foundation. Mr. Fiske listened carefully to Dr. Frankel's constructive ideas. Shortly thereafter, with the warm approval of the Metropolitan's Directors and Officers, he invited Dr. Frankel to join the Company's Official Staff.

The general program was greeted enthusiastically by everyone in the Home Office and in the Field. Dr. Frankel was given free hand to carry out his plans with the full force of Executive authority behind him; and in the fusion of their efforts a service of far-reaching value was created. The rich fruit that this work has borne is due, in large measure, to the recognition by these two men that a great business organization could be a powerful instrument for social good. It was an example, characteristic of the American way of life, of private enterprise promoting public welfare.

On February 1, 1909, the Welfare Division commenced its work. President Fiske informed the policyholders of this new service in the following words: "Today, the Metropolitan is launched upon a new era—an era in which it joins the battle against the forces of disease, and in which it hopes to lead the world in preserving lives from the ravages of mankind's insidious foes."

423

Henry Street Settlement Nurses in 1909

One of Dr. Frankel's first and most important steps was to organize the Nursing Service for policyholders in the Industrial Department. Early in 1909 he mentioned the work of the Company's Agents "whose business took them regularly into the homes of millions of the people," in the course of a talk before a charitable organization of New York City. In the audience was Miss Lillian D. Wald, the head of the famous Henry Street Settlement and brilliant social worker. His talk fired her with an idea, and afterwards she said to him: "Many of your policyholders aren't getting proper medical care. Why don't you engage Henry Street nurses to visit every (insured) family where Agents see or hear there is illness, so there will be accurate reporting, home instruction, and treatment." Dr. Frankel was quick to see that here was the solution he was seeking. He arranged for Miss Wald to tell the Metropolitan's Officers, about the work of the Henry Street nurses, and the great benefits to the families and to the community resulting from it. The Directors at once recognized the value that such a service would have among the Industrial policyholders, and it was not long before the project was launched.

On June 9, 1909, the first Henry Street nurse visited a sick policyholder. A revolutionary idea, indeed—that a visiting nurse should give bedside care to a policyholder at the expense of an insurance company. At the outset the Nursing Service was to be tried out for a three-month period in a part of the Borough of Manhattan. So valuable were the results that at the end of this time the plan was at once extended throughout New York City. Soon Managers, Agents, and policyholders elsewhere clamored for the new service. It was extended to the city of Washington on August 11, 1909, and then in quick succession to Baltimore, Boston, Chicago, Cleveland, and St. Louis. In all, 13 affiliations with existing Visiting Nurse associations were completed in that year. In the early part of 1910 Montreal, Worcester, Lowell, Trenton, Philadelphia, Harrisburg, Buffalo, and Cincinnati were added to the list. The establishment of the Montreal service was notable in that it was the first affiliation with the Victorian Order of Nurses, which now does most of the Metropolitan's work for English-speaking policyholders in Canada. Forty-seven nursing affiliations were completed by 1910, and 350 by the following year. Thus, an experiment that had started on a very limited scale grew by leaps and bounds. Later the service was extended to include Group policyholders (1918) and Intermediate policyholders (1926).

In setting up the Nursing Service the Company adopted the principle of utilizing existing public health nursing organizations wherever possible, instead of setting up separate and duplicating units of its own. As the demand for the Nursing Service spread, however, the Company organized its own staff to serve communities which had inadequate or no visiting nurse agencies. Thus, in St. Paul, Minn., in 1910, the Metropolitan first engaged its own Nurse on a direct salary basis. Today, the Metropolitan Nursing Service reaches 7,728 communities throughout the United States and Canada. It has contract affiliations with 819 public health nursing agencies, and its own staff of 571 salaried Nurses.

The Nursing Service has been acutely responsive to changing needs of the times. Skilled bedside care of the sick has been emphasized throughout the period, as has maternity care to women during the months before and after childbirth. But with the years, Metropolitan Nurses have more and more become instructors as well as healers. Their teaching has taken many forms, ranging from the correction of some ignorant, harmful practice in the home, to more general matters such as the diet of the patient's family or removal of accident hazards. Very frequently the Nurse has brought the physician into the home and has insisted upon and arranged for the patient's hospitalization. Her alertness and advice have often prevented the spread of disease to other members of the family. Her knowledge of community agencies and the services they render has often spelled the difference between hardship and adequacy for families under her care. When disaster strikes, Metropolitan Nurses are among the first to offer aid. In typical reports of emergency work, we find such terse statements as: "On duty practically 24 hours every day" . . . "I gave 1,500 inoculations against typhoid" . . . "No. doctor to help me, but an accurate check shows that most of my patients are safe."

No effort has been spared to keep standards for the individual Nurses and for the Service as a whole at a high level. The Metropolitan Nurse has been carefully chosen from the ranks of the well-trained and fully qualified professional nurses. She has been encouraged to keep up with developments in her field by postgraduate study. She has been a good citizen, has made herself familiar with local health laws and needs, and has lent effective aid to the health officer in community education and disease prevention.

The Metropolitan has not only encouraged additional training for its own Nurses, but has frequently joined with other interested agencies to sponsor projects for the improvement of public health nursing in general. To meet the pressing need for qualified French-speaking nurses in Canada, it helped to finance a public health nursing course at Montreal University. In cooperation with the National Organization for Public Health Nursing, it prepared a *Manual of Instructions for Visiting Nurses*. The Company has made many studies in this field, and recommendations growing out of these have been widely applied and have stimulated better all-around performance by nursing agencies.

Cumbersome and antiquated records were kept by some visiting nurse agencies in the early days, but generally the nurses carried records "in their heads." From the beginning of the service Dr. Frankel urged that records be kept in an orderly, uniform, businesslike way so that trustworthy figures might be obtained. These data have helped the nursing agencies to operate on sound business principles and have proved in dollars and cents the worth of the service. They have also helped ascertain how the Nursing Service can best meet the needs of the community, and have defined the methods, training, and supervision to accomplish the desired results. More recently accurate nursing records have provided valuable information on sickness prevalence and have proved to be important material for medical research.

Moreover, the development of a good working relationship between established nursing agencies and the Company, including equitable financial arrangements, has done much to raise the standards of public health nursing throughout the United States and Canada. Before Metropolitan nursing began, these agencies had been almost entirely dependent upon private philanthropy; as a result, their income was often precarious. It takes little imagination to see what a tremendous lift public health nursing received when a strong Company like the Metropolitan joined hands in its work. Since 1909 the Company has spent more than $80,000,000 on nursing service, about half of which has been paid to affiliated nursing agencies. This tremendous sum has not only helped to put the organizations on a firm financial basis, but by adding to the average earnings of visiting nurses and to the regularity of their employment, it has made this work more attractive to women interested in a professional career. Many of the newer visiting nursing agencies now available to the general public owe their founding to Metropolitan initiative and financing. The importance of this support may be judged from the fact that approximately one quarter of the nursing service budgets to which the Company contributes, represents compensation for services rendered to Metropolitan policyholders.

The modern concept of medicine has two aspects: the curative and the preventive. The Nursing Service was inaugurated to take care of the former; the Agency Staff was to be the pivot around which a great campaign of disease prevention was to be conducted. Dr. Frankel was at once alert to the potentialities of the Metropolitan Field Force, then numbering almost 10,000 men, as instruments to carry out the plans of the new Welfare Division. These men entered the homes of working people in almost every part of the United States and Canada, and visited millions of families weekly. Their friendly and regular contacts with the policyholders afforded a unique opportunity to spread health knowledge. Again and again these Agents had seen poverty and death as the result of sickness and disability. It is easy to understand why they became willing and useful co-workers in the Metropolitan's health program.

One of the first and most effective methods for bringing sound health information to the policyholders was through the distribution of welfare pamphlets. The publication of health information by the Company was not new. Even as far back as 1871 an article entitled "Health Hints" was published in a Company periodical. In 1892, when cholera was prevalent in Europe and health officials feared that the disease might be brought to this country by immigrants, the Company, in cooperation with the Health Department of New York City, published, and its Agents distributed, a popular circular giving facts about the disease and measures to prevent it. In March 1898 appeared the first of the Company's health booklets, A Friend in Need Is a Friend Indeed, published for the Canadian policyholders.

When Dr. Frankel launched the welfare work he knew that he must get simple, readable, and accurate information directly to the people. A series of booklets, planned and created by the Welfare Division and distributed to policyholders' homes by Company Agents, was his first step. The first Welfare pamphlet, issued in 1909, was *A War on Consumption*—one of the Company's pioneer efforts to turn people away from the self-diagnosis fostered by the old-fashioned "doctor book" and to direct them to a qualified physician. In the course of several years separate editions were published in 12 different languages, and eventually the circulation of this booklet exceeded 12,000,000 copies. Next came the beautifully illustrated pamphlet *The Child*, of which also millions of copies were circulated in American and Canadian homes. These were only the first of a long list of helpful publications, covering more than 100 separate subjects in the fields of personal and community health, and of disease and accident prevention. For the sizable groups of foreign-born or other non-English speaking policyholders, the Metropolitan has translated some of its booklets into German, Italian, French, Spanish, Polish, and Yiddish. From the very beginning requests for supplies of the Company's pamphlets have been received from official agencies in all health and welfare fields, and public health departments of States and cities, and school systems and social agencies throughout the world have made good use of them. Metropolitan health messages have found their way to the four corners of the earth.

These health pamphlets have been revised from time to time, so that the information they contain is literally up to the minute. Thus, Metropolitan health literature has interpreted medical discoveries so that the veriest layman may know of recent scientific progress, and he may learn what is useful and reliable and what is unreliable or outmoded. He has learned to lead a more healthful life; to protect himself and his children against disease; to avoid accidents in the home, on the streets, and at work; and to make good use of the medical facilities available in his community. It is difficult to measure the good done by these booklets, which find their way into thousands of out-of-the-way places in this country and Canada, replacing superstition and old wives' tales with scientific facts. No one can say how much sickness has been prevented—yet the

Metropolitan gets an indication of it sometimes through an occasional letter from some workman or from an obscure housewife, thanking the Company for a timely bit of information which has led directly to the saving of a human life.

In addition to health pamphlets as a tool for advancing public health, Dr. Frankel devised an even more dramatic and effective method—the town health demonstration. The attention of a whole Nation was thus focused upon a small community, which served as the laboratory for testing the efficiency of public health measures. His first major undertaking of this type was in 1916, when the Company launched a demonstration to show how a typical community with an average tuberculosis problem could bring the disease under control through the acceptance of reasonable rules of health, periodic examinations, and treatment where necessary. The 17,000 citizens of Framingham, Mass., and the National Tuberculosis Association joined the Company in carrying out this public health demonstration. Dr. Donald B. Armstrong, a young physician trained in public health work, was in charge of the experiment. His management was so admirable that soon after the close of the demonstration, Dr. Frankel invited him to come as his assistant with the Company.

The Framingham project lasted seven years, and its cost was largely borne by the Metropolitan, which put $200,000 into it. In the 10 years before the demonstration (1907–1916), the city's death rate from tuberculosis had averaged 121 deaths per 100,000 people; by 1923, when the project closed, the tuberculosis mortality had been cut 68 percent to 38.2 per 100,000. As a secondary result the infant mortality and general death rate were sharply decreased in the same period. The public-spirited citizens of Framingham have kept at the job, and in recent years Framingham has boasted a death rate from tuberculosis which is extraordinarily low for an industrial community of this size. The tuberculosis problem in this town is virtually solved. Out of this demonstration came a new and fully implemented conception as to how a community could organize itself effectively to fight tuberculosis,

Dr. DONALD B. ARMSTRONG
Third Vice-President

and hundreds of communities throughout the country have used it and benefited.

Thetford Mines, Quebec, was the scene of another notable test of the demonstration method. This French-Canadian community was in an area where infant mortality was extremely high. The Company set out to show how it might be reduced by educating the mothers in a few simple rules of sanitation and nutrition. At the end of three years the infant mortality rate had dropped from 300 per thousand live births to 96 per thousand. Largely because of the success of this demonstration, the Provincial Government of Quebec appropriated $500,000 for similar child welfare work in other communities, where the infant mortality rate was high. So effective has this demonstration method proved, that it has been adopted widely in the fight on other diseases.

A very considerable part of the Company's welfare work is carried out anonymously, so to speak—in cooperation with civic agencies, health departments, medical societies, parents' associations, and social groups. Managers, Agents, and Nurses have been active participants—often the key figures—in initiating or spurring on the local effort.

Most striking in its results has been the Metropolitan's campaign against diphtheria. This was waged first and most intensively in New York State, with the cooperation of official and private health and welfare agencies. In 1926, when the work was begun in this State, diphtheria caused 738 deaths, or at a rate of 6.3 per 100,000 persons. By 1930 the rate had been brought down to 2.8 per 100,000. The fight still went on, and the extraordinary results for 1941 marked the culmination of the splendid teamwork of the Health Commissioner of the State, the State Medical Society, the State Charities Aid Association, Metropolitan Agents and Nurses, and local health officers. Among the 6,000,000 people in upper New York State (excluding New York City), where the fight was concentrated, there were, in 1941, only six deaths from diphtheria—a rate of 0.1 per 100,000. Not a single case was reported in more than half the counties of the State or in two thirds of the cities. In like manner the persistent drive against diphtheria among Industrial policyholders generally has yielded extraordinarily good results, as will be described in the next chapter. The day is not far distant when we shall mark the virtual eradication of this disease.

The campaign against pneumonia has also had heartening results. Through its Welfare Division the Metropolitan has itself conducted or given financial support to much important medical research. The outstanding example is the work of its Influenza-Pneumonia Commission, which was constituted in June 1919 with Dr. Milton J. Rosenau, of Harvard University, as its Chairman. In the 24 years since its founding, this Commission of leading scientists has produced valuable results in the control of pneumonia and influenza and of related respiratory conditions. Its activities have contributed materially to the perfection of antipneumococcus sera and to the wide use of the new sulfa drugs, so effective in the treatment

432

of pneumonia. The amazing success of this new chemotherapy has caused the Company to redouble its educational efforts in this field. Through its national advertising; through popular and scientific literature; through its films, exhibits, and posters, the Metropolitan has sounded the message over the land that pneumonia deaths can be prevented by early treatment, and has thus undoubtedly saved many lives.

Another fruitful example of the Company's health research is the intensive study of diabetes made in cooperation with Dr. Elliott P. Joslin and his associates at the George F. Baker Clinic of the New England Deaconess Hospital in Boston. This project involved the analysis of records of many thousands of diabetics cared for in that clinic since 1898. The discovery of insulin greatly improved the outlook for diabetics, but to secure the full benefit of this discovery required the reeducation of physicians and patients in the treatment of the disease. The publications and scientific exhibits resulting from this joint effort of the Metropolitan with the George F. Baker Clinic have helped to stimulate interest in diabetes, and have brought many cases under early treatment when most can be done for them.

Since so many of its policyholders are industrial workers, the Company has also made a number of studies in the field of industrial hygiene. In 1916 it organized the Industrial Service Bureau, and began actively to work with employers to solve health problems in their particular industries. The growth of Group insurance has given great impetus to this work. The industrial hygiene activities have expanded rapidly, and at present include valuable technical services to Group policyholders to aid them in the control of occupational hazards. Detailed studies dealing with silicosis, asbestosis, and hazards in the ceramic, the leather, and other industries have been made for the benefit of such policyholders, and have been utilized by health officers and others in the field of preventive medicine. Industrial hygiene pamphlets and posters in popular style have likewise been issued for workers and their families. The maintenance of an exceptionally well-equipped laboratory in the Home Office has meant life-saving service to Group policyholders, and has resulted in important contributions to disease control in industry.

The Welfare Division has also a special Bureau to promote health education in the schools. It has been increasingly active in spreading knowledge on nutrition, as rapid advances in this field have stimulated the need for such a program. Technical publications of the Division, including monographs, special reports, and pamphlets, have been prepared to meet the needs of industrial managers, health officers, school admin-istrators, classroom teachers, and workers in preventive medi-cine, social service, and scientific research.

The story of the Metropolitan's contribution to popular health education would be incomplete without reference to its unique magazine advertising. Because it was not designed to sell Life insurance, but to bring important health informa-tion to all the people of this country, this campaign has won a host of new friends for the Company. The advertisements, dramatically worded and well illustrated, have continuously stressed three themes: the importance of keeping fit; the danger of neglecting even minor illnesses and injuries; and the need for periodic medical examination for the early detec-tion of chronic disease. The Company's advertising has ap-peared regularly in magazines with national circulations run-ning into the tens of millions; it has aroused such public interest that as many as 50,000 requests have been received in a single month for some health booklet referred to in an advertisement. This effective campaign has won prizes awarded by the advertising profession, and has, in fact, set a style for dignity and utility in institutional promotion.

Supplementing its advertising campaign, the Welfare Divi-sion has developed a series of motion pictures, exhibits, posters, and radio presentations to popularize knowledge on health and safety. The motion picture has been used very exten-sively. In 1924 appeared the Company's first professional film, "One Scar or Many," in which the value of smallpox vaccination was convincingly brought out. Other effective

434

Metropolitan films have dealt with diphtheria immunization, the value of periodic medical examination, the avoidance and correction of obesity, nutrition, and street and highway safety. The two most recent Metropolitan films, shown in theaters throughout the United States and Canada, are "A New Day," a dramatic presentation of the modern treatment of pneumonia, and "Proof of the Pudding," illustrating the value of proper nutrition in the promotion of health, growth, and vitality. The quality of these latest films is attested by the fact that the United States Public Health Service has joined the Company in sponsoring them. Professional Hollywood actors and producers have given them popular value as good entertainment as well as excellent public health education.

Metropolitan exhibits in the field of health and safety have been of two general types: popular exhibits for the use of industry and educational and social agencies; and technical exhibits for showing at scientific meetings. The lay exhibits for many years were prepared for showing at county fairs. More ambitious were those prepared for the New York World's Fair 1939 and 1940 and for the Golden Gate Exposition at San Francisco in the same years. At these Fairs the Company dramatized its work with charts and animated displays covering all its operations, but featuring especially the work of the Welfare Division. The attendance at the Company's exhibits at these two fairs was in excess of 6,000,000.

Although the Company's technical exhibits have reached smaller audiences, these have included picked groups of physicians, educators, public health experts, engineers, industrial executives, and others active in health and safety administration. Metropolitan exhibits on tuberculosis, diabetes, nutrition, and accidents have been shown at meetings of professional societies, including the American Medical Association, the American Public Health Association, the American Nurses Association, the National Safety Council, the National Education Association, and similar National and State bodies. Since these exhibits are generally based upon material growing out

435

LOUIS I. DUBLIN
Third Vice-President and Statistician

of the Company's own experience or research activities, they are recognized as important and valuable scientific contributions in their respective fields.

From the very beginning, Dr. Frankel insisted that the work he planned for the Company should justify itself by concrete results. He believed that progress could be achieved only on a basis of solid fact. He insisted at the very outset on accurate record-keeping and on sound analysis of the data collected. With this in mind, in 1909 he invited Dr. Louis I. Dublin, a young man fresh from his training in statistical methods, to furnish advice on how to measure the effectiveness of the work of the new Division. Dr. Dublin outlined a plan for the study of the nursing records and the death records of the Company. In 1911 he was appointed head of the new Statistical Bureau which has been closely associated with the Welfare Division as its research agency. Every year, it has collected and analyzed data on the millions of policyholders.

This has been not only a measure of the Company's efforts in lowering mortality, but has also served as a guide to new welfare projects. Statistical research based on this experience has been valuable to outside health agencies as well, and has stimulated and set standards for the use of such methods by Federal, State, and city health departments. Since the Bureau has made use of millions of records, it has developed one of the best organizations in the country for mechanical tabulation. So effective, in fact, is the Tabulating Section, that it has served as a laboratory for development of techniques which have become increasingly important tools in the conduct of business, government, and research throughout the world.

Through the Statistical Bureau the Company has been a force in the improvement of the Nation's vital statistics. When this Bureau was established in 1911, satisfactory data on births and deaths were lacking for large sections of the United States. In cooperation with others the Company sought to correct this situation. It even utilized its Field-Men to work with legislatures and local authorities for adequate registration of births and deaths. At present every State has machinery for the reporting and tabulating of such records. Furthermore, in order to improve the quality of mortality statistics, it has been necessary from time to time to modify the classification of causes of death, in order to keep abreast of new medical knowledge. For this purpose a representative of the Statistical Bureau has served regularly on the committee charged with the periodic revision of the International List of Causes of Death.

The Statistical Bureau has made studies of mortality according to occupation, and others on the frequency of physical impairments and their effect on longevity. Its library on vital statistics has been invaluable in the health research activities of the Company, and of service also to welfare workers and agencies outside the Company. The Bureau answers thousands of inquiries each year from physicians and others, even from distant countries, on all phases of vital statistics and demographic research.

The varied research activities of the Bureau are embodied in hundreds of reports and papers on mortality, population problems, sickness surveys, expectation of life, both in scientific publications and in popular articles. These articles and other researches have served as the basis for many books, notably, *Mortality Statistics of Insured Wage-Earners and Their Families* (1919); *Health and Wealth* (1928), which has been translated into several foreign languages and has spurred on public health efforts abroad; *The Money Value of a Man* (1930); *Length of Life: A Study of the Life Table* (1936); *Twenty-Five Years of Health Progress* (1937). Since 1920 the Bureau has published a *Statistical Bulletin*, in which are given current mortality data on the Company's policyholders, the results of Bureau research, and accounts of important developments in public health. The *Statistical Bulletin* is recognized as an authoritative source, and is probably the most widely quoted periodical of its type in the United States and Canada.

The Company over the years has conducted many original investigations into various social and economic problems. In 1915 it launched a series of surveys on the extent of unemployment in the industrial population of the United States. The data were collected by the Agents of the Company, and the findings constituted the first significant report on the amount and kind of unemployment in this country. The wide and practical results of this study demonstrated the feasibility of conducting similar investigations, and the next study was launched in nine different population centers, on the character and amount of sickness in wage-earning populations. Both investigations were made on behalf of the Federal Government and were later published by the U. S. Bureau of Labor Statistics. In 1922 the Company began a series of studies on the cost of medical care, and in 1929 gathered such information among its Industrial policyholders. These studies constituted a pioneer effort in this field.

In 1920 the Company helped to organize the Committee on Administrative Practice of the American Public Health Association, which made a systematic investigation of the

438

work of the larger health departments throughout the country. The work of this committee, originally financed by the Metropolitan, brought about much improvement in standards by developing methods of measuring the effectiveness of health departments.

The ability thus to evaluate city health work through accurate records has opened an approach to stimulate community leaders to more active public health campaigns in their own cities. This has made possible the City Health Conservation Contest, launched by the American Public Health Association in 1929, with financial support by the Metropolitan and other Life insurance companies and with the cooperation of the Chamber of Commerce of the United States. These contests bring out vividly the actual achievements of communities in the health field, as well as the improvements made from year to year. Since the project was inaugurated, more than 500 American cities have enrolled and without exception have reported improved health conditions and lowered mortality. Separate contests under other auspices have been developed for rural communities and for Canada, and have given great impetus to the health services of many outlying towns.

It is significant that Dr. Frankel's last effort should be concerned with the newer developments of social insurance in Europe and with its possible applications to American life. In the summer of 1931 he went abroad with Actuary James D. Craig to survey the scope and administration of such programs. This survey was an expression of a fundamental interest which dominated his life: to bring ever-increasing security to wage-earners through the medium of insurance. He was fortunately able to bring the work to a substantial conclusion before his sudden death in Paris on July 25, 1931. This study proved a fitting climax to a career of service to his Company and to his country. As was noted in chapter 18, it constituted the groundwork for new types of private insurance and helped in the development of our present Federal system of unemployment and old-age insurance.

It is difficult to evaluate a personality as fertile and con-structive as that of Dr. Frankel. His activities covered many fields, but he was always the servant of mankind. The creation of the Welfare Division of the Company was his greatest achievement. He put the mark of his humanity on the Metropolitan, helping to transform it from a typical busi-ness organization into an institution for social progress. The whole field of Life insurance has felt the effect of this effort. He also brought new vigor to American public health work, both official and voluntary. In 1919 he served as President of the American Public Health Association. He found new sources of financial support for it, and as a result the Association has grown in prestige and effectiveness. He was a prime mover in the formation of the National Health Council, which brought together various national associations in each field of public health, enabling them to further their common aims and to prevent wasteful duplication of effort. He held high office and served on important committees in virtually all the leading health organizations. His influence on the Ameri-can health movement has been deep and lasting.

In September of 1931 the Board of Directors designated Dr. Armstrong and Dr. Dublin, both of whom had been intimately associated with Dr. Frankel for many years, to carry on the health activities of the Company. Working together, they have continued the tradition of Dr. Frankel in the conduct of the welfare program and in stimulating and supporting a wide range of outside health organizations. The work Dr. Frankel envisioned has been richly fulfilled, and the Company has continued increasingly to be a force in the life conservation activities of the country.

This chapter would be incomplete without a tribute to the contribution of the Company's Agents. They have been of the greatest service in bringing sick policyholders under nursing care, and in carrying popular health education into the home. But their efforts have not been limited to propa-ganda alone. In the early stages of the Company's fight against diphtheria, it was the Metropolitan Agents who often set the example in the community by first having their own children inoculated. They have carried through many nation-wide educational campaigns against specific diseases and accidents. Working side by side with civic and health agencies, Metropolitan Agents have helped in vital research, such as the Company's unemployment and sickness surveys. They have given generously of their time and interest, and have labored fruitfully.

It is not surprising, therefore, that their welfare work has been a rewarding experience. Many Agents can tell of lives that have been saved and communities made healthier and happier places in which to live as the result of their efforts. Since the organization of the Welfare Division, in 1909, the policyholders on their debits have been enabled to share in the gifts conferred by recent discoveries of science, and by the operation of public health measures. Close to 25,000,000 people in the United States and Canada are now eligible to receive skilled nursing care during illness.

The welfare work of the Company has surely been worth while in terms of lives saved and deaths postponed, and in the consequent lowering of the cost of insurance. In the third of a century since the founding of the Welfare Division, its Nurses have made more than 92,000,000 home visits to approximately 20,000,000 policyholders. Considerably more than 1,200,-000,000 copies of Metropolitan health pamphlets have been distributed in this country and Canada. Its motion pictures have been seen since 1924 by nearly 127,000,000 persons at theaters, schools, and other centers. Certainly no one agency working alone could have reached out to change the health attitudes and practices of so many millions of individuals. In the movement which through the years has achieved longer and more abundant life for the American people, the Metro-politan is proud to have played its part.

CHAPTER 21

Progress in Health and Longevity

IN THE PERIOD of 75 years during which the Metropolitan Life Insurance Company has been operating, and especially the last third of a century during which its welfare work has developed, there has been phenomenal progress in the health of the Nation. Some of the death rates that prevailed in our population 75 years ago would, on modern standards, appear calamitous. In 1868, the year that the Company was chartered, the mortality in New York City was 28 per 1,000 population. In many cities death rates exceeding 30 per 1,000 were common. From such figures the step to current rates of about 10 per 1,000 reflects epoch-making advances in public health, medicine, and general standards of living. Infant mortality in those days was so high that, of every thousand children born, from 150 to 200 failed to attain their first birthday. Today infant deaths number only about 40 in 1,000 live births and even less in many areas, including New York and Chicago and some of our other large cities.

Time and again during the early period of the Company's history, epidemics of yellow fever, cholera, malaria, smallpox, typhus, and other diseases swept the country, with terrifyingly high crests. Particularly dreaded, years ago, were epidemics of diphtheria, which ravaged the child population. Today an epidemic of any magnitude from this cause is very unlikely indeed. Typical of the excellent current situation is the record in seven States covered by the Company's Pacific Coast Head Office, where only three deaths from diphtheria were reported among Industrial policyholders in the entire year of

1941. Typhoid fever, another disease that recurrently visited the country in severe epidemics, is now reduced to a minor position among the causes of death. That the occurrence of any epidemic of this disease, under modern conditions, is a sign of culpable neglect on the part of the community is attested by the fact that in some instances damage suits have successfully been brought against municipalities by victims of the disease or their surviving relatives.

As the result of the high mortality, the average length of life in the general population three quarters of a century ago was correspondingly low—only about 40 years as against close to 64 years today. This increase in longevity is due in considerable measure to the large reduction in mortality in infancy and childhood. It has been at the early periods of life that the improvement has been particularly marked. Yet it must not be supposed that the gains have been restricted to young persons. Appreciable reductions in mortality since the beginning of the century have been registered among white men at every age up to 60, and among white women up to age 80. We shall see later in the chapter that the increase in longevity among Metropolitan policyholders has been even more impressive than that for the population as a whole.

Only fragmentary statistical information on mortality, both for the general population and for Metropolitan policyholders, is available for the first 40 years of the period under survey. With the establishment of the Welfare Division in 1909 it was realized that full and accurate information regarding the mortality of policyholders was necessary. As was pointed out in the preceding chapter, the Company's Statistical Bureau was organized for this purpose.

The records prepared each year since 1911 by this Bureau tell a dramatic story of Metropolitan achievement in the field of public health. They show the progress which has been made in controlling a number of diseases, the most important of which have been tuberculosis, diphtheria, and pneumonia. Campaigns against each of these in turn have constituted a major objective in the welfare program at a particular period.

443

Moreover, these campaigns have generally been so conducted as to reach beyond the policyholder group to the general population. Thus entire communities and areas have bene-fited, and the downward trend of mortality in the whole country has been accelerated—a fact to be kept in mind when comparisons are made between improvements in the Metro-politan group and in the general population.

In 1911 the death rate from all causes among Metropolitan Industrial policyholders, ages 1 to 74, was 13.5 per 1,000. Current rates are less than half this figure. Today there are 6.1 deaths per 1,000 (adjustment being made here, and in the figures that follow, for changes which have taken place in the age and sex composition of the group). Speaking in terms of longevity, according to the mortality of 1911 the average length of life of these policyholders was 46.6 years. In 1942 it was close·to 64 years, a gain of 17 years. If we look back to the earliest records for the Company's Industrial policyholders covering the period from·1879 to 1890, we find that their average length of life was about 34 years. Thus the longevity of wage-earners and their families has almost doubled in the course of the Company's history.

These figures, striking enough in themselves, gain par-ticular significance when compared with the corresponding figures for the general population. Broadly comparable data for the two experiences are available only from 1920 onward. In that year the death rate among the Industrial policyholders, ages 1 to 74, was 10.4 deaths per 1,000 persons, as against 9.0 in the general population. Currently, the mortality in each of these groups is about 6 per 1,000. Thus, the Industrial policyholders, starting as they did on a considerably less favorable mortality level, have now caught up with the general population. This has naturally been reflected in the figures on longevity. At the beginning of this period the average length of life was more than four years greater in the general population than among the Industrial policyholders. Today, only two decades later, this advantage over the insured group has been virtually wiped out.

444

This remarkable achievement certainly is no accident, and is in part at least the result of the Company's welfare program. In gradually raising the health status of an economically less favored group to the level of the American people as a whole, we have a splendid example of the working of the democratic process. Moreover, over the years methods of underwriting Industrial insurance have greatly improved, and this, too, has undoubtedly been reflected in improved current mortality.

It must be remembered, however, that our Industrial policyholders consist primarily of wage-earners and their families. They are not wealthy people. They cannot, when the occasion arises, call in a famous specialist. These wage-earners engage in a variety of occupations, some of which involve exceptional risks to life, and many of which impose considerable wear and tear on the physical organism. Moreover, these policyholders are not a group selected by a strict medical examination at the time of insurance, though persons obviously ill or seriously impaired have been excluded. The great majority of the insured are urban dwellers, and urban mortality commonly runs higher than rural mortality. Yet today this Industrial group has achieved practically the same mortality experience as prevails in the general population of one of the healthiest nations in the world.

The improvement in mortality has been unevenly distributed over the various ages. The greatest advances have been made against those diseases which have been most amenable to public health control and which the Metropolitan has particularly attacked. A spectacular change has occurred in infant mortality, and this improvement shows up in practically all the major causes of death characteristic of the period of infancy. The most abrupt decline, in the first year of life, has occurred in the death rate from diarrhea and enteritis, formerly the outstanding threat to infant life. Today, thanks largely to the education of mothers and to the modern methods of preparation, handling, and distribution of foods, especially milk, this death rate has been reduced to just about one fifth the figure for 1920.

From the very beginning of the Company's welfare program, emphasis was placed upon maternal care. This work has been carried out through millions of visits by Company Nurses to maternity cases, through education of the family by the Nurse, and through special literature. In consequence, along with the marked improvements in infant mortality, there has been a marked reduction in the death rate from conditions incidental to pregnancy and childbirth. The maternal mortality was 19.0 per 100,000 policyholders in 1911, and had fallen to only 4.6 per 100,000 by 1941. Although part of this decline is attributable to the fall in the birth rate, a very large share of it represents an actual reduction in maternal mortality. Analysis of Company records shows that its extensive maternity nursing program has had a definite effect in lowering the death rate among the many mothers receiving such care.

In the childhood ages from 1 to 14 there has likewise been an extraordinary improvement in mortality—no less than four fifths for Metropolitan Industrial policyholders since 1911. Childhood is the period of life when mortality is at its lowest. In recent years the minimum point, at age 10, has fallen to less than one death per 1,000, and it is gratifying to find that conditions among the children of Industrial families are now as favorable as in the population at large.

Each of the principal communicable diseases of childhood— measles, whooping cough, scarlet fever, and diphtheria—has experienced a precipitous decline in mortality and has contributed its full share to the improvement in the death rate among children. But outstanding in this group is diphtheria. A news item in a Company periodical issued to our policyholders some 50 years ago described three claims paid on the deaths, within five days, of three children in one family, all victims of diphtheria. Even a single death from this cause today implies culpable neglect on somebody's part. The toll has been reduced to insignificance, thanks first to the extensive use of antitoxin in the treatment of the disease, and later to the general preventive inoculation against it. The Company has worked continuously and intensively in the popularization of these treatments. At every point in the campaign during the last 30 years, the Metropolitan has been active in educating mothers, stimulating health officers, organizing communities—in fact, whole States—toward the very desirable objective of "No More Diphtheria."

At the very beginning of its life conservation activities the Company directed its attention to the urgent problem of tuberculosis. The disease was the leading cause of death among Industrial policyholders in 1911, with a death rate of more than 240 per 100,000. Scarcely a family but counted one or more victims among its members. Death claim payments for tuberculosis accounted for more than one fifth of the total paid out each year, and were greater than for any other single cause. At present tuberculosis has been brought down to seventh place in the list of causes of death, with a rate around 40 per 100,000. The claim payments for this cause are now only about 5 percent of the total and, despite the great increase in the amount of insurance in force, are actually less in amount than in 1911. A particularly pernicious feature about tuberculosis in the past was that it claimed so many victims in the most productive ages of life. In 1911 it accounted for almost two fifths of the deaths in the age group from 25 to 44 among white men, and almost one third among white women. By 1941 only one seventh of the deaths in this age group were due to tuberculosis; the death rate from this cause, among white men, had been reduced to less than one eighth, and among white women to less than one seventh of its level of 30 years ago. The improvement in tuberculosis mortality alone has meant the saving of hundreds of thousands of lives among Industrial policyholders.

The successful attack against pneumonia, in which the Company has played a prominent part, has been described in the preceding chapter. The campaign against this disease has been one of the most brilliant triumphs of contemporary medicine. With the introduction first of serum therapy, and more recently of the sulfa drugs, the mortality from pneu-

447

monia among Metropolitan Industrial policyholders has been reduced to less than one half the levels of only a few years ago. The achievements in the field of chemotherapy are so new and so considerable that their full implications are not yet generally appreciated.

A discussion of pneumonia would be incomplete, however, without reference to the influenza epidemic of 1918–1919. Such epidemics have always produced a sharp rise in the pneumonia rate. It is estimated that more than 500,000 deaths occurred in the United States from influenza and pneumonia, or from their complications, in the winter of 1918–1919. The death rate from these diseases in the Industrial Department at the peak of the epidemic was more than 20 times the normal rate. For 1918 as a whole the effect of the epidemic was to increase the death rate from all causes by about one third over the rate of the prepandemic years. The extra claim payments by American Life insurance companies as a result of the epidemic amounted to about $200,000,000. Of this sum the Metropolitan alone paid out more than $26,000,-000; and at that time it had less than one sixth of the present amount of insurance in force. It was this epidemic, among other things, that spurred the Company to form the Influenza-Pneumonia Commission, whose work has contributed so much to the successful fight on pneumonia.

Past mid-life, the so-called degenerative conditions begin to figure prominently among the causes of death, and their control still presents many unsolved problems to science and to the medical profession. Nevertheless, the death rate has registered notable improvement since 1911, especially among white women. In these fields the effect of the Company's welfare work is also discernible. Many cases of degenerative disease have been prevented through the reduction in the frequency and severity of infections in childhood and early adult life; others have been postponed in their course through education in personal hygiene and in nutrition. Furthermore, Metropolitan Nurses have helped to carry many sufferers through acute phases of these chronic conditions, and such service on a large scale may well have had a salutary effect on the course of the death rate. All in all, the diseases characteristic of late life now constitute the major item in mortality, and their importance will increase with time.

With regard to cancer, another disease that claims its victims mainly after mid-life, the report is not too encouraging. Recently the cost of this disease to the Company, in terms of claim payments, has been more than $25,000,000 a year, or 14 percent of the total for all death claims; in 1911 the proportion was only 6 percent. It is true that among white women there has been a slight decline in the death rate from cancer, perhaps because some of the common forms of the disease in women are in relatively accessible sites, and thus amenable to surgery and X-ray or radium treatment. But among white men the death rate from this cause, *as reported*, has shown an appreciable increase in the past three decades. The increase in reported deaths from this cause is in some degree misleading, and must not be taken to mean that the extensive campaign of research and public education on the subject of cancer has been fruitless. In former years many deaths now reported as due to cancer would probably have been incorrectly diagnosed and attributed to some other cause. In this way increased accuracy of diagnosis has had the effect of raising the reported cancer death rate. But until greater success crowns the efforts to gain an understanding of the cancer problem, the most effective measures are early diagnosis and early treatment. This message has been a prominent item in the Company's campaign against the disease.

Diabetes, which is a fairly important cause of death past mid-life, presents a paradox in that the development of insulin therapy has saved the lives of many thousands of diabetics, while at the same time the death rate has shown an actual increase since preinsulin days. In explanation it must be remembered, first, that the very success of this therapy has drawn greater attention to diabetes, and has undoubtedly brought to light many cases which previously would have escaped proper diagnosis; and second, insulin has added to

449

the length of life of the average diabetic, without curing him. Deaths thus postponed tend to accumulate at the higher ages. An important fact, however, is that diabetics, thanks to insulin, can now generally lead normal lives. That many reap the advantage of modern treatment is in no small measure due to the efforts of the Metropolitan, which has spread the knowledge of the drug far and wide for many years. It has also made a number of important statistical researches in this field which have clarified the natural history of diabetes.

Appendicitis, a disease without a marked age incidence, has declined sharply in recent years. The current mortality among policyholders is the lowest in Metropolitan history. This improvement reflects not only important advances in diagnosis and surgery, but also productive efforts along public health lines by the Company and other agencies. These have disseminated information to the public to help them recognize the early signs of the disease, when prompt medical and surgical treatment is of most avail; and have prevented many serious complications by warning against the use of laxatives in the presence of abdominal pain. The extensive use of the sulfa drugs during the last two years in cases of appendicitis with peritonitis has also played an important role in bringing the death rate down to its present low level.

The record of achievement in disease control would be incomplete without mention of the virtual elimination of typhoid fever. In 1911 it was an important cause of death among Metropolitan policyholders, but for many years now mortality from this disease has been negligible. While community efforts, through the provision of pure water supplies and adequate sewage systems, are largely responsible for wiping out typhoid, the Metropolitan did yeoman service in organizing public sentiment in support of bond issues to pay for these sanitary improvements and in the promotion of other measures for the control of the disease.

Accidents have an importance for Life insurance companies beyond their actual magnitude as causes of death. The Metropolitan, as well as most other companies, has developed special benefits which provide for an additional payment equal to the face value of the policy in the event of death by accidental means. Industrial policies, with certain broad exceptions, grant this benefit without specific extra premiums to policyholders; Ordinary policies make this available to the insured at a small extra cost. Claim payments on the Double Indemnity provision currently average about $4,500,000 a year in the Metropolitan.

Just as the physician and the public health worker have been successful in their fight against disease, so various agencies, including the Metropolitan, have engaged in equally productive efforts to control accidents. The mortality rate from accidents in 1941 among the Company's Industrial policyholders was about six tenths of what it was in 1911. While accidents generally constitute a very considerable item in the total death rate, they rise to first place in the list of causes at ages 5 to 14 among girls and 5 to 39 among boys and men.

Accidents, like diseases, have their characteristic age and sex incidence. Even the infant in the very first year of life is exposed to hazards peculiar to that age, among them accidental suffocation. Nevertheless, the decline in accident mortality in early childhood has been greater than at any other period of life. There has been a marked reduction in the death rate from falls, burns, and drownings throughout the childhood ages. Even the frequency of automobile accidents among children has fallen off appreciably in the past decade or more.

In the main productive ages of life many of the accident hazards are occupational, especially among men. Great improvement has been recorded in this field, although the death rate from such accidents varies with the level of business activity. The lowest rates are usually recorded in depression years and the highest in boom periods. In wartime the death rate from job accidents is further adversely affected by the influx of large numbers of "green" workers into industry and by the speed-up of production. In recent years the mortality from occupational accidents among men insured in the Company has been about one third lower than the average for the 1920's, and about one half the maximum rate recorded in 1913. The minimum rate was recorded in 1939. This drop is notable because employment was much better in that year than in 1933, in which the previous minimum death rate from occupational accidents had been registered. A good part of the improvement in mortality from accidents on the job can be attributed to safer working conditions in industry, which, in turn, are to be credited largely to the stimulus of Workmen's Compensation Insurance and to accident-prevention programs. In the development of such programs, the Company has actively participated for more than 25 years.

The aged, though in some ways less exposed to risk because of their more sheltered lives, are, on the other hand, more vulnerable when an accident does occur; and among them the fatal accident rate reaches a high figure. The trend of fatal accidents among older policyholders has, however, been downward, largely as a result of the reduction in fatalities from burns, falls, and gas poisoning. Among these people even the rate for automobile fatalities in the last two or three years has been well below the peak and, in fact, is now lower than in the late 1920's.

The two revolutionary advances in transportation—the use of the automobile and the airplane—made since the beginning of the century, have brought with them new hazards. For many years now the automobile has been a major factor in the accident picture. Thus far, civilian aviation, because of its limited use, has caused relatively few deaths each year, but postwar development in this field may seriously affect the accident toll.

The death rate from automobile accidents among Metropolitan policyholders prior to the second World War reached a figure about nine times as high as that for 1911. For the Company as a whole, annual claim payments from this cause in the year 1941 have exceeded $8,500,000, a sum appreciably in excess of that paid out on account of tuberculosis. In order to see the automobile accident hazard in proper perspective

one must, however, note that since 1911 automobile registration has multiplied 50 times and that the use of these vehicles,
as measured by mileage, has increased in even higher ratio.
Safety education in this field and certain legal measures have
had an appreciable effect in curbing the rising trend of such
accidents, especially among children of school age. In this
effort the Company has also played a major role. However,
much remains to be done to safeguard life on our highways.

War is another major catastrophe for which Life insurance
companies must make provision. During this anniversary year
of the Company, Americans and Canadians are deeply engaged
in a second World War. The contingency of war entails
such possibilities of loss as to require the maintenance of special
reserves, as well as restrictions in policy contracts for new
applicants because many are likely to enter military service.
Because of our long record of peace, American Life insurance
companies generally paid little attention to war risks prior to
the first World War, and, in fact, most restrictions in policy
contracts written during that war were subsequently removed.
Since 1941, however (in Canada since 1939), restrictions on
account of war service were put into effect in all new policies.
But, except on newly issued policies, the Company has been
obliged to pay claims for deaths arising out of military service
during both major wars. Fortunately, the duration of our
active participation in the first World War was relatively
short, and the Company paid out, in all Departments,
$8,252,000 on account of deaths due to that war. In the
present war the Company has paid out, up to the end of 1942,
$3,500,000 on deaths among military personnel and among
civilians killed by enemy action.

The general mortality picture for Canadian policyholders
differs somewhat from that in the United States. More than
1,600,000 Canadians are insured in the Industrial Department
of the Company. Generally speaking, Canadian mortality
is a little higher at the earlier ages, but this is offset by a
balance in favor of the Canadians in later life. According to
the latest data available, the average length of life of the

Canadian policyholders is just about the same as that of the white policyholders for the Company as a whole.

The differences in mortality at certain ages are definitely referrable to specific causes of death. The disadvantage among Canadians at the younger ages arises mainly from the higher incidence of the communicable diseases — diarrhea and enteritis, tuberculosis, pneumonia, and typhoid fever. Canadian policyholders also have a higher death rate from puerperal causes; but the major part of this excess is attributable to the much higher birth rate prevailing among the French-speaking population. At the older ages Canadians enjoy the advantage of lower mortality from the degenerative diseases characteristic of this period of life, as well as from accidents, homicides, and suicides.

The mortality among Canadian policyholders has likewise shown marked improvement. In the past 10 years alone the total death rate (unadjusted for changes in age distribution) has declined more than 15 percent. For the principal communicable diseases of childhood as a group, and for diarrhea and enteritis, the reduction has been more than 70 percent. Approximately the same reduction has been brought about for typhoid fever. The death rates from pneumonia and from diseases of childbearing have been cut by one half, and that from tuberculosis by about one third in the decade. The recent improvement in health facilities throughout Canada has been marked, and promises even greater gains in the immediate future unless the country is adversely affected by the continuance of war conditions.

The excellence of the current mortality record among Metropolitan Industrial policyholders as a whole is surpassed by that for the Pacific Coast. There the death rate in recent years has been 6 percent lower than in the rest of the United States. The record is remarkably good with respect to childhood diseases, reflecting in part the lower incidence of the communicable diseases in Pacific Coast families. Diphtheria has been practically wiped out. In the past 10 years the mortality from puerperal conditions has declined 70 percent, and tuberculosis and the respiratory diseases generally have dropped to half their former levels. Likewise, the mortality in middle and later life from diseases of the heart and other conditions associated with hardening of the arteries, from cancer and diabetes, is somewhat lower than in the rest of the country. On the other hand, the record for violent deaths on the Pacific Coast has been worse, largely because of the high death rate from automobile accidents.

The Company's varied activities in the health field, although primarily designed for Industrial policyholders, have also been helpful in reducing mortality among those insured in the Ordinary and Group Departments. Among Ordinary policyholders the welfare effort has been largely, though not altogether, indirect. In so far as many of them are breadwinners and heads of families whose members are protected by Industrial insurance, they are reached by the Company's broad program of health education. Moreover, one fifth of them are also insured in the Industrial or Group Departments and thus receive the direct benefit of the Company's Nursing Service during acute illness. Finally, the practice of periodic health examination has been particularly encouraged among Ordinary policyholders and, under an offer first made in 1914, nearly 2,000,000 such examinations have been provided for owners of Ordinary policies at Company expense. There is some evidence that these examinations have had a favorable effect on the health and longevity of the policyholders using the Life Extension service.

Although, for technical reasons, we do not have the same detail of figures for policyholders in the Ordinary and Group Departments as in the Industrial, nevertheless some idea of their improved mortality is afforded by records running back to 1911 for those insured in the Standard Ordinary branch. Since that year there has been a reduction of approximately 30 percent in the death rate among Ordinary policyholders. (This figure is based on the facts for the broad age group from 10 to 74 years, adjusted to allow for changes in the age and sex composition of these policyholders). The death rate in recent years has been about five per 1,000 persons. The reduction has been roughly the same for men as for women.

The experience among the younger Ordinary policyholders during this period has been exceptionally favorable. The death rates of men under 35 and of women under 25 have dropped to one half what they were 30 years ago. In fact, the actual level of the rates at the younger ages among Ordinary policyholders is already as low as any likely to be achieved in the general population for many years to come, even on the most optimistic estimates. The chief reason for this remarkable showing lies in the select character of these insured persons. Death rates between the ages of 35 and 44 have declined about one third for each sex. There have been consistent reductions at every age past 45, but these have been smaller than among younger persons. This favorable trend in mortality reflects, in part, the improved methods of underwriting in the Ordinary Department.

For the most part, the trends of mortality from individual causes of death differ only in degree from those already reported for Industrial policyholders; yet certain features have a special significance. Outstanding in the improved mortality record of the Ordinary Department is the decline in the death rate from tuberculosis. Prior to 1910 tuberculosis was a leading cause of death even among policyholders of this group, and was responsible for nearly one quarter of the deaths at ages 15 to 30. In the last 30 years alone the death rate from tuberculosis among Metropolitan Ordinary policyholders has been reduced by more than two thirds. Current death rates among these insured are so low as to suggest that the virtual eradication of the disease is definitely in sight. Indeed, among women insured in the Standard Ordinary branch of the Department, the death rate is already well below 20 per 100,000.

Notable improvement has likewise been registered for other infectious diseases. Current death rates from pneumonia are only one fourth of what they were in 1911–1915; the rate of decline has been especially rapid in the last five years, reflecting the benefit of the sulfa-drug treatment among

Ordinary policyholders. Relatively the greatest decline has been recorded in the mortality from typhoid fever. Death rates from this disease are now well below one per 100,000, as compared with 17 in 1911–1915 among the Company's Ordinary policyholders, and with a rate of about 50 among policyholders of the large companies in the period 1885 to 1909.

The accident record among Ordinary policyholders, so important because of the supplemental Double Indemnity benefits available to them, has also shown a highly satisfactory trend. The death rate from accidents has declined one quarter in the past 30 years. This achievement is particularly gratifying because, on the one hand, workingmen form a large proportion of those insured in the Ordinary Department of the Metropolitan, and on the other hand, because the improvement in the death rate from all accidents combined has taken place in a period of sharply rising death rates from accidents due to the increasing use of the automobile.

The mortality from civilian aviation activities has thus far been but a small part of the accident toll in the Ordinary Department. Nevertheless, the Company pays close attention to this risk particularly because of the substantial extra hazard involved in nonpassenger flying and because the risk is greatest among those who carry relatively large amounts of insurance. The Company has been increasingly aware of the importance of aviation to the Nation, and has therefore taken active part in the investigation of aviation hazards. On the basis of its studies, schedules of ratings for those operating or using planes have been made and revised from time to time. The trend has been to liberalize rates as the statistics gathered have shown improvement in safety in commercial planes. Today, nearly all passengers using scheduled air lines in the United States and Canada are insured without extra premiums.

Declining mortality has a financial aspect of special importance to policyholders of a mutual Life insurance company like the Metropolitan. There is a direct relation between the death rate among policyholders and the cost of insurance. The reduction in mortality, when translated into claim payments averted or postponed, represents huge sums of money. In the Metropolitan it has meant a saving of many million dollars over the past 30 years. These savings have been reflected in the net cost of insurance to policyholders, and have made possible the addition of many valuable features to their policies. The importance of these reductions in mortality has never been greater than in recent years. For, as more fully set forth in an earlier chapter, they have helped to offset a part of the decrease in investment return resulting from the sharp decline in the interest rate. The Company's efforts in life conservation have helped to keep the cost of Life insurance at a level at which large numbers of people are able to purchase and maintain their policies.

Certainly no single figure can represent with any exactness the aggregate results of the Metropolitan's program of life conservation over the many years. It has unquestionably meant the saving of hundreds of thousands of lives. A significant proportion of these have been men and women at the most productive ages, when their family responsibilities were greatest. The economic value of these people to their families runs into billions of dollars. Their economic value to their country has likewise been conserved. The Metropolitan, together with other agencies, has played its part in saving for the war effort the lives of large numbers which might otherwise have been lost through premature death.

In the final analysis, however, the real measure of the Metropolitan's welfare work is not in dollars and cents. The true significance of the Company's welfare efforts lies in what it has contributed to human values, in what it has added to the sum total of human health and happiness. To appreciate this we must think of the thousands of families kept together and saved from want and suffering; we must think in terms of the many children who have grown up healthy in good homes under the loving care of their parents; of many people living on to a happy and productive old age. Who can assay the value of these blessings? Medical and public health authorities throughout the world look upon the Metropolitan's program of public health service as tangible proof of the value of such preventive activity.

And what of the future? It is clear that public health work will shift its emphasis from the infectious diseases of youth to the chronic conditions of middle and later life—to heart disease, cancer, and diabetes. Research currently being carried on in the field of nutrition and into the physiological action of the hormones may point the way to a further rise in the expectation of life—may indeed create a whole new concept of "the prime of life." To realize the promises implied in the current work, it is vital to bring this life-saving knowledge to the people and to teach them how to use it in their daily lives. It is a task for which the Metropolitan's organization is well equipped and in which it has proved its worth. And when the expectation of life has reached new frontiers, the Company must still labor unceasingly with its fellow workers to hold the territory which has been won.

CHAPTER 22

The People We Insure

PRESIDENT HEGEMAN, who was fond of picturesque language, enjoyed referring to the Company's policyholders as "Our Metropolitan Family." From the few thousand people when he joined the Company, this "family" has grown until today it includes more than one fifth of the combined American and Canadian populations. It includes a machinist in Bethlehem, Pa., his wife, and his two children at school, all of whom own Industrial policies. It includes a professor of history with wife and son, in Orono, Maine, who pays annual premiums on his $5,000 Whole Life Ordinary policy; a salesgirl at the notions counter in a Montreal department store, who shares in a Group policy; a grocery store-keeper in Davenport, Iowa, who knows that his Metropolitan Accident and Health policy will protect him in case of personal incapacity. "The Metropolitan Family" means all these people, and 30,000,000 more like them.

As the population of the United States and Canada has grown, and as its economic status has changed in the past three quarters of a century, the Company has always been ready to meet its varied insurance needs. Earlier chapters have described the many types of policies offered by the Company, each designed to cover a specific field of protection. How successful the Metropolitan has been in fulfilling all the Life insurance requirements of the American people is best gauged by the growth in number of policyholders, from modest beginnings to the present huge figure. Thirty million is impressive from its very size, and significant in the fact that one of every five men, women, and children in the two neighboring countries owns a Metropolitan policy. Indeed, if we limit the comparison to the population of urban areas in which the Company maintains Agency Offices, the proportion of policyholders is more than one in every three. In terms of insured families, the figures are even more impressive. Of the 38,000,000 families in the United States and Canada, almost one third carry some form of Metropolitan insurance; in the urban areas served by the Company, every other family benefits from Metropolitan protection. Thus, the Company serves a major need in more homes on this continent than does almost any other single business institution.

In its first few years as an Ordinary Company, the Metropolitan gave little hint of such potential scope. Even at its early peak of 19,000 policyholders in 1874, it was clear that Ordinary Life insurance, exclusively, had as yet a very limited popular appeal. Furthermore, the difficult times of the later 70's, as well as the severe competition from older companies, resulted in the loss of policyholders. It was only with the inauguration of Industrial insurance in 1879 that renewed impetus was given to the Company's business.

Starting almost from scratch at that point, the Company, scarcely four years later, had half a million policyholders. It counted one million only three years later, in 1886; two million by 1891; five million by 1901; ten million by 1913; twenty million by 1923; and thirty million policyholders at the start of 1943. In the last two decades much of the increase was accounted for by the development of the Ordinary and Group business. Moreover, while the rapid growth of policyholders has reflected an aggressive and resourceful management, it would hardly have been possible but for the rapid increase in the general population, especially in the cities. In 1880 the population of the United States was only 50,000,000, as compared with its present population of 134,000,000. Most of the people in the earlier period lived in rural areas, whereas today the majority live in cities and towns. Since 1900 the urban population of the United States and Canada has increased 2½ times, while the Metropolitan policyholders have increased more than sixfold.

For nearly 30 years after 1879 the history of Metropolitan growth was essentially that of its Industrial Department. By 1910 there were about 8,000,000 policyholders in that branch, and they continued to grow without interruption until, in 1929, they numbered more than 22,000,000. During the depression of the early 30's this number receded somewhat; but the growth of the Department was resumed and reached a maximum (including Monthly Premium policyholders) of nearly 23,000,000 in 1937. The number insured in the Industrial Department has remained fairly stable for the last decade, and at present its policyholders number about 22,300,000.

After the reorganization of the Ordinary Department in 1892, that branch of the Company's business grew fairly satisfactorily, yet at first not nearly at the pace at which the Industrial Department developed. Not until 1906 did the total number of Ordinary policyholders (regular Ordinary, Intermediate, and Special Class) reach the 500,000 mark. The millionth Ordinary policyholder came into the Metropolitan family seven years later, in 1913. Great impetus to the growth of this Department was given by the Government insurance program for soldiers during the first World War. The amounts of insurance purchasable under this program were larger than most men had previously conceived as necessary, and this "exposure" to a new point of view, combined with an era of prosperity, brought about a greatly increased demand for Ordinary insurance. Further impetus was given by the influenza epidemic, which brought home the immediate advantages of Life insurance in a most effective and striking way. By 1919 two million people were insured in this Department of the Company. Progress in obtaining new Ordinary policyholders was good throughout the prosperous 1920's. This favorable trend continued unabated even during the early depression years, so that by 1932 there were more than 5,000,000 insured in the various Ordinary branches. Today their number stands at 6,750,000, as compared with the 22,300,000 Industrial policyholders. About 1,500,000 of these people are insured in both Departments of the Company.

These figures for the Ordinary Department include the policyholders insured in its Intermediate branch. The growth of this branch since its inception in 1896 has clearly demonstrated the great need of protection for moderate amounts. Within a few years the number of policyholders with Intermediate insurance actually outnumbered those with Standard Ordinary policies, and the Intermediate branch continued to lead for many years. Not until 1919, when the Ordinary Department had 1,024,000 owners of Standard policies, did their number exceed the Intermediate policyholders. Since then, the holders of Standard Ordinary policies have gained an increasingly large lead, due, in part, to the higher level of incomes and, in part, to the liberalization of underwriting rules. Many applicants financially eligible for Standard Ordinary insurance, who worked at occupations formerly considered hazardous, or who had a personal history of disease or impairments once considered adverse, have been shown in the periodic investigations of the Company to have become good insurance risks. Thus, many large classes of applicants formerly eligible only for Intermediate or even Special Class insurance are now accepted for Standard Ordinary policies.

The growth of the Company during the past 15 years has been greatly stimulated by the writing of policies, both Ordinary and Industrial, on a Monthly Premium Debit basis. Premiums for such business are received by the Agents, as had always been the practice for Weekly Premium Industrial policies. First inaugurated in the Ordinary Department late in 1926 and in the Industrial Department at the beginning of 1927, Monthly Debit insurance proved its usefulness and popularity from the start. In the first four years—by the end of 1930—nearly 1,500,000 policyholders owned insurance on the Monthly Debit plan. Steady gains were made even during the depression years; between 1930 and 1937 the number of such policies in force was doubled. Today about 4,750,000 persons own Monthly policies in the Metropolitan, their numbers being equally divided between the Ordinary and Industrial Departments.

Although the Company has been extraordinarily successful in the field of Group insurance, progress at first was comparatively slow. The Metropolitan launched its Group Department in 1917, yet not until 1923 did the number of insured in the Group Life Department reach 500,000. During the 20's, however, the growth of this branch was rapid and the million mark was reached early in 1927. Naturally, this type of business moved slowly during the depression, and in some years there were actual setbacks. In the past few years the growth of the Company's Group business has again moved rapidly forward. At the end of 1942 about 2,500,000 workers were insured under Group Life certificates. Several other types of insurance protection, such as Weekly Health and Accident benefits, Hospital and Surgical benefits, and Annuities are written on Group plans, usually covering employees who also have Group Life certificates. The persons insured under various types of Group insurance, but who do not have Group Life insurance in the Metropolitan, now number about 300,000. Altogether, at present, the lives of about 2,750,000 men and women are insured under various Group policies of the Company.

About 2,000,000 policyholders, or one in every 15, are insured in more than one Department. As we have seen, policyholders in a Company like the Metropolitan build up their insurance programs as the family grows. Many are first insured, as children, in the Industrial Department; then as they grow up and join the ranks of workers or housewives, and as their economic circumstances improve, they in a sense "graduate" into the Ordinary Department, or through their job affiliations, become insured under a Group contract. This not only explains the relatively large number with insurance in more than one Department of the Company, but also is another indication that there are no hard and fast lines between the Departments.

This point is well illustrated by the insurance history of one Metropolitan policyholder, the head of a fairly average American family, whom we shall designate as Mr. J. S., aged 41, married, and the father of two growing children. The insurance history of this policyholder begins when, as a boy 3 years old, his parents bought for him an Industrial 20-Year Endowment policy for $100. In 1922 Mr. J. S., now a young man, bought his first Ordinary policy for $1,000. In the next year the Industrial policy matured. He used the funds to help pay for a course in textile manufacturing, and thus its aim was fulfilled. Now his insurance coverage was limited to $1,000 and stayed at this amount until the summer of 1925, at which time he got a job as shipping inspector in a textile mill and became insured for $4,000 under his employer's Group policy. Late in the same year he bought $3,000 of additional Ordinary insurance, raising the total in force to $8,000. In 1928 he was married, and supplemented his insurance by an Accident and Health policy, which protected him and his wife against sudden and serious burdens of expense that might arise in case of serious illnesses or incapacity due to accident. After the birth of his first daughter, in 1931, he purchased an additional Life insurance policy for $5,000. A second daughter was born in 1933. He bought an additional Ordinary policy for $6,000 in 1936 and another for $5,000 in 1941, so that his present insurance coverage totals $24,000. Except for the $4,000 in Group insurance, all his protection is in the Ordinary Department, although he began as an Industrial policyholder.

The roster of Company policyholders includes inhabitants of every State in the Union and of every Province in Canada. In some cities and towns, particularly in the East, an actual majority of the population own Metropolitan policies. This statement applies to cities as widely separated as Providence, R. I.; Schenectady and Troy, N. Y.; Cincinnati, Ohio; and St. Louis, Mo. Even in much larger areas covering entire States, almost half the entire population are Metropolitan policyholders. Generally, the proportion is highest in the New England and Middle Atlantic States, where about 4 in every 10 persons own Metropolitan insurance. Rhode Island leads with just about half of the population, and New Jersey, Connecticut, and Massachusetts have more than 40 percent insured with the Metropolitan. New York and New Hampshire fall just below this figure. In the urban population, in practically every State along the Atlantic seaboard as far south as Maryland a majority, or close to a majority, of the inhabitants are insured in the Company. In most States in which the Company has an Agency organization, at least one third of the urban population owns its policies.

As measured in actual numbers, the most populous States have, of course, the largest numbers of policyholders. New York has more than 5,000,000, Pennsylvania 3,000,000, Illinois nearly 2,500,000, while Massachusetts, New Jersey, Ohio, Michigan, Missouri, and California each have 1,000,000 or more insured with the Metropolitan. The Province of Quebec holds the lead for Canada, with about 900,000 policyholders.

The Metropolitan, as we have already indicated, insures, every section of the urban population. Its clientele, therefore, is representative of these people as regards sex, color, and age. Among the insured there are approximately the same number of boys and girls, and almost as many women as men. About one twelfth of the policyholders are Negroes, a figure practically identical with the proportion of Negroes in the urban areas of the United States. Children under 15 years of age and young adults between 15 and 25 each account for about one fifth of the Metropolitan policyholders. About 35 percent are people from 25 to 45, the period of life when most men and women carry family responsibilities; the middle and later ages, up to 65, account for another 20 percent. Older policyholders—those 65 years of age or over—comprise the remaining 5 percent.

The proportions vary considerably by Department. Women and children of the wage-earning population, by reason of their needs for lesser amounts of Life insurance, make up the larger number of Industrial policyholders. The Ordinary Department is composed mainly of men in the productive ages, although it also includes considerable numbers of self-supporting women, housewives, and even of children. By the very nature of the operations of the Group Division, its

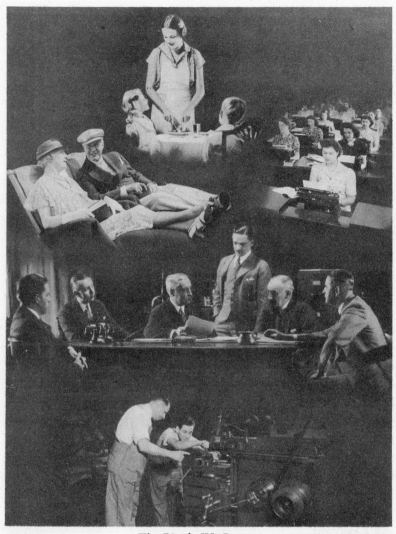

The People We Insure

policyholders are drawn from among men and women of working ages; of these, 85 percent are men.

Further indication of the representative character of the policyholders is found in the facts regarding their occupations. Taking the Company as a whole, employed and retired persons account for about 45 in every 100 policyholders, housewives and home-makers for about 30 in every 100, while students and children of preschool age make up the remaining quarter.

Virtually all occupations are represented, and their distribution definitely reflects the urban character of the Company's policyholders. The largest groups are the office workers —clerks, bookkeepers, and stenographers—of whom there are 1,750,000, and storekeepers and salesmen, of whom there are more than 1,250,000. Another million are employed as servants, maids, cooks, or waiters. One-half million policyholders work as chauffeurs, drivers, or deliverymen. About 400,000 are steam railroad workers, and about the same number are textile mill operatives. Carpenters and clothing workers each number well in excess of 300,000; miners number 150,000; and teachers, printing industry workers, painters, machinists, and workers in iron and steel mills and foundries are represented with 200,000 to 300,000 members insured in the Metropolitan. Men with jobs too hazardous to permit their acceptance as Life insurance risks constitute only a negligible fraction of the country's working force.

And what of those who work outside of the thickly populated areas—such as farmers? While proportionately they are not as well represented, their numbers are not inconsiderable. Nearly 700,000 farmers and farm laborers own insurance in the several Departments of the Company.

Inasmuch as the Company's policyholders come from all walks of life, ranging from unskilled laborers to top-rank business executives, the average amount of insurance owned by individuals in the respective groups varies from small amounts to hundreds of thousands of dollars. It is to be expected, therefore, that there would be considerable difference in the extent to which the various occupations are represented in the several Departments of the Company. In the Ordinary Department the predominant occupational types are the white collar workers, storekeepers, salesmen, and professional men. There are likewise goodly numbers of foremen, mechanics, and semiskilled workers. Laborers and servants make up a relatively small proportion of this total. In the Industrial Department the situation is reversed—laborers, domestics working either in private homes or hotels, and the lower-paid ranks of semiskilled and clerical workers constitute the great majority of the gainfully employed policyholders.

Changes in the operations of the Company in the course of its development have been reflected in changes in the occupational distribution of the insured. In the earliest days, when only Ordinary policies were written, Metropolitan policyholders were chiefly small-business men, mechanics, and other skilled workers. With the establishment and development of the Industrial Department to the point where it constituted almost the entire business of the Company, the insured were predominantly semiskilled and unskilled workers. Again, with the reorganization of the Ordinary Department in 1892, the number of business and professional men, skilled mechanics, and white collar workers insured under its policies increased. The introduction of the special $5,000 Whole Life policy in 1909 was particularly fruitful in bringing into the Company's membership large numbers of professionals and executives, as well as the better-paid office workers, for whom this policy was designed and among whom it found great popularity.

At present, when every effort is bent toward the successful prosecution of the war, there is temporarily a marked alteration in the occupational distribution of policyholders. Of the 7,000,000 insured men between the ages of 20 and 45, a large proportion must be serving with the armed forces of the United States or Canada, and hundreds of thousands in addition have shifted from their regular employment to jobs directly connected with the war effort.

The 30,000,000 policyholders of the Company now own close to $27,000,000,000 of Life insurance. If we concern ourselves only with those holding premium-paying policies, the average amount of Life insurance per policyholder for all Departments combined is close to $1,000. Since the amounts owned vary so widely according to economic circumstances, age, and family responsibilities, the averages have greater significance when analyzed by Department. Thus, in the Ordinary Department, including Intermediate and Special

469

Class policies, and in the Group Department, the average insurance holding approaches $2,000; and in the Industrial, a little less than $400.

Even within Departments there is great variation. For example, in the Ordinary branch the greatest average holding is on those who own the special $5,000 Whole Life policies. Together with other insurance in the Metropolitan, these men own on the average more than $7,000 of protection with the Company. If we exclude this group, the average for Standard Ordinary is about $1,600. The average for Special Class policyholders is slightly less than this amount, and for those owning Intermediate policies it is about $1,000.

These averages, it must be pointed out, necessarily reflect insurance programs in all stages of completion, from the single Industrial policy on the life of a young child, to the complete and elaborate portfolio on mature men who have accumulated a number of policies over a period of years. Thus, for white males at the productive ages 25 to 44 years, the average claim payment in the Industrial Department alone is nearly $600. In the Regular Ordinary Department (excluding Monthly, Intermediate, and Special Class) it is about $3,400 for married men at these ages. The latter figure reaches a maximum at ages 45 to 49, when the average exceeds $4,000.

Actually, even these figures understate the total amount of insurance owned by individuals, for many policyholders are insured in more than one Department. It is not possible to determine the total amount of insurance owned by each policy-holder from the routine records, inasmuch as these are based on individual policies and do not show the entire insurance outstanding for each insured. From special studies, however, we know that the averages, as given for the individual Depart-ments, are materially increased when the insurance program as a whole is considered. To give just one illustration, the amount of Metropolitan insurance on white men in the ages 25 to 44 is nearly $600 in the Industrial Department alone; when insurance in other Departments is added, the average is in-creased by more than 50 percent. Nor does this tell the whole story. A significant proportion of Metropolitan policyholders own insurance in other companies or in fraternal societies. As we shall see later, this adds materially to the total insurance benefits available to their families in the event of the demise of the family head.

Of even greater interest than the Life insurance coverage for individuals, is the insurance protection available for the family as a whole. Recent studies in families owning Metropolitan Industrial insurance show that frequently every member owns a Metropolitan policy suited to his age and position in the household. In all but a small fraction of these cases the head of the family owns some Life insurance protection, either in the Metropolitan or in another company or fraternal order. If he owns Industrial insurance, it is very likely to be in the Metropolitan. The average amount of Life insurance of all kinds, Metropolitan and other, on these heads of wage-earning families is about $1,500, or roughly the equivalent of one year's income. The amounts, however, vary from a few hundred dollars to many thousands, with about 7 percent owning less than $300 of Life insurance and 11 percent more than $3,000. The mother is insured in 90 percent of these Industrial families, and her insurance, usually Metropolitan Industrial exclusively, averages about one third that of her husband's, or about $500. In like manner, almost 90 percent of the children also have Life insurance protection, and again, almost all of it is in the Metropolitan. The average for the children, in the last survey made, was about $350, based on the amounts of insurance payable in the event of death. But, of course, appreciably larger amounts of benefit are paid to living policyholders as the policies mature.

Another study, this one on the Life insurance benefits left by deceased heads of Industrial families, throws additional light upon their income resources, and the extent to which their insurance has benefited them. The policyholders in question were married men insured in the Industrial Department of the Metropolitan who were between 21 and 65 years of age at death (average 53 years of age) and were survived

471

by their wives and at least one child. The average* family income, in the year before death of the breadwinner, was $30 a week from all sources, to which the deceased, usually the chief earner, contributed on the average about $20 a week. About 4 in every 10 of these families owned their own homes, and this was their chief asset other than their Life insurance. Only about one fourth had any savings accounts at all, and of these less than one half had more than $400 in their accounts. Less than 5 percent of the families had any business or investment, other than their real estate, worth more than $1,000. Consequently, only little more than 10 percent of the families had enough money saved to meet funeral and other costs entailed by the death of the head of the family, the amount of such expenses, not including medical costs, averaging just under $500. Families with so little ready cash on hand would be hit hard by the loss of the breadwinner were it not for their Life insurance benefits.

We have less information regarding the types of families insured in the Ordinary Department, their make-up, and their insurance coverage; yet such facts as we have, point out that in at least a third of the families, two or more members own insurance in that Department. The average is approximately 1½ persons with Ordinary insurance per Ordinary family. In at least one third of the families with Ordinary insurance, some member also owns Industrial insurance—in the great majority of cases, with the Metropolitan.

With respect to the amounts of insurance, the average person accepted for new insurance in the Ordinary Department of the Company buys close to $1,900 and already owns about $1,450 of Life insurance of some kind (in the Metropolitan or other companies), so that his combined insurance holdings average about $3,300. The figures for the Standard Ordinary cases (i.e., excluding Intermediate and Special Class) which comprise the bulk of the business, average somewhat higher. For this group the total insurance owned exceeds

*The type of average used in this instance is the "median," which corresponds to the middle item in a series arranged in order of size.

472

$3,600, a little more than $2,000 of which is new insurance and a little less than $1,600 is insurance in force at the time of the new application. In the combined Substandard branches (Intermediate and Special Class) the average total owned is approximately $2,250.

The data from these reports have been analyzed separately for applicants in families which owned no Metropolitan Industrial insurance and for those which did own such insurance. Applicants in the former group—"purely Ordinary" families—have appreciably higher amounts of insurance than the general average. For all such applicants the total insurance, including the new, was about $3,800, of which nearly $2,100 comprised the new insurance and about $1,700 the insurance in force. For married men in this group the average amount of insurance was greatest, namely, $5,700 for the new and old insurance combined. Among these married men between the ages of 40 and 55, the average figure was $6,200; and for those accepted for Standard insurance, the average was $7,350.

The steadily growing number of Metropolitan policyholders and their increasing amount of Life insurance are eloquent testimony of the vitality and character of the Company. That 30,000,000 persons have come to look to the Metropolitan for all or part of their Life insurance protection is, of course, a remarkable achievement. But what of the future? Has the growth of the Metropolitan reached its limit? By no means. While it would be rash to forecast just how many policyholders the Company will have even a decade hence, there is every reason to look forward to continued and substantial growth in numbers.

Such optimism is justified by the fact that the basic social forces which motivate the purchase of Life insurance will continue to operate in the United States and Canada. The formation of new families is one of these forces. Well in excess of 1,000,000 new families are formed by marriage each year in the United States. The birth of a child is another event which calls for an adjustment of the family insurance

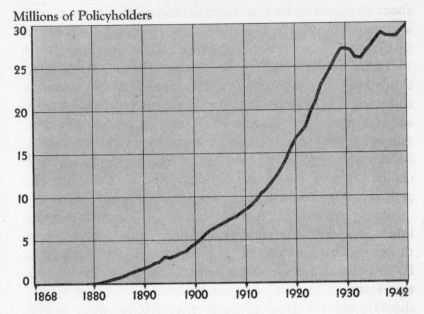

Millions of Policyholders

program. In the course of an average year, more than 2,000,000 babies are born into American families, thus adding to the responsibilities of the heads of these families. Parents have found Life insurance useful to provide for the education of the child, and thus give it a running start in life.

On the other side of the picture are the facts with regard to mortality. The number of deaths in this country in the past few years has averaged approximately 1,400,000. About 400,000 of these are married men, of whom one quarter, or 100,000, leave widows under 45 years of age. In the great majority of these broken families there are dependent children. Altogether, 220,000 children under 16 are orphaned each year by the death of their father, and relatively young widows have the responsibility for the care of these children. Even for older widows the economic problems may be acute, because many have never worked for a living and most of the others will have been out of the employment market for years.

The fact is that the majority of women eventually face widowhood, with its attendant problems. Even where bride and groom are of the same age at marriage, the chances are about 55 in 100 that the groom will die first. Since the groom is usually the older, the chances, in typical marriages, are that 65 of 100 brides will eventually become widows.

Still another motive for Life insurance is the protection of children against orphanhood. The chances that a newborn child will lose his father by death before the child reaches age 16 are not inconsiderable. On the basis of current mortality conditions, six of every 100 children born to 25-year-old fathers will become orphaned before they reach age 16. For children born to 35-year-old fathers, this chance is 10 in 100, and the probability mounts as the age of the father increases.

As in the past, a large field for future expansion of the Life insurance market in the Company will probably be among those already insured with it. The close contact of the Field Force with Metropolitan families and the increasing skill of the Agents in planning programs of security for their clients should result in more adequate coverage for them in the Metropolitan. Those even in the lower income brackets are becoming increasingly aware of the value of Life insurance as a means of keeping the family together.

The bulk of the billions of dollars of Life insurance in force covers the lives of family men who plan that, in the event of their death, a measure of their earning power may be continued for the benefit of their dependents. The sums needed to replace their earning power are far greater than is generally realized, as measured by the present value of their future earnings, with due allowance for the cost of their share of future family expenditures. Assuming normal mortality, and an interest rate of 3½ percent, the monetary value to his dependents of the average wage-earner of 30, whose maximum earnings during his lifetime will not exceed $1,000 a year— less than $20 a week—exceeds $10,000. For the middle-class man at age 30, whose income will eventually reach $2,500, the sum is $30,000, and for the $5,000 man, nearly $50,000.

The majority of American families cannot hope to replace the economic value of their breadwinners through Life insurance. As a matter of fact, in view of the difference between current income and possible maximum earnings and other considerations, insurance in the amount of the foregoing monetary values would generally be beyond the needs of such families and could not be obtained. However, steady progress has been made in narrowing the gap between what individuals need and what they can afford. In recent years also, Social Security benefits have further helped to close this gap. But private Life insurance can do still more. The job of the Metropolitan and of the other companies in providing adequate coverage for American families is far from complete.

The crisis through which we are now passing might seem to impede Life insurance expansion, and yet may actually spur it on. The need for Life insurance protection is as pressing in wartime as in peace. In fact, the Metropolitan and the Life insurance companies generally have forged ahead through previous wars and peacetime upheavals. After the last World War the Company, once peace was declared, experienced a growth greater than ever before in its history. More recently, the economic depression following the stock market crash in 1929 made the safe investment in Life insurance attractive to large numbers of people. At present, insurance serves as a constructive means of offsetting inflationary tendencies by absorbing part of the current excess purchasing power.

The extraordinary growth of the Metropolitan in recent decades is a good augury for the future. Further progress is favored both by the type and quality of the Company's organization. It has a large and well-trained staff of Field-Men, each serving hundreds of families whose problems and changing circumstances they know intimately. Day by day these men are extending their services to new families. Behind the Field Force is an able group of Executives in the Home and Head Offices whose function it is to improve the policies and plans which the Company offers, and to find more efficient methods of operation. Their dynamic energy is ever seeking to extend the field of the Company's coverage.

There are likewise factors outside the Company itself which favor the continued growth of the Metropolitan. The populations of the United States and Canada are still increasing and will continue to do so for some time. The Company has scarcely tapped the field of insuring the large rural population. The rising scale of employment at good wages should more and more stimulate the purchase of Life insurance. The systematic saving encouraged in the current war economy should have the same effect. With only half those employed in industry now covered under Group plans, the possibilities inherent in this type of protection likewise loom large. These abundant opportunities assure further expansion in the days ahead and constitute a challenge to the Field Force. So long as men and women build families and plan for the future of their loved ones, Life insurance will remain a vital force in our civilization. On this firm foundation is built the conviction that the Metropolitan will serve an increasing number of Americans and Canadians in the years to come.

477

List of Official Personnel

FREDERICK H. ECKER . . . . *Chairman of the Board*

LEROY A. LINCOLN . . . . *President*

CHARLES G. TAYLOR, Jr. . . . . . . *Vice-President*

SECRETARY'S DIVISIONS

JAMES P. BRADLEY . . . . *Secretary*

TREASURER'S DIVISION

HARRY C. HAGERTY . . . . *Treasurer*
ARTHUR W. MELLEN, Jr. . . . . *Assistant Treasurer*
LAWRENCE WASHINGTON . . . . *Assistant Treasurer*
EUGENE A. SCHMIDT, Jr. . . . . *Assistant Treasurer*
GILBERT STANLEY . . . . *Assistant Treasurer*

ACTUARIAL DIVISION

HORACE R. BASSFORD . . . . *Actuary*
REINHARD A. HOHAUS . . . . *Associate Actuary*
GILBERT W. FITZHUGH . . . . *Assistant Actuary*
HERBERT J. STARK . . . . *Assistant Actuary*
JAMES R. HERMAN . . . . *Associate Actuary*
W. PERCY BRENTON . . . . *Assistant Actuary*
EDWARD A. LEW . . . . *Assistant Actuary*
CHARLES A. SIEGFRIED . . . . *Assistant Actuary*
MALVIN E. DAVIS . . . . *Associate Actuary*
JOSEPH A. CHRISTMAN . . . . *Assistant Actuary*
FREDERICK P. CHAPMAN . . . . *Assistant Actuary*

ORDINARY DEPARTMENT
AND ACCIDENT AND HEALTH DIVISION

SAMUEL MILLIGAN . . . . *Second Vice-President*
EDWARD M. KEYS . . . . *Assistant Secretary*
LAWRENCE K. FARRELL . . . . *Assistant Secretary*
DOUGLAS S. CRAIG . . . . *Assistant Secretary*
HENRY E. WELSH . . . . *Assistant Secretary*

List of Official Personnel—Continued

GROUP DIVISION

ALEXANDER C. CAMPBELL . . . . Second Vice-President
JAMES M. CAMPBELL . . . . Third Vice-President
GALE F. JOHNSTON   . . . . Third Vice-President
WILLIAM J. BARRETT . . . . Assistant Secretary

INDUSTRIAL DEPARTMENT

FRANCIS M. SMITH . . . . Second Vice-President
J. EVERETT ROWE . . . . Assistant Secretary

FIELD OPERATIONS

CECIL J. NORTH . . . . Second Vice-President
ARTHUR W. TRETHEWEY . . . . Third Vice-President
GLEN J. SPAHN . . . . Field Personnel Officer
MAX C. FISHER . . . . Assistant Secretary

COMPTROLLER'S DIVISION

WILLIAM S. NORTON . . . . Comptroller
FRANCIS J. GEIST . . . . Assistant Comptroller
HOWARD I. DOHRMAN . . . . Assistant Comptroller

PACIFIC COAST HEAD OFFICE

HENRY E. NORTH . . Vice-President in Charge of Pacific Coast Head Office
WILLIAM P. SHEPARD, M.D. . . . . Assistant Secretary
LOUIS J. SCHMOLL . . . . Assistant Secretary
ARNOLD B. BROWN . . . Assistant Actuary and Assistant Manager
SAMUEL W. MEANS, M.D. . . . . Assistant Medical Director
CHARLES COLEMAN BERWICK, M.D. . . . Assistant Medical Director

CANADIAN HEAD OFFICE

EDWIN C. MCDONALD . Vice-President in Charge of Canadian Head Office
GEORGE V. BRADY . Associate Actuary and Assistant General Manager
NORMAN L. BURNETTE, D.Sc.S. . . . . Assistant Secretary
DENIS W. KELLY . . . . Assistant Secretary
WALLACE TROUP, M.D. . . . . Assistant Medical Director
HARRY BELL KIDD, M.D. . . . . Assistant Medical Director

LAW DIVISION

FREDERIC G. DUNHAM . . . . *General Counsel*
HARRY COLE BATES . . . . *General Counsel*
JOSEPH H. COLLINS . . . . *Assistant General Counsel*
CHURCHILL RODGERS . . . . *Assistant General Counsel*
BYRON CLAYTON . . . . *Assistant General Counsel*
CLETIS EUGENE TULLY . . . . *Assistant Secretary*

MEDICAL DIVISION

CHARLES L. CHRISTIERNIN, M.D. . . . . *Medical Director*
EARL C. BONNETT, M.D. . . . . *Assistant Medical Director*
ALBERT W. BROMER, M.D. . . . . *Assistant Medical Director*
*JOHN A. EVANS, M.D. . . . . *Assistant Medical Director*
*RAYMOND K. FARNHAM, M.D. . . . . . *Assistant Medical Director*
HAYNES H. FELLOWS, M.D. . . . . *Assistant Medical Director*
*REXFORD W. FINEGAN, M.D. . . . . . . *Assistant Medical Director*
JOHN T. GEIGER, M.D. . . . . *Assistant Medical Director*
JOSEPH C. HORAN, M.D. . . . . *Assistant Medical Director*
ALBERT O. JIMENIS, M.D. . . . . *Assistant Medical Director*
WILLIAM H. ORDWAY, M.D. . . . . . . *Assistant Medical Director*
*GEORGE P. ROBB, M.D. . . . . *Assistant Medical Director*
EDMUND W. WILSON, M.D. . . . . *Assistant Medical Director*

COORDINATION AND ADVERTISING

JAMES L. MADDEN . . . . *Third Vice-President*
ROY R. BENJAMIN . . . . *Assistant Actuary*

WELFARE DIVISION

DONALD B. ARMSTRONG, M.D. . . . . *Third Vice-President*
*ANTHONY J. LANZA, M.D. . . . . *Assistant Medical Director*
*WILLIAM J. McCONNELL, M.D. . . . . . *Assistant Medical Director*
GEORGE M. WHEATLEY, M.D. . . . . . . *Assistant Medical Director*

STATISTICAL DIVISION

LOUIS I. DUBLIN, PH.D. . . . . . . *Third Vice-President and Statistician*
ALFRED J. LOTKA, D.SC. . . . . *Assistant Statistician*

*On leave with the armed forces.

481

List of Official Personnel—*Continued*

ACCOUNTING AND AUDITING DIVISION

EARL O. DUNLAP . . . . *Third Vice-President*

JOSEPH J. CLAIR . . . . *Assistant Secretary*

FARM LOAN DIVISION

GLENN E. ROGERS . . . . *Third Vice-President*

BUSINESS RESEARCH BUREAU

WILLIAM A. BERRIDGE, PH.D. . . . . *Economist*

PERSONNEL DIVISION

HERBERT L. RHOADES . . . . *Personnel Officer*

SPECIAL ASSIGNMENTS

THOMPSON B. GRAHAM . . . . *Fourth Vice-President*

SUPERINTENDENTS OF AGENCIES

REGINALD R. LAWRENCE . . . . *Superintendent of Agencies*

SAMUEL D. RISLEY . . . . *Superintendent of Agencies*

LOUIS J. ZETTLER . . . . *Superintendent of Agencies*

JOHN H. BEHRMANN . . . . . . *Assistant Superintendent of Agencies*

AUSTIN T. SCHUSSLER . . . . *Superintendent of Agencies*

CLARENCE W. BETHEL . . . . . *Assistant Superintendent of Agencies*

EMILE P. ARNAUTOU . . . . *Superintendent of Agencies*

JOHN H. ALMY . . . . *Superintendent of Agencies*

W. S. J. SHEPHERD . . . . *Superintendent of Agencies*

G. HOYLE WRIGHT . . . . *Superintendent of Agencies*

FREEMAN D. SMITH . . . . *Superintendent of Agencies*

JAMES A. SMITHIES . . . . *Superintendent of Agencies*

J. O. KLEIN . . . . *Assistant Superintendent of Agencies*

OTHER OFFICIAL PERSONNEL

N. R. BLATHERWICK, PH.D. . . . . . . *Director*, Biochemical Laboratory

*JAMES M. DUNNING, D.D.S. . . . . *Dental Director*

GEORGE GOVE . . . . *Manager*, Housing Projects

RALPH T. HINES . . . . *Manager*, Printing Division

MICHAEL KLEY . . . . *Staff Assistant*, Welfare Division

H. W. McCLINTOCK . . . . *Manager*, Publication Division

JOHN B. NORTHROP . . . . *Manager*, Claim Division

*On leave with the armed forces.

Index

Applicants for Life insurance
 medical examination, 164, 240, 399–401,
  407–408
 number made in 1941, 407
 rating procedures, 407–410
 restrictions due to medical history, 408
Application Division, 240
Armour & Company, 174, 197
Armstrong, Dr. Donald B., 430–431, 440, 481
Armstrong Investigating Committee, 54–55,
  64–66, 153, 155, 169, 316
 vindication of Metropolitan, 64–66
Armstrong Laws, effect of, on
 deferred dividend insurance, 65
 Group Life insurance, 169
 Industrial insurance, 65
 Intermediate Branch, 153, 155
 Metropolitan, 64–66, 153–155, 169
 Ordinary Life insurance, 66–67, 169
Arnautou, Emile P., 482
Arnoux, Ritch and Woodford, 51
Assets of Metropolitan
 amount in 1943, 9
 table, 322
 investment of, see Investments
Association of Life Insurance Medical
  Directors of America, 385, 394, 403,
  408, 410
Association of Life Insurance Presidents, 64
Assumption of business of other companies,
  72–74, 284, 298, 303
Astoria housing project, 95, 349
Athletic Association, 249
Audit Division, 231, 364–365
Automobile accidents, death claims, 452–453
Aviation accidents, mortality experience,
  452, 457
Ayres, Francis O., 71, 153, 161, 365
Baker, George F., 28
Baker, George F., clinic, New England Dea-
  coness Hospital, 433
Band, Metropolitan, 250
Banting, Sir Frederick, 294
Barnes, William, 28
Barrett, W. J., 177, 480
Barry, James V., 368
Bashore, Frank L., 355
Bassett, Allen Lee, 44
Bassford, Horace R., 182, 200, 389, 390, 393,
  394, 479
Bates, Harry Cole, 366, 481

Beard, S. M., 8, 29
Beck, Thomas H., 232
Behrmann, John H., 482
Beland, Senator Henri S., 294
Benedict, Dr. Stanley, 411
Beneficial Life Insurance Company, 303
Benjamin, Roy R., 481
Bennett, Honorable Richard B., 293
Berridge, William A., 482
Berwick, Dr. Charles Coleman, 480
Bethel, Clarence W., 482
Biochemical Laboratory, 405, 410, 411
Blatherwick, N. R., 482
Blood sugar, tests devised by Metropolitan,
  411
Board of Design, Parkchester, 350
Bonds, investments in, see Investments,
  bonds and stocks
Bonnett, Dr. Earl C., 481
Bonuses to policyholders, 62, 70, 127–128,
  216, 220, 384
 amount paid, 210
 see also Dividends
Booth, J., 124
Boston night club fire, 1942, death claims paid
  by the Metropolitan, 371
Bradley, James P., 245, 479
Brady, George V., 395, 480
Brenton, W. Percy, 479
Bromer, Dr. Albert W., 481
Bronxville, Hall of Records, 245
Brown, Arnold B., 308, 395, 480
Buckman, David L., 365
Burnette, Norman L., 294, 480
Butler, Edward H., 234
Cahen, Isaac J., 151, 365
Campbell, A. C., 171, 175, 182, 191, 480
Campbell, J. M., 171, 480
Canada
 Life insurance in force per capita, 3–4, 279
 Metropolitan in, 279–296
  begins business, 258, 279
  employees, number, 286, 296
  Field Force, number, 286, 296
  Head Office opened, 91
  Investments in Canada, 279
  Life insurance in force in 1943, 279, 296
  mortality experience, 291, 453–454
  Nursing Service, 283
  policyholders, number, 279, 286

486

489

Investments—*Continued*
  bonds and stocks, 48, 322, 324-329
    Canadian Government, 95, 117, 284, 322
    U. S. Government, 48, 95, 117, 322
  depressions, effect of, 356-359
  effect on economic life of U. S., 106-109,
    331-338
  housing projects, *see* Housing projects
  interest rate, trend, 211-214, 218-219, 329-
    330
  mortgage loans, 47-48, 322, 339-359
    city property, 322, 339-343, 346-348
    farms, 322, 354-359
  principles, 19-20, 93-94, 103, 325-336,
    339-343, 346
  regulations on investments, 316, 325-327,
    339-340, 348
  T.N.E.C. Investigation of, 21-22, 106-109
  valuation policy, 103, 332, 340
Jimenís, Dr. Albert O., 481
John Hancock Mutual Life Insurance Com-
    pany, 27, 40, 44, 58, 122, 126, 134
Johnston, Gale F., 188, 480
Jones, Elias A., 29, 34
Jones, H. A., 8, 29
Jones and Laughlin Steel Corporation, 197
Joslin, Dr. Elliott P., 433
Kavanagh, James E., 71, 87, 169, 171, 181-
    182, 184, 191, 283, 292
Kay, Harry H., 285
Kelly, Denis W., 480
Keys, Edward M., 479
Kidd, Dr. Harry Bell, 480
Killington, William M., 264
Kimball, Ingalls, 184
Kingsport, Tenn., 191
Klein, J. O., 482
Kley, Michael, 482
Knapp, Joseph F.
  capitalization, efforts to increase, 41-42
  claim payments, supervises, 362-363
  death, 11, 49
  Field Force, interest in, 256-257, 261, 276
  Industrial insurance, first policy issued on
    life of, 257
  inaugurates, 41, 229-230, 363
  study of, 37-40, 122-123, 146
  influence on success of Metropolitan, 9, 11,
    29, 33-34, 41-42, 230-231, 363
  investment of funds, 314, 315
  Medical Examiners, 401
  One Madison Avenue, purchase of plot,
    48-49

President, elected, 33
selection of personnel for Metropolitan,
    33-34, 230, 247, 315
Knapp, Joseph P., 18, 68
Knight, Dr. Augustus S., 72, 404, 413
Labor Relations Act, U. S., 112
LaMont, Stewart M., 89, 200, 204
Lanza, Dr. Anthony J., 177, 481
Lapse rate
  Industrial Department, 23, 43, 60, 92-93,
    105, 109, 127, 130-135
  Ordinary Department, 22, 109, 161-162
  reduction of, 92-93, 105, 130-134, 271
Lapsed policies
  duration of policy, 133
  reinstatement of, 61, 132-133, 370
Law Division, 242, 243, 365-366
Lawrence, Reginald R., 482
LeBrun, Michel, 49, 236, 300
LeBrun, Napoleon, 49, 230
LeBrun, Pierre L., 49, 236, 300
Legal & General Assurance Society, Ltd., 182
Length of Life, A Study of the Life Table, 438
Level-premium plan, 144, 208
Lew, Edward A., 479
Liberalization of contract, 60-63, 70, 73-74,
    199, 370
Library, 245
Liens on policies
  Pittsburgh Life Insurance policies, 73
  Special Class insurance, 155
Life Extension Institute, 455
Life insurance
  and American way of life, 3, 144-145
  assets, U. S. and Canada, 4
  companies, number of, 36, 175
  counselors, 113-114
  in force, U. S. and Canada, 3
  investigations of, *see* Armstrong Investiga-
    tion; Industrial insurance investiga-
    tions; Temporary National Economic
    Committee
  moratoria on cash surrender payments, 20,
    101-102
  policies, *see* under name of policy
Life Insurance Adjustment Bureau, 134
Life Office Management Association Insti-
    tute, 249
Life Underwriters Association of Canada, 292
Lincoln, Leroy A., 479
  Field Force, meetings with, 111-112, 276-
    277, 292

490

494